The trade union rank and file

To my mother and father

Alan Clinton

The trade union rank and file
Trades councils in Britain, 1900–40

Manchester University Press

Rowman and Littlefield

© *Alan Clinton 1977*

Published by
Manchester University Press
Oxford Road, Manchester M13 9PL

ISBN 0 7190 0655 4

USA
Rowman and Littlefield
Totowa, NJ 07512

ISBN 0 87471 982 8

British Library cataloguing-in-publication data

Clinton, Alan
 The trade union rank and file.
 1. Trade unions – Great Britain – History
 I. Title
 331.87'2   HD6664

 ISBN 0–7190–0655–4

Printed in Great Britain by
The Scolar Press Limited

Computerised Phototypesetting by
G C Typeset Limited
166 Crook Street, Bolton BL3 6AS

Contents

Preface

This study began in 1966 from an effort to understand why it was that during the General Strike, forty years before, ordinary trade unionists showed a great deal more initiative and imagination than their leaders. When, during the late '60s and early '70s, a lengthening list of the achievements of the local organisations of trade unionism was being compiled, many familiar institutions began to disappear. In some places the term 'trades council' was replaced by some more awkward but allegedly more recognisable phrase such as 'trades union council'. Elsewhere well known organisations have been broken up or merged. In 1974 the London Trades Council, most famous of them all, was dissolved.

If in recent years historic landmarks have gone, one has nevertheless been continually reminded of the initiatives that could still be taken by ordinary trade unionists. In the summer of 1968, when research was being actively pursued, millions of French workers brought alive the strength and inventiveness of their class. The British trade union movement in the following period campaigned against and defeated the Industrial Relations Act, as their forefathers had dealt with the law of master and servant, and the legal judgements of Taff Vale and Osborne. Early in 1974 the miners, with the help of many other sections of the organised working class, forced out of office their traditional enemies in the Tory government. If the landmarks had been wiped out, and many of the forms had been changed, echoes nevertheless remained of the voices recalled in these pages.

Inevitably in the course of these years I have incurred many debts to friends who have borne with me, academic colleagues who have given me the benefit of their knowledge, and trades council officials and librarians who have helped me to uncover the past. A somewhat different version of chapter four of this book will be found in the *International Review of Social History*, XV, 1970. The research on which my original doctoral dissertation was based began while I was a student at the Department of Humanities of the Chelsea College of Science, and I owe much to the college, and in particular to Professor Harold Silver, who guided my work while I was there. I would also like to thank Professor Ralph Miliband, who acted as my supervisor, and professors Royden Harrison and Eric Hobsbawm, who made a number of useful suggestions in examining the original thesis. Working more recently at Leeds University, I also benefited from discussions with Tom Woodhouse, Bob Turner and Professor Vic Allen. I learnt most of all about the study of the history of the working class from the late and sadly missed Dr J. E. Williams.

Many individuals and institutions have helped me in looking through the various collections of documents on which this work is based. I would like to mention especially Mr E. Brown and Ms C. Coates, the librarians at the Trades Union Congress, Mr R. Simon and his assistants at the Labour Research Department, Mr V. M. Thornes of the Sheffield Trades and Labour Council, and Mr J. Ainley of the Coventry Trades Council. Many other trades council officials and delegates helped me, often as much by talking about their current preoccupations as by telling me what they knew of their history. I should mention Mike Knowles of Hackney, who wants to see that the local organisations have as great a future as they have a glorious past, Dai Stevens of Islington, who brought me up to date with the movement, and also Mr T. R. Holland of Northampton, Mrs E. May of Battersea, and Mr W. Fancy of Woolwich, who helped me in various ways. Howard Belton provided me with his notes on the minutes of the Oxford Trades Council, Josephine Smith discussed the unemployed movement with me and obtained some useful material on the St Albans Trades Council, and Judy Fincher Laird gave me some interesting references to the trade union reorganisation schemes of the 1890s. Robin Page Arnot also kindly told me what he remembered of the National Federation of Trades Councils of 1922–24.

My friends Alice and Jon Amsden, Alan Gillie, Brian Barber and Adam Westoby helped to sustain me throughout this work, though they, no more than anybody else mentioned, can be held responsible for the numerous imperfections that still remain in it.

London   *Alan Clinton*
16 August 1975

Abbreviations

AC	Annual Conference
AEU	Amalgamated Engineering Union
AR	Annual Report
ASE	Amalgamated Society of Engineers
ASLEF	Amalgamated Society of Locomotive Engineers and Firemen
AUCE	Amalgamated Union of Co-operative Employees
BSP	British Socialist Party
BSSLH	*Bulletin of the Society for the Study of Labour History*
CoA	Council of Action
CFT	*Cotton Factory Times*
CGT	Confédération Générale du Travail (France)
Cole Coll	Cole collection, Nuffield College, Oxford
CP(GB)	Communist Party (of Great Britain)
CTA	Class Teachers' Association
DORA	Defence of the Realm Act, 1914
ETU	Electrical Trades Union
FWC	Fair Wages Clause
GFTU	General Federation of Trade Unions
GMWU	General and Municipal Workers' Union
HYR	Half Yearly Report
IHES	Industrial Health Education Society
ILP	Independent Labour Party
IRSH	*International Review of Social History*
ISEL	Industrial Syndicalist Education League
JCC	Joint Consultative Committee
JS	Jubilee Souvenir
LNS	Land Nationalisation Society
LP	Labour Party
LRC	Labour Representation Committee
LRD	Labour Research Department
LRDMC	*Labour Research Department Monthly Circular* (called *Fabian Research Department Monthly Circular*, July 1917 to October 1918)
LRD Reply	Filled in circulars replying to the 1918 LRD survey
LWC	*Leeds Weekly Citizen*
MEA	Municipal Employees' Association
(N)MM	(National) Minority Movement

n.a.	not available
NCLC	National Council of Labour Colleges
NCLOAP	National Committee of Organised Labour for the Promotion of Old Age Pensions for All (1899–1908)
n.d.	no date given
NUR	National Union of Railwaymen
NUW(C)M	National Unemployed Workers' (Committee) Movement
PAC	Public Assistance Committee
PP	Parliamentary Papers
RCL	Royal Commission on Labour (1893)
RILU	Red International of Labour Unions
RSLO	Report of Strikes and Lockouts, issued by the Board of Trade Labour Department, and later by the Ministry of Labour
SDF	Social Democratic Federation
STUC	Scottish Trades Union Congress
STUC Report	Reports to and of the Scottish Trades Union Congress
T&LC	Trades and Labour Council
T&LRC	Trades and Labour Representation Committee
T&IC	Trades and Industrial Council
TC	Trades Council
TC&LP	Trades Council and Labour Party
TCAC	Annual Conference of Trades Councils, sponsored by the TUC since 1925. Reports published with the reports to the conference since 1932
(TC)JCC	(Trades Councils) Joint Consultative Committee
TUC	Trades Union Congress
TUC Report	Trades Union Congress Annual Report and Conference Proceedings
UAB	Unemployment Assistance Board
UDC	Union of Democratic Control
US	*Unemployed Struggles* (by W. Hannington)
VCH	Victoria County History
WEA	Workers Educational Association
WEWNC	War Emergency Workers' National Committee
W R&P	Webb Reports and Papers on the Relief of Distress 1914–16 (in the British Library of Political and Economic Science)
W TU Coll	Webb Trade Union Collection (in the British Library of Political and Economic Science)
YB	Year Book
YFT	*Yorkshire Factory Times*

Chapter one

Introduction
From revival to decline

This book is concerned to describe the development of a major facet of the British working class movement during the first four decades of this century. Local organisations to which the branches of various trade unions affiliate have been a feature of the movement since the mid-nineteenth century, and they continue to play their part to this day.[1] In recent years it has been maintained that trades councils 'do not fit comfortably into the structure of the trade union movement'. Their role has been described as 'anomolous', and even 'curious'.[2] Yet the position of these local organisations within the constellation of bodies that make up the trade union movement has not been established in any simple or preconceived way. The trades councils have developed within the complex and shifting dialectic in the trade unions between national and local, leaders and led, and between the active rank and file and the professional bureaucracy. A study of how these relationships have changed is essential to understanding the dynamics of the movement as a whole, but it will not reveal any tidy patterns or immutable distinctions.

The men and women who were, and are, active in the trades councils should not be confused with the mass of working people, with the passive trade union members mobilised only at great moments in the life of their movement. Nor should they be identified with those who hold leading positions in the unions, the Labour Party and the TUC. They have always been 'the active soldiers and non-commissioned officers who constitute the most vital element of the trade union army',[3] not the millions of ordinary members but the hundreds and thousands of the most active. This trade union rank and file stands at a strategic point within the working class. It transmits the impulses that come through the movement from its leadership and from society as a whole. At the same time, it absorbs the influences that alter the outlook of working people, and reflects their changing moods and aspirations.

Viewed against the perspective of more than a hundred years in the history of trade unionism, it is possible to see how the trades councils have changed from being essential constituents of a movement that still relied on local initiative to develop its strength and to win recognition for its interests. The local bodies have been transformed in our own day into humble instruments of a professional trade union leadership that is fixed in a long-accepted set of relationships with employers and the State. For all their subservience, the trades councils continue to thrive, to maintain in many instances a vigorous internal life, and to serve the interests of working people in numerous ways. This book covers the main period from which it is possible to explain this transition, from the time when their value seemed eroded to when their subordination was agreed and their useful functions established. During the nineteenth century the trades councils showed themselves unable to play a major role in bargaining with employers, and in the early years of the twentieth century it became clear that they could not alone run the local electoral machinery of the movement. Nevertheless, in the period covered by the chapters that follow, they showed that there were still industrial and political functions for them to perform. As the trades councils took up a wide range of the economic and social problems facing those they represented, as they tried to confront the great issues of international politics raised in the first world war and after, they found a part to play. In doing so they began to reflect that tension between acceptance and revolt that is a constant feature of the working class movement and came into conflict with those of its leaders who fought with some success to transform the trade union movement into a system of centralised command.

The very earliest forms of organisation in the British working class included bodies more akin to trades councils than to centralised trade unions.[4] Thus in 1818 a Philanthropic Society in Manchester brought together various groups of workers in the cotton industry to lend aid to 'any trade feeling the necessity of an advance in wages', and a London Philanthropic Hercules aimed more generally at 'the mutual support of the Labouring Mechanic'.[5] Similar temporary arrangements can be traced in the capital in the following period, and in most other main towns. The bodies thus established had such functions as the support of particular strikes, or making general propaganda in defence of trade unionism. Glasgow, Aberdeen, Sheffield and elsewhere could boast 'Committees of Delegates', 'Trades Combinations Committees' and the like in the years before and after the first permanent organisation was set up as the Liverpool Trades Guardian Association in 1848. During the 1860s trades councils became an important feature of the trade union movement in most of the main centres of population and industry, taking many important initiatives within the movement, in efforts to secure the repeal of the Master and Servant Act, as well as in calling the first meeting of what was to become the Trades Union Congress.[6]

A hundred years ago unrecognised working class organisations engaged in their first 'struggle for acceptance' relied heavily on the sorts of initiative which only the trades councils could provide. It was even claimed by the Webbs that the London Trades Council in this period brought together 'the beginnings of an informal cabinet of the Trade Union world', a 'junta' of the leaders of the main unions. If this characterisation overstates the homogeneity of union leaders in the metropolis during the 1860s, and the extent to which they acted together, it does at least draw attention to the importance for the movement of its best known, though somewhat atypical, local organisation.[7] By 1875 there existed 'a network of Councils throughout the country, most of them in contact with each other and in touch with the Parliamentary Committee of the TUC. They had petitioned Parliament, and helped to carry out the campaign against the Labour laws. They were generally recognised as being an important arm of the trade-union movement.'[8]

During the decade or so of severe contraction in the trade unions after the mid-'70s the trades councils suffered a parallel diminution of strength, and probably only a dozen of them survived. As the movement revived and expanded in the late '80s and early '90s more than a hundred local bodies were built with many thousands of affiliates. Their efforts to set up local bargaining machinery were everywhere unsuccessful, and in 1895 they were excluded from the very Trades Union Congress they had initiated. Yet the trades councils did not fade away, nor did they become moribund or unnecessary. They were now part of a movement which for the first time organised on a permanent basis large groups of workers who could not rely on their special skills or monopoly power in the labour market. The interests of such workers could be served only by looking well beyond their immediate work situation to the economic and social problems faced by all the poor. Both in the national arena and within their local communities, workers' organisations now had to deal with much more than the simple defence of the right to organise. They had to take up more general questions of concern to working people, such as unemployment, housing and public health. These new preoccupations pushed the trades councils away from the individualist and craft-oriented outlook of the nineteenth century to the wider sympathies and collectivist social policies of the twentieth.

The description of the development of local organisations from the 1890s to the 1920s in chapters two and three shows that when the trades councils found themselves unable to play a role in industrial bargaining they did not simply become the agents of electoral politics. They began to take an active role in the expansion and development of trade unionism. They became spokesmen and representatives of working people on a wide range of political and social issues, on all matters relating to the welfare of the poor. By the second decade of the century they played an important part in all those activities of working class organisations that go beyond the day-to-day consideration of wages and conditions of work, and extend mutual aid to workers as a whole, by taking up the needs of every section of that class, including the ill organised and the destitute. In other words, the central concerns of the trades councils were precisely those facets of the actions of trade unionism that make its diverse institutions a 'movement'. A study of the local organisations in this period is a living disproof of the statement of one group of writers that around 1910 the unions had shared concerns 'often apparent only to the discerning eye, rarely visible in day-to-day union business, and only very rarely powerful enough to override the self-interest of any individual union'.[9] If that was how matters seemed when viewed from the headquarters of the unions, they were quite different for the trade union rank and file.

In the early chapters some effort is made to go beyond the proposition, self-evident in the sources on which they are based, that there was a common range of attitudes and activities in trade union organisations in every corner of the land, which was not simply a matter of industrial bargaining or electoral politics. It is true that the unions of unskilled workers set up in the heroic years from 1888 to 1892 were for a long time weak and tender growths, and the break from Liberalism by the labour movement was a protracted process. Nevertheless, in a period when many sections of workers came into the unions for the first time, and when the working class emerged as an independent political force, many thousands, and eventually millions, of working men and women changed their conception of the world. A major transition in working class consciousness can be seen clearly in the local bodies of the organised movement, and some of its causes and results are described in chapters three and five. The trade union rank and file were subject to many influences, such as the changing views of the leaders of their movement, and the many pressure groups that tried to win their support from the outside. They were also affected by the heightened expectations of ordinary working people. As a result, the trades councils began to put forward more ambitious aims. The increasing support within the trade union movement for the chief propositions of collectivism and socialism in the early years of this century is not a phenomenon that can be precisely measured, but it is not difficult to outline its general form and chief results. New expectations in the working class brought into sharp relief the perennial conflict within the unions between the forces seeking accommodation with the established social order and those countervailing tendencies that try to confront and overthrow it. The middle chapters are devoted to describing how this process worked out in the trades councils in the 1920s.

In the years of Liberal reform and world war from 1906 to 1918 the working class movement obtained an unprecedented degree of recognition from employers and the State. Trade union and labour leaders took part in every form of industrial relations machinery, were given many political responsibilities, and were eventually even welcomed into government itself. There were parallel developments over this period in local communities. The trades councils provided a medium whereby the interests of various groups of workers were brought to bear on the increasing activities of the State in matters of social and economic policy. Local working class representatives were allowed to play a part in the machinery for the administration of welfare services which they had often themselves advocated. This process is described in chapter three, and the granting of a much wider range of functions, including quasi-administrative ones, is set out in the early sections of chapter four. Clearly, by about 1916 the working class movement had made important gains at both local and national level.

Against a background of disenchantment with the results of European war, and with the sharpening of class conflict at home, it was inevitable that the broadening expectations of active trade unionists would bring them into conflict with the new-found, but strictly circumscribed, ways in which the authorities allowed them to serve the interests of the poor. Within the trades councils this process assumed a further dimension. The local organisations had long provided a focus for those who sought to co-ordinate the efforts of diverse groups of workers, to centralise them, and to make them more militant. In chapter five there is a description of how these policies were advocated in the trades councils, and in chapter six an account of how they worked out in practice in the decade after 1916. During the 1926 General Strike the trades councils stood on the brink of challenging those who held social and political power in their local communities, but were faced with a dilemma which neither they nor their advocates were able to resolve. The changes the trades councils themselves recommended in the direction of centralisation and unification of effort within the trade union movement, when carried out, acted against the amplification of their own role that the local bodies had sought at the same time. Thus even when they showed themselves uniquely able to co-ordinate the most thoroughgoing industrial militancy they had little capacity for independent action within a movement that was already well on the way to limiting local initiative of any sort. In chapter five there is a description of the efforts, largely sponsored or taken over by the syndicalists and Communists, to co-ordinate the work of the trades councils on a national level. In the end such centralisation could be carried through only under the authority of a trade union leadership whose hegemony had never been questioned, but who had no desire to extend the powers allowed to local organisations.

Between the wars the trades councils stood at the centre of that process whereby the trade union movement came less and less to constitute a plurality of organisations and opinions, and began more closely to resemble a centralised command structure. Within individual unions the growth of the authority of groups of professional officials over disparate bodies of members can be traced back at least to the period of the so-called 'new model' unions of the 1850s. As the only meeting point of the collective trade union leadership and the mass of the active rank and file, the relationship between the TUC and the trades councils in the inter-war period expressed in its most general form the culmination of a process of developing central control within the trade union movement as whole. The history of these relationships is outlined in chapter five, which ends with their settlement by the establishment of the Trades Councils Joint Consultative Committee in 1925. A full account of the early years of this body is given in chapter seven, with particular emphasis on its function in establishing the authority of the union leaders within their movement. The 'black circulars' of 1934 sought with some success to dictate the political opinions of trades council delegates, though the comparative failure of the unemployed associations showed that the movement could still not yet be quite monolithic.

It would be wrong, however, to conclude this introductory survey simply by describing the process through which the subordinate position of the local organisations of the trade union movement was established. If there were inconsistencies in the views of the trades councils about how they should develop, and flaws in their achievements, they could hardly be blamed for failing to display an independence to which they never laid claim. As is demonstrated repeatedly in the chapters that follow, there remained a broad range of methods for the trade union rank and file to serve their movement and their class. The final chapter emphasises that at the end of the period covered by this book there was still room, within what were now well defined limits, for small and special heroisms of the trades councils. During the 1930s local organisations continued to bring new sections of workers into their movement, and to take up numerous issues of politics and social welfare on behalf of working people. They thus helped their class to take a few small and faltering but nonetheless definite steps forward.

One day another book should be written to set out the story of the local organisations of the working class beyond 1940. There would be something to be learnt from the activities of the trades councils during the second world war, from their further conflicts with the leaders of their movement in the early 1950s, and from their widespread reorganisation during the '70s. There would be much to tell of their internal life and of the important part they still play in the lives of many local communities. It seems certain, however, that the main lines of their activities were established in the first half of this century, and their relations within the rest of the working class movement will not be found to have changed much since the peak of their power and influence in the mid-1920s. The remaining chapters will try to describe how this came about.

Chapter two

Servants of the trade unions

Failure as bargaining agents

The structure of trade union bargaining in Britain today, it is often asserted, is a product of history. Disputes between capital and labour have come to be settled through a system of national and individual plant negotiation. This system did not grow up without attempts being made to manage affairs in other ways. Most notably, the trades councils played a conspicuous part in efforts to set up local bargaining machinery dealing with the problems of different trades. An account of this false start in the development of industrial relations machinery can do much to explain some important aspects of the work of the trades councils and to illustrate their position in the twentieth century trade union movement.[1]

In the mid-nineteenth century the movement could look in one of two ways in its effort to find a method of settling disputes. Either it could participate in local general bodies covering different trades or else it could fight for specialised national organisations familiar with the problems of individual industries or crafts.[2] To many at the time local general bodies seemed most likely to be successful. There were, after all, models. The *conseils de prud'hommes* in France were local general bodies where employers and workers could secure legally binding decisions about the interpretation of labour contracts. They were first developed as early as 1806 and were constantly referred to in Britain by advocates of industrial conciliation as worthy of emulation.[3] In 1845, before there was a single permanent trades council in Britain, the National Association of United Trades proposed 'the establishment of local boards of trade or councils of conciliation and arbitration to adjust disputes between employers and employed'. In 1856 at a House of Commons committee on conciliation machinery 'most of the witnesses

... appeared to be in favour of local bodies with power to deal with disputes in any area of jurisdiction'. William Newton of the ASE 'thought to have one board for each trade would be too complicated', and the committee agreed in the end that it would be best to set up local 'courts of conciliation'.[4] Support for such ideas was soon to be heard in the newly formed trades councils themselves. Both William Dronfield, a leader of the Sheffield Amalgamated Organisation of Trades, and William Gilliver, who performed a similar role in Birmingham, advocated the setting up of joint bodies by trades councils and chambers of commerce.[5]

Thus during the 1860s, when many trades councils were founded or became well established, they were actively involved in setting up local conciliation machinery. When the Manchester Trades Council began in 1866, it aimed 'to prevent strikes and lock-outs' by establishing 'Courts of Conciliation and Arbitration'. A Joint Court of Arbitration was set up with the Manchester Chamber of Commerce in 1868 whose object was 'to arbitrate on questions of wages and other matters referred to it' when the parties concerned could find no other way of settling their disputes. Like many later efforts, this body failed because of hostility from the employers, and separate arrangements were made for particular trades.[6] Similar courts were set up during the next two years in Aberdeen, Leeds, Nottingham and Sheffield, but they did not prove a success either, owing, it was said, 'to the employers' unwillingness to use them'.[7] This attitude was common when the employers used conciliation machinery mainly to impose 'substantial limits on the bargaining power of the operatives', and usually also wage cuts.[8] Thus in this period even efforts to set up conciliation machinery dealing only with the Leicester lace trade or the specialised metal industries at Sheffield proved no more successful.[9]

During the period from the mid-'70s to the mid-'80s, when trade union activity declined and many trade councils disappeared, there was still discussion about the best types of conciliation machinery, particularly by middle class writers. Although they varied in their view of whether compulsory settlements should be enforced, they were agreed that local joint organisations of employers and workers covering different trades had an important part to play.[10] When government agencies began to take an interest in settling industrial disputes they placed more emphasis on 'local councils of conciliation and arbitration' than on those bodies covering individual trades.[11] As a result of such influences, in the late 1880s and early '90s virtually every trades council in the land was involved in attempts to set up local conciliation machinery.

The most successful and best known local conciliation board in this period did not work directly with any trades councils, but many local labour leaders were actively involved. This was the London Conciliation Committee, set up in 1890 under the inspiration of Samuel Boulton, a chemical manufacturer and a member of the executive committee of the London Chamber of Commerce, who modelled his ideas on the *conseils de prud'hommes*. During its first year this conciliation committee, under the aegis of the Chamber of Commerce, settled disputes involving dockers, cement manufacturers, bargemen and French polishers. Although the London Trades Council declined to be directly represented, on the grounds that disputes could best be settled 'by the parties . . . meeting, as occasion may necessitate', leaders of the ASE, Watermen and Lightermen and National Union of Clerks in the metropolis were soon involved in setting up separate trade committees under the conciliation committee. Boulton also succeeded in persuading the Congress of Chambers of Commerce of the Empire to pass a motion in 1892 approving local conciliation boards.[12] In the following years the London Conciliation Board considered a steady stream of cases. In 1901 it claimed to have 'the general support and confidence of the working classes of the metropolis', and in 1904 it was said that on the Thames waterside at least it was 'becoming an established practice' to refer disputes to it. However, increasingly the work of the Board took the form of 'informal interviews . . . tending to the prevention of disputes rather than their settlement', and was considered to have a 'largely educational' character. It was found more and more that disputes were being 'dealt with by the particular conciliation boards concerned'.[13] It was still possible in 1914 to claim that fifty disputes had been settled in twenty-two years. 'The cases dealt with cover a wide range of questions, but were principally in connection with employment on the Thames and in the docks, and the Board literally "kept the peace" in the Port of London for upward of twenty years. The other trades which have benefited include such divergent ones as tailoring, printing, baking, coopering and ironplate working.' In 1915, when the last annual aggregate meeting of the Board was held, the thirty-eight union representatives present included Duncan Carmichael, soon to become London Trades Council secretary. It was claimed that, of the fifty-seven awards made in its history, 'only in one instance has the award of the Board been set aside or ignored'.[14] Although the Board continued in existence as late as 1929, it was then being referred to only in a number of rare cases where its work was still remembered.[15]

Although the London Conciliation Board was the most conspicuous example of local conciliation machinery, about 300 such local bodies were set up in the 1890s, often at the initiative of chambers of commerce, but nearly always with the enthusiastic participation of the trades councils. In 1889 and 1890 the TUC supported the setting up of such bodies, and the Labour Department of the Board of Trade reported in detail on their activities. In 1890 in Aberdeen a conciliation board was established by the Trades Council and the Chamber of Commerce. This could act only if both sides agreed to refer matters to it, and even then the trades council was not prepared to be bound by its decisions. In Manchester a similar body was set up by the local trades council and chamber of commerce on the model of the London Conciliation Board. It could intervene in any dispute, but as late as 1894 had not considered a single case. Other joint bodies found more to do, however. The Bradford Conciliation Board, set up in 1891, met seven times in its first year and claimed to have settled two strikes and prevented another. In near-by Leeds the Board proved useful not so much in settling disputes as in ensuring 'cordial relations between masters and men', although its services were frequently advocated at Trades Council meetings and the Workmen's Section was used to discuss inter-union disputes. The Liverpool body set up in 1892 elected the workers' side not through the trades council but by the separate trades. The Birmingham Conciliation Board, established on Trades Council initiative in the same year, intervened in disputes only when asked to do so, but does not seem to have settled any cases. It applied for registration under the 1896 Conciliation Act without success, but achieved more as an educational body, running, for example, a successful public meeting on the compulsory arbitration procedures in New Zealand.[16]

Despite the high hopes that were placed in these arrangements, their achievements were limited. In 1895 it was reported that the year before only in London, Liverpool and Halifax had the conciliation boards settled any cases, 'though Bradford, Dewsbury, Leeds and Newport offered their services'. In 1896 only twenty-five boards were known to survive, and only those in Blackburn and London had settled any cases. When the 1896 Conciliation Act was passed the local conciliation boards were virtually ignored, despite all the confidence that had recently been placed in them.[17] Between 1897 and 1906 local conciliation boards considered only thirty-three cases, twenty of them in London and nine in Aberdeen. Most local organisations had gone out of existence in 1908, including those in Leeds, Liverpool and Birmingham.[18] However, the London model continued to provide some inspiration, and in the year before the outbreak of the first world war new bodies were set up in Bolton, Bridgwater and Dundee, where it was said that four local cases were settled in 1913.[19] When a further revival was proposed in 1917 in Nottingham by the Chamber of Commerce to the Trades Council, 'on similar lines to the London scheme of 1890', it was decided that industry-wide bargaining such as was being proposed by the Whitley Committee was likely to be more successful.[20]

The story of these local conciliation boards is but a footnote in the history of industrial relations. Because so little was achieved they have since been largely forgotten. However, when they were revived in the late '80s 'for a moment it might have seemed to contemporaries that they were in the presence of a major development that would add a new organ to the body politic', especially as similar developments could be observed in Germany, France and New Zealand. For a time, at least, the trades councils appeared to offer 'the basis of an alternative system of labour organisation to that of the national unions'.[21] The failure of these hopes to materialise is not difficult to explain, but it is important in understanding the role that local trade union organisation came to assume.

British trade unionism first developed permanent roots among skilled workers who identified themselves not with those who worked around them but with others who shared their skills. Most bargains were agreed by finding a 'rate for the job'. Thus the centralising tendencies within industries themselves were reinforced in the way workers organised themselves to bargain with their employers.[22] This limited the role in bargaining of any organisations that were either localised or brought together workers from more than one craft. In France, where there were legalised procedures which were important, and the national movement remained weak, the trades councils' equivalent, the *bourses de travail*, could perform a comparatively important role in co-ordinating the movement. In Britain, where there was no legal compulsion in bargaining, 'outside machinery' was regarded with some suspicion. In Leeds the local conciliation board felt that anybody involved in making settlements had to 'thoroughly understand the technicalities of their trade'. As early as 1876 there was noticed 'the unwillingness of both masters and men to refer their disputes to anyone who has not practical knowledge of the particular trade in which the dispute has arisen'. Thus when satisfactory industrial relations machinery was set up it tended to specialise in the problems of particular trades and to cover wide areas, even the whole country.[23] Different types of workers in Britain found it very difficult to agree to bargain together, even if they worked in the same industry or the same town. Many of the trades councils reflected these divisions. In Leeds in the setting up of the conciliation board, although 'the older trade unions acquiesced', unskilled workers 'tended to hold aloof', and similar divisions were noted at Hull. In Cardiff the Trades Council refused to co-operate with any body on which non-unionists were represented.[24] Opposition from the employers to such arrangements was also an important factor, especially when they regarded conciliation machinery simply as an alternative to union recognition. Thus in Hull they 'showed no great enthusiasm' for the local conciliation scheme, and in Birmingham the workers indicated 'more readiness to accept the intervention of the Board'.[25]

Local conciliation machinery failed not simply because of the structure of industry or the attitudes of those involved. It failed also because of the weaknesses of workers' local organisations. The trades councils could not bind their members in any way; they had no financial or other sanctions with which to enforce settlements on their constituents. Their equivalents in the United States, the Central Labour Unions, were said at that time to be 'not organised on a plan that will enable them' to take part in bargaining.[26] The same was true in Britain, where their position in the movement and the powers they possessed simply did not enable the trades councils to play an important part at the centre of trade union activity in negotiating about wages and conditions. In 1922 the secretary of the Sheffield Trades and Labour Council noticed this phenomenon, but still saw a role for his organisation.

During the year, we have been called upon to give advice and assistance to several branches affiliated to the Council, particularly what is known as 'Local Trades'. On the large national questions, whilst we have been prepared to assist and advise, we are forced to recognise that as the various Unions strengthen themselves by amalgamation, the wage questions of the future will be settled more on a national basis than they have been heretofore. If that is going to be the case, the functions of your EC must in future be directed in helping to co-ordinate those local branches, so that they in turn will bring such pressure to bear on the National Executives that will make them feel when entering the Conference room, that the opinion of the rank and file have given them a mandate, which must be the guiding force in negotiation.

Although local leaders abandoned the role they once tried to assume as trade union bargainers, they still had many tasks to perform in the industrial work of the trade union movement, and these went well beyond putting pressure on the union leaders. It is the purpose of the rest of this chapter to describe and explain the nature of such activities.

A new industrial role

Although the trades councils had to leave to the unions themselves the main work of negotiating wages and conditions, they were still involved in industrial disputes. Most trades councils said in their published aims that they wanted to bring such disputes 'to an amicable settlement', often by acting as mediator. In the nineteenth century they sometimes told unions on strike to moderate their demands.[28] Trades council leaders could thus try to bring the parties in a local dispute together and even on occasion act as mediator. In Coventry it was said that the chairman of the Trades and Labour Council 'by virtue of that office, has been identified more frequently as peacemaker, in many local trade disputes'.[29] However, during the twentieth century, trades councils have taken up a somewhat different stance. As early as 1893 the president of the Sheffield Trades Council went to a great deal of trouble 'in bringing about settlements and preventing grievances in other trades from his own', but in most cases 'the Trades Council has put pressure on the employers on behalf of the men rather than acted as an impartial mandatory body'. Trades councils increasingly considered it to be 'their duty to help forward any movement which is for the benefit of the workers as a whole'. The Kettering body could only see its chief industrial aims as 'to gain advances; to prevent reductions; to gain a uniform price for the same class of work; and to resist encroachments effecting the rights of labour'. Thus trades councils came to see their role as aiming 'for the improvement of the conditions under which the workers live, by industrial action', or thought they should be 'organising trades in their various industries that they might take united action in disputes'.[30] It became the work of the trades councils, as the London secretary, James MacDonald, put it, to 'carry on the militant side of the movement'.[31] Pleas for help were supposed to be subject to the 'fullest investigation'. However, the Cambridge Trades Council secretary expressed what was assumed to be the position in most local bodies by the inter-war period in saying that 'as a Trades Council we have no right to interfere in industrial negotiations between workers and employers, but when negotiations have failed we have done all in our power to assist the worker'.[32] Support for workers in disputes became fairly indiscriminate. When there was some doubt in Liverpool in 1919 whether trade unionists could support policemen who had once themselves broken strikes, one delegate said 'they should support the P[olice] or any Union that went out on strike whether they were right or wrong'.[33] This attitude was common, and did not entirely disappear in the 1930s, when the TUC tried to persuade local bodies not to support strikes deemed to be 'unofficial'.

It is difficult to assess the extent to which the help given so readily to embattled workers was of value to them. The 'credentials' granted by the London Trades Council to those who asked its help in its early years have loomed so large in trade union histories that recent writers have sometimes disparaged their importance.[34] Although the material resources of the trades councils themselves were never great, they could often call on considerable outside help. In Leeds during the great struggle of municipal employees in the winter of 1913–14 it was thought 'desirable that a meeting should be called under the auspices of the Trades Council – the recognised body representing organised Labour in the City', and at Manchester in the 1940s the support of the Trades Council was always thought worth securing because it was 'the only body which can claim to have behind it the support of a large number of local trade unionists in a number of industries'.[35] Moral support could be important to a group of workers in a dispute, particularly if they were unused to the ways of industrial struggle. Trades councils could often give more than moral support. In 1898 the Birmingham body raised £1,220 for the locked-out engineers, and the London Trades Council ran a national conference to support them when the TUC refused to do so.[36] It was widespread support organised by the trades councils that helped the quarrymen of North Wales in their protracted dispute at the turn of the century with their obscurantist employer, Lord Penrhyn.[37] In exceptional cases the councils were even involved in running strikes. A sub-committee of the Liverpool Trades Council organised the great Liverpool transport strike of 1911.[38] In all the big national disputes from the engineers' lock-out of 1897–98 to the general strike of 1926 the trades councils were active in supporting the workers in every way they could. Their role was particularly conspicuous in the important disputes that preceded the first world war, when many groups of workers were involved for the first time in such action. Though not actually calling people out on strike or negotiating their return to work, the trades councils could obtain widespread moral support for embattled workers, and give them the benefit of their experience. During the Black Country strike of 1913 trades council leaders helped to formulate the famous demand for a 23*s* minimum, raised money, and tried to co-ordinate the scattered efforts of the strikers in the Midland Minimum Wage Council. In the Leeds municipal strike of 1913–14 it was the Trades Council leaders who mobilised support for the strikers, defended them in the press, and tried to stop the university allowing its students to be used as blacklegs.[39]

The role of local organisations in the industrial work of the trade union movement was not confined to participating in strikes. There were many other ways in which the movement could be strengthened. For one thing, meetings of trades councils were places where the conditions of different groups of workers could be compared and discussed. In one London trades council it was decreed that delegates could be 'appointed and empowered to enter Trade Union branches and other organisations with a view of an interchange of working agreements etc. as a means towards securing a united policy amongst the working class in this area'.[40] If few local bodies envisaged such formal arrangements, all discussed local conditions and must have been instrumental in the preparation of claims for their improvement. This applied particularly to issues which concerned more than one group of workers. In the United States 'the demand for a shorter working day frequently stimulated the formation of city central unions' because this was an issue 'common to all trades'.[41] In Britain too this was an important issue for local organisations. Tom Mann thought the London Trades Council was the best organisation in the metropolis for 'dealing with the "Eight Hour" question and generally advising the workers as to the most expeditious steps to be taken to secure the reduction of working hours in their respective callings'. In Oldham the main activity of the Trades Council in its early years, besides trying to defend the legal rights of trade unionists, was 'to reduce the working week'. Conferences were run on the eight-hour day and there were discussions of the evils of 'systematic overtime'.[42] In later years, especially during the first world war and immediately after, shorter hours were frequently discussed as a solution to the problems of unemployment, and the detailed schemes worked out in the trades councils must have had an effect on trade unionists in other parts of the movement.[43]

Trades councils could go beyond discussing ideal trade union conditions to trying to enforce those that already existed. They issued lists of firms who paid trade union rates, and although it was sometimes difficult to agree on which firms were fair, and although the TUC did not agree to the issuing of such lists at all, some successes were recorded.[44] In 1915 Everton Football Club was persuaded to stop patronising firms that did not pay trade union rates, and at Burton in 1915 the Trades Council got the local co-operative society to stop buying from an 'unfair' furniture firm. The secretary concluded that 'sweated labour will cease when we refuse to have anything to do with articles *produced by sweated labour*'.[45] Councils could also help union members by mounting boycotts of various kinds. Through the councils trade unionists were often exhorted to pay their insurance premiums only to collectors who were union members. Appeals to shop early in order to enforce half-day closing were also heard on behalf of shop workers, and on occasions there were calls for complete boycotts of the strongly anti-union multiple grocery chains. Blackpool Trades Council even appealed to trade unionists to stop taking their holidays there until there were decent conditions for the tramway workers.[46]

A more direct way in which trades councils could make themselves useful was by getting local authorities of various kinds to pay trade union rates, and to enforce these on firms who contracted for local authority work. The struggle for 'fair wages clauses' on public contracts began with the success of the London Society of Compositors in persuading the Stationery Office to enforce trade union rates in 1885. In 1886 the Compositors got the London Trades Council to protest about the failure of the London School Board to patronise 'fair' houses. Soon municipal candidates began to declare support for this policy, and in 1889 FWCs were adopted by both the London School Board and the London County Council. In the same year the Hull and Birmingham trades councils began to campaign on the question, and in 1891 these conditions were agreed locally as a result of the actions of the trades councils in Sheffield and Manchester. By 1894 150 local authorities had adopted fair wages resolutions.[47] Trades councils were particularly well placed to agitate on this subject. They could publicise cases of hardship in their own press or in reports of their meetings, and could lobby councils and elections in their role as local pressure groups. They could even take independent action by putting up candidates prepared to support these policies.

Their work did not end when local authorities adopted FWCs. They had to see to it that the clauses were enforced, and that the contractors who did not observe them were punished. In Oldham, Derby and Leeds they had special sub-committees which took up cases where it was not considered that justice had been done.[48] Trades councils consulted one another about the practice in their respective areas.[49] In Manchester in 1914 it was said to be 'becoming common practice for local governing bodies to apply to the Council for information respecting working conditions observed by firms contracting for public works', a practice described at Birmingham as a recognition of 'the important position occupied by Trades Councils'. At Leeds in 1917 employers themselves consulted the Trades Council about approved conditions.[50] Another important task for the local organisations was to see that FWCs were always framed so that they could not be ignored. In Oldham, after many years of effort, the Trades and Labour Council got a penalty clause included in the contracts in 1909. In Crewe, even though the corporation adopted an FWC in 1893, it was not until 1906 that the Trades Council got trade union rates enforced through the contracts. In Liverpool there was an FWC in 1892, but in 1896 the Trades and Labour Council secretary said he thought it 'so subtly drawn up as to be ineffective in its operation'. Numerous amendments were introduced both by the lobbying of the Trades and Labour Council and by Labour councillors acting on its behalf, until a nationally approved model clause was passed in 1913. At Leeds in 1912 the Trades Council led a campaign against a particular firm so that it would have to pay the standard rate not just for those contracts which it secured from the town council.[51] There were many such cases in every part of the country, which showed that by lobbying, agitating and negotiating trades councils could directly affect the wages and conditions of some important groups of their affiliates, and indirectly those of many others.

Another important method of strengthening the bargaining power of the workers in the localities was to recruit more members to the unions. In the nineteenth century the trades councils had catered mainly for people who were already union members. It was never true that trades council leaders were hostile to those newly involved in union organisation.[52] However, their attitude changed with the development of a type of trade unionism which depended on mass recruitment rather than on the support of workers in small occupational groups. Winning new members then became an obvious method of strengthening the position of those already in the unions, and from the 1890s onwards was a common activity in the trades councils. The process later described in Nottingham was a general phenomenon.

As the workers in all the various trades developed organisations, the kind of organising work the Council found itself best able to do, was in assisting societies already formed to increase their membership ... With the adoption of more intensive organising methods by many of the unions and the appointment of permanent organisers another change took place in the organising activities of the Trades Councils. While work is still sometimes done for particular trade unions, the appeal is made more general. This is shown by the running of Recruitment Campaigns, Trade Union Weeks, etc., when the non-unionists are urged to join their *appropriate trade union.*[53]

By the turn of the century trades councils often set up union branches, especially among unskilled workers and those difficult to organise. In Hull in 1894 the Trades Council established a branch of the General Labourers' Union among local dockers. A branch of the Workers' Union was set up by the Coventry Trades Council in 1899, and the secretary for a time acted as organiser. Branches of the Workers' Union were also set up by the trades councils of Oxford in 1912, Aylesbury in 1913 and Northampton in 1917.[54] Many trades councils, especially outside the main urban areas, took a major share in trade union recruitment in their district. In 1906 the Crewe Trades and Labour Council invited the secretary of the Gasworkers' Union to address local meetings of unskilled workers, and organised metal and furniture workers. When the Cambridge body was revived in 1912 it 'started a campaign in the town and surrounding countryside to organise general and unskilled workers', and set up branches of the Carmen's Union, the National Amalgamated Union of Labour and the Agricultural Labourers Union. In Motherwell at the same period the Trades Council set up branches of the Gasworkers and Municipal Employees that soon became the largest in the district.[55]

Within two decades of the new unionist upsurge of the late 1880s the responsibility for trade union recruitment was assumed by all trades councils. At Newport in 1909 it was said that the Trades and Labour Council would help unorganised workers, and 'consider it to be one of its prime objects to place at their disposal the benefit of the experience of its members to assist them in forming a Union upon a solid basis'.[56] Increasingly such activities were carried on through general recruitment campaigns during short periods specially set aside. 'Trade union weeks' were held in Huddersfield in 1911 and in Aberdeen, Manchester and Leeds in 1912. In the Manchester campaign there were fifty-four dinner-hour and evening meetings. It is interesting to note that in Leeds the ASE and the Postmen's Federation opposed such activity being carried out by a trades council, and the secretary justified it not simply as an effort to win over new trade unionists but also 'to demonstrate to the powers that be that Trade Unionism was a force that had come to stop in Leeds and intended to make itself felt in the near future'.[57] Trade union recruitment could often give rise to suspicion on the part of individual unions, and scepticism about results which were difficult to measure. It did, however, allow the trades councils to play a useful role in strengthening and defending the trade union movement.

Defence of trade unionism could take other forms also. For example. the local trades council got the mayor of Leeds to apologise in 1904 when he falsely asserted that high house prices were being caused by the wages paid to building workers.[58] Throughout their history trades councils have had to defend the working class movement from more serious attacks than this. The struggle against anti-trade union laws has often been important. Opposition to the Master and Servant Acts in the 1860s has been mentioned elsewhere. The 'important question of altering the laws affecting Trade Unionists' was discussed at the first meeting of the Bristol Trades Council in 1873. Such issues were the reason for the establishment of the Bradford body in 1872, and defence of 'the right to strike' was the 'most important single issue' in the early years of the Oldham Trades Council. In Nottingham it was said in 1931 that 'anti-trade union enactments of Parliament, and consequent decisions in the courts of law, have from the beginning been a source of great provocation to the movement, and the cause of some of the hardest work and bitterest fighting'.[59] The decision to fine the Amalgamated Society of Railway Servants in 1901 for striking against the Taff Vale Railway Company caused many local protest meetings, and the Birmingham Trades Council sent delegates to London to argue with MPs about it.[60] The Osborne judgement of 1909, which made it illegal for the unions to give money to the Labour Party, was opposed even more bitterly. The secretary at Sunderland thought it was 'TRADE UNIONISM, and not merely Labour Representation, that is hit', and the one at York said it 'upsets all previous conception of majority in our Unions'.[61] Some branches of railway workers left trades councils for a time for fear of being associated with their electoral work.[62] When the legal position was reversed by the 1913 Trade Union Act the Aberdeen Trades Council secretary thought that such successful agitation could 'only be effectively accomplished through Trades Councils'. It was no doubt in part at least the pressure from local trade union bodies that prevented the enactment of the many proposed anti-union measures of the period before 1914. The Yorkshire Federation held a large conference against these proposals, and the Liverpool Trades and Labour Council threatened a 'down tools policy' if restrictions on picketing were carried into effect.[63]

Within the movement itself the trades councils were called upon to settle inter-union disputes, and many made provision for doing so.[64] These disputes were usually about demarcation for recruitment, or sometimes about alleged blacklegging. The Webbs give the impression that efforts to resolve these disputes by the trades councils were always doomed to failure. However, powerful local bodies could arrange successful settlements, at least temporarily. In Aberdeen in the 1880s and '90s a number of arguments were successfully settled by the Trades Council. In Liverpool in 1908 the plumbers and whitesmiths were persuaded to resolve their differences, and in Edinburgh in 1918 unions catering for women workers also arrived at an agreement. In 1923 the Birmingham Trades Council arranged meetings between local branches of the Workers' Union and the AEU, and it was 'agreed that a better understanding had been recorded' as a result.[65] Such efforts did not always succeed. In Aylesbury in the 1920s branches of the Workers' Union and ASLEF withdrew because of unsatisfactory adjudications by the Trades Council, and something similar happened with the G&MWU in Northampton in 1924.[66] The position was such that in 1913 the Lancashire and Cheshire Federation decided that 'in view of the friction and ill-feeling often caused by poaching and demarcation of Labour questions being brought up at Trades Councils, to advise the Councils, except in very extraordinary and purely local cases, to decline to discuss such questions, but to refer the disputants to their respective local and national unions'.[67] A more centralised trade union movement tried to deal with these disputes at a higher level than the trades councils, although it is not clear that anyone else had a better record in resolving them. The Municipal Employees' Association, which was considered by some of the general unions to poach on their members, was nevertheless supported by the Liverpool Trades Council against elements which, it was said, were backed by the Conservative Party. Similarly at Rawtenstall a branch was set up by the Trades Council in 1915. The Amalgamated Union of Co-operative Employees had a similar reputation, mostly because of the success of its militant tactics, which persuaded people to leave other unions. The TUC became hostile, but the trades councils were often persuaded to expel local branches only after protracted debate.[68]

There were other ways too in which the trades councils could play an important part in the trade union movement. There were a few issues on which they could speak for the whole local labour force. Thus in some of the northern textile towns they were able to negotiate local factory holidays with the employers.[69] Trades councils were also called upon to negotiate on the question of cheap fares for those travelling to and from work. Although workmen's fares existed in most areas long before 1900, the trades councils often had them improved. In Birmingham in 1899 the Trades Council had these facilities extended to some new suburban areas, and in 1923 performed a similar task for those doing night work at the new car factories. In 1908 and 1910 the Liverpool body lobbied and called meetings against a local tramway company which, because of 'the sordid interests of a wealthy minority', refused to arrange any cheap fares for workmen, or even for schoolchildren. Similarly at Oxford in 1902 the Trades Council secured improvements in the 'inadequate and unsatisfactory' workmen's fares available in the town, and the Oldham body in 1917 negotiated the restoration of a train service on which such fares were paid.[70]

As well as negotiating in this way locally on behalf of the whole movement trades councils could provide more direct service to local trade union branches. They could improve their morale by arranging a show of strength in May Day demonstrations. As part of such activities the trades councils at Peterborough and Swindon both ran bands.[71] More material services were also provided. Trades council offices, where such existed, could be used by all sections of the local trade union movement. The Bradford office provided 'assistance to scores of trade unionists' and at Manchester it was 'the Recognised Clearing House for Trade Union officials and members'.[72] Nearly every trades council at one time or another discussed the setting up of a trades hall; in the majority of cases it was found impossible. This happened in Oldham in the 1870s, at Manchester in the 1880s, at Warrington in 1904 and at Stockton in 1911.[73] Sometimes, however, the local bodies could proceed. As the initial expenses involved were nearly always far beyond the resources of any trades council, it was usually in co-operation with others that permanent trades halls were established. In Croydon the Trades and Labour

Representation Committee obtained a house in 1914 as the result of a bequest from a sympathetic local Quaker, and at Blackpool a Trades Hall was set up in 1920 when the Trades Council worked in association with the local electoral and co-operative movements.[74] In some places the trades councils obtained halls by running them partly as social clubs. Such was the role of the Trades Hall in Leeds purchased by the Trades Council in 1901, which served the local trade union movement until recent times. There were similar arrangements at Hebden Bridge and Hull, and at Barrow it was said to be the only way the institution could be kept going.[75] It is perhaps surprising that the trades councils did not work with the Club and Institute Union; such co-operation was rare, perhaps because of the reactionary political image of the Union.[76] The financial liabilities incurred in running such halls were often considerable,[77] but where they were solvent they could be of great value. At Spen Valley the Trades Hall was 'a boon' during strikes, for branch meetings, and was used by men signing on for unemployment benefit through their unions. At Aldershot in the 1926 General Strike the Labour Hall was 'small, but very useful'. Also a success was the Trade Union Hall at Watford, which took ten years to build by direct trade union labour and was opened by the Prime Minister in 1931.[78]

Another important service which the trades councils rendered the trade union movement was in helping local labour newspapers. Again, these were rarely set up by the trades councils alone, but local trade union organisations supported the ILP's *Leicester Pioneer*, the Labour Party's *Woolwich Pioneer*, and the *Willesden Call* and *Southern Worker* of the SDF and BSP. The *Bradford Pioneer* was sponsored jointly by the Trades and Labour Council, ILP and local Labour Party, and £20 together with four representatives on the controlling body were the contributions of the Trades Council to the *Leeds Weekly Citizen* when it was set up in 1911. The Birmingham Trades Council was always an active supporter of the *Town Crier*, which existed from 1919 to 1951, at times only continuing through the donations of rich sympathisers. The *Wolverhampton Worker* was praised by the local Trades and Labour Council as showing that the movement was not 'confined to the narrow limits of the workshop'.[79] Trades councils were also actively involved in the *Hull Sentinel*, set up in 1928, and in the *Sheffield Forward*, which still exists. They were keen propagandists for the national papers of the movement, both for the brief and abortive *Daily Citizen* in 1913 and for the *Herald* in the various phases of its history from 1911.[80]

Finally there was the trades councils' role in training future leaders of the trade union movement. It is certainly true that the local bodies offered a method of 'instruction on social and industrial matters to the younger generation of trade unionists', as well as 'an excellent opportunity for the gaining of experience in the administrative and executive affairs of the movement'. It is difficult to assess in any systematic way the effect of this training, despite the assertion of one trade union leader, Charles Dukes, that 'practically everyone who has attained any position of prominence in the trade union movement has had an early grounding and training through the medium of Trade Council activity'.[81] It is certainly true that many well known personalities were active in trades councils, perhaps especially those who led the movement between the wars. Bramley and Citrine, successive TUC General Secretaries, were active in Bradford and Liverpool respectively in their earlier years, Charles Dukes of the GMWU was secretary at Warrington, Ernest Bevin the chairman at Bristol, and Emmanuel Shinwell, later to make his career on the political side of the movement, found his experience at Glasgow 'formative and educational'. Other trades council leaders often achieved civic office, and numerous delegates became mayors. In Manchester it was said that by the 1950s there had been altogether among the delegates nine union general secretaries, thirteen members of the TUC Parliamentary Committee or General Council, eight MPs and three mayors.[82]

Aid to special groups

As well as providing all these general services to the trade union movement, trades councils were of particular value for groups of workers outside the mainstream of trade union development. By the early twentieth century it might be said that there were many workers who had powerful national organisations to protect them. Even unskilled groups had unions that had secured some recognition if not yet great bargaining strength. At least one trades council secretary was aware of the existence of 'other unions, not so well organised, and we, as a Council, must be prepared to help them'. Aid to such small groups was described as the 'most important work' of another local body.[83] Musicians, insurance collectors and many public employees needed the support of the trades councils because of their inexperience in organisation and negotiation and because of the difficulty they often faced in being recognised as legitimate trade unionists.

Entertainers of various sorts were often aided by the trades councils. Musicians were the most important of these before the 1920s. The Amalgamated Musicians' Union, established in Manchester by Joseph Williams in 1893, often sought such help.[84] In Hull as early as 1895 the Trades Council advised trade unionists to boycott the Grand Theatre during a fifteen-week lock-out of musicians, which ultimately secured

improvements for them. Similar boycotts were called by the Birmingham
Trades Council in 1913, in Leicester in 1914, and by the Plymouth body
in 1915 and again in 1923. The small Trades and Labour Council at
Hyde in Cheshire arranged a regional meeting of trade unionists in
support of musicians in dispute against the Stoll theatre chain, and found
that 'after several months of kid-glove fighting, viz., peaceful picketing
and persuasion, solidarity won the day'.[85] In some cases the trades
councils negotiated for the musicians, as at Liverpool in 1896 and at
Bolton in 1923.[86] Trade union organisations were also exhorted to employ
only union bands, and competition from military bands was deplored.[87]
Other groups of entertainment workers were also helped. The
Birmingham Trades Council secretary presided at the inaugural meeting
of a branch of organised actors in 1909, and in 1915 the Liverpool body
negotiated with the employers in a dispute with a local branch of the
National Association of Theatrical Employees, another branch of which
the Trades Council later established.[88] The Variety Artistes' Federation
had a successful struggle in London in 1906 to improve their conditions
through strike action, but it was not until the 1920s that the activities of
this group of workers seem to have become nationally important. In
1924 the Birmingham Trades Council helped the Actors' Association 'by
means of sandwich men, leaflets and picketing' in their efforts to displace
a company union known as the Stage Guild. This routine trade union
activity was unusually rewarded when trades council delegates were
invited to a performance by the company of Mr Arthur Bourchier at the
Theatre Royal. In the same period similar support for organising work
was given by the Wolverhampton Trades and Labour Council, and at
Manchester delegates were also thanked through special visits to see the
Bourchier company.[89]

Trades councils could do much to help various types of service
workers. Perhaps most frequently mentioned in this category were
insurance agents. Trades councils often helped in setting up branches of
their organisations, and in a large number of cases negotiated with
employers on their behalf. During the first world war letters were written
to many employers protesting at the failure to pay 'war bonus', and at
Stockton in 1924 the Trades and Labour Council claimed to have 'very
materially assisted' in negotiating improvements for the Britannic
agents.[90] During the course of disputes involving the agents, and
sometimes as a simple organising method, trades council delegates were
frequently exhorted to pay their premiums only to agents who were union
members. The effectiveness of such action was rarely assessed, but it was
often advocated.[91] Boycotts and the threat of them were frequently used
to help shop workers. These could be in attempts to secure early closing

on one day of the week, or to put pressure on employers to grant union recognition. Again, it is difficult to measure the rate of success, but the trades councils of Swansea, Cardiff and Liverpool are said to have reduced the hours of local shop workers.[92] Political agitation of various sorts in supporting legislative improvements in shop workers' conditions, lobbying, sending letters, and on some occasions directly negotiating with employers, were other methods used.[93] Another service group in whom the trades councils took a particular interest were the employees of co-operative societies. In Oxford the Trades Council spent over a decade trying to enforce union membership on Co-operative employees, and in 1908 put up candidates in Co-operative elections pledged to achieve this. By 1915, although the society could not be persuaded to enforce membership, nevertheless enough employees had joined the union to make it possible to drop the matter. Elsewhere trades councils negotiated successfully with local societies on behalf of their employees, although for a time these activities were hampered by disputes between the AUCE and other unions who were trades council affiliates.[94]

Trades councils frequently took an interest in the organisation of women workers, especially when they joined the work force in large numbers during the first world war. The special Women's Trades Council in Manchester, which co-operated with the main body and eventually merged with it, is a well known example.[95] There are many examples of trades councils fighting 'the indifference of the male trade unionist to female organisation', and often members were exhorted 'to use all their influence to persuade their lady relations to join a Trade Union'.[96] In south London early in the war a number of trades councils set up branches of the National Federation of Women Workers, and at other periods there were special efforts on behalf of cafe waitresses in Liverpool and nurses in Halifax and Great Harwood.[97] Trades councils were also often eager to help schoolteachers, 'a profession which has not hitherto been associated with the general trade union movement'. The National Union of Teachers obtained a substantial vote for TUC affiliation as early as 1895, and some branches worked with trades councils in the following period. Such participation remained rare, however, despite the constant concern of the trades councils with educational questions, and frequent efforts to persuade branches of the union to affiliate. More success attended efforts to persuade the Class Teachers' Association and the National Union of Uncertificated Teachers to join, when the trades councils took up their separate grievances, and at Liverpool it was said that the Trades and Labour Council played some part in recruitment to the teaching unions.[98] In some areas the trade councils also took part in the organisation of agricultural workers.[99] They could also apply with success some of their own methods of political pressure and agitation on behalf of workers in bakehouses. The Birmingham Trades Council ran a big publicity campaign about the conditions and fearsome hours endured by workers of this kind, and other bodies supported legislative efforts to combat these evils.[100] Trades councils also applied pressure on local authorities and other employers to get work for painters in the winter.[101]

Another group of workers that the trades councils could help through local lobbying and negotiation was the blind. They applied pressure for general concessions on behalf of the blind on humanitarian grounds, and often got them reduced fares or free travel on public transport.[102] However, trades councils sympathised closely with the militant stance of the National League for the Blind, whose organiser told the Leeds Trades Council that he 'stood for State aid and State control, not for charity and voluntarism ... He represented a Trade Union, which belonged to the Trade Union Federation, and not any charity organisation.' Local bodies supported the efforts of this group by trying to get public control of all blind workshops. When the Bolton workshop was municipalised in 1933 the Trades Council was 'delighted' at 'a measure we have agitated for for nearly half a century'.[103] Elsewhere conferences and marches run by blind organisations were supported, and negotiations were carried out with local authorities and others running institutions to improve the conditions of blind workers.[104]

It was probably the employees of public authorities that the trades councils could aid most effectively. Much has already been said about the FWCs that trades councils secured and enforced for those working for local authorities. Trades councils also set up union branches for tramway workers, normally local authority employees, and sometimes negotiated for them.[105] At Liverpool the Trades Council negotiated improvements for council scavengers in 1892, and in 1916 tried to get wage increases for employees of the public health department. They were also actively involved when local authorities employees went on strike, as in Oxford and Leeds in 1913. One president thought that trades councils could do more for council employees than could Labour councillors.[106] In the early and semi-illegal years of trade unionism in the Post Office the Liverpool Trades Council fulfilled an important role in setting up branches of the relevant trade unions. In later years trades councils often passed motions to show public concern at the grievances of postal workers.[107] The conditions of employees in Admiralty dockyards were also often a cause for protest by trades councils, and in 1912 the Portsmouth body was instrumental in the formation of a Dockyards Grievances Committee which provided the first substantial bargaining machinery for this group of workers.[108]

However, perhaps the most spectacular work of the trades councils in the organisation of public employees came during the brief period when genuine trade unionism existed among police and prison officers.[109] In this case trades councils used all their negotiating experience and resources for moral and material support in an unsuccessful effort to secure recognition for the Police and Prison Officers' Union, supporting them in their strikes in 1918 and 1919 and helping those who were victimised as a result. Although there were various efforts at improving the conditions of policemen before that time,[110] it was only during the first world war that the Police and Prison Officers' Union began to achieve national support. As early as January 1917 the Liverpool Trades Council agreed to support the local branch after a debate in which the action of the police against strikers in the past was mentioned, but it was agreed 'that if the Police then had a Union things might have been different'. By the end of the year six branches were affiliated to the trades council. Similarly, in Manchester, 300 members affiliated. At Ràwtenstall there were already collections for men disciplined for attending meetings, and at Watford support for 'a trade union in its infancy' was commended to union members.[111] It was from the London Trade Council that the most substantial effort came. Though it is perhaps an exaggeration to say that this body was 'largely responsible for creating the union', nevertheless in the strike of August 1918 the 'guiding hand of the London Trades Council was evident' in the way 'the Union leaders displayed a surprising knowledge of how to run a major industrial stoppage'. At a meeting on Tower Hill on 30 August Duncan Carmichael, its secretary, could tell the strikers 'in the name of the London Trades Council that they had the hearty support of organised labour generally in the London district'.[112]

After the success of this strike in achieving all its demands, except recognition of the union, branches sprang up in every part of the country. At Birmingham in October the Trades Council president ran the opening meeting. In the same month a branch affiliated to the trades council at Ashton and the Lancashire Federation urged that 'every trades council with a borough force could and should organise a branch'. The union had now received enough recognition in the movement to affiliate to the TUC early in 1919.[113] Its legitimacy as a union was now agreed by the movement, but not by the authorities. During the course of 1919 it was defeated by a combination of cunning on the part of government and police chiefs, division of leadership and lack of support from most leading figures in the trade union movement.[114] By the time of the second and last strike run by the union in August 1919 so many threats had been made and so many concessions granted that many union members did not come out, and little support proved forthcoming from the rest of the trade union movement.[115] In Liverpool, where the strike was most extensively supported, the Trades Council continued to declare 'common cause with the police', and a meeting was convened by the youthful Walter Citrine of the trades councils of Liverpool, Bootle and Birkenhead, together with the Transport Workers' Federation, a group which had often combined for militant action in the past. But by the time of this meeting there was little that could be done except to plead for the jobs of the dismissed strikers.[116] Such soon came to be the role of other local bodies, collecting money for the dependants of the former policemen and trying every method to negotiate the reinstatement of those so cruelly treated for their steadfastness to the principles of a movement they had so recently joined.[117]

Although the experience in organising the police was not a happy one, it nevertheless illustrated the fact that, despite the centralisation in the bargaining activities of the trade union movement, there was still a place for local organisations in its industrial work. In the first two decades of the new century, even when large and stable organisations had been established by the workers in many industries, the movement still could not manage without the efforts of the trades councils in recruitment, and in winning a place for trade unionists both with their employers and in the wider community. Such industrial activities alone do not, however, explain the continued vigour of the local organisations. They proved their usefulness to the movement perhaps most effectively in the way they were able to deal with political and other matters often far beyond their preliminary concern with wages and working conditions. It is with this aspect of the work of the trades councils that the next chapter will deal.

Chapter three

From individualism to social reform

Changing aspirations

In the mid-nineteenth century trades councils reflected the narrow craft orientation of a movement whose basic strength derived from the ability of unions to establish and maintain the scarcity of workers' skills. In the 1870s and '80s organisations were set up by unskilled groups whose aims and methods had to be broader. At the same time radical and socialist ideas gained a following in the movement. These influences made the unions look beyond narrow industrial concerns to more general political and industrial questions affecting all sections of the poor. In the trades councils, especially in the early years of the present century, this transition can be clearly seen, and it is the purpose of this chapter to describe and explain it.

Even in the 1860s, when there were those who opposed 'trades meetings being mixed with politics', the Glasgow Trades Council could not agree 'as long as trades societies are amenable to law'. In 1876 George Howell wrote that the usefulness of the trades councils would 'be greatly enhanced in proportion as they are able and empowered to deal with matters above and beyond mere questions of wages and labour'. From the 1890s onwards it became more and more the case that local organisations were concerned not simply with 'the working part of [their] members' lives, but also ... those influences and environmental conditions which effect men and women when the factory, workshop and mine have been left behind'.[1]

In the nineteenth century it was not difficult to find expressions of snobbery and craft prejudice in the trades councils. Perhaps the most extreme case that can be quoted is that of the Manchester body in 1879 opposing the reduction in prices at Town Hall organ recitals in case 'certain classes of people whose company is distasteful might find their way into the hall'. In 1890 of the secretary of one trades council it could be written that 'in his heart of hearts he has little sympathy with the working man', and in the same year the leaders at Liverpool 'looked askance' at a strike of dockers in the port. In Leeds the unskilled workers even felt obliged to set up a separate trades council for a time.[2] Divisions on similar lines partly accounted for the separate trades councils which existed in both Nottingham and Sheffield for long periods. However, few councils remained hostile to unions of unskilled workers. The secretary at Cardiff thought that 'our brother-toilers engaged in lesser skilled industries' showed 'the breath of life of genuine trades-unionism', and at Swansea the local body 'opened its doors, largely through pressure from without, to all organised workers'. It was simply that unskilled workers took such a long time to get well organised. There were few trades councils which had more than a tiny group of unskilled workers affiliated before about 1910, and as late as 1918 at Liverpool the majority of branches affiliated still came from skilled groups – 119 to 107.[3] However, the very different and broader aspirations of the new unions rapidly had an effect on the older trades councils. The secretary at Liverpool thought 'the objects of the Old and New Unionism are identical' despite 'a certain amount of friction', and considered each group had something to learn from the other. The sincerity of these sentiments was shown by the fact that by the mid-'90s the Trades Council expelled the Plasterers' Society for blacklegging on a group of labourers.[4] The spread of these attitudes continued during the following years. The trades councils were seen as able to 'give expression to the desire of the strong societies to help the weak', and their meetings became 'educational in a direct sense'. The councils began to consider it necessary to take into account the needs of all groups of workers, including sections with limited bargaining power, and even those who were not members of unions at all. Trade union activity could not be conceived by those with limited bargaining strength as narrowly as before. Soon local bodies went well beyond the narrowly conceived industrial activities that had once been their main role. It was thus that it could be said of the Oldham body after the 1880s that 'where previously it had concerned itself solely with trade union matters, it now became involved in the broader politics of the town'. Elsewhere a trades council considered itself 'an organisation that can focus and give expression of opinion from a Trades Union point of view upon many matters appertaining to legislation that effects the interests, and tends to the welfare, of the labouring classes generally', and another local body was concerned 'to organise public opinion upon all questions effecting the well-being of the working class, and the general interests of the community'.[5]

The change in the outlook and activities of the trades councils in this period was not just a matter of the recruitment of the unskilled. Other influences were acting on local organisations to change their attitudes from the individualist, craft-bound ideas of the nineteenth century, reflecting something of artisan production, to a more broadly based, collectivist approach favoured by workers involved in larger-scale production. The historian of one trades council has described this process as 'Self-help to Social Reform', and others have noticed in the local organisations a greater 'consciousness of social injustice and a determination by trade unionists to set themselves higher targets of life style'. The Webbs thought that in general the new unionism brought with it 'a more generous recognition of the essential solidarity of the wage-earning class', and others saw the development among trade unionists of a 'consciousness they were all members of a single class'.[6] It was in the trades councils that these changes were most clearly reflected. They were the best forums in the movement for discussions of 'a moral and educational value, calculated to be most valuable to trades organisations'.[7] It was through such discussions that opposition to the friendly-society aspects of Victorian trade unionism and hostility to middle class philanthropy could be developed. The move away from treating the poor as evildoers, and the growth of hatred for such attitudes in the working class movement, have often been noted.[8] The gradual inculcation of this outlook in local working class organisations through such agencies as the Fabian Society and the syndicalists can also be traced. Affiliation to organisations like the National Housing Council, the Anti-Sweating League and the National Committee for the Prevention of Destitution, and taking part in their activities, had a strong effect on local attitudes.[9] More and more often trades councils could be heard protesting against public collections for hospitals, calling for unemployment to be dealt with as a national concern, and in many ways indicating a change of attitude from their forbears on all the problems of poverty and human misery.[10] The effect of these attitudes is discussed in more detail later in this chapter, but first more should be said about the growth of collectivist notions of a more general kind.

Well before the end of the nineteenth century trades councils tried to secure municipal control of certain public utilities, often with some success. The municipalisation of the trams was supported in a strong campaign in Glasgow in 1888, and in 1899 the Yorkshire Federated Trades Councils were urging local authorities to put 'the good of all' before 'individual profits' in this matter. In 1903 the Birmingham Trades Council claimed to be a 'powerful factor' in the decision to take over the tramway system in that town, and similar efforts were made in Oxford in

1905.[11] Such was the pride of the Bradford Trades and Labour Council in these and other achievements of municipal enterprise that in the early part of the century many delegates in organised parties visited the local technical college, baths, gasworks, electricity station, fire station and the recently acquired tramway undertaking. There was also widespread support for direct labour by local authorities.[12]

Working class organisations began soon to go beyond the simple aims of municipal ownership to wider collectivist aims, as can be illustrated by the developing support for the Land Nationalisation Society.[13] This organisation, set up in 1881, aimed at State ownership of all land and its leasing to tenant farmers as far as possible. Although started by Liberals, it came to rely increasingly on the support of the working class movement, especially from the trades councils. In the 1890s it began to send out 'yellow vans' in order to convert the urban and rural masses to the efficacy of its solution for social ills. In 1893 it got the support of the Labour Electoral Congress, and soon of leading Labour figures such as Keir Hardie. In 1895 meetings were run under the auspices of the trades councils at Halifax and Leeds, where there was an 'almost entire absence of hostile treatment', and there was support from trades councils and other trade union organisations throughout the north of England.[14] In 1896 the Leicester Trades Council indicated its support for the movement, which was to remain unshaken for well over two decades.[15] During 1899 there were visitors from the yellow vans at twenty-six trades councils, and special conferences were run by the trades councils of Newcastle, Sunderland, Leicester and elsewhere. Such activities continued in the following years. It is interesting to notice that soon LNS conferences began to broaden their scope beyond rural concerns. In 1900 and the following years the Society ran 'Housing and land reform' conferences which centred around the demand for the implementation of the 1890 Housing Act, and campaigned for municipal housing schemes. Trades councils always supported such activities, and in many cases directly sponsored them.[16] Support for the general views of the LNS can be found throughout trades council meetings and reports. 'Perhaps the worst and greatest of all monopolies is the private ownership of land,' it was thought at Oldham, and at Warrington it was considered 'necessary to have efficiency rather than the landlord class'. At Dorchester the land was said to be 'the common social inheritance of the people'.[17] There was a further spate of land nationalisation propaganda activity in the period before and after the end of the first world war. Many local conferences were held. In 1917 ten trades councils were affiliated to the LNS and twenty-five others associated themselves with it by making regular donations; by 1920 these numbers had risen to fifteen and thirty respectively.[18]

Although the support in the working class movement for the ideas of the LNS in some measure represented the yearning of urban workers to return to an unattainable rural past, these ideas nevertheless helped to push working class leaders towards collectivist views of a more general kind. From municipal ownership to land nationalisation, it was but a short step to the view that there should be other forms of public ownership. The Railway Nationalisation Society, set up in 1908, directed itself largely to the working class movement and found much support in the trades councils.[19] Soon collectivist solutions of various kinds were being put forward in local organisations to other problems. In 1905 the Glasgow Trades Council ran a demonstration which agreed 'that unemployment and poverty are inseparably bound up with the private ownership of land and capital'. In the same year at Accrington it was said that mines, railways 'and other monopolies' should be nationalised, and in 1908 the secretary at Newcastle said he thought that soon 'public ownership will be admitted to be the only solution' to social problems. The Birmingham Trades Council thought that there existed 'a quiet yet determined resolve, by combination among the workers, to secure control of all the means of life, that things socially needed shall be socially owned'.[20] During the 1914–18 war such aims grew broader. At Leicester it was thought that all the major industries 'should be taken over by the Government and managed by joint boards representing the Government and the workers concerned in the interests of the State'. The retention of national control over those industries in which the State had intervened during the war was considered the 'only hope' for dealing with the post-war economic problems, and the only way to replace the dole by 'the production of useful and needed articles'. As a result of such sentiments trades councils were naturally enthusiastic participants in the 'Mines for the nation' campaign in 1920.[21]

The changing atmosphere and attitudes in the trades councils was not just a matter in this period of the growth of collectivist ideas about the running of the welfare services and industry. It was also indicated by more humanitarian views on other matters. Support for the kind of free speech campaigns normally run by the SDF and the ILP were voiced by the trades councils in London in 1893 and in Liverpool in 1915.[22] Trades councils protested against the imprisonment of Tom Mann in 1912 for urging soldiers not to break strikes, and supported those involved in such cases abroad, such as Tom Mooney, the trade unionist who languished in jail in the United States for many years.[23] Support for generally progressive causes such as female suffrage could always be assured in local bodies.[24] Such feelings could at times be given an internationalist complexion, with growing support for self-determination in Ireland and

India in the trades councils.[25] It is hard to say how internationalist-minded they became. Many local organisations supported the campaign against Chinese workers in South Africa that dominated the 1906 general election. They later also joined protests against the employment of foreign labour on British ships, and even opposed 'coloured labour' altogether.[26] On the other hand, local organisations protested against Belgian rule in the Congo and welcomed the Chinese revolution of 1911. Trades councils largely abandoned the views they previously expressed in the 1890s at Blackburn, Liverpool and Leeds against the immigration of 'alien paupers', mainly Jews from Russia. The Manchester Trades Council demonstrated against anti-semitism in 1903, and with other local bodies protested against the visit of the Czar to Britain in 1910. Trades councils in London, Leicester, Brighton and Peterborough expressed opposition to the Boer war on the grounds that it worsened the conditions of the workers, and local bodies and their leaders at Aberdeen, Bradford, Keighley, Reading, Southport and Darwen protested in a more general way.[27] The numerous motions passed by trades councils before 1914 promising a general strike in the event of war were also a testimony to the strong feeling that existed in the local bodies, if not to their ability to act on those feelings.[28] However, many trades councils did much to welcome and win support for the trade union leaders deported from South Africa to Britain in the spring of 1914. The London Trades Council organised a demonstration of 100,000 that gave 'the deported leaders such a London welcome as had not occurred since Garibaldi's visit to this country', and the Birmingham Trades Council executive spoke of 'an unscrupulous gang of traders and mineowners' trying to maintain 'their power to exploit labour, black and white alike'.[29] Although internationalist feelings of this kind temporarily evaporated with the advent of war in 1914, social discontent and radical propaganda soon ensured their revival.

Many of the political ideas adopted by the trades councils in this period were not far outside the ambit of the most elementary defence of working class and democratic rights, and many were shared by sections of the Liberal Party. They do represent, however, an important manifestation of a transition in the working class movement from the confines of advanced Liberalism to modern Labourism, a change easier to pinpoint in the trades councils than elsewhere in the movement. For the councils themselves they also represented a major shift in the types of function they expected to perform.

New functions

Perhaps the most striking way in which the attitudes and activities of local bodies changed was in dealing with unemployment. Before the 1890s this was not a matter in which they took an interest. As was often to be the case in the future, it was the left wing political organisations in the working class movement that first made serious efforts to organise the unemployed, to agitate to improve their conditions, and to secure the economic changes that would increase the number of jobs. In Hull in 1884 the Trades Council would have nothing to do with local agitation on the matter, and in 1892 the Liverpool Trades Council refused to join the Association for the Unemployed. In London it seems that the matter was never mentioned before 1889, and elsewhere it was still often left to others. The first 'hunger march' at Leicester in 1906 was led by members of the local clergy, and, more typically, at Crewe local agitation on the question was led by the ILP as late as 1914.[30]

From the 1890s a gradual change could be noticed. At Hull in 1894 the Trades Council was prepared to support a campaign which two years earlier it had rejected. At first, efforts on behalf of their less fortunate brethren involved trade unionists in activities which they later came to oppose. For example, the Leicester Trades Council in 1894 and 1895 raised charitable donations, and in Leeds in 1895 the Trades Council joined a committee with the Chamber of Commerce.[31] By the winter of 1903–04, when unemployment again became a major issue, local organisations were working on it in new ways. At Birmingham the Trades Council engaged in both national and local political agitation for public works schemes, and at Bradford the Trades and Labour Council persuaded the local council not to sack those who would only be thrown into the ranks of the unemployed.[32] Although the initiative for agitation, and the establishment of local Right to Work committees in the following period, were the work of the SDF, the trades councils were now enthusiastic participants in these activities, and they were supported in Carlisle, Oxford and many other towns.[33] Most local organisations were not happy about the Unemployed Workmen Act of 1905, even though they were often represented on the local distress committees set up under it to survey the situation and initiate remedies such as setting up labour exchanges. The Birmingham Trades Council thought it 'a Shop Window Act', and leading trade unionists regarded it as 'a menace', since the exchanges would attract 'the inefficient worker and the cheap labour employer'.[34] The type of solution now being advocated can be seen from the statement of the Sunderland secretary in 1909 that 'modern civilisation' should be able to provide more than 'spasmodic charity' for the 12,000 unemployed of his town: 'Unemployment is more a social than an individual question, society must therefore accept responsibility for its own neglect and find a solution.'[35]

The development of attitudes in Liverpool over this period provides an illustration of the kind of change that was taking place. Besides the negative attitude of 1892 already mentioned, in the following year the secretary attacked delegates for attending a confence on behalf of the unemployed although prepared to donate £86 to their welfare. However, by 1902 the Trades and Labour Council sponsored regular visits to the homes of the unemployed and put forward a long list of public works for the local council to undertake. In 1906 a special committee was set up at the behest of the affiliated Socialist Society, and in 1908 this was re-established to complain of the 'stereotyped callousness and indifference to the needy and the suffering which has at all times distinguished Liverpool public bodies from all others throughout Great Britain'. By the time of the beginning of the post-war depression in 1920 the Liverpool Trades Council was able itself to undertake the organisation of the unemployed.[36] This change from individualist to more general and humanitarian attitudes, combined with efforts to achieve collectivist solutions for social ills, was to show itself in other aspects of the work of the trades councils in this period.

On the issue of the health of affiliated members local organisations showed most clearly the way in which their interests broadened beyond the immediate concern with wages and working conditions. In the 1890s the main interest of the trades councils was in securing liberal measures of workmen's compensation. In 1893 twenty-seven of them wrote to the Home Office asking that employers should not be able to contract out of the legislation that was then being proposed. After the Act was passed in 1897 local organisations spent a great deal of time complaining about its inadequacy, particularly about how few people were entitled to benefit from it. Such efforts resulted in shop workers, clerks and others being included in a 1906 Act. The Bradford Trades and Labour Council claimed to have been responsible for the inclusion of some of the new groups in the 1906 measure, and later sponsored some of the first prosecutions under it. By 1915 the Yorkshire Federated Trades Councils put forward a complete programme, including special doctors to help adjudication and a national system of insurance.[37] Some local bodies in the meantime spent a great deal of effort over the years in doing what they could under the measures that did exist. In Bradford from 1882 there was a fund, originally collected for the victims of a local mill disaster, which was used to help other victims of industrial accidents. After 1897 this money was employed almost exclusively in fighting cases through the courts, and by 1906 it was claimed that £3,450 had been secured for injured workers with the expenditure of less than £100 a year by the Trades and Labour Council. In Birmingham the Trades Council raised money to advise societies, and the Huddersfield body employed a legal adviser to help members. In Halifax there was a special fund like the one at Bradford, which in 1914 was used to fight eighty-three cases involving £4,000, and in 1928 twenty-five cases involving £2,600. The special fund continued until 1935, when it was abandoned, perhaps under TUC pressure.[38]

Matters such as these might normally have been expected to concern trade union organisations, but trades councils began to go beyond them. At first they were simply involved in charitable efforts on behalf of local hospitals.[39] This soon led to involvement in local Hospital Saturday Funds, which provided forms of insurance in voluntary hospitals. Saturday funds were originally set up in the 1850s as a workmen's alternative to the Sunday funds run by the Churches, though the relationship of the working class movement to them seems to have varied a great deal. In Belfast the Trades Council simply received delegations from the fund about the need to support it. At Liverpool the Trades and Labour Council put pressure on a local equivalent for such measures as lunchtime surgeries in 1908, and in 1914 was trying to get representation on its ruling committee. The Birmingham body also complained about lack of representation, though at times encouraging people to support it. The Oxford Trades Council attacked the fund on the grounds that all hospitals should be publicly run, although the Leicester body had a representative on a local committee and worked closely with it for many years.[40] After 1918 these funds grew less important, and the trades councils became involved in such activities in different ways. In 1920 the Blackpool Trades Council set up its own hospital scheme to finance improvements at the local voluntary hospital, and in Edinburgh the Trades Council established a League of Subscribers to the Infirmary after it had been granted increased representation on the board of managers. In Sheffield the Trades and Labour Council was involved in the Joint Hospital Council from 1919, and some years later was thanked 'for the real live interest they have taken in the hospital movement during the last few years', mention being made of the 'high standard' of their work in the field.[41] These examples are enough to show how the interest of the trades councils in the Saturday funds led to a concern with hospital administration in general. Such general concerns also developed when local bodies took up cases of alleged ill treatment. Some had sub-committees which considered many such cases, others strongly pursued individual complaints.[42] It was not long before efforts in this direction led the trades councils to seek, and often to obtain, representation on the governing bodies of local hospitals. By about 1910 such representation was being increasingly secured, either by election or through direct co-option.[43] Sympathy was also shown for the Manor House Hospital, run in association with the trade union movement itself.[44]

Leading on from such interests as these, the trades councils began to show an increasing interest in public health in general. Calls for more public control over the hospital and health system grew more insistent as local organisations came into closer contact with the voluntary system and with those who proposed more attractive alternatives. Interestingly enough, the discussion of industrial diseases does not seem to have been very common, except perhaps at Bradford in the case of anthrax, the wool sorters' disease, which was to some extent a special local problem.[45] In general such subjects were left to the unions. However, a whole range of other matters of public health were considered by the trades councils, and in most cases public control was advocated. For example, during the first world war there was widespread agitation for the setting up of municipal maternity centres, and also a great deal of interest in venereal disease after the 1916 report of the Royal Commission on the matter and the setting up of a National Council for Combating Venereal Disease.[46]

It was but a short step from an interest in public health matters of this kind to a concern with housing conditions. In the first place, many local bodies considered it to be their duty to protest about bad conditions where they existed. In Leeds the Trades Council wanted the abolition of back-to-back housing as early as 1909, and at Hull in 1903 the Trades and Labour Council supported the Medical Officer of Health in his efforts to have all privy middens converted to water closets, a reform which was not in fact carried out until the 1920s. The Hackney Trades Council, when established in 1900, began to 'agitate for better housing for the workers', and at Aylesbury it was said that after the council's foundation in 1911 'the most important duty of a delegate was to go round the town seeking complaints about drainage and bad housing'. At Clydebank in 1913 there were complaints of 'A HOUSE FAMINE' and at Ripley, Derbyshire, two years later a special survey by the Trades and Labour Council revealed 'a scarcity of houses, closets and watertaps, and too many privy middens'. A special meeting of the local council was secured, and, if no new houses were built, something was done to improve sanitary conditions. In Crewe in the same period it was said that the Trades Council, together with the ILP, 'made the question their own'.[47] Such discussion and agitation increasingly resulted in the adoption of collectivist solutions by the trades councils, and, under the influence of the Workmen's National Housing Council, they called for new houses to be built by the local authorities.[48] Municipal housing was proposed to the candidates in the Birmingham local elections in 1896, and at Oxford in 1900. Careful surveys resulted in the formulation of detailed schemes at Bradford in 1913 and at Ripley in 1915. In both Carlisle and Wolverhampton in 1914 local authorities adopted some of the ideas of the trades council. House building was suspended from 1914 to 1918, however, and it was only after this that any real successes in the campaign for public housing could be claimed. In 1918, however, the Rawtenstall Trades Council actually helped the local authority to formulate a scheme once it had been decided to start one.[49] Many trades councils from 1914 onwards went beyond simply putting collectivist policies to reluctant local authorities, and began actively to organise tenants to improve their situation. The passing of the Rent Restriction Act in December 1915 has sometimes been portrayed as resulting simply from the rent strikes that took place on the Clyde.[50] However, before the war even started there were rent strikes in which other local movements were involved, and at Leeds it was thought that 'the raising of rents by the landlord class offered a splendid opportunity for ridding themselves entirely of the landlord class. It was quite as easy to strike against paying rent altogether as to strike against it in part.' In the opening days of the war the Camberwell Trades and Labour Council told tenants, 'Do NOT worry if you are unable to pay your rent.' After the passing of the Rent Restriction Act both the Woolwich and Coventry bodies claimed to have been responsible for it, and during the course of 1915 virtually every trades council ran meetings and demonstrations on the question.[51] After the passing of the Act, however, trades councils found that their work had only begun. Numerous leaflets were issued publicising the Act, particularly for the benefit of landlords who claimed to be ignorant of it. Many individual cases were taken up, and even fought through the courts, and Tenants' Defence Leagues were set up to serve the interests of those involved. The Oldham Trades and Labour Council found that at one stage 'almost all' the time of the full-time secretary was spent in advising tenants, and reversing illegal increases, work which the secretary justified, since although it 'may not appear to be strictly the work of a Trade Union', nevertheless it was 'the duty of the Council to attend and assist not only the Trade Union branches but its individual members also'.[52] Such statements could often have been made on many other aspects of the work of the trades councils. Their efforts on rents certainly showed results. At Hartlepools the Labour League secretary asserted early in 1918 that 'we can justly claim to have saved the workers of this town thousands of pounds', and in Hull the figure of £25,000 was actually specified after the war.[53] In the following years trades councils were actively involved in many types of activity on behalf of tenants. At Preston the Trades Council established a Tenants' Defence Bureau in 1919, and in Doncaster in 1920 a special department was set up to deal with tenants' problems. Elsewhere trades councils established and supported organisations of tenants themselves. The Manchester body was actively involved with such an organisation during the war, and continued to support it during the 1920s, when housing, along with unemployment, was said to be its main preoccupation. In Birmingham there was a complex organisation of at least fifteen local tenants' associations, for which the Trades Council provided information and advice. In Northampton the Trades Council was less actively involved with the Tenants' Defence Association but nevertheless lent it cordial support.[54]

The issue of housing and rents shows the way in which the comparatively narrow concerns of the nineteenth century became broadened during the twentieth, and how the trades councils, as well as fighting for housing policies which were to have an important effect in the future, also did something on behalf of the tenants among their affiliated members. The interests of the local bodies in educational policy broadened in the same way, from the narrow preoccupation with some problems of working men to a concern for more general aspects of education, and to action as pressure groups and as working class representatives in local communities.

During the nineteenth century the trades councils interested themselves in provisions for technical education. In Coventry it was considered necessary to save it from the 'faddists'. The passing of the Technical Instruction Act in 1889 and the setting up of local Technical Instruction Committees gave a role to local organisations in discussing details of technical courses to be arranged, and often in being represented on the committees.[55] When the Wolverhampton Trades and Labour Council ran a conference on apprenticeship with the local chamber of commerce it was agreed that for each apprentice there should be provision for 'the full practical and technical instruction necessary to his trade'.[56]

It was not long before such discussions as these were expanded into other aspects of education as well. The interest in securing the representation of working men on local administrative bodies resulted in the candidates being put up by the trades councils for the School Boards that existed from 1870 to 1902, generally on a platform of opposition to the dominance of education by various religious factions.[57] Trades council representatives were elected to School Boards in Hull in 1883, and in Leeds, Bristol and Nottingham in 1886. In Birmingham the 'plumping' method – allowing people to vote for one candidate as many times as there were vacancies – was used to secure trades council representation in the 1890s.[58] The trades councils took an active part in the wide-scale discussion of educational issues that preceded and followed the 1902 Education Act. They defended the Higher Grade Schools against the attacks on them by judiciary and local authorities. They also bitterly opposed many aspects of the 1902 measure, especially its abandonment of the elective principle. The Birmingham Trades Council was against it not only because of this but also 'because it failed to meet the urgent needs of the country for the better supply of secondary education and because it proposed to give further grants of public money to schools without proper public control'. The Bradford Trades and Labour Council obtained the agreement of 111 trades councils, representing 750,000 trade unionists, to 'free unsectarian education of the fullest character, the machinery of which should be entirely under popular control'. At Swindon feeling was so strong on this issue that the failure to stop the 1902 Act seems to have been as important a factor in converting the Trades Council to the need for independent representation as was the persecution of the Taff Vale railway strikers.[59]

Despite their opposition to the 1902 Education Act, trades councils soon found that the Education Committees it set up could provide them with an important extension of their functions in speaking for working men. Not for the last time, local organisations found their rebellion mollified by responsibility. At Manchester and Birmingham the powerful local trades councils were soon represented on the local committees, and at Liverpool there was a delegate who was elected by the Trades and Labour Council every three years and who had to give a detailed account of his stewardship in the annual report. Trades councils at Warrington and Cheltenham also played a part in local Education Committees.[60] Such representatives often at first interested themselves in what might be termed the welfare aspect of education. They advocated medical and dental inspection as well as smaller classes.[61] Trades councils also took up the campaign initiated by the SDF for free meals for schoolchildren. In Birmingham in 1905 the Trades Council got the local authority to pass such a measure, and the London, Bradford and Liverpool bodies were active in supporting conferences for it. After the Education (Provision of Meals) Act was passed in 1906 many local organisations spent a great deal of effort in discussing the details of the meals provided and in trying to get local authorities to carry out the service.[62]

As well as increasing their work in the field of education for the young, trades councils also took an increasing interest in adult education for their own members and others. Traditional working class measures of self-improvement were obvious from their support for the university extension movement in the nineteenth century and also for evening classes run by local authorities.[63] Early in the twentieth century, with the expansion of the working class education movement, the trades councils began to play a more significant role. In 1899 Ruskin College was established to provide a residential education for working men in Oxford, and in 1903 the WEA began to provide a liberal education. The Central Labour College was set up in 1909 in opposition to both of these, to run an education that was independent of such capitalist institutions as universities – the Plebs League and later the NCLC made propaganda on behalf of these ideas. The founder of the WEA wrote in 1907 of the difficulty he had had in persuading the leaders of the unions to interest themselves in educational activities, an attitude which changed only because of 'the influence of trades councils, and the advanced position of many of their leaders'. The local organisations were certainly active from the start. The Birmingham Trades Council was involved in sending two students to Ruskin in 1903, and the Bolton Trades Council sent one in 1905. The Reading branch of the WEA, its first and model local organisation, had a trades council representative on its board from the time of its foundation. The Belfast branch was set up when the Trades Council approached the university jointly with the Co-operative Society, and the trades councils at Leicester, Northampton, Derby and Blackpool convened the meetings that started local branches there. The Glasgow Trades Council also began the WEA in Scotland.[64] In Leeds trades council and university co-operated happily in the WEA until some of the WEA figures in the university condoned blacklegging in the 1913 municipal strike.[65] Local bodies were not just involved with the moderate wing of the working class educational movement. Often 'sleepy' trades councils 'were astonished by a violent clash between rival WEA and "Plebs" propagandists'. At Blackpool the issue raised such passion that a meeting 'for the only time in the history of the Council, broke up through non-observance of the Chair'.[66] In general, however, the local organisations were broad-minded, and often affiliated to both parts of the movement, as at Bolton, Northampton and Leeds, or worked closely with them, as at Nottingham.[67] In South Wales local bodies seem to have been broadly sympathetic to the aims of the Labour College movement, and similar support could sometimes be seen elsewhere.[68] Some trades councils ran classes themselves for their own members, independently of either faction.[69]

Interest in all these aspects of education soon led local organisations on to other activities in the field. In Liverpool the Trades and Labour Council interested itself from the 1880s in the discussion that eventually led to the foundation of the university. The establishment of Birmingham University in 1899 was celebrated in 1901 by a special exhibition run by the Trades Council, and the proceeds from this were used to finance a scholarship there from 1903 to 1948.[70] Local working class leaders soon became so involved in such questions as these as to be considered experts in their own communities on adult education matters.[71] Discontent with the results of the 1902 Education Act stimulated an ongoing concern in local organisations in the following years, and they took part in the widespread discussion that preceded the 1918 Education Act. At Nottingham there was a special advisory committee, at Huddersfield and Swindon there were visits from H. A. L. Fisher in 1916 and 1917, and at Middlesbrough a policy was formulated for 'a free educational highway from the nursery school to the University' as necessary to 'satisfy the needs of a democratic community'.[72] As early as 1916 the Bradford Trades and Labour Council could claim many achievements in the field. Besides a campaign on child feeding they were 'pioneers' in getting free scholarships in local secondary schools, and had secured 70 per cent of free places, as well as some maintenance scholarships. At the 1917 Labour Party conference it was the Bradford Trades and Labour Council, claiming the support of thirty to forty other trades councils, that proposed a full range of policies on education and child care. By then it had set out a detailed programme for free education at all levels, for better treatment of teachers, for more physical education for schoolchildren, and for the co-ordination of advanced technical and university education.[73] Such policies as these, worked out after years of discussion and under a variety of political and other influences, indicated how far the trades councils had travelled from the narrow preoccupations of an earlier period to a general effort to cater for many aspects of the lives of working people and their children.

Workers' representatives in the welfare services

In the early part of the twentieth century trades councils began to discuss and agitate about a wide variety of questions to do with the welfare of their members. During this period some at least of the policies advocated by these local bodies as well as by other sections of the labour movement came to be adopted. Despite preliminary suspicion, the councils were often persuaded to take part in the administration of them in one form or another. Their dislike for the 1905 Unemployed Workmens Act has already been mentioned. Yet in many cases they were involved in the local committees set up under the Act. Chesterfield Trades and Labour Council called a meeting in 1905 to set one up, and at Reading, Leicester, Portsmouth and Birmingham the trades councils had representatives on the local equivalents, in some cases devoting a great deal of time to discussion of their work. But, although there were 118 local committees in existence in 1908, by 1914 there were only sixteen.[74] Trades councils also tried to carry out such representative functions by getting some of their leaders appointed as JPs. Such appointments began in the 1870s, when local trade union leaders first found that their fight against 'class justice' could be combined with securing 'a means of advancement to some prominence in the community'. The Bolton Trades Council had a representative on the judicial bench in the 1870s, the Nottingham body had one in 1887, and the Birmingham Trades Council got three of its nominees selected in 1906.[75] There was also some importance in the representation which trades councils secured on the Education Committees set up under the 1902 Education Act. Real changes could be noticed, however, when the welfare legislation of the 1906 Liberal government seemed to show the success of the campaigning efforts of the local organisations and at the same time a recognition of their ability to speak for working people. Many of the measures of the Liberal government represented in one form or another a response to what the local bodies advocated, even if never quite in a form of which they wholly approved. However, in nearly every case the trades councils were reconciled to the new schemes, mostly through the representative responsibilities which were granted to them.

The first welfare provision with which the trades councils were actively involved was the granting of old age pensions in 1908. The earliest 'pension proposals came from persons of middle class origin and not from the ranks of labour'. Canon Blakely set up a National Providence League with this aim in 1878, which secured the support of Joseph Chamberlain in the following decade. His organisation was superseded by the efforts of Charles Booth, who began to advocate such pensions in 1890 when he found that old age was the largest demonstrable cause of poverty. Under these influences a number of government and parliamentary enquiries in the 1890s grew increasingly favourable to the idea.[76] In the 1890s the working class movement itself began to support the measure, the TUC doing so in 1896.[77] However, it was in the trades councils that support for old age pensions was perhaps most strongly and actively canvassed, and it was as much their efforts as those of any other part of the labour movement that built up public support in the following decade. In 1899 Booth published his *Old Age Pensions and the Aged Poor, a Proposal* and this captured the imagination of F. H. Stead, brother of the great Liberal journalist, who contacted George Barnes, General Secretary of the ASE. Together they called a small group of trade unionists to London to discuss the scheme, including representatives of the trades councils of London, Bristol, Hull and Leeds. It was agreed that there should be a series of local conferences addressed by Booth. These seem always to have been organised by local trades councils, and took place in Newcastle, Leeds, Manchester, Bristol, Glasgow and Birmingham. The result of all these conferences was the setting up of the National Committee of Organised Labour for Promoting Old Age Pensions for All (NCLOAP).[78]

In the years from 1899 to 1908 there was continuous propaganda in support of old age pensions, and the trades councils played a prominent part. In Birmingham the Trades Council operated as the local branch of the NCLOAP. It had already itself in 1896 supported a non-contributory scheme of 5s a week for all those of sixty-five and over, opposed the contributory scheme favoured by Joseph Chamberlain, and set up a sub-committee to deal with the matter. The 1899 Birmingham conference was run jointly with the local philanthropist George Cadbury, and was described by the Trades Council delegates as 'one of the most interesting and valuable conferences ever held in Birmingham'. In the following years nearly all the meetings and other activities to win public support in the Midlands were carried out by the officers of the Birmingham Trades Council.[79] Similarly the trades councils of both Glasgow and Edinburgh operated as branches of the national organisation, and the Yorkshire federation had a representative on its national committee. In the general elections of 1900 and 1906 numerous trades councils in every part of the country presented candidates with lists of demands among which old age pensions was prominent.[80] After the election of the Liberal government in 1906 interest in the matter increased, and the TUC even began to ask local organisations to organise demonstrations on the issue. In 1905 it was the efforts of the London Trades Council that gained the support of the Derbyshire miners for the need to continue agitation on the issue. As a result of many such activities, after the 1906 general election there were few outside the Conservative Party and the Charity Organisation Society who were not convinced of the need for the measure, and further efforts after the election finally persuaded the government to introduce old age pensions in 1908.[81]

When this reform was introduced the reaction in the trades councils to the granting of only 5s at seventy was usually one of disappointment. At Sunderland it was said that 'while all trade unionists will welcome the starting of the scheme, its details are not likely to be accepted in their entirety. The age limit is too high, and the discrimination by the medium of the income limit is objectionable.' The Liverpool body, which had expressed worry about the delay in introducing the measure, now considered it 'an insult and a mockery to the veterans of industry', and called on trade unionists to have nothing to do with it unless it was much modified.[82] But, although such objections as these were widely expressed it was not long before trade unionists became involved, albeit to a limited degree, in the administration of the Act. In order to keep the working of the pensions away from the poor law, local Old Age Pension Committees were set up in the larger urban centres to work in co-ordination with pensions officers. Local interests were supposed to be represented on these committees, and though there was no systematic effort to bring in trade unionists, trades councils often found a place.[83] One of those who led the struggle for old age pensions later wrote of how the local organisations had been kept out of mischief by their efforts:

perhaps no agitation before has so brought out the value of the Trades Council. The Trades Council was once looked upon as the happy hunting ground of socialistic cranks. Our work has shown it is capable of becoming the local organ of a great national movement. Again and again has the Trades Council . . . made audible the voice of the non-articulate . . . The Trades Councils of Great Britain have won national honours over Old Age Pensions.

Although it is doubtful whether 'socialistic cranks' had much influence in the local organisations before that date, it is certainly true that trades councils played an important role in the whole campaign for this measure, and, whatever their reservations when it was passed, were assured of a place in its administration when their campaigning was over.

When labour exchanges were introduced in 1909, partly arising from the work of the local committees under the 1905 Unemployed Workmen Act, the reservations in the trades councils were much more pronounced. The exchanges closely affected the functioning of trade unions, and it is not surprising that many were suspicious that they might be used to break strikes or to keep down wages. It is certainly not true, as one recent writer has claimed, that the 'dogmatic hostility' to labour exchanges from the SDF was not shared throughout the working class movement. The secretary of the Bradford Trades and Labour Council made this clear in 1912:

Up to the present the management of the Exchanges has been anything but satisfactory and unless there is a great improvement in the methods adopted by *certain* heads of departments, they are more likely to be Union smashers than Work Finders; we have asked for bread, and as usual, an unsympathetic government has given us a *stone*. The Labour Exchanges fail on the most crucial point. *They do not find employment* . . . Labour Exchanges *ought not to be allowed* to supply labour where there is a dispute in progress, or send anyone to a firm where they do not pay the *Standard Rate of Wages*.

At Liverpool, York and Birmingham similar suspicions were expressed.[85] It is clear, however, that there was a systematic effort by the authorities to reconcile trade unionists with the new institutions. This was done in a number of ways. In Leicester the Trades Council was convinced that they were 'a blessing to the working classes' by having their former secretary appointed the first local deputy manager. Another way of winning over trade unionists was to have local officials visit the trades councils, or even write in their annual reports to explain that the exchanges 'do not interfere with, make no attempt to regulate, the terms of the bargain between employer and workman'.[86] It is interesting to notice that at York such a visit convinced the Trades and Labour Council secretary of the need for trade unionists 'to take an active interest in their administration if they are not to be used as instruments against the interests of organised labour'. The Birmingham Trades Council was prepared to express cautious support if 'in framing the regulations for administrative control . . . a just and adequate share may be allotted to the Trades and Friendly Society representatives'.[87]

Trade unionists were given a share in the administration of labour exchanges from 1910 through Juvenile Advisory Committees. The Huddersfield and Plymouth trades councils secured local and area representation on these bodies. In Liverpool, despite a row in 1910 about local representation, by 1916 the Trades and Labour Council was convinced of its value. In Oxford, however, such representation was found to be futile, and was eventually abandoned, because of the lack of power of the Advisory Committee.[88] In 1917 Local Employment Committees were set up to represent 'influential citizens, chosen from among the leading employers and from the workers' organisations who could command the confidence and support of the public'. In later years they dealt with many aspects of the work of the exchanges, and trades councils were often represented on them, though sometimes after a struggle.[89] By the new period it seemed that working people had been reconciled to the labour exchanges. Some of the smaller unions began to put their lists of unemployed in the exchanges.[90] However, the original suspicions had by no means been allayed. In 1916 the Lancashire federation condemned the new Advisory Committees as 'mere puppets of the Board of Trade'. This suspicion was felt particularly strongly among trade unionists in the cotton industry, but calls for the abolition of the labour exchanges were also heard in Blackpool and Gainsborough in 1921, and at Birmingham in the following year.[91] Such criticism became so insistent that a committee of enquiry was set up in order to report that the labour exchanges were working well, at least for the unskilled.[92]

The authorities also found it difficult to secure the agreement of trade unionists for the National Insurance Act of 1911. In 1888 the General Secretary of the TUC, Henry Broadhurst, said compulsory unemployment insurance would 'strike at the root of trade unionism', and similar views were often heard on the trades councils.[93] They normally

reflected the older 'friendly benefit' type of trade unionism, and by 1911
many of the newer societies did not consider insurance an important part
of their work. This is not to say that they favoured compulsory
insurance, which their members could ill afford. When the matter was
discussed at the Liverpool Trades Council in 1911 the Lithograph
Printers expressed the view of the older organisations in saying that
unemployment insurance would 'undermine the autonomy and
independence of the Trade Unions'. The Trades Council as a whole
would not agree to this attitude, though opposing compulsory insurance.
In Birmingham a combination of old-fashioned trade unionists opposed
to State insurance and a group not prepared to agree to the contributory
principle on any terms almost managed to get the Trades Council to
oppose the 1911 measure altogether. It was agreed, however, that the
employers ought to pay all the contributions.[94] When the Bill was going
through Parliament local organisations took a great deal of interest in its
passage, two at least sending delegations to London to discuss it with the
Local Government Board. Though a great deal of suspicion continued to
be expressed, and at Aberdeen it was feared that union officials would be
'reduced to mere stereotyped agents working strictly within the compass
of bureaucratic institutions', nevertheless considerable interest was taken
in the 1911 Act. In Leicester 'a large proportion of the time of the
Council' in 1912 was spent in discussing the details of the measure, and
the Insurance Commissioners often arranged courses of lectures run by
trades councils. At Birmingham 400 people wanted to attend such
lectures, and at Manchester there were three special meetings and two
lecture courses on the Act. After a long period of this discussion the
Bradford Trades and Labour Council decided the Act was '*Good, Bad*
and Indifferent'.[95] In general, however, opinion gradually grew more
favourable. At Liverpool the Trades and Labour Council urged affiliated
unions to become 'approved societies' for the purpose of the Act. The
Leicester body also decided to support the measure and the more
conservative of Sheffield's two trades councils called it 'the most
democratic of modern times'.[96]

This growing support for a measure towards which there had initially
been considerable suspicion was caused in part at least by the
responsibilities which trade unionists came to assume under the Act. The
first part of the National Insurance Act, dealing with health insurance,
involved most of the working population being insured through friendly
societies or trade unions acting as 'approved societies'. Trades councils
tried to get their members to insure through their unions or the GFTU,
and in Bradford actually set up an approved society themselves.[97] More
important for the trades councils were the local Insurance Committees

set up to supervise the administration of medical and sanatorium benefits under the Act. These were set up in each county and county borough, and were supposed to be independent of the local authorities, while representing all the interests involved.[98] Trades councils often worked with the unions themselves to ensure that acceptable people were appointed to the Insurance Committees, and at Plymouth and Carlisle they co-operated with the local friendly societies on the matter.[99] The second part of the Act, dealing with unemployment insurance, involved a smaller group of just over two million workers and a somewhat different method of administration. Most of the work locally was done by insurance officers, but appeals against their decisions were allowed to courts of referees which were supposed to represent both employers and workers.[100] Although there were some successes in securing representation acceptable to organised labour, discontent at the powers and decisions of the courts of referees grew so great during 1917 that a number of trades councils in Lancashire withdrew their delegates, and advised those on the Labour Exchange Advisory Committees to resign also.[101]

The Liberal welfare legislation completed a process by which local working class organisations moved from being outsiders and agitators in favour of a limited number of collectivist measures to being successful proponents of important reforms and well recognised representatives of working people. By 1913 the Liverpool secretary could write that his council was 'represented on every principal body in Liverpool, educational, administrative and social'.[102] Few other trades councils could claim as much, but all had some part of this power, which they tried to exercise to the full.

Electoral work

There is one other aspect of the political work of the trades councils in this period which has only briefly been referred to so far, and that is their work as agents for the election of working men to local and national administrative bodies, Boards of Guardians, School Boards, local councils and Parliament. This is not an aspect of their work which will be covered in great detail, since to do so would be to move into aspects of local working class organisation far beyond their work as trade unions. However, it is necessary to say something of how the electoral work of the trades councils affected their internal development and their relations with other parts of the working class movement.

During the last years of the nineteenth century trades councils gradually became convinced of the need for independent representation, and began themselves to put up candidates, increasingly in opposition to the Liberal and Conservative parties.[103] Something has already been said about efforts in this direction in relation to School Boards, and the councils made similar attempts to secure a place for working men on Boards of Guardians. What is most interesting about this is the way in which the gradual expansion of the movement for the representation of working people always relied heavily on the trades councils. The Labour Electoral Association, which existed from 1887 to 1895, tried to secure working class representation, not necessarily independent of the Liberal Party. It relied almost entirely on the affiliation of trades councils, and said that all candidates had to be endorsed by them. The Bristol branch was called the Trades Council and Labour Electoral Association, and a London Labour Electoral League was set up by the Trades Council there in 1891.[104] Although only two trades councils were represented at the founding conference of the ILP, it was they who became 'the organisational unit on which the West Yorkshire ILP was based', and in London trades councils were established at Hammersmith, West Ham and Woolwich primarily to promote labour candidates.[105]

Against this background it is not surprising that the trades councils played a conspicuous part in the early years of the LRC and Labour Party. The first conference in 1900 elected James MacDonald and Harry Quelch, leaders of the London Trades Council, to the exeecutive, and soon trades councils in the main cities began to affiliate. At the second conference of the LRC one trade union delegate said he thought the organisation 'would have to work largely through the Trades Councils'.[106] Although in the following years local LRCs and Labour Parties were set up, the main electoral work was still carried out by the trades councils themselves. Until 1905 only trades councils could affiliate to the Labour Party, and after that date electoral organisations could affiliate only in areas not covered by trades councils. In 1908 local electoral organisations were allowed to affiliate in areas where they covered the jurisdiction of a number of trades councils. In 1906, when the LRC became the Labour Party, although there were over 100 local electoral bodies, very few were affiliated. As late as 1914, when seventy-three LRCs were affiliated, as against eighty-five trades councils, the latter covered all the main industrial centres of population. In Accrington and Carlisle in 1904 local trade unionists could not be persuaded to hand over any power on elections away from the trades councils to the LRCs. At Chesterfield the local unions provided most of the finance for candidatures but nevertheless considered that the only proper channel for nominations was through the Trades Council. At Leicester it was said that the local Labour Party confined its functions very narrowly to fighting elections.

It made no declaration of policy other than that of maintaining an independent party, enlisted no individual section, and made no attempt to create a social life or to organise systematic propaganda ... In all matters other than purely electoral ones, the ILP was the source of all local Party activity.[107]

The reason why the Labour Party leaders at first encouraged this position is not difficult to understand. Their new organisation needed to rest for its support on well tried and accepted parts of the working class movement rather than on bodies often regarded with suspicion by trade unionists. Party leaders thus wanted local efforts at getting support for independent representation to centre on the trades councils. The debates at the 1903 and 1905 LRC conferences are interesting in showing the suspicions against any non-trade union organisation being associated with electoral work.[108] Efforts to give over electoral work and affiliation to LRCs were always fiercely resisted, as at Grimsby and Liverpool in 1906.[109] However, soon the successes in the 1906 general election made it seem that the future now lay with purely electoral organisations. J. R. Clynes, secretary of the Oldham Trades and Labour Council, thought that 'Some of the work done by the Trades Councils has been lessened and made more effective during the past twelve months by the presence of the Labour Party in Parliament.' Elsewhere it was thought that industrial action was becoming obsolete.[110] Against this background the national Labour Party began in the period up to 1914 to try to set up strong electoral organisations in the main cities, and to get these affiliated to the Labour Party with full local trade union support. This was carried on despite the difficulty of local Labour Parties getting union affiliation at all after the Osborne judgement. It met with stubborn resistance. In Manchester the Trades and Labour Council simply refused to give up any of its power to the LRC, both because it considered itself the main trade union body in the area and because delegates 'were not prepared to hand over their powers to a body which represented the socialist element'. In North Staffordshire the LRC was affiliated only after the Trades Council had left it, and in Newcastle affiliation of the electoral organisation was agreed on the assumption that the Trades Council would continue to run it. In Leicester such affiliation was arranged in 1910, but the Trades Council president was careful to point out that his organisation would continue to perform the same work as before.[111]

By 1913 efforts to work out an effective form of local Labour Party organisation had still not proved successful. Trades councils 'of a primarily political type' were becoming important, it is true, but the problem of affiliation had not been effectively solved. The national leaders of the Labour Party now decided to encourage the merging of local electoral and industrial organisations. At Liverpool in 1913 the secretary explained that this would avoid 'overlapping' and 'the selection of candidates at hole-in-the-corner meetings'. One delegate later said that 'many of the societies believed that the Council fails to provide that complete representation which the movement needs'. There followed an increasing co-ordination of industrial and electoral activities in Liverpool, and eventually the merging of the two organisations in a way that continued for many years. Similar mergings were effected at Rochdale in 1913, at Oldham and Birmingham in 1914, at Burton in 1915 and at Woolwich in 1917. At Oldham it was made clear that the main reason for this change was to make the Labour Party more efficient, and at Woolwich the trend to unification of forces had gone so far that the shop stewards' movement was involved.[112] By 1918 many local organisations had experienced a period of close co-operation between all sections of the working class movement and became strong supporters of it. At Bury St Edmunds it was thought best to have 'one local party only, having committees for all things appertaining to labour', and at nearby Ipswich in the same period the Trades and Labour Council secretary looked forward to 'the unification of those forces into an organisation so complete that its power would be inestimable'.[113] Other influences besides the leaders of the Labour Party were involved in the formulation of such views, and the propaganda for the unification of local working class forces by Tom Mann and Tom Quelch will be considered in a later chapter. However, even at the end of the war these aims had not won universal support. At Clydach, Hendon and Hereford in 1918 it was still considered preferable to have separate organisations, and in London there was never any merging of the two main wings of the movement. At a conference run by the Fabian Research Department on the trades councils in March 1918 there was vigorous opposition to unification on the grounds that the trades councils needed all their time for industrial work.[114]

The trend to unification in the working class movement was confirmed in 1918 by the new Labour Party constitution. The changes have been seen as an attempt partly to suppress the left-wing elements in the trades councils.[115] It is probably more accurate to see them simply as attempts to streamline Labour Party organisation and to try to concentrate the interests of trade unionists on getting people elected to local and national office. From now on the Labour Party leaders, and particularly those responsible for party organisation, hoped that the trades councils would fade away. Under such headings as 'Trades Council or Labour Party? Which is it to be?' they argued that trades councils were 'played out' because the struggle between the workers and their opponents would be carried out 'in the political field', and that they should give up all their other functions and become 'fighting political machine[s]'. They claimed that the amalgamation of forces was bringing with it an increased interest in the work of local organisations. They tried to portray the trades councils as 'out of date' and 'dear delightful old Talking Shops where we solemnly sat, or stood, and talked and talked and talked, but never DID — unless one smoked, which one did with a vengeance'.[116] If this picture had been true in the 1890s it was certainly not so in the 1920s, when a wide range of new functions had transformed the 'talking shops' into lively and effective bodies. It was then that those on the left began to regret the unification of forces which they had formerly advocated.[117] It was not surprising that Herbert Morrison sneered at them:

Recently an effort appears to have been made by various people, among whom Communists and Guild Socialists tend to be prominent, to revive the separate existence of local Trades Councils . . . it is not without humour to observe that our "advanced" friends who are behind this movement, are making a big effort, not with the purpose of going forward, but of going backward to a type of organisation more appropriate to the middle of the nineteenth century. [118]

Despite the views of Herbert Morrison and other Labour Party organisers the work of the trades councils could not be confined to getting people elected to various local and national offices. The councils had already shown that they could do much more besides for the benefit of working people, and increasingly they found it necessary to organise themselves specially for non-electoral work before the 1927 Trade Disputes Act forced a more rigid separation of functions on them. Thus although the trades councils were electoral organisations at one stage in their career, they ultimately abandoned this role to concentrate on other political and industrial activities.

Chapter four

Recognition and radicalisation
1914–18

In the period from their exclusion from the TUC in 1895 to the beginning of world war in 1914 the trades councils expanded their work as local organisations in the trade union movement and as workers' representatives in their local communities. The war saw important developments in this process. National leaders of the movement were consulted on social and economic questions, and even accepted into government. Meanwhile the war saw 'much local initiative' through 'the local committee or tribunal, with powers over matters varying from the determination of the genuineness of a young man's claim to have a conscientious objection to war, to the ploughing of pasture land'. Although these committees mostly 'marked an Indian summer of power and glory for the traditional local bigwigs', they also indicated a new acceptance of local labour organisations, and an attempt to encourage local as well as national working class collaboration with government policy.[1] The trades councils, however, often found their role on the committees unsatisfactory, either because they did not feel they had sufficient representation or else because they did not entirely approve of what they were called upon to do. Thus from about 1917 onwards the attitudes of those active in the councils grew more and more radical, and their activities brought them into sharper conflict with government and employers.

War relief, refugees and pensions

The brave words that were often heard in the trades councils before 1914 about what they would do in the event of war have been quoted already. The promised strikes and widespread anti-militarist activities did not materialise, although there were some half-hearted efforts along these lines at first. In Birmingham the Trades Council secretary discussed with the local ILP 'preliminary steps for a "Stop the War" agitation', but under pressure from local and national Labour Party leaders dropped this, and decided to concentrate on unemployment and the relief of distress. In Oldham, too, the Trades and Labour Council soon became 'more concerned with the practical than the moral questions raised by the war'. The Nottingham secretary typified the determined but slightly shamefaced attitude of local leaders in the opening days of the war.

We find ourselves plunged into catastrophe without our knowledge or consent. This action is not of our seeking, nor is it the will of the Industrial Workers of those nations now urging war, neither can the people at this stage stop the war, although they may at any rate do much in the direction of mediation at the appropriate time ... in the meantime people are suffering as they always suffer. Most of us will not only lose those who are near and dear to us, but also wives and children will undergo privation.[2]

It was to concerns such as these, and to the powers and responsibilities that flowed from them, that the councils addressed themselves in the early months of the war.

The beginning of war was widely expected, both inside and outside the working class movement, to lead to widespread social distress. Thus the trades councils immediately began to discuss and agitate about the problems they expected their members to face. The government also acted rapidly, and on 4 August set up a national committee for the relief of distress under the patronage of the Prince of Wales. Two days later local authorities were told to establish, on the same pattern as the 1905 Unemployed Workmen Act, distress committees which would 'consider the needs of the localities and co-ordination and distribution of such relief as may be required'. Among those definitely to be represented on these local committees were trade unionists.[3] The government thus began by making a conscious effort to secure the co-operation of trade unionists, locally as well as nationally, in solving the problems brought on by war.

In the opening days of the war also a War Emergency Workers' National Committee (WEWNC) was established by most of the leaders of the political and industrial working class movement.[4] This body tried to see that local organisations were aware of their rights, and circularised them urging them to claim representation on the relief committees. The situation faced by local organisations on the matter of representation varied a great deal, depending on the strength of the movement and the attitude of the local authorities. In Liverpool there was a conference between the mayor and local working class leaders on 5 August on the relief of distress, so that when a local committee was set up there were twenty-one labour representatives on it. In Peterborough the Trades Council was asked to send eight representatives to the local committee, an event which it later saw as its 'first recognition as an authoritative body'. The Scottish TUC thought that, generally speaking, the WEWNC had 'succeeded in getting a fair representation of the Trades Councils throughout Britain'.[5] Such was not always the case, however, as can be seen from the story of what happened at Camberwell, where the newly established Trades and Labour Council was under the secretaryship of Arthur Creech Jones, later an important figure in the Labour Party. On 12 August a town meeting summoned by the mayor set up a relief committee of twenty-nine persons, including three representatives of labour. None of these was considered acceptable by the Trades and Labour Council, and it was reported that 'in Trade Union circles, complaints regarding their non-representation are very bitter indeed'. A full-scale local dispute developed, large meetings were held by both sides, and at the end of October it was said that 'the Mayor of Camberwell had expressed his intention to resign rather than to appoint the nominee of the Camberwell Trades Council'. It was not until after the end of his term of office in November that the Trades and Labour Council secured six representatives on the committee.[6] Many such disputes were to occur in the future before the rights of the trades councils were established.

Soon, however, other problems arose, chiefly because of the seriousness with which local organisations viewed their work. In Edinburgh the Trades Council set up a Labour Emergency Committee before the war had even started, and at Huddersfield the Trades and Labour Council had a committee that was prepared to formulate the claims of anybody who wanted to apply for relief. In Grimsby the Trades and Labour Council, after threatening to boycott the local relief committee in a successful effort to increase its representation from three to six, claimed that before the end of 1914 it was responsible for getting the press admitted to committee meetings, for increased scales of relief, and even for getting one sub-committee to pass by fourteen votes to three a motion for the national control of food supplies.[7] Despite these successes, complaints were also heard. In Wolverhampton the Trades and Labour Council complained that they had only three representatives, and had also 'suffered disrespectful treatment ... at the hands of the Mayor'. A separate trade union relief committee was proposed 'if better treatment is not meted out in the future and the business democratically carried out'. One writer sympathetic to the attitudes of working class organisations wrote late in 1915 that local committees consisted largely of 'social workers', of those who have been connected with the Poor Law, the Charity Organisation Society and other relief agencies. The Labour representatives ... were nearly always swamped by the mass votes of the officials and charity-mongers.

The attitude in the working class movement to the relief agencies and the poor law has already been described, and it can be illustrated by the complaint from the Bethnal Green Trades Council that the work of their local relief committee had 'the degradation of the "charity taint" and decent people are largely deterred from applying'.[8]

Many working class representatives became dissatisfied with the work of the relief committees. They were continually protesting about the scales of relief, about the categories of those entitled to it, and the inadequate publicity given to those in a position to claim it. In Rushton the Trades Council was horrified when the local relief committee began its work by advocating the release of children of thirteen from school to take the jobs of men who had enlisted. In Southampton and Hebden Bridge labour representatives objected when men who were adjudged capable of military service were refused relief. This, it was said, 'makes the committee into a recruiting sergeant, and, as only the poor were affected, the principle involved was worse than the adoption of conscription'. There was strong objection to giving aid to the dependants of soldiers, who should have been maintained from public funds. In Fulham the Labour Council even persuaded the mayor to organise a demonstration on this issue.[9] There was also considerable friction about how the local committees carried out their duties. Although Sidney Webb characteristically reminded the working class members of local committees that the use of food tickets was 'an old-fashioned device, now discredited by administrative science', many local committees adopted such methods, under instructions from the government. They were used in Bethnal Green and elsewhere, in the face of opposition from the working class members of the relief committees. The tickets were abandoned, however, after cases were reported of families 'sitting in the dark with parcels of dry tea and uncooked meat, because they had not a penny for coal or gas'. 'All over the country the Relief Committee earned an unpopularity that did much to irritate the workers.'[10] In Motherwell the secretary of the Trades Council reported that within a month of the operation of the relief scheme there was 'a growing suspicion that the spirit of the provisions proposed by the government is being departed from', and in Cardiff in the following January suspicion was clearly deepening when the Trades Council urgently demanded the publication of the full accounts of the National Relief Fund.[11]

However, grievances of this kind did not come to a head, because the distress which the relief committees had been formed to deal with did not materialise, except for a short period at the beginning of the war, mainly in textile areas. Within a year nearly all local relief committees had suspended their activities, and the National Relief Fund was mostly used subsequently not to help the poor at all, but those who suffered from air raids, or lodging house keepers who lost their living because of the war.[12] However, the trades councils found there were many other ways in which they could represent the interests of their members.

In the early period of the war trade unionists interested themselves in the influx of Belgian refugees. On the whole they were welcomed by local working class leaders, though 'not as cheap labour'. A Belgian musician was used in a trade dispute at Burnley, and Belgians were used to replace local musicians at Nelson. Despite these incidents trade unionists tried to bring the refugees into their movement. At Coventry the Trades Council set up a special branch of the Workers' Union for Belgian metalworkers, and a similar union branch affiliated to the Letchworth and Luton bodies.[13] Despite the obvious concern of trade unionists with the employment of this group, it is interesting to see that many local authorities at this stage of the war did not feel the need to take account of their views. During August and September 1914 local reception committees were set up, at first spontaneously, and later at the behest of the Local Government Board. By the end of the year there were at least 1,400 such local committees, initially simply finding accommodation for the refugees but later charged with looking for jobs for them as well. Though separate from the relief committees, these bodies often consisted of much the same people. In November the LGB circularised local authorities on the constitution of the committees, recommending that they should include representatives of labour. A Board of Trade departmental committee, however, soon found that little was being done to carry out this suggestion. There were no working class representatives on many of the committees, and the Manchester committee was said to be 'quite unrepresentative of feeling in the district'. At Sheffield the committee chairman was not even sure whether there were any working class representatives there. The government was prepared to agree with C. W. Bowerman, secretary of the TUC Parliamentary Committee, that 'anything of this kind was not complete without the trade unions being represented on it'. Presumably as a result of the activities of the departmental committee, the trades council secretaries at Oxford and Newport were soon taken onto their respective local committees, and by the end of 1914 the Wrexham Trades and Labour Council had three representatives.[14] From that time it came increasingly to be assumed that there would be working class representation in 'anything of this kind', and government pressure became less necessary to establish it.

Local working class organisations at the same time had to show their effectiveness as campaigning organisations, and this they did in efforts to secure war pensions. This was an issue the trades councils made their own, and were recognised as playing an important role. The demand of £1 a week for all widows and dependants of soldiers, as well as for discharged and disabled soldiers themselves, was probably first heard at a conference run by the Poplar Trades Council on 2 September 1914, but the whole problem first became widely publicised with a letter from George Barnes to the *Daily Citizen* in the following month. The £1 demand was subsequently put forward in many localities, often in conferences organised by trades councils under the auspices of the WEWNC.[15] In November the government set up a select committee to deal with war pensions, and a year later the Naval and Military War Pensions Act was passed, which established a National Statutory Committee and local bodies to administer government-provided finances. The local committees, which were to include 'women and representatives of labour', were given quite wide powers. They could inquire into specific cases, and give supplementary and urgent grants to those entitled to them. Provision was also made for local sub-committees consisting solely of representatives of employers and workers. This legislation involved trade unionists in directly administering policies they had advocated, and gave them powers which they had not previously secured in their representative work. It also gave them for the first time a real stake in the welfare services.[16]

The government again wanted to be certain of trade union co-operation with the work of the war pensions committees. The Statutory Committee, in a circular to local authorities, showed an awareness of some of the problems about representation which had arisen before, particularly in the case of the relief committees, and emphasised the importance of 'Trades Councils in which the local trade unions are usually combined'. Local authorities were warned that what was important was

not merely the presence on the Committees of persons who are cognizant of working class conditions or who themselves belong to the manual working class, but the representation on the Committee of working class opinion and the cordial and continued co-operation of working class organisations in the work of the Committee.[17]

Despite such admonitions as these, and the clearly stated provisions of the Act, many local organisations found that the path to representation was not always an easy one. The secretary of the Edinburgh Trades

Council said there were many cases where the desire of the Statutory Committee that there should be one-fifth trade union representation was ignored, and that 'the Association of County Councils practically recommended that the injunction be ignored'. However, after some effort, the Trades Council got seven representatives locally, and also helped to secure two for the Midlothian Trades Council. The Edinburgh secretary considered that 'by such vigilance . . . we gain both respect and influence' and thought that this work had a 'direct bearing on social conditions'. In Warrington the borough council at first objected to the Trades and Labour Council representatives because they had expressed opposition to the war, but the matter was cleared up after appeal to the Statutory Committee. More typically, the Leicester Trades Council was asked to appoint five representatives to the committee, an invitation which was 'readily accepted . . . as this marked a new feature in legislation, where Labour appointed representation'.[18]

The work of the war pensions committees often took up a considerable amount of the time and energy of the trades councils during the war, and afterwards. It was even an aspect of the work of the local organisations in which the TUC took an interest, setting up a special war pensions department and circularising the local organisations about the importance of securing representation, though after most of them had already made efforts to do so.[19] It was later claimed by those sympathetic to the older forms of voluntary charity that

representatives of labour organisations and local officials have not, as a matter of fact, taken an active part in the work of local committees, but in most places the same people who were doing the work before the creation of the Statutory Committee continued to do it under a new name.[20]

This statement is certainly not borne out by any investigation of the activities of the trades councils. War pensions were constantly discussed at their meetings, and representatives were carefully selected, frequently reported on their work, pressed for changes in government policy, and met working class representatives from other areas. For example, at a meeting of the local branch of the National Association of Discharged Soldiers in September 1917 the representatives of the Hartlepool Trades Union Council on the local committee asked delegates to publicise the work of the local committees and 'to let it be known that the members of the committee were eager and ready to assist all legitimate claimants to obtain their rights'. In Northampton the Trades Council claimed the credit for increasing the amount payable in numerous individual cases, for preventing evictions, and even for stopping the local committee from soliciting charitable donations, though this was in fact government policy. The Ayr Labour Council got the powers of the local committee increased and found that the work 'admits the exercise of many of our ideals'.[21]

Despite a great deal of such activity and effort, many local representatives were not satisfied with their achievements. The Liverpool Trades Council delegates found their work hampered by the 'domination of middle-class ladies of the charity organisation persuasion'. In general this was not so much of a problem as it had been with the relief committees, since, as the same representatives reported, 'the work is mostly of a dry and routine nature . . . [and] there is little scope for our sympathies'. The Dewsbury Trades Council secretary, Ben Turner, found that the tasks of a labour representative involved 'heartbreaking work' in the absence of such measures as a minimum rate of allowances for the dependent mothers of soldiers. The Hampstead Trades and Labour Council reported that there were numerous cases where the regulations did not allow adequate pensions to be paid in deserving cases, and the representatives on the local committee had to confine themselves to informing people of the rights they possessed, though they considered them inadequate. In Finchley the representatives of the Trades Council, together with those of the Discharged Soldiers' and Sailors' Federation, after a running battle with the majority of the local sub-committee, withdrew their representatives in 1919, and hoped that after the boycott was over 'a firmer and juster policy will be the result'.[22] An example of the reaction produced by the work of trade unionists in this field can be seen from the views of one writer who thought that private relief agencies should have been used because they spent less. He considered that the local committees had 'brought the unhealthy atmosphere of local politics into relief work', and that this applied particularly to

some of the delegates from working class associations who are too class-conscious to be a success in any judicial position. Working men, when administering their own funds, show very careful regard for economy, but when administering public money, some of them appear to think that virtue only lies in open handed benevolence.[23]

From these comments it would appear that the trades council representatives, whatever their own feelings of inadequacy, succeeded in doing something on behalf of those who had suffered most in that terrible war. They were demonstrating their ability to speak and act effectively for those whom they represented.

By the middle of the war the representative powers of the trades councils were so well established that they were valued not only by the local organisations themselves but also by the government. This is illustrated by the case of the local employment committees, whose establishment in 1917 was described in the last chapter. One local London secretary described what happened in his area.

It was rather amusing to find that such a newly proposed body for dealing with local industrial distribution and conditions of employment should be so fastidious in desiring to ignore the Trades Council as a representative body of the organised workers. Recourse had to be had to the Ministry of Labour, who politely instructed the Committee to 'recognise' the Trades Council. Two representatives were subsequently elected, but it was found that, like so many bodies constituted by the capitalistic governing class, no useful function can be performed by this committee, although the representatives of the workers are doing their best under the biased circumstances. [24]

This combination of the assumption that the trades council always had a right to representation, and at the same time the growing disenchantment with the results of such efforts, became more and more common as the war went on.

Conscription and prices

On these two issues both the power and disenchantment of the local organisations grew. For conscription local organisations were given powers they had little desire to wield, and on rising prices powers they never considered adequate.

Efforts to fight conscription were begun by the national leaders of the movement, taken up with enthusiasm locally, and then dealt a series of humiliating blows with the retreat of the national leaders, which considerably eased the task of the government in imposing the measure.[25] Eventually the local trade union leaders found themselves forced to modify in practice policies which they found extremely distasteful. The basic opposition to conscription dated from well before the war and derived, in part at least, from a fear of the powers it would place in the hands of employers, since it could lead to 'industrial conscription'. This remained the chief and often the only argument of trade unionists against military conscription, both before and after it was introduced. The efforts of Lord Roberts and his National Service League in the immediate pre-war years were never favourably regarded in the trades councils. The Liverpool Trades Council thought that conscription 'would be the master stroke of capitalism, backed up by landlordism, and bolstered and supported by war material mongers'. Though it was correctly prophesied that some labour leaders would support the measure, nevertheless there was a remedy to hand. 'The strike of the future will be the national strike against any form of compulsory military service.'[26]

During 1915 the Northcliffe press and others began to campaign seriously for the introduction of conscription. The demand was often linked with charges of drunkenness and indolence against workers, charges which came ill from those who had seldom in the past shown much concern with the welfare of working people, or with the defence of their organisations. Naturally enough, this attitude provoked a flood of bitterly hostile motions from virtually every labour meeting in the summer of 1915. Typical was the motion passed by the Coventry Trades Council on 17 June, which said that conscription was 'contrary to the sentiments and principle of the British people; subversive of the free democratic character of their traditions, and involves a serious menace to the freedoms of the labour movement'. Motions with an identical form of words were passed at Poplar, Shoreditch and Liverpool. At the Newcastle and Gateshead Trades Council on 26 August there was no support whatever for military conscription, but some alternatives were suggested. 'Conscription of wealth and land in the interests of the whole people, however, is receiving much support on Tyneside.' Before the end of the summer it could be said without obvious exaggeration that all 'the Trades Councils of Great Britain are unanimous in their opposition to conscription'.[27] This view was shared by every other working class organisation.

In the autumn, however, the situation changed. In October the government launched the 'Derby scheme' of recruitment, which aimed at virtually every means short of compulsion to persuade unmarried men to enlist. At the same time some sections of the trade union leadership launched a recruitment campaign of their own. Both of these efforts were put forward as the only possible alternative to military conscription. On 4 November W. A. Appleton, secretary of the GFTU, spoke at a meeting of the Manchester and Salford Trades Council and proposed that union officials should become recruiting agents, working closely with the army. These developments led to considerable heart-searchings in the trades councils, who were almost equally divided on whether to support recruitment as the only alternative to conscription or to wash their hands of the whole business. In Northampton the Trades Council changed its mind during the course of the year, just avoiding resignations from the executive committee when it agreed to support recruitment. The Birmingham Trades Council claimed to have been 'chiefly instrumental in the success of the Derby scheme', which was 'the alternative to conscription'. In Carlisle the Trades and Labour Council refused to take an attitude on the question, and among the trades councils which remained actively hostile were those at Clydebank, Huddersfield, Bristol and Sheffield.[28]

Most of the national leaders of the movement, with the help of diplomatic efforts by the government, before the end of the year replaced their opposition to conscription with an enthusiasm for increasing the size of the army. On the whole the local labour movement did not show the same change of heart. At the September TUC the strongest speeches against conscription came from John Stokes and Duncan Carmichael of the London Trades Council. The London Trades Council delegates also moved the motion to reject conscription at the Central Hall conference of labour organisations on 6 January, held after the first measure of conscription had been announced. This involved the enlistment of unmarried men. However, although the Manchester and Chorley trades councils were not prepared to agree to conscription in any form, the more conservatively inclined bodies from Oldham and South Shields were prepared to accept such limited measures. Despite the strong opposition to conscription he expressed at the Central Hall conference, Henderson remained in the Cabinet and summed up for the government on the second reading of the Military Service Bill. In the light of this it was hardly surprising that the Labour movement's demand for 50 per cent representation on the tribunals to administer exemptions could be brushed aside by the government with the promise that such representation would be 'adequate'.[29]

This sequence of events had an important effect in increasing the general mood of disillusionment and disenchantment in the local organisations during these years. Once the first measure of conscription had been adopted the national leadership of the movement did not consider it necessary to do anything more to oppose it. The Labour Party conference late in January refused to continue the campaign against conscription, and the Parliamentary Committee of the TUC would not even have considered the matter further had it not been for a communication from the London Trades Council.[30] The attitude in the trades councils was very different. In Glasgow in January there was a vote of ninety to three to continue to protest on the matter, and in Walthamstow in the following month the secretary called upon branches 'to support any action in the direction of repeal which may be decided upon by Trade Unionists'. The Birmingham body agreed to sustain anyone who wanted to defy a law which was simply 'a conspiracy against the social, industrial and political advancement of the British people'. At Woodford the secretary found himself driven to some uncomfortable reflections. 'Surely something will be done of a drastic character or are the votes at Labour and Trade Union conferences simply pious expressions of opinion?' In Liverpool, when the Trades Council in conjunction with a number of other local working class organisations prepared to hold a meeting late in January in support of the decisions of the Central Hall conference, they were assailed by the local press as 'pro-German', and interviews with the Labour members of the government were used by the papers to reinforce support for conscription and to encourage the breaking up of the meeting. The Trades Council was much aggrieved by this, especially as it had co-operated with the Derby scheme, and was only carrying out what were, after all, official Labour policies. The meeting, held on 23 January, was a success, and 2,000 people pledged to continue the fight against conscription. The Trades Council's delegate to the London conference reflected a growing mood of bitterness when he asserted that 'we were sold by our MPs like pigs in a poke'. The Huddersfield Trades and Labour Council also felt 'obliged to deprecate the attitude taken by the majority of the Labour Party from whom we feel we have a right to expect better things'.[31] As long as conscription continued, local organisations did not cease to express bitter opposition. The Colchester Trades Council issued a strongly worded leaflet in May 1916 which ended 'ENGLAND SHALL BE FREE', and in the same month the Reading Trades Council felt it necessary to protest 'against the actions of those leaders who have assisted in fastening the chains of conscription upon the workers without first obtaining the will of the rank and file'. More general protests continued to the end of the war and after.[32]

These sentiments were prevented from coming strongly to the surface by a government strategy now becoming invariable in these cases — giving the trades councils some limited power in carrying out the measure to which they objected. In many cases this resulted in trade unionists spending as much energy in 1916 in making conscription work as they had spent in 1915 in opposing it. When local tribunals were set up in November 1915 to administer the Derby scheme the LGB president was careful to see that they were broadly representative.

I desire in particular to refer to the representation of labour. The work of the Tribunals will closely concern the working classes, and it is imperative that they should be adequately represented on these Tribunals . . . what is desired is that the Tribunals will contain a member or members of the working classes in which the latter will have confidence.

It was these tribunals which, when conscription was introduced, were transformed from recruiting agencies into bodies that had to consider claims for exemption, occupational, 'conscientious' or otherwise. By the end of February 1916 there were over 2,000 tribunals, and they had already obtained a reputation for 'bias and injustice' which, if not entirely merited, has remained with them to this day.[33] The LGB sent out a further circular to local authorities on 31 January 1916 insisting that 'a fair proportion of the tribunal should be direct representatives of labour'. Nevertheless in Harrow labour representatives were specifically excluded, and at South Shields the local Labour Party 'emphatically protested' at the composition of the tribunal there.[34] In general even though trades councils were often consulted local authorities seem to have been more interested in appointing people of whom they approved rather than those who had the support of trade unionists. One account of the tribunals says that only labour men known for their support of the war were appointed, and that efforts in furthering the Derby scheme were 'a passport to appointment'. In Oxford the town clerk maintained that the labour representatives did not have to be trade unionists, though he later agreed to appoint the secretary of the Trades and Labour Council. At Boston the Trades and Labour Council nominees were rejected on the grounds that there were already labour representatives, despite the fact that these representatives had 'no connection whatsoever with the Trade Union and Labour movement'. In Rawtenstall anti-war delegates were not reappointed by the local authority in 1917. Even when, as at Crewe, the trades council had three representatives, these were outweighed by the two Liberals and four Conservatives.[35] A good number of representatives did not guarantee that trade unionists could achieve much in such disagreeable work. They found they could not even prevent the conscription of their own officials.[36] In both Huddersfield and Glasgow meetings of local tribunals were interrupted by the singing of 'The red flag', and at Leeds mutterings about 'treacherous labour representatives' were heard from the public gallery. At the Yorkshire appeal tribunal Ben Turner complained of the regulations being broken, an issue which led to the resignation of one of the labour representatives at Leeds.[37] Dissatisfaction was rising to a level where the value of such representative work was being questioned altogether, and these activities were found not to have the automatic value to the movement that had previously been assumed. Soon, however, there were new representative responsibilities that did something to assuage these fears.

Rising prices, particularly of food, were probably the most discussed topic in the trades councils during the war years. The drastic remedies they advocated included government control, price fixing and rationing, and were eventually adopted in part as the policy of the government, largely because of the agitation in which the local organisation played a prominent part. It was in no small degree the responsibilities which flowed from these policies that prevented the trades councils from becoming very disillusioned indeed about the course of events in these years.

The sharp rise in prices in the first days of the war was followed by a period of constant inflation, with the result that by the middle of 1917 prices in general were about twice what they had been at the beginning of the war, and food prices had risen even faster. Though average earnings may have risen more than this, wage rates did not, and few trade unionists were convinced that their wages were keeping pace with the cost of living.[38] From the first days of the war the trades councils discussed and agitated about rising prices. On 7 August 1914 the Bradford Trades and Labour Council met

to consider the effects of the panic action of the capitalist class who rule the destiny of the workers . . . [We] at once began to investigate retail and wholesale prices of foodstuffs and the result of our efforts disclosed that the workers were being exploited to the utmost.

Within weeks the same solutions to these problems were being put forward by trade unionists in every part of the country. In Gloucester, Aberdeen, Burnley and Camberwell, trades councils called for government control of food supply and prices.[39] Much of the inspiration for this campaign came from the WEWNC, who issued propaganda and initiated numerous local meetings in the early part of 1915.[40] National leaders of the movement took a great deal of interest in the campaign, perhaps especially because of their self-denying ordinance on the question of wages. For local organisations the campaign was also important. It brought together all sections of the movement, including the co-operative societies, as no such issue had done in the past, and provided a role for the trades councils in co-ordinating them. Thus they could speak on behalf of all sections of the labouring poor, and assert their authority both within the trade union movement and in their local communities. However, the campaign in the early part of 1915 was a failure. The government did nothing, and prices continued to rise. G. D. H. Cole, writing later in the year, spelt out the consequences. 'The Labour unrest that followed the prices campaign was to be a great extent the result of its failure.'[41] The policies of the labour movement at this stage were not even considered by the government.

Although the food price campaign abated to some extent after the middle of 1915, other related matters were still considered. The Liquor

Control Board, established late in 1915, was viewed with an enthusiasm that seems to have diminished the farther south one went. There was some support for the restriction of drinking hours in the north of Scotland, but little elsewhere. The Bethnal Green Trades Council 'thought that organised Labour could take action on more vital questions than the drink controversy', but the trades councils were sometimes represented on the local committees because of their work in establishing industrial canteens, a step for which there was considerably more widespread enthusiasm. The second report of the Liquor Control Board praised the work of local organisations on the matter, saying that they had to note 'in the frankest and most cordial terms, the loyal support given to the Board by Trades Councils and other Labour organisations'.[42]

During 1916 the general question of food prices again began to be seriously considered, partly because prices began to rise more steeply than before. Another cause was probably the change in government and in the general political atmosphere. In the summer a report of a departmental committee of the Board of Trade called for 'a large measure of public control' as the only solution to the problem. Now that 'the tide of collectivism was definitely in flood' not only was the problem growing more acute but a satisfactory solution seemed more likely.[43] During the summer and autumn of 1916 numerous local meetings and conferences were held, though not apparently nationally co-ordinated. In this period 'cries of hands off the people's food ... [were] heard at mass meetings held by labouring organisations throughout the country'.[44] When it became clear that the government had little intention of acting on such demands the tone of the meetings grew distinctly sharper. The Castleford Trades and Labour Council in June asked the government 'to take over all the necessities of production and exchange, and so prevent the unnecessary fleecing of the workers'. A special conference called by the Walthamstow Trades Council before the end of the year called for a general strike if there were not immediate government action. The appointment of Lord Devonport as Food Controller and the tentative government efforts at control in the early part of 1917 did not serve their purpose of impressing the labour movement. The sudden growth of food queues caused considerable alarm and was described by one trades council secretary with some exaggeration as 'probably the greatest scandal brought about by this terrible Armageddon'. It emphasised how little was being done to solve the problems of which trade unionists had complained. At a meeting sponsored by the Chatham Trades and Labour Council and the local ILP, Robert Williams denounced the 'masterly inactivity' of the government. The vast unofficial 'May strikes' which followed were an eloquent testimony of the discontent of working people. The Commissioners for Industrial Unrest in the following months consulted numerous trades council officials, and every witness agreed that food prices were 'the chief cause of unrest'.[45]

In seeking a solution to these problems the government looked from the first to the organised labour movement. There was an effort to persuade Robert Smillie to be Food Controller, perhaps to silence one of the most vociferous critics of government policy, but ultimately Lord Rhondda was appointed to replace the ineffective Devonport, and J. R. Clynes, sometime secretary of the Oldham Trades and Labour Council, became his deputy. During 1917 maximum prices were fixed on a wide range of foodstuffs, and 2,000 local authorities were told to set up food control committees to enforce them. In August 1917 it was suggested that these local committees should have twelve members, including at least one trade unionist and one woman. A year later it was said that there should be two or three labour representatives in the larger towns. In general a fairly high level of representation was accorded to the labour movement. By November 1917 it had one-eighth of the members of these local committees, though private farmers and traders had over 27 per cent representation. Within a year the representation of women and the labour movement almost doubled.[46] Despite these concessions to working class opinion, a meeting of the Lancashire and Cheshire Federation of Trades Councils on 29 September 1917 heard of some familiar problems.

Complaints were stated . . . that Labour 'representatives' on Food Control Committees had been chosen by Town Councils . . . It was not the number that was the primary grievance but the selection of Labour men by bodies who had no claim to choose them . . . It was agreed that in no case where 'labour representatives' had been co-opted by local authorities would the Councils recognise them as 'labour representatives' and it was reported that in several cases those chosen had refused to act.[47]

Local organisations were dissatisfied in other ways too. The Bury Trades Council thought that 'private interests ought not to be represented', and at Leicester it was claimed that this aim had been achieved. At Plymouth, however, only shopkeepers were on the committee. In Luton the struggle over working class representation was particularly intense. Not only did the Trades Council demand six seats on the local food control committee, it also wanted the original body completely reorganised to fight for a programme of full municipal control of the food supplies. Early in 1918 the Trades Council called a large demonstration on the issue, and there was also a strike.[48] More substantial grievances were also expressed. The Edinburgh Trades Council found that the food control committees had 'little power and initiative allotted to them', and at Ayr it was considered that 'until the Government take control of the whole supply and distribution of food nothing can be done by these committees'. In Aylesbury the Trades Council was still calling in January 1918 for a full national system of rationing, and later in the year the trades councils at Manchester and Swindon supported strikes against rising food prices.[49]

However, the work of the food control committees did provide a safety valve for trade unionists, especially as important initiatives were often taken under their prompting. In many areas the committees began requisitioning and rationing without recourse to higher authority. For instance, in November 1917 sugar rationing was introduced by the Gravesend Food Control Committee, and under the direct influence of the Trades Council in Birmingham tea, butter and margarine were rationed in the city on the first day of 1918.[50] Fear of the violent manifestation of working class discontent was an important influence on all official actions. The north-west regional controller later explained how he dealt with the problem. He appointed to his staff a man called C. H. Pearce, who in his capacity as someone 'well acquainted with the leading men of the Labour and Trade Union movements' was deputed 'to act as peripatetic lecturer to Trades and Labour Councils and other similar bodies'. In his travels Pearce 'had all the latest information and corrected misapprehensions and rumours – all complaints made were taken up'.[51]

The trades council representatives found that their activities involved a great deal of work, and many local bodies discussed the activities of the food control committees in considerable detail. The Nottingham body saw its local prestige much increased. It was in connection with food control that the Trades Council was 'for the first time in its history honoured by a visit from the Mayor', together with the town clerk and sheriff. This civic deputation was offered 'the fullest measure of support'.[52]

The government tried to involve the trades councils in some of the other measures to deal with food distribution and prices. There was little or no enthusiasm for the 'food economy' committees which were first established in the autumn of 1917.[53] Another related activity for which the trades councils showed less than complete enthusiasm was the encouragement of saving. As part of efforts in this direction local war savings committees were set up which were supposed 'to explain to the people the economic situation and the necessity for saving'. In Leeds the local Labour Party considered its efforts in the campaign to be a step forward in its 'participation in local finance', and at Liverpool a small committee was set up by the Trades and Labour Council to assist in such work. By March 1917 over 1,000 local committees and associations of various kinds had been set up, and 2,236 out of 20,777 members – over 10 per cent – were from trades councils and other local labour organisations. However, the vast majority of members of the committees were employers, bankers and others hostile to the working class movement, so it is not surprising that working class opposition grew. The Fulham Labour Council 'felt that, in view of the ever-increasing cost of living, it would be a betrayal of our trust to take part' in the campaign, and at Hartlepool a similar invitation was declined on the grounds that 'wages received will not meet the cost of foodstuffs, consequently we have nothing to save'.[54] National kitchens and profiteering committees were also of interest to the trades councils but increasingly provoked disillusionment and bitterness. The national kitchens were publicly run restaurants set up by the food control committees, largely under pressure from their trade union members. Where they survived they were usually taken over by the co-operative movement.[55] The 'profiteering committees', set up just after the war, were supposed to punish shopkeepers who were making 'excessive' profits. Their main purpose was not, of course, to perform this impossible task at all but, as one civil servant later put it, 'to ease the public mind', mainly as it had been expressed by the trade union movement. Seventy-five per cent of the cases considered by the 1,800 local committees were dismissed as irrelevant, and only £2,000 was ever exacted in fines. The Leeds Trades and Labour Council representative thought his work so useless 'that he did not consider the representation of the Council was worth the cost'. The Smethwick Trades and Labour Council decided to withdraw, 'as they considered the whole administration of the Act was a farce', and later rejoiced when the local committee collapsed altogether.[56] Thus, although the trade councils were often apparently granted quite wide powers in dealing with the discontent of their members, in the end they seldom found themselves satisfied with the results.

Changing attitudes in war and after

The period of the war did much to strengthen the position of the trades councils as widely accepted spokesmen for the poor, and to show their value to the whole working class movement. At Middlesbrough it was considered that the period had shown 'the usefulness of the Council in focusing the aspirations of the workers, and emphasising the necessity for Labour solidarity', and the Northampton secretary thought that representative work had shown that his organisation was 'prepared to play its part in very necessary administrative work', and also 'that its meetings are not merely held for passing pious resolutions of protest or condemnation'. At Newport the secretary was also enthusiastic about what could be achieved. Through 'representation on all possible governing bodies' trade unionists could make themselves

so persistent that public opinion will force the most antiquated and sleeping body to move, and make them realise the workers are a body to be considered, and our claims for justice and right must be accounted to.

Such activities not only did something for the workers, they also improved the position of their organisations in the local community, as another secretary found.

The Hereford Trades Council has had an uneventful career for several years until 1914, when circumstances arising out of the war brought into prominence the workers[,] making it the medium for pressing [their] interests forward before the various authorities and by its means the trade unions have secured representation [on] War committees . . . Owing to the rapid growth of the Council even the Conservative and Liberal Parties are becoming more friendly.

The consequences of such increasing friendliness often included a lessening of the independence of the trades councils, as is made clear by the comments of local representatives on war pensions and food control sub-committees in the suburbs of Liverpool, who found that

the work in connection with these committees is interesting and educative and an opportunity is afforded for coming into contact with people of widely divergent views from ours ... we have always experienced every courtesy and consideration from our fellow members ... our relation is of a harmonious character ... the differences of opinion are frequently of an educative character.

Clearly the aristocratic embrace could make itself felt right to the humblest levels of local administration![57]

Not everyone was so happy with what happened. Some of the discontent which arose as a result of the work on local employment committees, war pensions committees and other bodies has already been mentioned. These local committees, although often set up to take account of trades council pressure, usually had very limited powers, or were dominated by those hostile to the trade unions. As early as the spring of 1916 it was already clear at least to the secretary of the Bournemouth Trades Council that the new powers being granted to the trade union movement were not necessarily in its best interests.

We have seen sweeping changes taking place in the wholesale recognition of Trade Unionism by the State, the entrance of labour into the Cabinet and the admission by the Government of our rights to representation on public bodies. The things that we have been fighting for [for] years are given to us with a lavish hand, and yet — there remains a suspicion that the total results of all is that the governing classes and capitalistic interests have but tightened their grip on labour . . . Samson has been lured and shorn his strength.

In 1918 one trades council delegate said he thought 'Pensions Committees, the Military Service Tribunals, and similar bodies, should be composed of at least one-half Labour members', since working class representatives 'were hopelessly outnumbered because of the presence of large numbers of reactionaries on the different Committees'. The story of some boycotts and withdrawals from this work has already been told. The mood of many of these actions can be gathered from the statement of the secretary in Northampton in 1920 in leaving the local War Pensions Committee:

Owing to the curtailment of the powers of the Committee, it was felt no useful purpose would be served by the Council's representatives remaining merely to register the decisions of the Government as expressed by the Regional Officer, . . . [and] they felt there was no option but to resign.[58]

The even sharper feelings over the worse than useless profiteering committees in the period just after the end of the war showed a spirit of revolt in the trades councils and a questioning of previously held assumptions. Thus the war period did not confirm the ability of the trades councils to act as part of the local administration of welfare and related services quite as easily as some of their leaders had hoped. Trades councils had to remain to some degree campaigning bodies, aiming to 'keep the workers alive to the dangers which threaten them and their organisations', able to 'awaken the consciousness of the people to their own needs'. By the middle of 1916 one trades council secretary could claim that on such matters as food prices, conscription, rents and wages 'public opinion has been largely influenced . . . by the actions of the Trades Councils throughout the country'.[59] On rents, indeed, the local organisations had apparently gained a great victory in the Act of 1915, although by the end of the war price rises in other commodities made this victory seem hollow. Another field in which success was taken from the grasp of the trades councils was in the organisation of ex-servicemen. The first local body to take action in this direction was the Blackburn Trades and Labour Council, which on 13 September 1916 sponsored a meeting that set up a Union of Ex-servicemen. Very soon this became a national organisation operating mainly through the machinery of the trades councils, with branches in the main industrial areas in Lancashire, Yorkshire and South Wales. By the latter part of 1917 the National Federation of Discharged Sailors and Soldiers held its first annual conference. Twenty-one trades councils were represented at this meeting, which was 'very desirous that it should be a purely working-class organisation, and that the position of the discharged men should not be exploited by the capitalist class'. Though espousing only policies on the lines of the official trade union and labour movement, it was in direct competition with the officially approved National Association of Discharged Soldiers and Sailors.[60] The relationship between the trades councils and the ex-servicemen's organisations varied considerably. On the one hand the Great Harwood Trades Council simply declared itself a branch of the Federation in October 1916. Other trades councils, at Oldham, Reading and Hebden Bridge, set up branches of the Federation in the latter part of 1917. The Middlesbrough Trades Council also set up a branch early in 1917, but soon left the organisation to the ex-servicemen themselves when there were enough of them to run it. By the end of the war virtually every trades council was associated with an ex-servicemen's organisation, even, in some cases, such as Chesterfield, with those generally hostile to the working class movement such as the Comrades of the Great War.[61] Despite all these efforts, however, the plans of the labour movement were frustrated by conscious official efforts to keep the ex-servicemen away from their influence, which culminated in the isolation of the Federation and the establishment of the much less militant British Legion in 1920.[62] These events must have caused some frustration in the local organisations.

During the course of the war many other grievances combined to increase the discontent of the trades councils. Increasingly the conduct of the war itself and the general political problems facing the working class were enough to cause resentment. In the first year of the war the Birkenhead secretary said that trade unionists were 'torn between defending their country and defending their conditions'. Although trade unionists did not at first express much hostility to the war, they were not prepared to forget the defence of their conditions. By the end of 1915 the Treasury agreements, which had at first been seen as an important recognition of the position of the trade union movement, were taken as showing how the leaders were 'so readily agreeing to surrender the rights of Labour while the employers are permitted to exploit the people at will'. The munitions tribunals, in which the trades councils occasionally became involved, sometimes providing representatives of labour, became more and more the objects of discontent. By November 1916 the Coventry Trades Council circularised other bodies to secure the release from prison of the local organiser of the Workers' Union for an offence which seems to have amounted to refusing to carry out the dilution schemes that had been agreed on by the national leaders of the movement.[63] The Munitions Act, the Defence of the Realm Act and the general erosion of civil liberties were matters constantly discussed in the trades councils, and their protests grew increasingly strident as the war went on. Early in 1915 the Rotherham Trades and Labour Council was already pointing out that its support for the war did 'not mean that the rights of free speech and criticism have been abated'. Trades councils were constantly protesting against the breaking up of pacifist and anti-war meetings, even at times when they refused to have anything to do with such meetings themselves.[64] They also attacked the treatment of conscientious objectors, particularly in the cases of Charles Dukes, secretary of the Warrington Trades and Labour Council and of the Lancashire Federation, and George Beardsworth, a delegate to the Blackburn body. The vice-president of the Brighton Trades Council was also imprisoned for his beliefs. The Liverpool Trades Council and Labour Representation Committee opened a fund for the welfare of Beardsworth and Dukes with a large donation of £10, but was careful to make its own position clear, since 'most of our people, including the writers, dissent from their views', but nevertheless opposing 'the Prussianisation of the British army'. Concern for such questions in a general way also grew. Many trades councils supported the Trade Unions Rights Committee set up in 1915 by Tom Quelch, William Mellor and others, as well as the short-lived earlier version of the National Council of Civil Liberties, which grew out of the movement against conscription. In affiliating to the latter body the Chatham secretary wrote that this was part of 'safeguarding what few privileges are left us'.[65]

This growing militancy was related to, but not of the same character as, the main sphere of trade union militancy in this period, the shop stewards' movement. It is not true, as one book dealing with working conditions in the period says, that 'Trades Councils . . . [in] character and attitudes . . . leaned rather to the shop stewards than to the Central Executives'.[66] Trades councils were largely organisations of the trade union machinery itself, not in any way adapted to the workshop problems which arose in the period and expressed themselves in the shop stewards' movement. Though largely ignored at the time by trade union leaders, the trades councils as a whole reflected their policies and attitudes, if usually in a somewhat more radical form. Thus the relationship between the trades councils and the shop stewards' movement was one of occasional co-operation rather than active support. In Sheffield, where there was a comparatively stable workers' committee, there was joint agitation on such general issues as food queues and conscription. Something similar happened in Coventry on food prices in 1917. On the other hand, Clyde shop stewards consciously abstained from participation in the powerful Glasgow Trades Council, probably because they equated it with the official trade union machinery.[67] The publication of the views of two leading local stewards by the Paisley Trades and Labour Council in 1918 was an unusual act for a trades council. In general the councils remained sympathetic outsiders. When the Southampton Trades Council considered the first of the Clyde strikes at its meeting on 3 March 1915 it was thought that the Scottish workers had been 'unpatriotic', but nevertheless had shown 'what the workers were prepared to do'. Later a deputation of deportees was received by the Sunderland Trades and Labour Council, and they were made 'freemen' of the Liverpool Trades Council in 1916 during their enforced sojourn in the area.[68] Later on the Chorley Trades and Labour Council thought that shop stewards should 'come to the Trades Councils', and the Birmingham Trades Council in 1918 heard delegations of both local and national leaders of the movement. The reaction to the visit in July of J. T. Murphy, a leading theorist of the movement, typified the warm but somewhat remote sympathy that existed in the local organisations in showing that the Trades Council

unanimously agreed that these Committees inside the shops and various industries were a step in the right direction towards proper control, further, that they should be properly recognised by the Trade Union Executives and Employers ... All must realise that there are brains, determination and enthusiasm behind the Shop Stewards movement – qualities which the Trade Union leaders must encourage, foster and wisely guide.[69]

A tendency to militancy on industrial questions in the trades councils can be illustrated by their rejection of the various schemes for permanent harmony between employers and employed which proliferated towards the end of the war. The Liverpool Trades Council in 1918 set up a sub-committee on the Whitley schemes, which leaders of the movement had helped to formulate. The sub-committee condemned

the persistent efforts now being made, and in very dubious quarters, to convince the organised workers particularly that there is a delightful and satisfactory identity of interest as between Capital and Labour.

The Trades Council itself supported this view, and condemned Whitleyism as 'simply machinery for the consolidation of capital'.[70]

The growth of radical views in the trades councils was reflected not simply in their industrial policies but also in their attitude to political developments. In 1917 there was rejoicing at the overthrow of the Czar, an old *bête noir* of the working class movement, and many resolutions were passed and meetings held in support of the Russian revolution. More will be said later about the consequences of this support, and also about the Leeds convention of June 1917, which brought together 207 delegates from trades councils and local Labour Parties to celebrate the revolution and much else besides.[71] Increasing feeling against the war was also developed by the activities of the Union of Democratic Control (UDC). This organisation, established early in the war, campaigned on generally pacifist lines for such 'democratic' measures as the end of secret diplomacy. From the start it sought to 'extend its influence ... in the ranks of organised labour', aiming its propaganda primarily at 'trades councils and local branches of the ILP'. In May 1915 Egerton Wake, who had previously represented the trades councils on the Labour Party national executive; became 'special commissioner' for the UDC and by the following autumn had spoken at eighty-five trades councils and Labour Parties, securing the affiliation of thirty of them. By the beginning of 1916 forty-nine such local organisations were affiliated.[72] Although at first the trades councils were suspicious of 'middle class peace men', gradually support grew more widespread, until by the end of 1916 the UDC leader, E. D. Morel, could cite the support of trades councils in such major towns as Glasgow and Bradford as an indication of growing support for his policies. It is certainly true that by the middle of 1917 most councils, whether affiliated or not, were calling for a declaration of war aims and a negotiated peace, on the same lines as the UDC. Those in the highest reaches of government were well aware of this, and Milner wrote to Lloyd George in 1917 of 'the very systematic and active propaganda of the pacifists' which was 'capturing the Trades Councils and other bodies'. In 1917 an uncompromising anti-militarism could be associated with such local organisations as the Poplar Trades Council, and at Bradford in the following year a poll arranged among the 30,000 affiliated members of the Trades and Labour Council found a majority of fifteen to one in favour of peace by negotiation. Developing opinions of this kind could mean that by the end of the war 'British labour was a most important political force behind a drive for a league of nations'.[73] The Nottingham secretary well reflected the mood of troubled determination with which trades councils faced the peace:

we entered into this awful war not only because ... agreements made between our nation and others have been broken with imminent danger to ourselves, but also with the determination that there should be no future wars. The real guarantee of no future wars can only be made by peoples and not by rulers and Governments.[74]

Many of the influences which caused feelings of disenchantment and militancy in the trades councils have already been described. It is also important to remember the context in which the councils operated from the time of the enormous and unofficial strikes of May 1917 to the general strike of 1926. These were years of amalgamation and centralisation in the trade union movement, including efforts to establish a Triple Alliance that would concentrate the industrial power of the working class movement. They were years in which mutinies in the army and the police were followed by the enormous struggles of the railwaymen in 1919, the miners in 1921 and the engineers in 1922. In the period just after the war many of the trades councils were actively involved in local strikes for the shorter working hours they had often discussed at their meetings.[75] They were also active in efforts to stop intervention against the Russian revolution, in ways which will be described in chapter six. These were years in which revolutionary struggles swept away ancient dynasties throughout Europe, and when nationalist movements in Ireland and India were for the first time attaining some success against the British Empire.[76] In this situation it is not surprising that leaders of the working class movement were talking of 'the determination of Labour to challenge the whole existing structure of capitalist industry', and *The Times* could fear that behind 'labour unrest' lay 'a conscious revolutionary movement which aims at a complete overthrow of the existing social order, not in some uncertain future, but here and now'. In this situation the Cabinet itself felt it necessary to have regular reports on the state of working class feeling and the activities of revolutionary organisations.[77]

The changing mood of the working class movement in this period was naturally reflected in the trades councils. A sense of grievance predominated in many local organisations. One secretary thought that the war had 'brought with it in increased intensity the cry of the poverty-stricken and downtrodden'. Few trade unionists thought the policies of the government had done enough to solve these problems. The secretary at Huddersfield in 1916 wrote in a way that showed great bitterness.

During the past twelve months the position of the working class has been put back a century and the outlook is far blacker than it has been at any time since Waterloo. The shackles of Military and Industrial Slavery are being rivetted on us, and we shall have to take steps we may think necessary, in order that we may pass on to our children as goodly a heritage as our forefathers handed to us.

A strong feeling of disillusionment made trades council leaders assert that

the rights and privileges won by our forebears, and upheld by ourselves for so long have been wrested from us by false pretences, aided by the laxity and short-sightedness of our leaders, without any adequate guarantees.[78]

The end of the war was long expected to produce the profoundest social conflicts. At Wrexham early in 1916 it was prophesied that it would lead to 'an economic crisis unparalleled in the history of trade unionism', and everywhere 'industrial war' 'between organised labour and the employers' was expected. When the war did end, the trades councils were determined not to lose these battles. The Liverpool secretary made this clear.

Now that the war is over there is evidence, from every quarter, that the harassed, worried and exploited people are determined that they will no longer be the tools and victims of the employing class. The restrictions of DORA, the poor food, the strain, the shameless profiteering, the inaptitude of the Government, the millions of extra profits, the loss of kindred, the home-coming wounded, the meanness of the Pension Authorities, the flaunting display of the wealthy, have produced a determination that a life of freedom and comfort is a common heritage of all, and the more we are unified the more difficult it will be to keep us out of it.

The Northampton secretary also expressed a common view. 'Looking back to 1914, and remembering the great, unparalleled sacrifices made by all people, who can be anything but disappointed with the results?' Others saw a remedy to hand, hoping 'that the workers will have to adopt a more aggressive attitude and enforce their decisions'. They became convinced of 'the need to organise trade unions to overthrow capitalism', because there could be 'no harmony between capital and labour'.[79] Many saw the trades councils as important instruments in this struggle. In 1917 the Commissioners of Enquiry into Industrial Unrest for South Wales thought that trades councils had 'become centres of *social* and *political* activity more potent, perhaps, than any other of the social movements in the community'. The Manchester and Salford Trades and Labour Council set out how the local organisations could go beyond this.

The work of the Council in the future will be on very different lines from that in the past. Trade Unions will no longer be merely defensive organisations against the encroachments of employers and capitalists but are directing an offensive against the very citadel of capitalism itself. The fight immediately in front of us is not for higher wages and shorter hours only, but for issues of a fundamental nature, industrial control and management, the elimination of the wages system, and the substitution of complete industrial democracy. If the fight is to be successfully waged, this Trades Council and other Trades Councils in the UK will be powerful organs of intensive industrial propaganda, if so organised as to include and co-ordinate all trade union forces.

These were years when trade unionists became convinced, as one of the leaders of the Leeds Trades Council put it, of 'the great importance of direct action' and of the fact that the 'Sidney Webb definition of trade unionism could not hold good any longer'.[80]

Against this general background and with these feelings in the trades councils it was inevitable that everywhere the local organisations would find much to do. 1918 at Luton was a year of 'phenomenal activity', and 1919 saw 'ever-increasing activity' at Bolton. By the end of 1920 the Manchester secretary doubted 'if the Council or trade unionism itself has ever before experienced the same combination of complexities, uncertainties and industrial difficulties.' Truly the war had been 'removed from the fields of France to the industrial centres of the United Kingdom'.[81] The events of these years and the conspicuous role of the trades councils in them will be described in detail in chapter six. Having seen the growth in the power and influence of the local bodies in the decades up to this period, it is necessary to devote some time to discussing further the ideological and other influences acting on the trades councils and shaping their attitude to the world in the period up to the 1920s, both from the radical wing of the movement and from its increasingly powerful official leadership.

Chapter five

Ideology and organisation
1890–1925

New Unionists, syndicalists, guild socialists and Communists

The period between the 1880s and 1920s saw big changes in the size and constitution of the trade union movement, and many new groups of workers joined it. Trades councils were the only institutions in the movement besides the TUC itself that brought together organised workers of every type, so it was not surprising that they should be given some prominence by those who wanted to see a more permanent and thoroughgoing unity between different groups of trade unionists. The councils became instruments for all those with ideas that emphasised the need for working class solidarity, and for those who wanted to see a working class movement that was more democratic, less bureaucratic, and concerned with political questions beyond the mere winning of elections. It is possible to trace such theories back a long way.

Before the great majority of workers in Britain could even aspire to belong to a trade union, and before there was a national body that catered for the interests of more than a tiny minority of the working class, the president of one of the best-organised trades councils in the country told his delegates that he

trusted that the members would forget that they were masons, joiners, and so many different groups of tradesmen, and that they would keep in mind that they were all workmen and therefore had an interest in the general cause of labour and whatever tended to the advancement and elevation of the workman.

The first historian of the trades councils also found that from the earliest period they were 'pioneers of Trade Union solidarity', and gave the unions a sense 'of the solidarity of labour and of the existence in the

Trade Union movement of something larger than its component unions; something bound together by a real unity and striving for a verifiable ideal'.[1] Throughout their history trades councils have called for unity of effort within the trade union movement, and have often seen themselves as playing an important part in effecting that unity. More detail will be given later of local discussion on these lines, but for the moment some of the ideas commonly expressed in the trades councils during the nineteenth century should be noted. They often called for the centralised organisation of trade union efforts. In Manchester in 1898 there was talk of the need for 'a federation of all trades and labour organisations', and at Leeds in the same period it was asserted that the employers were so well organised that 'it was now a question as to whether the single trades unionisms were powerful enough to compete with the federations of employers'. Thus there was a need for 'some scheme of Federation for all organised workers of the United Kingdom'. The trades councils themselves were often seen as having an important function in developing trade union unity. Not only that, but they could also play a directly political role. Thus the Chesterfield Trades Council, when set up in 1893, hoped that 'it would become the "boss of the show" instead of the Town Council'.[2]

In the period of rapid union expansion that began in 1889 there were many who looked to the trades councils to continue the transformation of the movement. One working class paper spoke of the 'real life' and 'splendid possibilities' in the trades councils, and of the role they could play in 'grouping kindred trades for concerted action; promoting amalgamations where clashing and overlapping exist, and in many ways pointing out the common good which we all know is somewhere under our feet'. In the same paper George Barnes of the ASE said the trades councils 'afford the next field for united action'.[3] In 1892 further ideas for strengthening the unions were discussed in another of the movement's papers. Leonard Hall, at that time a trade union organiser in the Manchester docks, and later a member of the syndicalist movement, said he thought that the trades councils were the

latest, most successful, and most promising development of the English combine movement. .. In my judgement ... the 'amalgamation of all trades' lies first through the trades councils ... I venture to predict that this line of co-operation, as the most natural, will therefore be the most practical.

In the discussion that followed this statement others saw a possible future movement where trades councils would organise conferences of a national organisation of all the trades.[4] Tom Mann, recent hero of the

London dock strike, also looked to the trades councils for much besides simple trade union goals.

> There is no reason ... why the London Trades Council should not become two, or three, or five times as powerful as it is now ... If there were twenty thousand amongst London trades who looked upon Trade Unionism not merely as a means of maintaining the present rate of wages at a minimum of cost and trouble to themselves but as the germ of the organisation that is capable, by a full exercise of its industrial, educational, and political powers, of completely freeing labour and making him the master of his fate, and destroying not only material poverty but poverty of mind and spirit ... the London Trades Council would be immensely more powerful, numerically and financially, while one could hardly exaggerate the influence it could exert.

Mann also advocated the use of trades councils to break down craft divisions and campaign for the eight-hour day. Together with Ben Tillett, he thought that the London Trades Council could defeat craft unionism, become 'the real centre of organised industry in the metropolitan area', and take on the role of 'London's Labour Parliament, nothing less, where every affiliated union having a difficulty could turn to for, and obtain, real and substantial help'. Mann continued to have faith in the trades councils, and in making predictions for the twentieth century saw them as an important 'part of the advancing democratic forces making for the socialisation of industry'.[5]

In the next period, when Mann was away from England, he was a delegate to the Melbourne Trades Council. As soon as he returned in 1910 he met Guy Bowman and went with him to Paris, where they 'examined thoroughly the principles and practice of the CGT and the syndicalists in France'.[6] On their return from France in July 1910 Mann and Bowman set up the Industrial Syndicalist Education League. They had learnt much from the localised nature of the French movement. Local trade union organisations, *bourses du travail* established in the main towns from 1887, played a more important role in the movement than in Britain. This was due partly to municipal encouragement of their work as labour exchanges, partly to the localised traditions in all aspects of French life, and partly to the support of the syndicalists, especially Ferdinand Pelloutier, for local initiative within the movement. The Fédération Nationale des Bourses du Travail of 1892 merged with the CGT in 1902. The local bodies played an essential role in building the trade union movement, as one contemporary realised. 'Avant la bourse du travail l'existence des syndicats était absolument précaire.'[7] The *bourses*, as well as being 'the creative arm of the labour movement' and the centre of much local working class activity, were also seen by

Pelloutier as 'the institutional nucleus for the construction of a new order from the old'.[8] Mann absorbed these and other ideas from the French movement and tried to adapt them to British conditions. For the local movement he translated *bourse du travail* as trades council and tried to get them to act along the same lines.[9]

In Britain, as elsewhere, the syndicalists had a whole body of ideas other than those concerned with local trade union organisation.[10] Especially in Britain, these notions were often combined in a somewhat eclectic and inconsistent way. In general, however, they believed in building industrial unions as a step to the One Big Union that would replace the institutions of the existing capitalist society. An important corollary to these efforts was the expansion of local trade union organisation in order to replace the existing local authorities in a future socialist society. One of the earliest British statements of syndicalist aims said that there should be in future, 'for purely local matters, industrial district councils composed of all industrial unions in a given district, similar to the existing trades councils'.[11] In their more immediate opposition to the lack of democracy and militancy within the trade unions the syndicalists also looked to local initiative. Thus Mann advocated the affiliation of every local union or branch to a trades council, 'whose work should be primarily for educational and general purposes other than fighting'.[12] Trades councils were seen both as instruments of local struggle in the short term and as future organs of government.

The first congress of Mann's Industrial Syndicalist Education League took place in Manchester in November 1910, and sixteen trades councils were represented. *The Times* reported that 'several of the cotton towns were represented by their Trades Councils', but derived some consolation from the fact that 'several were not'.[13] Nevertheless the trades councils present, including those of Manchester, Ashton, Stockport, Derby and Walthamstow, represented a fair cross-section of different types of local bodies. Not only this, but the trades council delegates were among the most militant of those present and most hostile to trade union officialdom. W. G. Kerry of the Brighton Trades Council thought that the leaders of the unions had 'betrayed them again and again in the past' and 'would betray them again'. Another trades council delegate expressed such feelings even more strongly.

In the trade union world they had a set of officials determined to keep their seats. ... One of the things they ought to work and fight for was to take out of the hands of the Executives and leaders the power they now have, and they could do it by getting among the members. The majority of trade unionists he talked to were dead-sick with the present rate of progress.

This mood of disillusionment, though by no means universal in the trades councils, was common among younger trade unionists in this period. Although there were some at the conference who thought that the trades councils 'were fighting sectionally all over the place', and would therefore have to be replaced, most agreed with Mann that the positive qualities of the existing organisations could be adapted to the ends of militant trade unionism.[14]

After the Manchester conference, support for syndicalist ideas grew in the trades councils. Early in 1911 the Derby Trades Council 'decided to act as an Education Committee for the promulgation of syndicalist principles', in particular for the amalgamation of the unions of railway workers. The Walthamstow body, having heard a report from the conference, decided that 'the Trade Unions must organise in order to provide the necessary machinery for the conduct of industry in the future'. More and more other local bodies, even if they did not attend the conferences, came to support ideas of which the syndicalists would have approved. At Stockton early in 1912 it was agreed that

Important as are many of the questions dealt with, the question of Federation of Trade Unions is infinitely greater and is the real work of the Trades Council, not as an end, but as a means to an end. Until this is accomplished, the work will still be to do.

In Leicester at the same time the Trades Council decided that it was 'in favour of efforts being put forward to bring about the Amalgamation of all sectional Trade Unions' and called for the services of Mann to speak at a meeting on the industrial unrest.[15] Early in 1912, when Mann's organisation began to produce a normal printed paper, he and others were prosecuted for advising soldiers not to shoot at strikers. The main result of this was to give more publicity to syndicalism and to increase interest in it within the working class movement. It was not true, for example, that the members of the Walthamstow Trades Council 'lost their initial interest at this point', since they continued to be represented at syndicalist activities.[16]

In the following period, through the medium of their paper, the syndicalist leaders developed in greater detail their theory about the trades councils. This was particularly the task of Bowman, who was further from orthodox trade unionism than Mann, and more acquainted with anarchist theories and the French experience.[17] He wanted a 'National Federation of Trades Councils' that would 'take the place of the Municipal Councils of today, and form the Industrial Councils of tomorrow'. Bowman explained that the trades councils were the only

places where 'the general problems of Labour may be discussed without
the narrowness of view which in individual unions is apt to permit only
the immediate selfish interest of each craft to be discussed'. After the
overthrow of capitalism they would become 'part of the National Council
of the society of the future and will partly take the place of the
Parliament of today's'. Bowman went on to quote Pelloutier direct, and
said that the trades councils as well as the *bourses* 'reflect the state of the
soul of the working-men's groups' and 'give body to the secret desire of
the workers to shake off all tutelage and to henceforth draw from
themselves the elements of their emancipation'. Bowman told syndicalist
supporters how to develop these policies.

What they have got to do is to augment the functions of these Trades Councils,
which are thus seen to be the natural discussion ground for Labour in its general
interests . . . there must also be built up a systematic and intelligent campaign for
the constant reinforcement of the workers in both their trade struggles and their
individual struggles with . . . local capitalists. The spirit of comradeship must be
constantly manifested.

Finally he called for the setting up of a national federation of trades
councils without delay.[18] A trade unionist who had been active in the
trades councils thought the setting up of a federation would be 'most op-
portune' and that
The linking up of all Trades Councils into one body is a policy that all Trade
Unionists must strive for, and it remains for Trades Councils which see the
wisdom of such a policy to at once take active steps to bring about the desired
federation. If syndicalist propaganda can lead to this then it must truly be said
that it has done something extremely useful for the future of labour in this
country.

   Such sentiments as these could also be heard in the local movement
itself during 1912. At Bournemouth the paper brought out by industrial
and political sections of the movement indicated its sympathy, and at a
meeting in July to celebrate Mann's release from prison the Leeds Trades
and Labour Council spokesman welcomed him by saying that 'the
organisation of Trades Councils was far more powerful than the average
Trade Unionist imagined', and that despite advances in political representation by this method 'the organisation of industry, through the Trade
Unions, would have to be developed a great deal more than it was
today'.[19] The syndicalists themselves were not slow to draw out the implications of these feelings of support. Trades councils, it was said

should be the real centres of union agitation and propaganda . . . they should be
the starting-points for preaching the class struggle, raising it to the utmost

revolutionary height as expressed in the Social General Strike for the Expropriation of the Capitalist Class.

There was also support for the setting up of a national federation from the trades councils of Walthamstow, Wimbledon, Woolwich, West Ham and Runcorn.[20]

At the second conference of the Industrial Syndicalist Education League, held in London in November 1912, the role of the trades councils was again given prominence. Bowman said that the 'purely technical considerations which were often discussed in the trade union branch room' did not have a place in the trades councils, where workers' problems were 'dealt with in a broader spirit' which made it possible to 'emphasise the *Class* character of the Trade Union movement as apart from craft interests'. At the conference two motions on the trades councils were passed, one calling for their use in the 'building up of the Trade Union movement as a movement of wage workers', and the other again for a national federation. In the debate on the latter motion Mann again outlined his hopes on the ultimate future of the trades councils, to 'substitute for our present Borough Councils', so that eventually 'the working class will function so effectively through these Trades Councils that there will be an utter impossibility for the fuctioning of . . . the London County Council and so on'. A more immediate possibility of using discussion in the trades councils and in union branches as a means of 'getting rid of "dud" officials' was mentioned by a railwayman delegate.[21]

It was at this point in the history of syndicalism in Britain that 'the different elements in a largely cohesive movement since 1910 moved apart on the basis of international issues'.[22] In 1913 Mann went to the United States and lost interest in syndicalism, although those who remained active continued to argue for the importance of the role of the trades councils, for example to the local bodies at Crewe and Huddersfield. The emphasis on the importance of the trades councils remained so strong in the writings of some syndicalists that it was attacked by others, who considered it necessary to transcend the existing trade union machinery.[23]

However, although syndicalist organisations disintegrated or became very small, syndicalist ideas continued to exercise an important influence throughout the trade union movement. It is impossible to agree with one writer who argues of the syndicalists, that 'events in 1912 and thereafter showed that they had little influence on union policies'.[24] It is true that union leaders were hostile to calls for direct action and amalgamation of the unions, but they were certainly affected by them. Nor is it enough simply to say that syndicalism was 'what those who called themselves syndicalists thought and did'.[25] There are certain quite specifically syndicalist policies which can be defined, and which can be observed at about the same time in many countries. Most of these policies had an influence, particularly on the trades councils. Syndicalists were normally opposed to electoral politics, and although trades councils rarely shared this view they showed a similar hostility in some cases to those leaders of the movement who made careers as politicians. Other syndicalist notions were, however, almost universal in the trades councils. They agreed with the call for more militant action by the trade union movement; they called for greater solidarity among different groups of workers; they often saw the trade unions as embryonic organisations for the new society; and they tried to reorganise the trade union movement. It is true that some of these ideas existed before syndicalism did. However, it was the syndicalists in the years of working class militancy just before 1914 who articulated these policies in such a way as to give them enduring effect. The periods of industrial militancy around 1912, 1919 and 1926, the amalgamation of many unions, and the spread of revolutionary ideas in the working class movement would have taken place without the syndicalists; but all these developments would have had a different form and definition had it not been for the syndicalist movement. At the same time, in the trades councils themselves, it is to the syndicalists that can be traced the idea, the nomenclature and the chief conceptions of the National Federation of Trades Councils. The organisation eventually established in 1922 certainly owed much to what the syndicalists put forward in 1911 and 1912.

Some of the special features of the industrial unrest that preceded 1914 can be attributed to the syndicalists and seen in the trades councils, notably the widespread distrust of trade union officials and the joint action of different groups of workers. Thus in this period trades councils were heard to 'rejoice at the Great Labour Unrest' and to call for *'Solidarity of the Workers'*. Their role as 'co-ordinating and supervising bodies' in national strike action was advocated. In the Nottingham Trades Council it was noticed that 'the barrier that hitherto seemed to exist' between different groups of workers was dissolving at all levels, and workers were 'at length realising that an injury to one is an injury to all'. Such feelings led to 'a growing tendency for closer unity between the societies that comprise each industrial group'. At Halifax in this period the Trades and Industrial Council aimed to 'unify the forces of Labour and strengthen the working class movement with a view to obtaining control Politically and Industrially'.[26] Trades councils made propaganda for trade union unification, and took active steps to effect it. Thus in the period from about 1910 to 1920 virtually any trades council in the land could be quoted as favouring 'the greater unionism' and the ending of 'our snobbery, our craft feelings and our petty jealousies'. The steps towards trade union unity were often seen as a means towards 'the unity of all workers', and ultimately it was thought necessary to fight for

the amalgamation of all Unions into one body, for the purpose of resisting the encroachments of the ruling class upon the liberty of the workers, to secure more adequate remuneration for their labour, and to extend a fraternal hand to the workers of all nations who are struggling for their emancipation.[27]

There were many both inside and outside the trades councils who saw the local organisations as important instruments in this work. In 1912 one local commentator thought that the trades councils would 'play a prominent part' in the unification of trade union forces. In Liverpool, although a syndicalist speaker 'failed to grip the minds of those present', the Trades Council nevertheless did and said much of which the syndicalists would have approved. It was actively involved in discussions for the unification of local unions, and supported the establishment of a Building Trades Committee in the city as a step in 'the trend towards the combination of all labour forces into one harmonious whole'. It also considered that there was a 'need for the drawing together of all kindred trades into federations or committees as a preliminary step'. The syndicalists would also have supported the prominent role that the Trades Council itself was given in this process.

Every effort will be made in the coming year to bring about a unity of forces in Liverpool, and in taking this step the Council will show no desire to ignore or stultify the work of other bodies. But we do feel that the Trades Council, holding as it does the premier position, should be recognised as the CENTRE in giving public expression in things that are and should not be, and also to be the pivot on which should swing the whole Labour movement in Liverpool.[28]

Elsewhere trades councils took active steps 'to organise by industry grades of workers'. Thus the Portsmouth Trades and Labour Council supported the setting up of a Building Trades Federation in 1912, and like the Oxford body actively encouraged the Provisional Committee for Metal Engineering and Shipbuilding Unions which ultimately helped to bring together many of these unions into the AEU. At Reading a conference of unions was called on the general question of organising such mergers, and at Leeds the Trades Council, whose leaders in 1912 doubted that 'single trades unions were powerful enough', continued to support the Amalgamation Committees during the war despite the opposition of some of the affiliated unions. As late as 1932 Walter Citrine considered that there was still 'not a more popular idea in the [trades councils] than the amalgamation and federation of unions'.[29]

Another radical influence on the trades councils in this period was provided by the guild socialist movement. The writings both by and about it are much more extensive than those relating to syndicalism, but guild socialists had few original ideas about what trades councils should do. Some of them simply saw them as 'local democratic assemblies', or as representatives of producers, or even as bodies that could arrange 'the effective and economical distribution of labour'.[30] However, others in the movement did envisage a role for the trades councils on the same lines as the syndicalists. Cole wrote in 1915 that 'the Trades Councils of today will grow into the producers' local authorities, co-ordinating supply locally as the Guild Congress controls it nationally'. He later advocated the expansion of their functions and recommended them as 'in many ways the soundest part of the labour movement, the most imbued with class spirit'.[31] The guild socialists spoke or ran conferences with trades councils at Colchester, Croydon, Waltham Abbey and Battersea, and Duncan Carmichael of the London Trades Council was an active member of the movement. In 1917 the Leicester Trades Council thought that the guild movement was 'receiving the attention of thoughtful men and women'. Although guild socialists had nothing new to contribute to the development of the trades councils themselves, they helped to develop ideas that already existed there. By 1920 guild socialist theorists were hoping that they would continue the development of the movement 'free from the rule and domination of officialdom', and advised revolutionaries who talked of soviets to look no further than the 'effective use of the well-established machinery already in existence' in the trades councils.[32]

After 1918 new preoccupations shaped radical attitudes towards the trades councils. The unification of trade unions in engineering, the Post Office and elsewhere, the setting up of centralised organisations in the Labour Party and the TUC, these steps seemed to carry through much of what radical groups in the movement had been striving for in the previous period. However, the increasingly militant attitudes in the trades councils from 1917 found new outlets. Those who sought radical solutions to the problems of the working class movement looked no longer to the theories of French syndicalism but to the proven successes of the Russian revolutionaries.[33] In every part of Europe revolutionaries became convinced that 'the success of the Russian Revolution of 1917 appeared to be bound up with the Councils system'. In Germany Councils of Soldiers and Workmen temporarily posed a threat to the capitalist State until absorbed into the established industrial relations machinery of the Weimar republic. In Italy also, Antonio Gramsci, founder of the Communist Party, saw the factory council as 'the model for the proletarian State', and in France the newly established Communist Party drew some more general conclusions from the Soviet experience.

Quelles formes nouvelles prendra la lutte? C'est la seule question qui se pose. Et il apparaît tout de suite que l'expérience acquise par le prolétariat de l'Europe Orientale et Centrale nous offre de précieux enseignements.
    Le plus considérable, à notre sens, est celui qui concerns les Conseils ouvriers. *Partout où le prolétariat s'est vu obligé de prendre en mains le pouvoir ou de s'engager la lutte décisive, il est organisé au sein des Conseils ouvriers.* En Russie, les Conseils forment la structure même du nouveau régime. En Allemagne, en Pologne, en Autriche, c'est au sein des Conseils ouvriers qui se concentre la lutte contre la bourgeoisie.[34]

In Britain also radical sections of the working class movement began to try and imitate the soviets in the period after the Russian revolution. At first the theories of the syndicalists and the experience of the shop stewards' and workers' committee movement created a predisposition to look towards factory organisation for the development of British soviets. The Socialist Labour Party, for example, thought that the soviets were 'in the nature of the Clyde Workers' Committee'. J. T. Murphy, the chief ideologist of the shop stewards' movement, wrote about the workers' committee in similar terms.

It would be similar in form to a trades council, with this essential difference – the trades council is only indirectly related to the workshop, whereas the workers' committee is directly related. The former has no power, the latter has the deriving power of the directly connected workers in the workshops.

Murphy also said that he chose the title 'workers' committee' to distinguish the organisation he was describing from the trades councils.[35] The workers' committees of 1916 and 1917 did not survive the war, however, and some of the hopes that had been centred around them were transferred to the trades councils.
    During the first world war some attention had already been paid by those on the left wing of the movement to the potentialities of the trades councils as revolutionary organisations of the workers. The *Herald* published reports of their activities in the period, and encouraged the development of new functions and of contacts between local bodies. In *The Federationist*, the paper of the GFTU, Tom Quelch, from the new generation of a family that had been in the British Marxist movement since its inception, set out a theory and practice for the trades councils which was widely discussed. With the advent of the war, he said, they 'should seize every opportunity to push their influence and develop their power', and thought that they

should aim at covering the whole range of the worker's life. They should cater in every way for his needs, and give expression to his aspirations, seeing first of all that his economic position is well maintained, they should encourage and invigorate his social life in all its ramifications.

Quelch thought that the trades councils should aim 'to improve the living and working conditions of the people, to develop working class organisation, and to pave the way for the rule of democracy'.[36] Others who were soon to join the Communist Party were also studying the possibilities afforded by the trades councils. Robin Page Arnot, for example, gave them an important future in a scheme he put forward in 1919 for the reorganisation of the trade union movement.

At the present the great industries tend to move very much within their own orbits without much thought for their fellow workers. It is the business of the new Trades Councils to correct this tendency. They can counteract it by holding educational classes, by organising Trade Union Campaigns, by rallying all the industries to the support of any one union that is hard pressed, by arranging for better distribution of Labour papers, and, finally, by conducting all general industrial work in the district.[37]

These proposals in themselves did not involve profound changes. However, the central role of the trades councils in the councils of workmen and soldiers' delegates of 1917 and the councils of action of 1920 — incidents described in greater detail in the next chapter — gave the activities of the local organisations a more profound significance in the eyes of militants and revolutionaries. At the first Congress of the CPGB A. A. Purcell, a former syndicalist who had once been active in the Manchester and Salford Trades Council, advocated 'the Soviet (or Workers' Council) system as a means whereby the working class shall achieve power and take control of the forces of production'. More often now 'the search for a potential "Soviet" in Britain' ended in the trades councils, and leaders of the Communist Party developed an expansive view of their possibilities. One of them saw that the councils of action in 1920 'outlined a plan of local institutions which would have been capable of becoming a most important administrative organ had a revolutionary crisis taken place'. As will be indicated in the next chapter, such a view was not without justification, and led to the hope that a widespread transformation of the whole movement would come through the trades councils.

The comparative weakness of the Trades Councils has been a weakness of the whole Trade Union movement . . . In the creation of strong local Labour bodies, in planning and fighting for their creation, the whole labour movement will recreate itself. If the coming of workshop branches with full power to deal with every matter affecting any or all of the men in the workshops will be the rebirth of each Union, the creation of a plenipotentiary in each town will have no less effect.[38]

Besides the syndicalists and other socialist organisations, there is one other influence on the councils' development that should be mentioned. In their *Industrial Democracy* the Webbs outlined an attitude to the trades councils which will be discussed in more detail later. However, after setting up the Fabian Research Department, later the LRD, in 1912, the Webbs took a great deal of interest in the trades councils. Beatrice Webb initiated a survey of their work which began in 1917, and G. D. H. Cole, also active in the LRD, was 'associated with attempts to use the trades councils as the basis for new industrial organisation'. Many of the others who were involved in the LRD survey, notably Arnot, joined the CP and played an important part in the development of trades councils' activities in the early '20s.[39]

These and other influences came together in the early CP, which in 1921 launched a campaign to transform the trade union movement.[40] The Communist Party in this period, wrote one of its members later,

wanted a real Congress of Labour based not on the trade unions alone but on a whole system of shop and works committees, grouped around the local Trades Councils. Thus reinforced, the Trades Councils would function as the authoritative local agencies of a genuine General Staff.

These policies, owing something both to the Webbs and to the syndicalists, were the main ones put forward by the party in the period, and linked the concentration of power in the General Council of the TUC, the development of factory organisation, and industrial unionism with the strengthening of local forces around the trades councils. Trades councils said the leaders of the Communist International and RILU 'should have authority to act as the General Staff of Labour for the given locality'.[41] In a statement of party industrial policy probably produced in 1922 it was said that Communists 'everywhere must seek to gain control of the Trades Councils, by ousting the reactionary leaders, transforming these Councils into real Councils of action'. As 'fighting organs of the class struggle' based on factory organisation and without careerists the local organisations would be able to play a significant role in the emancipation of the proletariat. Tom Quelch also stated the policies of the party on the trades councils. They should 'permit the affiliation of all bona-fide working class organisations in the locality'. Through this individual local bodies could be 'transformed from a Trades Council, with peculiar and limited industrial functions, to a Workers' Council', and also 'the supreme central body in the locality'. As for the municipal authorities, which were 'an integral part of the capitalist system', a trades council 'which will locally express the needs and requirements of the workers will supersede them.' Quelch explained why he had developed such views beyond those he had formerly expressed.

This conception of the ultimate object of the Trades Council, or Workers' Council, is supported by the available evidence we have of the further development of our movement. The rise of the Soviets, or Workers' Councils in Russia is the startlingly supreme example.[42]

These statements make clear the influence of syndicalism, of ideas which had to some extent been worked out independently by Quelch himself, and of the example of the Soviet Union. Efforts to put them into practice were developed further with the establishment of the British Bureau of the Red International of Labour Unions in the latter part of 1921. During the lock-out of engineering workers it was said that the trades councils should organise, 'in conjunction with the local lock-out committees, the complete massing of the organised workers to help the locked-out men'. Quelch outlined further work for them in organising the unemployed, acting as information offices, and bringing together all aspects of the working class movement.[43] J. T. Murphy was now fully convinced that the trades councils were 'the means of drawing all the labour forces together for a class resistance providing we will use them'. The London committee of the RILU circularised its members about how this work could be carried out. It was above all necessary for revolutionaries to 'capture the trades councils'. This was because in 'times of crisis, these councils play a very important part'. Revolutionaries should aim to expand the basis of representation in the local organisations, see that the unemployed were affiliates, and every affiliated branch 'should see that its delegate is a revolutionary who realises the potentialities of the council'. Considering their role in recent industrial crises, 'it is easy to see that in the very near future the trades councils will play an ever-increasing part in the class war'.[44] These statements show a keen awareness of the potentialities for militant struggle that did exist in the trades councils in this period, and, as is discussed elsewhere, involved accurate predictions on many activities of the local organisations. In the meantime it was an earlier syndicalist dream, the establishment of a national federation, that was to come to fruition and provide a field for the influence of the CP.

Trade union officialdom and the trades councils

Although left-wing elements in the working class movement had an important impact on the development of the trades councils – and more of this will be examined later in the chapter – it was the leaders of the trade unions and those sympathetic to them who were in the end to have the final say in their fate. It is to their attitudes and their theories that it is now necessary to turn.

The role of the trades councils in setting up the TUC in 1868 is well known. It is interesting to notice, however, that even then leaders of the main unions were hostile to the trades councils and to their participation in the national working class movement. During the 1872 campaign against anti-trade union laws 'sharp rebukes were issued to provincial Trades Councils that dared to show any initiative'.[45] Many union leaders were hostile to the local organisations. John Kane of the National Association of Ironworkers thought that national organisations should not even join, because 'large and wealthy societies, with important interests at stake, can never submit to having their members linked with the discretion of local and irresponsible bodies'. In 1874 Thomas Halliday, secretary of the Amalgamated Association of Miners, suggested that the trades councils should not be represented on the Parliamentary Committee of the TUC, and at the same time most trade union leaders were said to be against their being represented at the Congress at all. The *Beehive* expressed support for this view, largely because of its opposition to the leaders of the London Trades Council, one of whom later wrote of how the 'jealousy with which the governing bodies of the Unions regard any interference with their distinctive authority is permanently felt by the Trades Councils; it moulds their policy and controls their action in every movement in which they take part'.[46]

During the course of the nineteenth century the balance of forces between local and national organisations in the movement began to change. Thus although in 1885 the Sheffield Trades Council was still unable to raise money on behalf of national unions, in the previous year the ASE had begun for the first time to allow its local branches to affiliate to the trades councils. Increasingly from that time there was an acceptance of a more centralised trade union movement, and of a subordinate position for the councils. By the 1890s it was said that most trades council affiliates were 'branch societies, with limited powers, and whose Executives would not be disposed to entertain any idea of a local authority with the power to levy contributions in the event of a strike'.[47] This was the basis for the exclusion of the trades councils from the TUC in 1895, an event which has accurately been described as 'a mere incident in the fierce warfare then raging between the old and the new leaders of the Trade Union movement'.[48] The exclusion of the trades councils was part of a series of changes at the TUC, such as the introduction of the card vote, which were aimed at reflecting the strength of the largest and most important affiliated unions. The trades councils were expelled not because they were socialist, nor yet because they supported independent electoral politics or new unionism, but because they no longer had a role in the centralised movement that the leaders of the main unions wanted to see.[49] These developments were part of a general process of trade union centralisation, as could be seen from contemporary events in France already described, and from the fact that in 1895 also the five-year-old General Committee of the German trade unions similarly abandoned the affiliation of local organisations.[50] For trade union leaders throughout Western Europe, local organisations represented an alternative source of power within the movement which could not be allowed to threaten the centralised and streamlined movement they wanted.

The efforts the trades councils themselves made in the decades after 1895 to break out of the isolation imposed on them will be described below. Meanwhile it should be noted that at a time when their functions and their usefulness to the movement were increasing most union leaders hoped they would simply confine themselves to electoral work. In 1924 the TUC itself said that since 1895 there had been 'no point of contact except occasional calls upon them for assistance during national campaigns and special assistance always rendered by the local Councils at the place of meeting for the Trades Union Congress'. In 1902 the Parliamentary Committee actually refused a request to involve the trades councils in a campaign against the Education Bill. At Leeds in 1910 the Trades Council got a model FWC from the TUC, although they had already been campaigning on the matter for some time, and in the same year there was an instruction to have nothing to do with the outcast MEA. In 1916 the local bodies were urged, rather late in the day, to take an interest in the war pensions committees.[51]

Whatever general reservations or criticisms they may have had, this negative attitude of the union leaders was reflected in the writings of the Webbs. In the first edition of their *History* they admitted that the original establishment of the trades councils in the 1850s and '60s 'was an important step in the consolidation of the trade union movement' but went on to quote a description by J. Burnett, a former leader of the ASE, of the working of a typical trades council, an account which cast doubt on its capacity for any effective action. It was asserted that except in the case of the Fair Wages Clause, and in getting workmen elected to borough councils, they could achieve little:

> the crowded meetings of tired workmen, unused to official business, with knowledge and interest strictly limited to a single industry, is useless as a Court of Appeal, and ineffective even as a joint committee of the local trades ... they have no recognised authority in the Trade Union world; they are rigidly excluded from all participation in the government or trade policy of the Unions; and their influence on political questions of a national scope has hitherto been infinitesimal.[52]

Writing a little later, the Webbs themselves were even more damning about the usefulness of the local organisations.

> Without leadership, without an official programme, and without any definite work, the Trades Councils have become, in effect, microscopic Trades Union Congresses, with all the deficiencies of organised public meetings. Their wild and inconsistent resolutions, no less than their fitful and erratic action, have naturally increased the dislike of the central executives, and of the salaried officials who dominate the Parliamentary Committee.

Despite this disparagement of their current importance, however, the Webbs thought there was a possible role for the local organisations in a more centralised trade union movement.

> The local Trades Council without interfering in general policy could find abundant occupation in organising and educating the local Trade Unionist electors; in carrying out the frequent instructions received from the skilled political staff of the Parliamentary Committees; in watching and criticising the action of the Parliamentary representatives of the constituency, to whatever party they belonged; in supplementing and supervising the local work of the mines sanitary and factory inspectors.[53]

In a work published by the Fabian Society which set out to popularise the Webbs' views, the subordinate position of the trades councils was particularly emphasised. It was said that they should take no part in the formulation of the national programme of the movement:

> Their function is to explain and advocate locally the measures put forward by the Congress on behalf of the Trade Union Movement. The Parliamentary Committee should keep itself in close touch with the Local Councils, supplying them with all possible information regarding the work of the Congress, guiding and instructing them, and seeking their active co-operation.

It is interesting to note that it was in this form that the work of the Webbs was studied by the youthful Walter Citrine, to whom was later allotted the 'task of bringing the Councils and the Congress into correct structural relationship'.[54]

In the years after the appearance of the first editions of their books on the trade union movement the Webbs gradually revised their attitude to the trades councils. In successive editions of the *History* they noted the increase in their size and numbers.[55] In preparing the 1920 edition they found that some of their younger assistants thought they would have to take a different view altogether.[56] Margaret Cole and R. Page Arnot had recently been involved in the LRD survey of the trades councils, and had also investigated the attitudes of some of the leaders of the unions. As a result they considered that the earlier editions had 'understated the value and work of the Trades Councils'. They maintained that the larger ones were not primarily concerned with electoral work, that most unions actively encouraged their branches to affiliate, and that those union officials who did not take much interest in the trades councils took little part in other local matters. They also pointed to the contrast between the attitudes of various unions towards the trades councils. Branches of the Durham Miners and of the Amalgamated Society of Gas, Municipal and General Workers never affiliated, and the Workers' Union and the Postmen's Federation issued no specific instructions to local branches. But many others – especially those who frequently called for the support of the trades councils, either in small local disputes or in obtaining legitimisation in the eyes of their employers and of other trade unionists – were keen and active supporters of the councils. These included shop workers, insurance workers, the AUCE and the NUR, which was said to be 'the life and soul of the TC movement'. The increasing importance of the trades councils was reflected in the new edition of the Webbs' *History* in 1920.

> The character of their active membership, their functions and their proceedings have remained much as we described them thirty years ago; but they have, on the whole, increased in strength and local influence, as well as in numbers and membership. ... It is more and more on the political side that they are in some degree succeeding in uniting the energy of the Trade Unions of a particular town ... so far as Trade Unionism itself is concerned, their direct influence on questions of national scope is not great.

The Webbs went on to describe the role of the councils in training the new generation of union leaders, in recruiting to the unions, in occasionally settling industrial disputes, and in developing links between the trade union and co-operative sections of the working class movement.[57] Thus while prepared to concede that the trades councils had grown in importance, those who reflected the views of union leaders envisaged only a limited role for them in the future. In the years immediately after the 1920 edition of the *History* the leaders of the trade unions and TUC found it more necessary than before to pay attention to the councils. Another commentator noticed how between 1918 and 1924 they had 'greatly increased in numbers and activity'.[58] The Central Hall conference of January 1916 against conscription and the efforts of August 1920 against the government's Russian policies confirmed that the trades councils had a role to play in the national labour movement beyond electoral matters. In the early '20s the leaders of the TUC found that the trades councils could be useful in many fields. The local organisations were enthusiastic supporters of the 'Mines for the nation' campaign in 1919–20,[59] and the equally unsuccessful 'Back to the unions' campaign of 1923 convinced TUC leaders that there was something to be said for the activities of the trades councils.[60] Nearly every local body expended a great deal of time and energy in attempts to win back to the unions some of the millions who had left it with the onset of unemployment in 1920. At Manchester this campaign was 'the great event of the Trades Council's year'; at Cardiff 20,000 attended meetings and 100,000 people received propaganda. At Birmingham such work secured 'good results'. The Leeds Trades Council said that these efforts showed the TUC that the local organisations which they had neglected could still be of value to them. TUC Secretary Fred Bramley warned the trades councils against describing the campaign as a 'fiasco', though in general it probably was.[61] As well as being involved in work sponsored by the TUC, trades councils in the early '20s also took part in activities the inspiration for which came from other sources altogether. Some of these, and the response to them of the trade union leaders, the rest of this chapter will describe.

Early efforts at national organisation

The strong support for tendencies to unification in the working class movement that existed in the trades councils has already been indicated. The idea of a national organisation for the councils themselves also has a long history. The Glasgow and Edinburgh trades councils proposed amalgamating all Scottish trade unions, as early as 1861. The TUC was originally conceived as including only trades councils and other federated organisations, though it soon became dominated by the leaders of the major unions. This situation led the leaders of the London Trades Council as early as 1873 to propose the setting up of a federation of trades councils quite independent of the TUC, and the idea was supported at a meeting of other local organisations held during the 1874 congress. The Bristol Trades Council call, at its foundation in the same year, for 'a federation of trades through the Trades Councils of the kingdom' no doubt owed something to this discussion, but at the time nothing further was heard of it.[62] Similar proposals were sometimes put forward in later years, often in association with the notion that there ought to be an organisation more powerful and less exclusive than the TUC itself. Such proposals were discussed at Birmingham, Liverpool and Manchester in 1879 as part of an effort to bring together organisations of workers into a national federation that would operate through the trades councils.[63] The 1889 TUC was told by a delegate from the Sheffield Trades Council that there ought to be 'a strong combination of the Trades Councils of the United Kingdom', and in 1891 the Bristol body wanted the Parliamentary Committee 'to frame a working federal constitution for trade unions with trades councils as local executives'. In 1893 the London Trades Council argued that such an organisation should 'raise a central fund for the purpose of an important trade dispute' and to 'watch legal cases which effect Trade Unionists'.[64] The establishment of the generally ineffective regional trades council federations in the following period was the main concrete result of these aspirations. In 1893 the Yorkshire Federated Trades Councils was established in the hope of a closer unity than could ever be secured. Similar federations were set up in the Midlands in 1894, in the south-western counties and in the north-east in 1896, in Cheshire in 1897 and in Lancashire in 1898.[65]

During the 1890s other efforts to set up a national organisation for trades councils resulted from their activities as electoral agencies, and from their exclusion from the TUC in 1895. Many local bodies felt strongly about the latter event, the Liverpool Trades Council talking of 'the "Stuart Kings" of the Parliamentary Committee', and of the exclusion 'as a blow at the smaller unions who are unable to be represented except through the Trades Councils'.[66] Outside the 1895 Cardiff congress itself, seventeen trades councils met and agreed to set up a national federation, and it was decided that the London Trades Council should organise further meetings. However, on consideration, little further enthusiasm could be found for the proposal. In Leicester and Leeds it was decided to oppose it. The main reason was probably that given by the Leeds secretary to the Webbs in 1892; a national federation 'would frighten the National associations away from them'.[67] Another important reason for failure was probably the feeling of local organisations that they were too poor to finance a system of communication among themselves or the travelling that would be necessary to maintain such an organisation. Nevertheless the Federation of Trades Councils set up in the south-western counties in 1896 originally adopted the title of National Federation of Trades Councils in the vain hope that others might join it.

These efforts of the 1890s did, however, have at least two other concrete results. In 1894 the Dublin Trades Council convened the first meeting of what became the Irish Congress of Trade Unions.[68] In 1897 the Scottish trades councils, frustrated at the failure to set up an all-British organisation, called a conference of their own at which the Scottish TUC was established. It is interesting to see the consequences of the existence of a body to which both unions and trades councils were affiliated. There can be no doubt that the main result was that in the period from the mid-'90s to the 1920s the Scottish trades councils became much weaker than their English counterparts and showed little of the same initiative or development. It was often said that with the coming of the 1918 Labour Party constitution the Scottish trades councils had 'a complete orientation towards becoming a wing of the Labour Party', and that 'many trades councils had allowed their industrial activities to die out'. By 1925 it was clear that trades council representation at the STUC was maintained 'largely because of sentiment'. The situation was so bad that the General Council of the STUC said that 'the manner in which some of the important business is dealt with by the Councils does not warrant a general and continued recommendation being made that Trade Union money be passed to them as affiliation fees'. The British TUC, however hostile to the trades councils, never went as far as this. The Scottish General Council in 1925 proposed the setting up of special Industrial Committees under its direct control to recruit to the unions and carry on other industrial activities which were being neglected by the regular trades councils. These were set up in nineteen areas, including the few places, such as Edinburgh and Aberdeen, where there were flourishing trades councils. Trades councils and local union branches were hostile to the industrial committees, and although they did some recruiting they gradually disappeared or were absorbed into purely industrial trades councils.[69] This story of trades councils that remained closely integrated with the national union organisations shows the probable fate that would have awaited the trades councils in Britain as a whole had they not been excluded from the TUC in 1895. It also to some extent provided a foretaste of what was to happen when eventually a permanent organisation of trades councils in England and Wales was set up in 1925.

In the meantime, however, the trades councils throughout Britain continued to make efforts to set up a national organisation. The syndicalists were powerful advocates of a National Federation in the years before the first world war. The expanding role of the local organisations during the war increased the desire for such arrangements. In 1916 the London Trades Council was again discussing the need for a national conference of trades councils, though it did not agree that it was necessary at that time.[70] In the following year a more serious effort was made to set up a National Federation. At a meeting of the newly formed Essex Federation of Trades Councils on 2 June 1917 the East Ham Trades Council proposed 'the formation of a national central organisation of Trades Councils', and promised to obtain the support of national union leaders to this end. The Federation agreed to get in touch with others with a view to furthering the scheme, and later in the year it called a conference of trades council federations, of which probably a dozen existed at that time.[71] This meeting took place on 27 October at the headquarters of the GFTU, with George Appleton, its general secretary, presiding. The response to the call for a conference must have disappointed the organisers, however, because although there were messages of support from four trades council federations, just a few trades councils in the London area, representing a total of only 35,000 members, bothered to send representatives. Nevertheless a 'National Federation of County Federations of Trades Councils' was set up, aiming to organise new trades councils, to prevent old ones overlapping, to organise all trades councils into federations, and 'to consolidate the position and influence of the Trades Council movement'. The conference also set up a provisional committee and asked the Essex federation to call a further conference in the following January.[72] This conference did not take place, and it is not difficult to see why. The lack of response to the first conference showed that there would have to be much greater preparation for a national conference. The association with the GFTU, whose leaders adopted a thoroughly 'patriotic' attitude to the war, no doubt discredited the venture in the eyes of many local leaders. Attacks on the new organisation appeared in both the *Herald* and *Labour Leader* on grounds of this sort.[73] Finally, the discussion of the new Labour Party constitution which began towards the end of 1917 pre-empted much of what the Essex federation seemed to be striving for. After the failure of these efforts the GFTU became more hostile to the trades councils, ceasing to report their activities in its paper and even attacking them for making such allegedly impossible demands as holidays with pay.[74] The notion of a 'Federation of Federations' was still of interest to the trades councils, however, and was actively supported by the Earlstown and Eccles bodies in 1919.[75]

National Federation and Joint Consultative Committee, 1922–25

By the 1920s, after many abortive efforts to set up a national organisation for the trades councils, there were at last two successful moves in this direction. The first derived directly from the left-wing influences described in the first part of this chapter, and the second and more permanent effort was initiated by those leaders of the unions and of the TUC, whose rather more narrow and restricted view of the matter has also been discussed. These events took place in the early '20s, by which time the trades councils had found a new and important role in the movement from which they had been apparent outcasts in 1895, and had come to find tasks to perform other than the narrowly electoral ones envisaged for them in the 1918 Labour Party constitution, or the even narrower industrial ones to which the TUC tried to confine them.

It was in Birmingham that the first successful initiative came. At the Trades Council meeting on 2 October 1920 there was much discussion of the fact that the fighting policy being demanded by the rank and file of the movement was not being carried out by the leaders, and at the end of the year the cautious and moderate secretary F. W. Rudland said he thought that the Trades Council was a place where it could be discussed that 'Trade Unionism, to be effective, must be prepared to consider new ideas and adopt methods that will not leave their organisation at the mercy of the class-conscious capitalist system'.[76] It was in this spirit that in May 1922 H. Parsons, local orgainiser of the Furniture Trades Association and left-wing delegate to the Trades Council, proposed that the Trades Council should do something active about the continued depression and unemployment. His motion proposed 'a special Conference of the Trade Unions in the city' which would 'discuss and promote schemes for unifying the whole of the Unions, either by amalgamations or other such means as may be considered best'.[77] The conference duly took place on 6 July 1922, and was presided over by Jack Mills, MP, after unsuccessful efforts to secure the services of Tom Mann, G. D. H. Cole and William Mellor. There were 237 delegates present, representing eighty-seven local trade union organisations.[78] The local trade union paper thought that 'its success as a thoroughly representative gathering was unqualified'. The views presented at the conference were revealing. The Trades Council's president began by asserting the need for the co-ordination of trade union activities in a way 'which would supersede the present method, or, rather, lack of method', by means of 'less unions and more unity'. This sentiment won unanimous support at the conference, as can be seen from the motion that was eventually passed by it.

That this conference is of the opinion that an entire change in the objective and method of organisation of the Trade Union movement of the country is imperative if the combination of the employers and the concentrated attacks of organised Capitalism upon the position of the workers is to be met. We therefore recommend:

(*a*) That the existing unions be merged into a small number of National Industrial Unions to be further linked together in a single body such as the General Council of Trade Unions.

(*b*) Locally, each Industrial Group shall have the fullest measure of local autonomy consistent with the industrial national policy. Further, the local groupings should follow the national lines, with District Councils for each industry, welded together in local General Councils, such as the Trades Council.

Such ideas clearly owed more to the propaganda of the syndicalists than to any other influence. It is interesting to note that the members of some of the large general unions present simply wanted a move towards one union for all workers, and that a speaker from the West Bromwich Trades Council compared the proposals in the main resolution to the structure of the French CGT. As well as discussing these matters the conference set up a co-ordinating committee, and agreed to circularise trades councils to call a national conference and to ask the TUC in the meantime to call regional conferences of the local bodies.

The committee elected at the July 1922 conference acted quickly, and soon invited all trades councils to a conference in Birmingham on 14 October.[79] This conference was attended by 126 delegates from sixty-seven trades councils, and about sixty others wrote to express their support for its objects. The chairman this time was Alex Gossip, left-wing general secretary of the Furniture Trades Association, who considered sectional trade unionism 'a direct menace to the best interests of the workers' and attacked Fred Bramley for maintaining the importance of pride in craft and work. The conference considered a motion which had many similarities to the one passed in May, but this time called for immediate steps to be taken towards the creation of One Big Union. Parsons of the Birmingham Trades Council, who moved it, said that they opposed 'any system of bureaucratic control' and instead wanted all the leading bodies of the movement to begin work on 'a thoroughly democratic system, in which the interests of all classes of workers would be safeguarded'. So radical was the temper of this conference that those who wanted industrial unionism or local committees to propagate it as a step towards the One Big Union were voted down. It was then proposed by the very moderate secretary of the Bristol Trades Council, E. H. Parker, and agreed unanimously, that this should be the first Annual Conference of Trades Councils. It was also agreed that the TUC should be asked to admit the local bodies into affiliation.

In this way was born the National Federation of Trades Councils. It is important to point out at this stage that it arose more or less spontaneously from the initiative of the Birmingham Trades Council, that it expressed ideas which had at least a decade of history within the labour movement, and that it secured a widespread measure of support. Thus it is not true to say that the establishment of the National Federation was part of 'the Communist attempt to secure power within the trades councils', although it did to some extent become this. At the original meeting in May 1922 which began the process leading to the beginning of the new body, it was said that the CP delegates constituted a 'ridiculously small' minority of those present. It is interesting to note that at Sheffield also, quite independently of the events at Birmingham, the Trades and Labour Council early in 1922 was supporting efforts in the direction of 'One Big Union' almost without dissent at the same time as opposing advances from the local Branch of the Red International of Labour Unions. Also, the paper of the Union of Post Office Workers, one of the new industrial unions, greeted the 'Unification Campaign' with pleasure and hoped it would be a step towards a 'National General (or Industrial) Council' which could be 'the workers' parliament' and 'the chief hope for the future of Trade Unionism'.[80] After the two conferences of 1922 strong support came from local organisations also. The secretary at Sheffield said that during the year they had 'persistently urged the necessity of more power being allocated to Trades Councils', had called for all local branches to hand over their powers to them, and had supported the National Federation. At Wolverhampton it was agreed that 'an entire change in the objective and methods of organisation of the Trade Unions in this country is imperative', and the Trades and Labour Council proposed that all 'existing Unions shall be merged into one national organisation for all classes of workers'. The Stepney Trades Council also called on the TUC General Council 'to amalgamate the existing Trade Union organisations into one National Union'.[81] Thus not only did the National Federation come to birth quite independently of the Communist Party, it secured widespread support from many trades councils, and from other sections of the trade union movement as well.

Although the Birmingham conferences of 1922 and the National Federation secured general approval in the trade union movement, they did not find favour with the leaders of the TUC. Fred Bramley described the proposals of the first of the conferences as 'utopian', and after the second conference the TUC leaders affected to ignore the existence of the Federation, even refusing to reply to local bodies that sent in motions putting forward Federation policies. It was said that the General Council 'of course takes no cognisance of resolutions coming from these Councils', and that the idea of 'organising Trades Councils in a Federation with a separate annual conference . . . obviously overlaps with the National Assembly of the Trade Union movement'.[82] The leaders of the National Federation approached the TUC in all good faith and were somewhat bewildered by the hostile response they occasioned. The joint secretaries nevertheless thought that their agitation for union unity had resulted in some of the steps towards amalgamation over the past year, and pledged to go on fighting for 'the establishment of a completely co-ordinated industrial organisation' on the assumption that 'forging the weapon of emancipation' was 'the special function of the Trades Council'.[83] In this situation the Federation was virtually driven for support to the LRD and the Communist Party.[84] The schemes for reorganisation of the unions being put forward at that time by the party were not very different from those of the National Federation, and the industrial policies of both derived from the pre-war syndicalist notions which have already been described. Thus it is not surprising to find that the second conference of the National Federation of Trades Councils, held in Birmingham on 17 November 1923, was organised by R. Palme Dutt of the LRD and presided over by Harry Pollitt of the RILU, both leading members of the Communist Party.[85] Despite the opposition of the TUC leaders the conference was attended by 103 delegates from seventy-one trades councils, together with some from the Lancashire and Cheshire federation and the LRD.[86]

The general tone of this conference was more moderate than that of its predecessors, particularly on the questions of trade union organisation. Harry Pollitt's opening address[87] simply called for trade union unity 'on the only basis on which it can be established – the industrial basis' and not in the same thoroughgoing ways that had been mentioned before. Pollitt asserted, however, that the trades councils had an important role in voicing 'what at present has no voice or expression in the movement – the feelings of the rank and file'. He thought they could 'take the initiative in endeavouring to force a lead upon the central organs of the movement', but was careful to point out that they were 'not out in antagonism, as is falsely suggested, to the rightful central body of the movement, the Trades Union Congress'.[88] The committee set up by the previous conference reported that it had compiled a list of trades councils, campaigned to support building workers on strike, and secured 'an extraordinary response' to the call for affiliation to the TUC. The meeting began with a number of generally political speeches and motions which reflected the views of the Communist Party but would not have been out of place at the meetings of any of the individual trades councils represented. These included fraternal greetings from the RILU and the Workers' Welfare League of India, and a motion against the recent French invasion of the Ruhr, calling for the setting up of councils of action to oppose it. On the question of union reorganisation, the conference passed motions supporting industrial unionism and centralisation, and reflected many of the ideas about trades councils that had been put forward not just in the previous year but for over a decade by syndicalists and others. One motion said that the trades councils 'should become the leading propagandist bodies in the country', and urged the affiliation to them 'of all bone-fide political, industrial, co-operative and social working class organisations'. The debate on this showed a wider division of opinion than at the previous conferences. One speaker spoke of how, at Woolwich, 'the place-hunters and reactionaries were eliminated', but others worried about the inclusion of working men's clubs, or the unemployed, or even that they might break the recently agreed Labour Party rules by allowing the affiliation of CP branches. However, the motion was carried by twenty-nine votes to twenty. Next, although the conference refused to condemn the TUC leaders for their attitude to the National Federation, it nevertheless called unanimously for there to be two representatives of the Federation on the General Council. Another motion passed in line with Communist Party policy was the call for a national convention of working class organisations. Other motions discussed would not have been opposed in any trades councils, such as one calling for State aid for the blind, or another which wanted relief schemes run by the trade unions themselves as a solution to unemployment. The provisional committee was again re-elected, with Pollitt as chairman, and it was agreed that there would be another conference before the next TUC.

The widespread impact of these discussions during the next period can be traced easily. The trades councils themselves, even those who had not attended them, often advocated policies which the conferences had helped to formulate. In Manchester, where the 1923 conference was described as simply being about 'the need for the unification of trade unions', a special report was prepared and circulated to other local bodies. The Bolton Trades Council was also much affected by these ideas, and thought that by the beginning of 1924 'the old idea of individual trade unions being able to control the varied interests of their members is being rapidly dispelled and replaced by the co-operative policy as expressed in the combination of all local activities under the guidance of the Trades and Labour Council'. The council continued to campaign along these lines despite the opposition of some of the affiliated unions. In Wolverhampton a detailed scheme for organising the unions of the area into six groups was put forward in the local movement. At Sheffield it was said that although there had been a lot of criticism of the General Council at the 1923 conference 'on the whole it was helpful criticism', and even those local bodies which, like the Liverpool Trades Council, had not attended any of the conferences, thought that the trades councils should become local organs of the TUC on an 'all-inclusive working class basis'. At Cwmamman the Trades and Labour Council included affiliation to the National Federation in its new draft rules, and at Hull the industrial section of the Trades Council and Labour Party was prepared to pass motions on general industrial topics emanating from the Federation. At Birmingham itself it was considered that the Federation had played a part in the adoption of the generally more militant policies of the 1924 TUC meeting in Hull.[89] It was with some justice that early in 1924 the Federation leaders could claim to be 'leading a fight for a programme that covers all the issues now being faced by the workers'. The appeal of working for these policies through the local bodies is clear from one local paper, which argued that the trades councils were 'free from the exclusiveness of the craft-union and from the dogmatism of the political sect'. Moreover, since they consisted largely of 'simple workers in daily touch with the stern realities of capitalism, they do not readily develop a bureaucratic outlook'.[90]

This wide diffusion of the ideas of the Birmingham conferences and the growth of interest in the work of local organisations meant that the CP could soon claim with some justice to be responsible for the 'increased influence of the trades councils'. It could also be said that this work had increased support for industrial unionism and for a more fighting policy by the General Council, although claims by the RILU to have revived organisations that had up to then been 'eking out a miserable existence', or to control most of the trades councils in the London area, were somewhat more far-fetched.[91] The launching of the Minority Movement by the RILU in 1924 led to the intensification of work around such issues as those that had been discussed at Birmingham, and the new organisation at its opening conference noted 'with approval the revival that has recently taken place in the Trades Councils'.[92] In this period the Communist Party and its various associated movements discussed and put forward further policies for the work of the local organisations. Tom Mann, now Minority Movement president, said that the RILU was 'determined to take up and largely reorganise the Trades Councils of this country'. The Minority Movement also thought that the trades councils had a role to play in establishing alternative political machinery for a workers' take-over. Among other policies put forward for the trades councils were the affiliations of co-operative societies, working men's clubs, the unemployed, and other non-trade union organisations, as well as the reorganisation and centralisation of the trades councils in the London area.[93] Mann thought that the National Federation conference in November 1923 could serve to create 'a permanent organ of rank-and-file expression without being subject to the stifling and skilfully arranged "platforms" such as those at Labour Party conferences and Trades Union Congresses'. Tom Quelch also developed the views he had been expressing for at least a decade. He suggested that, with factory committees being affiliated, they could take over the task of 'disciplining and indisputably controlling the actions of working-class representatives', and could become 'leading organs of the class struggle' through their role in co-ordinating the actions of workers involved in disputes.[94] Quelch outlined his policies in their most complete and developed form in a pamphlet issued by the Movement in 1925, and later twice reprinted, entitled *The militant trades council. A model constitution for trades councils*. Here he emphasised the importance of all-inclusive organisations that would develop all aspects of the life of the workers. In summary he said that 'our conception of the Trades and Labour Council is a body which will gather together all the organised forces of the working-class movement ... and give them *all the time* bold and militant leadership'.

These ideas about the development of the trades councils had an effect beyond the ranks of the Communist Party and its associated organisations. A Plebs League textbook issued in May 1923 thought the trades council revival offered 'the best line of activity at the present moment' in the working class movement, since each council could go beyond the role of selecting people to be representatives on various capitalist administrative bodies and become 'the local working-class parliament'. Thus it

could bring together local sections of unions ready for amalgamation, and carry out local campaigns against non-Unionism ... It could lend a hand to the Guilds in the industries where they are possible, and link the Trade Unions up with the Co-operative Movement; the workers and the workless could be kept together under its auspices. All the Trades Councils could meet together as a national *class* parliament to supplement the work of the large national industrial groupings.[95]

The Plebs League also discussed these developments in its paper. The militancy of the trades council conferences was compared favourably by some to the moderate policies agreed at the 1923 TUC. On the other hand H. Drinkwater, the editor of *Labour Organiser*, reflecting the views of Labour Party leaders, thought that the trades councils would be only 'talking shops' if they were not exclusively devoted to electoral matters. In the same discussion the president of a trades council in the West Riding said that his organisation had repudiated the work of its councillors and operated independently and successfully on industrial matters ever since.[96] These discussions, and others that followed, did much to illuminate attitudes. Firstly, the established leaders of both industrial and political wings of the working class movement were not interested in developing the work of the trades councils. There is little evidence that they even took seriously such compromise proposals as those put forward by the *Daily Herald*'s industrial correspondent, for trades council attendance at Congress through area representatives.[97] In the second place, and partly because of this, left-wingers in the movement began to consider the possibility of separate trades councils and local labour parties.[98] Thirdly, the contradiction in the attitude of supporters of the National Federation became clear.

R. Palme Dutt, the organiser of the 1923 conference, said that it had given a 'genuine opportunity of common expression of the working class in this country', and that in future the conference, representing as it did 'many of the best, the keenest and also the most practical of the active workers' could be 'not only of the Trades Councils' but also of 'all the foremost and class-conscious sections of the workers' movement'. Dutt still maintained that such activities should be seen 'not in opposition to the Trades Union Congress but as a complement of the official body in whose hands the power rests'. But the TUC leaders were not prepared to show similar tolerance, as he pointed out: 'the machine', as he put it, had decided 'that the only policy is to endeavour to trample out the Conference as having no right to exist'.[99] Other Communist Party leaders were inclined to blame the trades councils themselves, considering that the Federation was 'as active, nationally, about as much as a dead fish'.[100] However, the dilemma of claiming to be subordinate to a body that refused even to recognise its existence was too much in the end for the National Federation, and it could only collapse when the TUC decided to take active steps to end it. As Ellen Wilkinson put it, they could not 'urge unity and then complain when it is achieved'.[101]

Although as late as the spring of 1924 the leaders of the TUC were still asserting their opposition to 'calling into being another organisation overlapping the one already in existence', they nevertheless feared 'that a separate organisation of Trades Councils would . . . grow up to challenge the authority of the Trades Union Congress on its own ground'.[102] Thus within a month of the November 1923 Birmingham conference the General Council sub-committee on the Defence of Trade Unionism was considering how to grant the 'maximum of recognition with safety'.

Bramley even announced that he might be prepared to meet leaders of the National Federation.[103] The next step was to call together representatives of the largest trades councils, including most of those who had been actively concerned with the Federation. A meeting took place in Caxton Hall, Westminster, on 7 May 1924, and delegates from twenty-five trades councils agreed to set up a Joint Consultative Committee including six representatives of the trades councils and six of the General Council. All six trades council representatives had supported the Federation, including Parsons from Birmingham, who had initiated it. The first meeting of the Joint Consultative Committee took place at the TUC headquarters on 10 July, and there it was agreed that the trades councils 'should act through their secretaries as the Labour correspondents of the Trades Union Congress General Council' and should 'act as the circulating agencies for all the special propaganda publications issued by the Trades Union Congress General Council'. It was also agreed that trades councils could issue general statements of TUC and Labour Party policy, and that the TUC would publish reports on their activities.[104] The significance of these events was that the TUC had now outflanked not only the Communist Party but also the trades councils themselves. Leaders of the CP were forced soon to admit that the Federation was 'not as healthy as it might be', and by the middle of 1925 it had clearly been abandoned altogether.[105]

The leaders of the TUC, however, had no intention of developing the work of the trades councils in the way the Federation had tried to. The local organisations continued to call for 'a forward industrial policy', and hoped that 'the machinery would be created to enable the Trades Councils not only to work but to have a say in the forming of policy'. There was no possibility of this happening now that the General Council was firmly in control.[106] At first Bramley told the trades councils that the new arrangements would, 'at all times, make due allowances for differences of opinion', but there is little evidence that the Joint Consultative Committee was ever allowed to make serious provision for this.[107] The 1924 Congress quickly pushed aside any suggestion of representation of the trades councils at Congress or on the General Council.[108] The first national trades councils conference run by the TUC made it clear that there too the TUC leaders were in control.[109] This conference, held in Denison House on 27 February 1925, had 126 delegates attending, including Tom Mann, representing Woolwich, and among other well known Communists J. T. Murphy represented Ealing and J. J. Vaughan Bethnal Green. The conference was opened by Alonzo Swales, current General Council chairman, with what Murphy described as 'a speech every Communist could applaud'.[110] It referred to the extension of the work of the local organisations not only in political matters but also on such industrial activities as union recruitment, and expressed the 'need for us to clarify our conception as to what a trades council should be, and as to its rightful place in the movement'. However, Swales made it clear that all debate would be strictly controlled. He asked delegates to confine 'discussion to the actualities, to the matters contained on the Agenda', referred to the General Council even the question of whether his speech should be printed, and refused to allow discussion at all of the question of affiliation to the TUC. Resolutions were proposed, and agreed, making the trades councils local correspondents of the TUC, receiving all General Council circulars. Complaints were heard that these stipulations 'put the trades councils almost in the position of lackeys, and excluded them from taking part in moulding policy', and there was also talk of how 'the trade union official element was often disruptive' to the work of local organisations. In general, however, the proposals of the General Council were agreed without much dissent, and other policies of the preliminary meetings were reaffirmed along with a general motion on trade union unity moved by Mann. A more specific motion that called for unity with the Russian trade unions was not allowed. Walter Hannington of the National Unemployed Workers' Committee Movement then addressed the conference on working closely with his organisation, which was at that time associated with the General Council. Further motions advocated the implementation of the Washington convention on the forty-eight-hour week and put forward the aims of the Industrial Workers' Charter, formulated at the recent TUC. Support for the co-operative movement and for 100 per cent trade unionism therein was also agreed, as well as a number of other motions on lines often heard in the trades councils themselves. It was also agreed to hold trades council area meetings, and new council representatives were elected to the Joint Consultative Committee, with Tom Mann top of the poll.

This conference finally buried the National Federation of Trades Councils and ended any trades council activity independent of the official trade union movement. It is certainly true, as one delegate maintained, 'that all the limitations on the agenda were made to stop the Communists from coming forward with resolutions and amendments which could be sympathetically heard and probably accepted'. However, when the CP perspective for the trades councils was still that they should 'use their influence to bring pressure upon the leaders to line the workers up for industrial action against the capitalist class' there was little anybody could do but accept the new situation. Thus Murphy thought that, 'when all allowance is made for the childish tone of the General Council, the conference marks an important step forward'.[111] For the local organisations themselves the conference could be seen as 'historic', 'a great stride in the way of co-ordinating industrial efforts', and it was hoped that the new arrangement would be the means of 'bringing about a better understanding between the Trades Councils and the Trades Union Congress'.[112] The Joint Consultative Committee was not to have so untroubled a future as its founders hoped, despite the diminishing power of the trades councils. The problems which arose will be discussed in chapter seven.

Chapter six

The 'hour of glory'
1917–26

Workmen's councils and councils of action

In the years from 1917 to 1926 the trade union movement expanded more rapidly than for two generations, reorganised itself from top to bottom, and was continually involved in bitter conflict with employers and government. The trades councils were very much part of this expansion, militancy and rapid change. Within the local organisations a feeling of disillusionment and bitterness at the end of the war prepared them to act in many of the ways that left-wing propagandists proposed to them. At a number of points in this period, after the Leeds convention of 1917, during the struggle against the war of intervention in 1920, and in the 1926 General Strike, the trades councils showed the resourcefulness and organising skill of rank-and-file trade unionists, and their potential power both within the working class movement and in their own local communities. On these occasions also the local organisations showed their limitations when they came into conflict with the organised forces of the State, or with those within the trade unions who were hostile to any increase in their power.

Long before this time the secretary of the London Trades Council, James MacDonald, had maintained that the trades councils could 'carry on the militant side of the movement', since they were less encumbered by financial and other responsibilities.[1] The Liverpool transport strike of 1911 showed clearly how this militancy could develop. The strike committee, which was a sub-committee of the Trades Council, allowed the movement of food and other essential goods by the issue of permits, and these were used by postmasters, shipping companies and others. Though it is an exaggeration to claim that this 'meant nothing less than working-class control over the means of distribution', it was nevertheless a significant portent of the sort of power that the trades councils could exercise in the future.[2]

The aftermath of the Leeds convention of May 1917 showed the wider significance that the exercise of independent power by the trades councils could assume. This meeting was called by the left-wing political organisations in the working class movement, and was attended by 207 delegates from trades councils and local Labour Parties, including 'practically every one of authority'.[3] At the convention it was decided to set up councils of workmen and soldier delegates which, according to Robert Williams of the Transport Workers' Federation, aimed at the 'dictatorship of the proletariat' and wanted 'to break the influence of the industrial "machine"'. Sylvia Pankhurst thought these bodies would prepare for a 'Provisional Government, like the Russian Socialist Government'. The trades councils themselves hoped for great things. The Liverpool delegates thought that the convention would be 'a landmark in the labour movement's history', and the secretary at Chatham said it promised 'to be epoch-making in its results'.[4] The new councils were supposed to function as extended trades councils, with membership from other sections of the working class movement besides trade unions and with a more positive role in co-ordinating all the activities of the working class. For Tom Quelch, who was a member of the national committee set up by the convention and responsible for establishing the new councils, this was consistent with what he had been saying for some time. Local conferences were called to set up councils of workmen and soldier delegates, and Quelch emphasised the importance of gathering support through the trades councils, saying that 'where sympathetic', they 'should take the initiative'.[5] In practice the trades councils were actively involved in the many local meetings that took place in efforts to set up the new organisations. In London forty-one trades councils were represented, and at Swansea twenty-six. Trades council delegates also attended local conferences at Portsmouth, Bristol, Leicester, Norwich and Manchester. In Glasgow the authorities imposed a ban on the local meeting, but the Trades Council arranged a large demonstration within a day.[6] These meetings did not achieve much, for a number of reasons. In the first place, they were often either banned by the authorities or else broken up, with police connivance, by 'patriots' gathered from near-by public houses. Secondly, the leaders of the ILP, including those present at the convention, were not happy to see the growth of new organisations which might challenge the powers of their local branches. Thirdly, the precise functions of the new local organisations were so vague that it was difficult to say in just what way they would replace the existing ones. At the Leeds meeting to set up a local council of workmen and soldier delegates these issues came out clearly. John Bromley said that the existing national organisations were 'not a reflex of the rank and file', and this could be proved by ordinary trade unionists 'taking things into their own hands'. However, the Leeds Trades and Labour Council itself thought the new bodies 'primarily propagandist', and considered that such work 'will best be done by existing organisations'.[7] Thus the local organisations could not expand in ways which were considered necessary by the movement in times of crisis unless they had a clearer view of their role and also were prepared to oppose many of the attitudes of the leaders of the working class movement. This was not to be the last occasion when these problems arose.

The period after the Leeds convention included militant action of all kinds by the working class movement, and the trades councils were always actively involved. Sometimes they simply supported such struggles, as in the January 1919 strike in Glasgow demanding a forty-hour week. On the other hand, in Belfast when workers struck for forty-four hours it is said that as the dispute proceeded the Belfast Trades Council was increasingly 'looked to as the leadership of the people'. More significant still, the Trades Council 'formed itself into a "Council of Action", and to a great extent had control of the movement of goods in the city'.[8] Not only is this perhaps the first mention of a new name, it is also the first occasion of many in these years when it seemed that some of the hopes that syndicalists had invested in the trades councils were proving to have some basis in practice. The big strikes and lock-outs of 1919 also had the support of the trades councils, and local bodies did what they could to help policemen, miners, engineers, cotton workers and others. The most intense activity took place during the strike of railwaymen in October and November. At Middlesbrough there was a special meeting, and at Finchley the Trades Council was 'galvanised into instantaneous activity' by the struggle. At Huddersfield there was a particularly interesting development when a special emergency committee was set up

comprising the EC and representatives from all the societies directly affiliated. Proposals were submitted for dealing with the existing situation in regard to provisions and other necessaries. It is singular to note that these functions very nearly approached the functions of the recently formed Councils of Action. Fortunately, the public were sufficiently well informed of the justice of the railwaymen's demand, that the strike terminated without the necessity of these methods being resorted to.[9]

Events were forcing the trades councils into adopting methods of organisation which went beyond the bounds of what they had tried before, and which had serious implications for their role in society.

The sympathy shown by the trades councils to the Russian revolution in its early stages also played an important part in these developments. Such bodies as the Committee for Anglo-Russian Co-operation, the

Peoples' Russian Information Bureau and the Hands off Russia Committee issued detailed accounts of British military intervention in the Soviet Union, and had a widespread influence on trades councils, which were nearly always hostile to war in any case and sympathetic to the new regime.[10] Thus the view of J. R. Clynes, expressed to the Oldham Trades Council in 1918, that a terrible fate awaited those who ceased to fight the Germans, won no answering echo in local organisations. As early as the summer of 1919 the Chatham and London trades councils supported efforts by socialist organisations to organise strikes against the war of intervention. Many other local organisations passed motions, affiliated to the protest organisations, and supported meetings against the intervention.[11] These actions derived not just from opposition to war but also from what one secretary called 'full sympathy with the Russians'. In Huddersfield the intervention was attributed to the 'policy and sinister designs of cosmopolitan financiers' and was seen as an illustration 'of what an intelligent democracy may experience when they have to assert their rights to the fruits of their labour'. Another secretary thought that the atrocity stories that had been published 'serve to show the press of this country in their true character, i.e. agencies of capitalist domination'. At Bradford it was thought that the beginnings of depression and unemployment were 'largely due to the failure of the Government to secure resumption of trade with Russia and East Europe'.[12] Besides drawing such conclusions as these, local organisations expressed sympathy for the Soviet Union with increasing intensity. At Northampton it was thought that 'Labour should keep its eye on the East on the horizon of a new day'. In 1923 the Liverpool Trades Council celebrated the sixth anniversary of the revolution by greeting 'the heroic stand made by the International Workers' Vanguard against the Capitalists of the World', and early in the following year the Birmingham Trades Council mourned the death of Lenin, 'who had devoted his life to the downtrodden and oppressed of all lands'. At Blackpool the Trades Council even withdrew its support for the League of Nations because it did not include the Soviet Union.[13]

These attitudes had an important influence on many of the things the councils did in the inter-war years, notably at the time of the Council of Action of August 1920.[14] In May the London dockers refused to load a ship with arms which were intended to help the Poles fight against the Soviet Union, and on 4 August, the sixth anniversary of the opening of the first world war, Arthur Henderson circularised all local Labour Parties with a telegram urging them to organise 'citizen demonstrations' against the supply of men or munitions to Poland, and to call for peace negotiations, the raising of the blockade and the resumption of trade relations.[15] Over the following weekend, 7–8 August, there were numerous local demonstrations, and in the week after there were emergency meetings of TUC and Labour Party leaders and discussions with the Prime Minister. On Friday 13 a national conference of working class organisations set up the Council of Action. This conference, like the national anti-conscription conference of January 1916 and the Leeds convention of June 1917, comprised as large and miscellaneous a group or workers' representatives as could be convened at short notice, and the 1,000 delegates included 355 from Labour Parties and trades councils. The conference called for strike action against any possible military intervention, heard speeches supporting these policies from such well known opponents of them as Clynes and Thomas, and set up a Council of Action consisting of the national leaders of all sections of the movement.[16] It was after these events that the trades councils began to act.

On 17 August the Council of Action issued a leaflet headed ' FORM YOUR COUNCIL OF ACTION!'[17] This proposed that trades councils and local Labour Parties should act together and call local conferences at which there would be formed all-inclusive councils of action. Considerable restrictions were placed on the activities of these local organisations on lines which were to become familiar in 1926.

Care should be exercised as to the functions of Local Councils. They are not in any way to usurp the functions of Trade Union Executives, especially so far as the withdrawal of labour is concerned, but are to act as centres of information – that is to say, they are to keep the National Council informed of any developments in their respective districts and to disseminate information received from the National Council and act in accordance with any instruction received from the National Council.

These limitations could not easily be enforced, and there were soon warnings that 'the call for action may be issued at any moment'. Local organisations called for their activities to be extended, but the national body considered 'the Council's mandate strictly limited'.[18] One of the members of the national Council of Action argued that the effectiveness of this body lay precisely in its ability to avoid any action.[19]

The local councils of action were prepared to go well beyond the limits set for them by their national leaders. One commentator thought that 'the Labour movement showed an excellent capacity for improvising local organisation'. In both Glasgow and Liverpool preparations were made for possible strike action, the executive committee of the Liverpool Trades Council deciding 'to use all possible means in its powers to stop recruiting and transport of munitions'. At Oldham the Council of Action

set up various strike sub-committees.[20] In all the main towns in the
country organisations were set up during August which included both
electoral and industrial wings of the working class movement. Such was
the case at Bradford, and at Leeds the co-operative societies were
included. At Manchester there was a member of the 1924 Labour
government in a body which also supported 'the national campaign
against government policy in Ireland', and which efforts were made to
revive in 1921 before the mining dispute. At Smethwick also the Council
of Action wanted to campaign on Ireland.[21] The Birmingham Council of
Action set up at a meeting of all sections of the local working class
movement on 17 August, constantly went beyond the limits set for it
nationally by making provision for strike action, by dealing with a wide
range of subjects besides the war against Russia, and by acting with
other local bodies without the sanction of the national Council of Action.
On 8 September the Birmingham council called on the national body to
set a date for strike action if all the troops were not withdrawn from
Russia and peace negotiations begun. At the same time it called for
'drastic steps' to secure the release of Terence MacSwiney, Lord Mayor
of Cork, at that time going through his ultimately fatal hunger strike. On
18 September the executive committee called for a national meeting of all
local bodies, and two days later circularised them all with a leaflet that
maintained the continued urgency of the campaign against the war on
Russia. A successful public meeting was run by the Council of Action on
26 September where its policies were endorsed. On 12 November it
continued to demand that it should be allowed to deal with the Irish war
and with unemployment, and protested 'against the apparent inactivity of
the National Council of Action and their failure to keep us informed
either of their decisions or proposals for some considerable time'. The
national organisation had long since decided to give up its activities, and
soon the local one did the same, although there were some attempts by
left-wing delegates during 1921 to revive it.[22] The Sheffield Council of
Action seems to have continued in existence longer than most other local
bodies, although in the end it suffered the same fate. It was originally set
up on 15 August on the initiative of the Industrial Executive of the
Trades and Labour Council, and included representatives of the joint
executive, local shop stewards, and the co-operative society. On 14
September at the Trades and Labour Council executive

It was resolved that a letter be sent to the Secretaries of the Central Council of
Action urging upon them that in the opinion of our Executive they should take
action in respect to Ireland in the same way in which they did in regard to
Poland, viz by stopping all munitions going to that country.

In October the work of the Council of Action sub-committees was still being discussed, and in January 1921 it was resolved to keep the body in existence 'in order to go into the question of unemployment and the opening of trade with Russia'. In the following month there was still talk of the Council of Action campaigning on these issues, but this was the last that was heard of it.[23]

The story of the councils of action of 1920 shows that local organisations of the working class movement were capable of acting with greater initiative and firmness than their national leaders, and could go beyond the organisational and political limits that their history imposed upon them. It was also made clear, however, that the local organisations could not act in this independent way for very long. Thus the theories that had been propounded by Mann, Bowman and Quelch were seen to have practical relevance, but also important limitations. It was possible to develop all-inclusive working class organisations which could concentrate some of the militancy that developed in the working class, and even the revolutionary aspirations, but local organisations were unable by themselves to exploit the potential power that their actions gave them. Nevertheless the experiences of 1920 ensured that this would not be the last occasion on which these issues would arise. Nearly every local body was convinced, whatever the truth of the matter, that their actions had 'undoubtedly prevented official war with Soviet Russia'.[24] It was also obvious that what happened had a significance beyond this issue alone. At Merthyr Tydfil the network of sub-committees that centred around the Council of Action covered every phase of the lives of the workers, and was said to be necessary because 'the normal functions of trade unions are over and there is no machinery to take up the functions in a systematic way, preserve order and carry on the administrative work that is necessary then'. The syndicalists could not have put it better, and this particular development was later described by a CP member as 'a plan of local institutions which would have been capable of becoming the most important administrative organ had a revolutionary crisis taken place'.[25] Other Communists saw these developments in the same way. Lenin said that although the Council of Action did not call itself a Soviet 'that is what it was. It was the same kind of dual power as we had under Kerensky from March 1917 onwards.' This description applied more to the local than the national organisations, and the Directorate of Intelligence, writing to the Cabinet on 16 September and describing some of the local strike preparations, said that the councils of action were 'taking on more the form of Soviets and in some areas [were] forming plans for the seizure of private property and means of transport'. Confirmed defenders of the established social order thought that the

Council of Action on a national scale was trying 'to usurp the functions of Parliament and practically impose the rule of the Soviet', and that it was a 'challenge to the whole constitution of this country'. An American observer of the British labour scene considered that workers did not understand the policies of the Council of Action, but were happy that it was 'against the government', and the leader of one of the largest unions said that 'the council does not regard the government as representing the will of the people'.[26] The implications of this widespread feeling were drawn out by one trades council secretary who spoke of the need now for the trade union movement to go forward on 'issues of a fundamental nature, industrial control and management, the elimination of the wages system and the substitution of complete industrial democracy'.[27]

There is a continuous thread running from these developments at the end of 1920 right up to the General Strike in May 1926. This can be seen first in the 'Black Friday' crisis of April 1921, when the Triple Alliance of railwaymen, transport workers and miners was threatening to strike together in defence of the miners. Though in the end they failed to do so, trades councils everywhere prepared to take action in case they did.[28] Efforts were made in Manchester and Barrow to re-establish the councils of action, and at Liverpool the Trades Council called for 'sympathetic action' in defence of the miners, demanding an emergency TUC to begin a general strike.[29] In Doncaster the 'machinery of the Trades Council was offered to local units of the Triple Alliance when the dispute threatened to assume serious proportions, but it was not required'. At Bradford also 'preparations for complying with the call of the Triple Alliance' were actively discussed.[30] In Birmingham the preparations for strike action went further. On 14 April there was a meeting under the auspices of the Trades Council of local full-time officials and leaders of the unions in the Triple Alliance, and a 'Birmingham Joint Trades' Union Emergency Committee' was set up, with a Food and Permits sub-committee. Before the crisis ended on 'Black Friday' these special bodies had already prepared permits for the transport of food to be used by union members and were discussing the issue of food vouchers through the Co-operative Society.[31]

During the lock-out of engineering workers in 1922 many trades councils took steps in the co-ordination of local action that went well beyond what the movement did on a national level. Thus at Northampton the Trades Council formed a joint committee with the local AEU to publicise the case of those in dispute, and at Leeds the Trades Council executive was instructed by a delegate meeting 'to do whatever was possible to secure united Trade Union action on the wages question, instead of leaving each section to be attacked in turn'. At Birmingham a

further effort to revive the Council of Action was narrowly defeated, and
at Smethwick the Trades Council ran a Joint Lock-out Committee that
functioned throughout the dispute.[32] In Sheffield it was found that some
of the forty-seven unions involved would not co-operate with Trades and
Labour Council's efforts to co-ordinate their activities, causing the
conclusion that

leaders, if they are wise, will lead to *concentration*, if they do not they must be
left by the wayside. Concentration nationally and the greater local power given
to Trade[s] Councils to act for the national concentration in an executive instead
of a purely recommendatory capacity in areas throughout the country will give
power and confidence to the workers in the industrial field.[33]

One result of these feelings was some effort in this period to reorganise
the trades councils themselves. In 1922 the Brighton Trades Council
worked out a complicated scheme for the establishment of a 'Council of
Industries', with nine separately functioning industrial groups, and a
'Publicity and Propaganda Council' including political, educational and
co-operative organisations, as well as a 'General Council' to co-ordinate
the efforts of them all. This scheme, which collapsed after three years,
and was not really much more than an attempt to operate in a way
resembling some of the larger local bodies but nevertheless showed 'the
desire of one Trades Council, at all events, to remedy the present defects'.
In 1926 the stronger local unions were operating independently of the
Council of Industries, though they did agree to co-operate with it during
the General Strike.[34] In Barrow a similar new constitution discussed by
the Trades Council in 1923 aimed to make it

the recognised co-ordinating body for all local industrial activity. Within the
Council seven groups will be set up, representative of all trade of the town; in an
industrial dispute the group directly affected will formulate its own policy and
call on the whole council for support. Representatives of Shop Stewards, district
committees and co-operatives will be added to the existing delegates.[35]

Related to these organisational experiments was the setting up of a
permanent disputes fund by the Kendal Trades and Labour Council in
1924. The discussion around the National Federation of Trades Councils
in 1922–23 showed strong support in the local organisations for a
continued reorganisation of the whole trade union movement, and at the
same time Tom Mann claimed widespread agreement in the trades
councils for an immediate general strike.[36]

Between August 1920 and May 1926 there were constant calls for the
re-establishment of the councils of action. Some of these have already

been mentioned, but the Communist Party and its allies also campaigned for the re-establishment of these organisations at the time of the Middle East crisis in the autumn of 1922, when the French invaded the Ruhr early in the following year, and later in 1923 when the British government again adopted an aggressive stance in Poland. On the latter occasion local bodies of some sort were set up at least in Nottingham, Liverpool and Newcastle. There were further efforts in this direction on the question of China in 1925.[37] However, events closer to home led to more important developments in the trades councils. Disillusionment with the 1924 Labour government caused a feeling in the working class movement and elsewhere 'that the next few years may be years mainly of industrial effort'. A reduction in the level of unemployment also made industrial militancy easier, and there was certainly a 'left-wing interlude' at the TUC in 1924 and 1925 when socialist policies and greater powers of central direction were approved.[38] In July 1925 there was a further episode of crisis in the coal industry when the government threatened to cut off its subsidy. In contrast to 1921, the trade union leaders held firm to their threats, and the government was forced, on 31 July, 'Red Friday', to agree to continue the subsidy. Part of the strength of the labour movement on this occasion was provided by the actions of the trades councils. At Oldham on 27 May trade union officials set up a Council of Action to resist wage cuts, and another such body was set up jointly by the Trades Council and Labour Party in Northampton. The Liverpool Trades Council ran an 'industrial conference' in July that set up a 'Provisional Council of Action' and called on other local bodies to do the same. The Birmingham Trades Council demanded that the TUC definitely call a general strike if the subsidy was not continued.[39] These examples are sufficient to show that the trades councils at the time of 'Red Friday' developed some of the same policies and forms of organisation that had been seen on a number of occasions in the recent period and were to be of the greatest importance in 1926. They would bring them into conflict once again both with past conceptions of their role, and with the main leaders of the trade unions. These questions could not but come to the fore at the highest point in the history of the trades councils, in May 1926, their 'hour of glory'.[40]

The General Strike, May 1926

The actions of the trades councils in the General Strike are the best known of their whole history. The considerable success of the local organisations in combining all sections of the working class movement for this struggle is often discussed. Some would say that the councils even came close to seizing political power. These aspects of the situation are described in all the major works on the General Strike.[41] E. Burns later in 1926 produced a survey of the activities of local organisations entitled *The General Strike, May 1926. Trades Councils in Action,* based largely on the replies of local secretaries to a questionnaire sent out by the LRD. All the trades council histories say something of their role at this time, and there have been a number of studies of their actions in the north-east based on a document entitled *The General Strike. An Account of the Proceedings of the Northumberland Joint Strike Committee* written by C. R. Flynn.[42] There are also a number of local studies dealing with events during the strike in Merseyside, Leeds, Birmingham, Nottingham and Oxford.[43] There has been some attempt to assess the significance of the work of the local organisations during the General Strike[44] and there are a number of collections of relevant documents, particularly in the TUC Library, that make it possible to study further local activities in a general way.[45] For the purposes of this study it is intended to illustrate again how the role of the trades councils in the General Strike had been foreshadowed and to some extent even predicted in the years before 1926. It is also intended to concentrate particularly on the relationship between local and national leaders during the struggle, and to try to assess how much power was actually exercised by the local organisations both in the trade union movement and in their own local communities.

It is well known that the leaders of the TUC had not 'a single preparation made for extended industrial action on behalf of the Miners when the subsidy ended in May'. One union official justified this by saying that the movement 'was not like a Government machine which can be perfected in private and orders given and obeyed'.[46] However, it is certain that there were many local organisations that would have been prepared to respond to any kind of lead from the TUC. In September 1925 the president of the Birmingham Trades Council urged delegates 'to be fully prepared for the coming struggle', and early in 1926 the Bradford leaders said they 'strongly urge Trade Unionists to make preparations for the coming fight'. Trades councils also called for arrangements to be made with the co-operative societies to cover possible future struggles.[47] Many local organisations made some preparations, usually at the behest of Communist Party and Minority Movement members. Soon after Red Friday the Minority Movement issued a call for a militant policy in the workers' movement which included the establishment of councils of action, capable, amongst other things, of 'carrying out the essential services for the working class in the event of a dispute'. In the following period, although the Movement on occasion emphasised the less popular demand for workers' defence corps, it is fair to call its efforts on this matter 'modest but useful'. The 'Special Conference of Action' held on 21 March, at which fifty-two trades councils were represented, did something to publicise further the need for strike preparations.[48] The efforts of the CP were not always successful, however. Party members at St Helens tried to get the Trades Council to set up a council of action but failed. On the other hand, CP members and their sympathisers were responsible for the bodies that existed before the strike began in Coventry and Leeds. The development of the latter body showed some of the problems involved. It existed throughout the period from 'Red Friday' to the General Strike and tried to act in defence of embattled textile and engineering workers and on a number of other issues. However, since it 'consisted mostly of "left wing" members and possessed little authority', it seems fair to conclude that it was 'more concerned with creating the atmosphere favourable for a General Strike amongst the workers rather than setting up machinery when, and if, it occurred'.[49] On the other hand, the Joint Council of Action at Bolton before the end of 1925 was 'pursuing enquiries with a view to definite preparations being made for any national or local industrial upheaval', and the body at Glasgow made efforts to recruit people to the unions. The councils of action set up in engineering centres like Birmingham in March when a big national dispute was expected also took concrete steps to help the workers in dispute.[50] Local bodies in Preston, Huddersfield and Liverpool were also prepared for action. In Nottingham, however, the Council of Action was dissolved before May because national union leaders did not support it, and at Manchester the body that existed up to then proved too unwieldy, and had to be re-formed in May. If it is inaccurate to say that 'no preparatory work of any kind had been undertaken before the call was issued', it can be asserted, in the words of the Middlesbrough secretary, that 'the necessary organised machinery for directing strike activities' did not exist, even if efforts had been made to construct it in a number of places.[51]

To some degree, at least, for the local organisations this lack of preparation did not matter. One local publication found that the problems they faced at the time forced 'scientific organisation' on them. 'What would have taken years in pre-strike days has been accomplished this week under the direct pressure of the class struggle.'[52] Thus within a day or two of the opening of the strike in nearly every town in the land there existed an organisation to oversee activities during the strike, usually on an all-inclusive working class basis, such as had been envisaged by the left wing in the past. The title 'Council of Action' was adopted by a substantial number of the special organisations, but in probably the majority of cases some such title as 'joint strike committee' was used. Most of these organisations were set up by the executive committees of trades councils together with representatives of the unions on strike. Such was the case at Birmingham and West Ham. At Stockton the local working class electoral organisation was involved, at Derby shop committees were affiliated, and in a few places co-operative societies were affiliated. The functions of the body thus established at Birmingham was 'co-ordinating the work of the various Strike Committees in the City, issuing "permits" for the release of foodstuffs etc., to Union labour; regulating the position of factories and workshops where difficulties arose carrying out TUC instructions; and mounting a dispatch service'.[53] This in general described the main work carried out by the councils of action, although in most cases they issued strike bulletins, and they also arranged meetings and social activities for strikers. Because of efforts by union leaders to run the strike through the machinery of their individual unions there was often considerable confusion locally, and many cases of uncertain and divided responsibility. At Crewe the Council of Action considered it possible only to 'work in conjunction with the various strike committees locally', and at Middlesbrough the Central Strike Committee 'could only hope to act as a co-ordinating and not as a directional body from the outset'. At St Albans the Emergency Committee did little more than run a distress fund and distribute the *British Worker*, leaving 'important matters' to the different unions. In other places there were a number of different strike committees with conflicting powers. Such was the case at Leeds, where the GMWU and the transport unions ran separate strike committees that refused to acknowledge the authority of the Trades Council. In Sheffield the CP ran a parallel and independent strike committee.[54] Many such difficulties arose in relation to the transport unions and will be considered later. In some areas the actions of local strike committees were co-ordinated. The East Glamorgan Federation of Trades Councils kept a number of local bodies in communication with one another; the Merseyside Council of Action issued a joint *Strike Bulletin* for a few local bodies; and the Northumberland and Durham Joint Strike Committee brought together local organisations to discuss common problems. Efforts by the CP to set up a similar body in London were defeated by trade union officials, though they were more successful at Glasgow and in Lanarkshire.[55]

It was clear to anybody who was seriously trying to win in a general strike that 'decentralised organisation' was essential, and the government prepared to break the strike on that basis. Walter Citrine at least thought the struggle could not be 'effectively organised without the Trades Councils being made the nucleus of the strike organisations'. This view did not meet with the approval of the union leaders, especially in transport.[56] Ernest Bevin of the Transport Workers was determined that all effective decisions in running the strike should emanate from the headquarters of the unions. The leaders of the railway workers also fought to retain control of their members during the struggle, and on 3 May told them to 'allow no disorderly or subversive elements to interfere in any way' with the conduct of the strike. J. H. Thomas of the NUR said that what he 'dreaded about the struggle more than anything else' (including presumably defeat) was that power 'should have got out of the hands of those who would be able to exercise some control'.[57] These unions, acting together, set up a National Transport Committee and a London equivalent which were supposed to issue all permits for the movement of goods, and to send orders to local joint committees of the unions' branches about what they should do.[58] This was but one example of efforts 'to maintain a control over provincial activities which was, in the circumstances, simply unworkable'. At Chatham confusion reigned. 'NUR telegram directs no permits. TUC directs full permits. What is to be worked to?' Similar confusion at Swansea led to understandable but incorrect conclusions. 'Telegrams are being received at intervals, cancelling one another and signed by leaders of different unions ... is government concocting conflicting telegrams to mislead Strike Committee?'[59] As a result of the efforts of the leaders of the transport unions to control the situation the transport committee was said to be more powerful than the Council of Action at Darlington, and to be independent and at least as powerful at Dorking, Cheltenham and Gloucester as the joint strike committees.[60] In other areas things were different. At Westminster the Council of Action could claim to be 'in SUPREME CONTROL of the strike in this district', and in Bolton 'the Council was the sole authoritative body all through'. In Coventry the Transport Permit Committee was entirely under the control of the Trades Council, and in Birmingham the Emergency Committee issued all permits and the Transport Committee was affiliated to it from the start. The situation was similar at Huddersfield, Exeter, Peterborough and Burton on Trent. At Kendal a deputation from the Strike Committee met members of the Transport and General Workers' Union late on the night of 3 May 'and prevailed on them to act to instructions'. At Bristol all the separate strike organisations had been dropped in favour of a central committee by 7 May. Thus it seems fair to conclude that 'most of the Joint Transport Committees chose to operate as subsidiaries of a central strike committee', whatever the instructions of the union leaders.[61]

Although in theory all unions yielded their powers to the TUC during the strike many of them acted independently both nationally and locally.

The GMWU, although claiming to have 74,394 strikers on 4 May, and later saying it 'played its full part' in the struggle, was clearly less than enthusiastic in its efforts. At Stone and Dartford no instructions at all were received from the union leaders. At Nottingham members worked with blacklegs, and at St Helens the local organiser tried to get glass delivered to Pilkington's against the wishes of the Council of Action.[62] The Typographical Association also seems rarely to have co-operated with other unions during the dispute, in many cases refusing to agree to print local strike bulletins, and even showing considerable hesitation about producing local editions of the *British Worker*.[63] Thus besides the difficulties with the transport unions, local co-ordinating bodies found some unions 'afraid to put their business in the hands of the Trades Council' at Dunfermline, or actually 'prepared to tell the Committee to mind their own business, and to leave the members to their respective officials' at Sheffield. There were, as it was put to one trades council, 'too many Executives at work'.[64] With the union leaders so jealous to maintain their power, the functions they proposed for the trades councils during the General Strike were restricted to 'organising the trade unionists in dispute in the most effective manner for the preservation of peace and order'. Such guidelines proved quite unpractical, since they did not mention many of the problems that confronted local organisations, and matters were made worse by the contradictory and confusing instructions that often came from the leaders of the individual unions. Despite these problems, local organisations were loyal to their leaders. At Newcastle they 'felt themselves bound to carry out the Trade[s] Union Congress decisions no matter how many misgivings they might have'. At Dartford TUC instructions 'were accepted without question and the faith and confidence in that body was a religion'. At Brighton they 'stood strictly to the TUC bulletins and instructions', and a message to the TUC on 5 May said, 'Birmingham has full confidence in the General Council; we accept their directions and await victory.'[65] Despite this faith in the leaders of their movement the trades councils were nevertheless accused of going beyond their powers. It was said that 'enthusiasm' caused them 'to overstep their duties', and that in some cases trades councils even 'called out people they should not have called out'. Charles Dukes of the GMWU asserted:

every day that the strike proceeded the control and the authority of that dispute was passing out of the hands of responsible Executives into the hands of men who had no authority, no control, no responsibility, and was wrecking the movement from one end to the other.

One writer has commented that 'whether this was a reference to the Communist minority or merely to untried local individual trade unionists is not made clear'. Such ambiguity was important for the trades councils in the future, but in the meantime there were union leaders who watched CP influence in the councils very carefully.[66] Any power trades councils secured within the working class movement during the General Strike, however, was the result much less of a conspiracy on their part or on that of the CP than of the weaknesses, vacillations and confusions of the union leaders.

Many local organisations during the dispute and subsequently complained about the 'lack of definite instructions and contact with the General Council', and others found that what messages they did receive were 'harassing and contradictory'. Such confusion resulted in one factory being called out three times in nine days at Lewisham. At Wolverhampton problems arose with 'each Union sending down different circular letters to their branches', and at Nottingham as a result 'differences of interpretation arose'. At Doncaster because of 'lack of direct instructions' the Council of Action at one stage broke down completely, though it was restored when the transport unions agreed to accept its authority.[67] On the whole the national leaders of the unions were a definite impediment to the effective running of the strike. In Liverpool there were complaints about the lack of contact with the TUC, while in London itself efforts were 'very badly handicapped' by the proximity of the national strike leadership.[68] Thus local strike leaders were thrown on their own resources, however limited their desire to function independently. Individual union branches could not exercise any of the power that union leaders tried to invest in them, and it was inevitable perhaps that in the confusion of authority within the working class movement their affiliates would turn to the trades councils as the only bodies in any way prepared for the role of strike co-ordinators.

One matter on which the trades councils and councils of action did exceed their powers was in issuing strike bulletins. This at least was something where the instructions from the centre were unambiguous. Local bodies were 'requested to refrain from making public statements of any sort' and to confine themselves to material supplied by the TUC publicity committee, adding 'nothing in the way of comment and interpretation'. All printed bulletins were ordered to stop, and as late as 10 May one trades council was told that 'production of any unofficial newspaper or bulletin would be contrary to the policy that the General Council has been following'. This statement was made after the majority of strike committees had produced bulletins of some sort, and in a number of cases these were printed, thus incurring the particular wrath of

the General Council.[69] The efforts of the union leaders to maintain
control over the issue of permits also failed in most cases, thus giving the
trades councils and councils of action powers beyond those they
anticipated. Some of the decisions on picketing, and also on the
establishment of workers' defence corps in the few cases where this was
done, also went beyond what the local organisations were supposed to
do. Perhaps the most important power which the trades councils are said
to have exercised during the struggle was that of calling people out on
strike. There were frequent complaints from union leaders that this was
done in cases not authorised by them. In practice, however, it was a rare
occurrence. Far more common for the local organisations was the
'nightmare' of pushing people back to work who wanted to come out, like
the action of left-wing building union leaders at Lewisham in pleading
with men to return to work and carry out TUC instructions.[70] Few local
bodies possessed or even wanted the power which the Birmingham Trade
Union Emergency Committee exercised in calling out a branch of the
Central Ironmoulders against the wishes of their own executive. It was
the ambiguity of their instructions rather than any desire to appropriate
the authority of others that led the Merseyside Council of Action to order
workers to strike 'where blacklegging of any kind was being performed',
and caused the Bristol body on 10 May 'to call out everyone except those
whose services are essential to the City'. Similarly, it was only the
division of responsibility among the unions that made it possible for the
Engineering Trades Advisory Committee of the Birmingham Emergency
Committee 'to call out all the Trade Union labour at an additional
number of large industrial works' on 7 May. At Leeds it was also fear of
victimisation through some people being on strike in individual factories,
and others not, that led to engineering workers being called out before the
'second line' was called out nationally. Even greater practical difficulties
faced electricians at the power stations in obeying the instructions sent to
them. They were told to remain at work and negotiate with the
authorities about emergency supplies. The authorities usually refused to
negotiate, so one local organisation was forced to 'plead' for 'direct
instructions to all ETU members to cease work', and in the end to call
them out anyway.[71] Similar difficulties arose in deciding who were
transport workers for the purpose of the strike call, and the precise
nature of the building work that could still be undertaken. In Coventry
trade union members making cars held a meeting on 9 May demanding
to be called out as transport workers, though there is no evidence that
they intended to act unilaterally. Many local bodies wanted more
workers to be called out, but showed no inclination to organise this
themselves. Messages calling for the TUC to extend the strike were sent

from strike bodies in Warrington, North Staffordshire, Southampton and Abertillery, always asking that the TUC itself take the initiative.[72] It was no doubt in response to pressures such as these that the TUC decided on 7 May to call out a 'second line' of strikers.

After 12 May, when the General Council called the strike off, local strike organisations were again forced to take the initiative, not because they wanted to but because the General Council and many of the union leaders had abdicated from all further responsibility. It was in the bitter struggle against victimisation that the trades councils showed their greatest independence and their most spectacular successes. At York on 12 May messengers were sent round to tell railway and transport workers to stand firm and not return to work. On the following day the *Gloucester Strike Bulletin* boldly proclaimed 'STRIKE STILL ON', and at Wood Green 'there was a unanimous decision not to return'. On the 14th the BBC still thought there was 'no general resumption of work', and *The Times* reported that in Scotland dockers, tramway workers and printers were still out. At Leeds few returned before the 15th, at East Ardsley nobody until the 16th, and at Erith 'the majority of workers never returned until May 24th'. The Merseyside Council of Action was involved for some weeks in rearguard actions on behalf of various groups of victimised workers. Although many strikers, especially in the transport system, went back to work with conditions inferior to when they came out, it was the determination of the local organisations and 'the extraordinary unity shown by the rank and file' that prevented matters from being much worse.[73] It was only at this stage, after the bitterest disappointments, that the trades councils and councils of action began to express hostility towards their national leaders. There was some hesitation at first. At Aldershot the Disputes Advisory Council secretary said of the return to work that 'we expect it was for the best, but we cannot understand it yet'. Soon, however, there was talk of 'disapproval', 'disappointment' and even 'shock'. Then motions condemning the General Council were passed by local bodies at Glasgow, Keighley, Blackpool, Sheffield, Rawtenstall and many other places. The Newcastle Trades Council of Action said that 'Never in the history of working-class struggle – with the exception of the treachery of our leaders in 1914 – has there been such a calculated betrayal of working-class interests as has overtaken us this week'. The call from Newcastle for the strike to be continued was echoed at Cardiff, Swansea, St Albans and elsewhere. The Coventry Council of Action sent a delegation to the General Council to demand 'the recall of the General Strike in the name of the workers of Coventry'. One of the delegation found that A. A. Purcell, 'the mighty leader whom I had known as a fighter . . . was cowed and beaten . . . The iron man . . . had feet of clay.'[74]

There can be no doubt that during the General Strike the local organisations assumed great power within the trade union movement. The trades councils and the bodies that worked in co-ordination with them issued policy statements, called people out on strike and ran many activities independently of the national union leaders. But the main reason for the assumption of these increased powers was not desire on the part of the trades councils to exercise them so much as the sheer timidity of the national leaders of the unions, who were less concerned with effective strike organisation than with trying to see to it that as much as possible of the power of running the strike remained in their hands. Even at the end, when the trades councils began for the first time to express widespread hostility to the actions of the union leaders, they assumed increased power in the working class movement only when they were forced to do so by the need to defend their members. The leaders of the local organisations of the movement showed a resourcefulness and skill during the greatest test in their history which was not manifested by the national union leaders. Yet, although they had to some extent been prepared for this greatness, when it came it was largely thrust upon them, and it was abandoned as soon as it was assumed.

The limitations of the role of the trades councils in the General Strike can perhaps best be indicated by showing the comparatively restricted part they were able to play in defeating and replacing established governmental authorities. This was, after all, the moment of which syndicalists and others had dreamed, when through the struggle to defend the living standards of the workers local organisations would be able to take social and political power away from the ruling classes. Many thought at the time and since that this was what happened. It is certainly true in some sense that everywhere 'there existed two authorities, the Council of Action or Strike Committee and the city municipal authority or controller under the direction of the government'. In the 'Theses of the Communist International on the British General Strike', published soon afterwards, it was said that

The Councils of Action organised by the trade unions actually developed into District Soviets. The Departments organised by the General Council already resembled in their structure and functions, the departments of the St. Petersburg Soviet in the period of so-called 'dual power' (February–November 1917).

Others have said that local strike organisations 'logically constituted an attempt to establish a rival authority to the local and national governing bodies', and that 'there began to develop an *embryo* alternative centre of Government, something like a type of "dual power" ', which saw 'the passing of authority as far as the strike permits for transport were concerned, and in other ways as well, from the hands of the Government and its agencies into the grasp of the Strike Committees and Councils of Action'. The trades councils have also been seen as 'practically sharing control with the authorities in running towns and cities', and even as trying 'to seize control of affairs', with some success.[75] The potential for such developments clearly existed in some of the things local organisations did during the General Strike, and there were some limited ways in which local trade union organisations did exercise quasi-political power. In a number of places it was said that newsagents were persuaded to take papers run by the strikers instead of the *British Gazette* or any of the various local anti-strike papers that appeared. There were reports of this happening at Coventry, Chester le Street and Cwmamman.[76] Another form of activity that threatened established authority was the rent strikes which were advocated or discussed by local bodies at Croydon, Westminster, Wandsworth and Dartford.[77] A more effective method of challenging for control of the life of local communities organised by strike organisations was in the mass picketing that was mounted, particularly in the north-east and Scotland. At Cowdenbeath in Fife all motor traffic passed only with the permission of the Trades Council. Farther south, at Newcastle, it was said that mass picketing was necessary 'to carry out the instructions of the General Council', and even regular passenger transport was stopped by this method. Similar mass picketing took place throughout Northumberland and Durham, and at Doncaster and Falkirk.[78] A more formidable challenge to authority was involved in the establishment of Workers' Defence Corps. Such a body at Methill, with 700 members, was 'organised in companies under ex-NCOs' and prevented police interference with pickets. A smaller force at Sowerby Bridge succeeded in 'maintaining peace in the streets and highways' and at Fife 'special platoons' prevented the authorities from doing 'anything foolish'. At Cheltenham also there was a 'well supported' Workers' Defence Corps, and at St Pancras a similar body was called the 'Workers' Vigilance Corps'. At both Gloucester and Chatham there were special pickets to protect meetings. All these local organisations formed under the auspices of trades councils and councils of action represented a clear challenge to the established instruments of law and order, and in a few isolated areas and in some limited ways they mounted such a challenge. The CP pushed hard for the establishment of the defence corps, often giving the demand precedence over the establishment of council of action themselves. The protracted struggle between right and left in the Birmingham Trades Council before the General Strike, ultimately rescinding a previous decision to set up a defence corps, showed that many were aware of the potential importance of the issue. In general, though, even when they organised to defend themselves, local organisations did not see themselves as acting in rivalry to the already established forces of law and order. At both Willesden and Selby workers' defence organisations were said to be 'in complete harmony' with the police.[79] Where defence corps were not set up, co-operation with the police was even closer. At Lincoln 'the police asked us to supply the whole of the Special Constables – which we did'. In the Forest of Dean the strike committee wrote to the chief constable offering co-operation, and at Rawtenstall there was 'splendid harmony'. Some of this concord may have been the result of police sympathy with the strikers, and this was perhaps behind what happened at Swindon, where the police sided with the strikers against an 'autocratic mayor'.[80] There can be no doubt, however, that had the strike gone on for very much longer the sympathies and loyalties of both strikers and police would have been tested more severely. Many writers have pointed to 'the very evident tightening up of police measures throughout Britain during the last weekend' and to the increasing violence in the last days of the struggle. In Bristol and Airdrie the issue of permits was stopped by the police, and at Birmingham, where there was a long history of police harassment of working class organisations, the whole of the Emergency Committee was arrested on 12 May.[81] These incidents show that the amity that existed between strikers and police in the first week of the strike could not have continued long into a second week. What they also show is that for the local organisations of the working class movement the question of defeating or replacing the forces defending the established social order did not seriously arise, and they came nowhere near to challenging them other than by implication.

The most important question regarding social control during the General Strike related to the supply of food and essential materials. To the government and its more determined opponents it was obvious that 'Who feeds the people wins the strike!'[82] On 1 May Citrine told Baldwin that 'the General Council is prepared to enter into arrangements for the distribution of essential foodstuffs', but since the unions had made no effort to prepare any alternative supply network the offer was simply ignored. The co-operative societies were the obvious sources for any alternative supply system through the working class movement, but arrangements with the societies were hardly even considered by the national leaders of the movement, and anyway the co-operative movement was often hostile to the strikers. There was some joint action in a few places, with co-operative directors on councils of action and credit offered to strikers – in Derby, for example. Even for the most radical, however, the idea of local organisations assuming 'control of food on behalf of the workers' was a somewhat distant one. The General Council also advocated efforts at joint control of power supplies, but in most cases such approaches were ignored, and although many power workers went on strike they were usually adequately replaced by blacklegs.[83] The only way in which the unions could then exert some power in the community was by deciding which goods were essential and which were not, and trying to get union members to produce, transport and deliver those deemed essential. By the use of picketing and the issuing of permits many trades councils and local strike organisations did manage to see to it that trade union drivers were employed in transporting essential goods. At Nottingham, Blackburn and Birmingham such actions by local strike organisations had some effect, and at Edinburgh large numbers of vehicles had to be impounded for the want of trade union drivers, so that it was hoped that the strike committee would soon be in 'practical control of the road traffic' of the city. In a number of places the use of permits also prevented the transport of 'inessential' goods, and employers were given a hard time in their efforts to get permission to move any goods at all. The Swansea Trades Council even stopped the movement of potatoes to Birmingham, and the Darlington Rota Committee would not allow the co-operative society to move bananas.[84] However, since the only purpose of the government plans was to keep essential supplies moving, local picketing and the issue of permits did not have much effect on the strength of the strike itself. Thus very soon, against the confusion engendered by national efforts of union leaders to maintain control over the issue of permits, more and more local bodies suspended their issue altogether. The Merseyside Council of Action decided to stop issuing permits on 7 May because 'they have been repeatedly abused', and on the same day the National Transport Committee in 'its first and only pronouncement of importance' urged local bodies to 'review' their permits, an admonition which many local bodies took to mean as ceasing to issue them altogether.[85] Although these decisions no doubt created difficulties for the authorities, they were also in a sense an admission of failure, since the strike-breakers were now left to their own devices, and it was tacitly assumed that they would be able to provide for the needs of the community. Even in the famous events at Newcastle, although the authorities were forced to negotiate with the local Council of Action, in the end there was no agreement even for joint control, and there were still blacklegs working on the docks at the end of the strike.[86]

It has often been said that during the General Strike trades councils were on the way to being rival governmental authorities. One writer declared that, for all the moderation of the national leaders, 'the *orders* of the General Council, as interpreted by the various strike committees throughout the nation and as put into practice by them, did logically constitute an attempt to set up a rival authority to that of local governing bodies'. Whatever the logic of the situation, however, few local bodies saw themselves as seizing power or in any sense establishing a rival authority. Thus although one union branch secretary could shout at a blackleg bus, 'We are your masters now' he and others like him did little to exercise such power in a systematic way. In one place in the early stage of the strike a local body could claim to be 'maintaining the food supplies to the people without assistance from other quarters', but usually local strike organisations saw their ability to carry out such tasks as a potential rather than a real possibility. Thus at Eccles the Trades and Labour Council showed 'it had the personnel and ability to take control', and at Lewisham there was constructed 'a machine, if things had gone our way, capable of administering the borough'. Even at Bradford, where trade unionists 'scoffed at the puny efforts of the authorities to get the work of the world done without them', they did not see themselves in any way aiming to take over social or political power.[87]

The real point about the power exercised by the local organisations of the working class movement at this supreme moment of their history is that, whatever had been proposed in the past, they did not even consider seizing political power. It is true that there was some distinction between 'Right-wing Committees' who 'refused to assume serious control of the strike' and more radical bodies 'prepared to adopt all methods for controlling' it, but as a matter of fact 'revolutionary action was not considered' even 'by the militants' at the time.[88] Despite the view of its official historian that 'the essential part of the Communist Party's assessment would seem to remain correct' the CP in fact did very little to bring out the revolutionary implications that existed in the situation.[89] In the last party publication before the beginning of the strike it was proposed that councils of action 'should not take over any of the duties which ordinarily belong to the Trade Unions', and in the first statement after it started militants were told, 'All it needs now is for every man to stand fast and the fight is won'. The early slogans of the party 'could not be construed as a call to revolution', and as it proceeded 'the Communists maintained a strictly constitutional attitude throughout'. One of the leaders of the party at the beginning said he was unconcerned 'with any wider horizons', simply with 'our limited objective'.[90] It cannot be claimed that anyone was putting forward to the trades councils policies which would make them consider taking over the running of their local communities. The influence of the Communist Party was not overwhelming, but there were many member on local strike committees, and many also were arrested.[91] Even they, however, did not call for action independent of the leaders of the TUC until the last day of the strike. They called for emergency meetings of the councils of action on 13 May, and on the following day for a national meeting of local committees which, among other things, would consider 'the question of changing the leadership of the Labour Movement'. It was only afterwards that party theorists began to maintain that it was 'not enough for the workers to give greater powers to the General Council, or the local Trades Councils acting under the General Council', and that it was necessary to go beyond this to 'the defeat of the Labour bureaucracy'.[92] Since nobody advocated such policies at the time, it is not surprising that the trades councils did little to win any kind of real power.

After the General Strike many of the councils felt that they had done something to prove themselves. At Eccles it was considered that the Trades and Labour Council had rescued itself from a 'position that some had scoffed at' and showed its importance 'in the life of the Borough'. At Plymouth the Trades Council 'did derive benefit from the short period of greater responsibilities', and at Wednesbury the Trades Council thought that it was 'now looked upon as a greater factor, particularly by political parties'.[93] Such sentiments again emphasised how little the councils saw themselves as alternatives to the established authorities. Their actions had posed more of a threat to the leaders of the trade unions, and may do something to account for the almost fanatical force with which in the future any flicker of independence on their part was suppressed. Within their local communities, however, they showed that all they wanted was to be recognised and to share in some very limited forms of decision making. The dreams of the syndicalists had not come true, and the trades councils had lost for ever their independence and initiative, and their position on the brink of limitless social and political power.

Chapter seven

The establishment of authority
1926–40

The work of the Trades Councils Joint Consultative Committee

The TCJCC was established in 1925 as a centrally controlled alternative to the left-wing National Federation of Trades Councils, and in the years after 1926 it played an important role in unifying the activities of the trades councils. The General Council was determined that the local organisations would be their 'labour correspondents' rather than the co-ordinators of militant local action, and much of what they did for the trades councils was devoted to this end. There were many benefits for the councils in the new arrangements. Walter Citrine spoke of 'the consciousness created among Trades Councils that there is some central body to whom they can appeal on points affecting either policy or administration', and one local secretary thought the set-up gave his organisation 'a good deal of prestige and some little authority'.[1] It is the nature and effect of this situation, and some of the conflicts within the trade union movement that it engendered, which this chapter will describe.

The JCC consisted of six members of the General Council and six delegates elected by the trades councils. The latter members usually consisted of the secretaries of the local bodies at London, Manchester, Bristol and Leeds, together with those from two others of the larger bodies. From 1927 candidates stood by area, with the whole conference voting for each one, and this method continued after 1929 despite a vote at the Trades Councils' Annual Conference against it.[2] One effect of voting in this way, as at the TUC itself, was that representatives of minority opinions had little chance of being elected. The chairman of the JCC was always a General Council member. From 1925 to 1933 A. Conley of the Tailor and Garment Workers occupied that position, in

1934–35 George Hicks of the Builders, in 1936 Charles Dukes of the GMWU, and after that J. Marchbank of the NUR. The head of the TUC organisation department always served as secretary. From 1925 this was Vincent Tewson and from 1931 E. Harries. The most cursory study of the activities of the JCC makes it clear that the General Council members of the committee entirely dominated its proceedings. There is no case recorded in this period of a decision being taken against the will of the General Council nominees, although there are a number of incidents when decisions were made in the name of the committee without even the knowledge of the trades council representatives.

The annual conferences of the JCC were of value for the trades councils in stimulating 'an intelligent interest in the problems which confront us today'.[3] From 1935 to 1938 efforts were made to direct the proceedings by introducing discussion around a memorandum on aspects of the councils' work, but this was unpopular. The delegates preferred to discuss all manner of general political and social topics in the same way they did at their own meetings. The JCC helped the work of the local bodies themselves by providing them with information, particularly on the workings of the welfare services and on the activities of other trades councils. In June 1925 a *Trades Council Monthly* was established for purposes such as these, but it appeared for little more than a year.[4] It then became *The Industrial Review*, which included reports on trades council activities, articles on their history, and other related matters, and appeared from January 1927 to February 1933. It is hard to measure the success of this periodical, though at the time of its demise it was said to have a circulation of less than 2,500, which allows for only a few copies for each local body.[5] From March 1933 the *Industrial Review* was merged with *Labour*, a more general TUC publication which included some news about trades council activities. Besides these publications the General Council arranged local conferences usually addressed by experts from the TUC staff on questions of interest to the trades councils such as industrial diseases, workmen's compensation and unemployment insurance. The TUC was well pleased with these conferences, and reported in 1931 that their 'size and representative character' reflected 'great credit on the machinery employed'. In the following year over thirty were arranged. The TUC also began to deal directly with trades council educational activities through a series of weekend schools which began in 1933. These meetings dealt mostly with trade union organisation, despite complaints that they could do more 'to instil ... some measure of class-consciousness'. They also propounded the views of trade union leaders on political questions by dealing with topics like 'Dictatorship: the threat to industrial democracy'. By 1939 each federation was organising such a school in alternate years, usually run by full-time TUC officials.[6] From 1937 trips to the TUC headquarters for trades council secretaries were also arranged, aiming to give them 'a better understanding of its work and of the relations between the Trades Councils and the General Council'.[7] The General Council arranged professional and amateur performances through the councils of *Six Men of Dorset*, a play making general propaganda in support of trade unionism. There was also a brief and apparently unsuccessful attempt in 1932 to arrange 'wireless groups'.[8] The provision of sports facilities, first advocated at the 1925 conference, was successfully undertaken by some councils, and they were helped by the General Council. Equipment was provided, and some teams went abroad to compete against other countries. Efforts in this direction were, however, restricted by the refusal of the TUC to co-operate with a body known as the British Workers' Sports Federation in 1928 because it would not exclude non-trade union bodies. It later supported another body called the National Workers' Sports Federation, to which in 1936 it was said 'several ' trades councils were affiliated.[9] In 1932 the JCC also became associated with the National Playing Fields Association. This was despite a claim at the Congress that the organisation was 'composed mainly of persons- whose ancestors took land from the people'. The General Council asserted, however, that involving the trade union movement in it would make it more 'democratic', and by the following year some trades councils had been persuaded to affiliate.[10]

The JCC also allowed the TUC to help the trades councils in some of their important tasks, notably recruitment to the trade unions. It was said that in this period the General Council came to regard the trades councils 'as the recruiting agencies for the movement', and the local bodies were provided with resources for these efforts, including leaflets, posters and loudspeaker equipment. At first special 'weeks' such as trades councils had often held in the past were advocated, and in 1933, fifty-five were organised in different areas. In later years more continuous efforts were proposed, concentrating on the recruitment of particular groups, notably women and young persons. Special help was given to recruitment in new industrial areas like Slough, or among groups who were particularly difficult to organise, like those covered by Trade Boards in Birmingham. At the initiative of the General Council trades councils also made surveys of places in their areas where organisation was particularly needed. The annual conferences allowed detailed discussion of the problems involved in this work.[11] Despite all these methods of helping recruitment through the trades councils, most of these activities would probably have gone on quite independently through the local organisations. What the TUC did that was new was to secure the assistance of the unions themselves. The General Council regarded support 'from full and part time Trade Union officials in the locality' as a 'first essential' for recruitment campaigns, and tried to arrange it for the trades councils.[12] It was not always successful. The GMWU, despite the work of Dukes in the JCC, was always hostile to recruitment by the trades councils, partly because it opposed decentralisation in any form and partly because of their well known preference for industrial unionism.[13] No union organiser could have been happy with the admonition received from the Sheffield Trades Council to aim at 'winning people back to Trade Unionism, and not attempt propaganda on behalf of his own Union'. It is not surprising that one trades council secretary in Yorkshire reported that union organisers seemed 'to regard any effort on the part of the Trades Council as encroaching upon their work, even though the Trades Council impress upon them that they are only too anxious to assist them'. In some towns rival unions refused to join committees concerned with recruitment, and trades councils had constantly to ask the General Council 'to encourage the Executives of some of the larger Unions to take notice of the Trades Councils in the localities'.[14] There can be no doubt that the existence of the JCC did help the General Council to take steps in this direction, though there is little evidence of conspicuous success.

Another important way the General Council helped the trades councils was by persuading union branches to affiliate to them. This matter was a 'hardy annual' at the Trades Council Annual Conferences, and though some secretaries complained 'of the treatment of Trades Councils by certain large unions' others thought that the 'importance' of the local bodies was understood because they were 'now recognised as local agents of the Trades Union Congress General Council and should receive the active support of every union branch in the district'.[15] The General Council did make some serious efforts in this direction, but it faced numerous difficulties. For one thing, many union branches said that they had to be financed by regional or national offices for affiliation, and used this to excuse themselves. Although the TUC issued directories of trades councils from 1931 there were constant complaints that local bodies would not reveal the full details of their membership to allow pressure to be placed on national union leaders to get their branches to affiliate. From the returns that did come in, however, it seemed that in 1935 the worst unions in this respect were the AEU, with at least fifty-three branches not affiliated, the NUR, with thirty-eight, and the Amalgamated Society of Woodworkers, with thirty-four. The list is surprising, all the more so since all three of these unions were often active participants in the trades councils, and the unions in mining and cotton were much more notable for their absence from the proceedings of local bodies. However, through the issue of such statistics, and such other methods as the passing of motions at Congress, efforts were certainly made to foster trades council affiliations.[16]

There were a number of other smaller ways in which the General Council helped the trades councils through the JCC. It brought pressure to bear to get trades councils represented on such bodies as local employment committees. It arranged for visits to their meetings by people from the factory inspectorate and labour exchange administration. The trades councils were helped in getting representation on judicial Benches, making sure that Fair Wages Clauses were rigorous enough, and organising the employees of local authorities.[17] The General Council also did something to help the trades councils with their own organisation. From 1927 onwards it tried to put the trades council federations on a more systematic basis than had been the case in the past. The federations, however, never became strong enough for trades council membership of them to be made mandatory.[18] Also somewhat uneven in application was the TUC effort to formulate model rules for the trades councils. The first of these were published in 1926, and the main emphasis then was on making a clear distinction between industrial and electoral functions, and obtaining the general adoption of a grouping system, despite objections from Sheffield and elsewhere. The General Council commended the 'eagerness' with which these model rules were adopted, but there is little evidence of this happening, except at Eccles, Redcar and Southampton.[19] Of greater significance were the model rules put forward from 1934. The most important purpose of these from 1935 to 1943 was to exclude from the trades councils members and supporters of the Communist Party. This aspect is discussed later in the chapter. The model rules also aimed to get the trades councils to drop all functions which some of them still claimed in the field of industrial relations, though not always with success, and to stop affiliating any organisations other than trade union branches.[20]

The new arrangements in force after 1925 were not just methods of helping the trades councils undertake activities they had long since performed, and would have continued. The TCJCC also aimed to keep the work of the local organisations within limits prescribed by the union leaders. Thus, despite the hopes at the time of its foundation that the JCC would enable the trades councils 'to function in scores of ways that at present [are] impossible',[21] there was none of the same expansion in the work of local organisatons after 1925 as had taken place in the three previous decades. The nature of the new relationship was carefully defined by one of the employees of the TUC as ending the 'suspicion and jealousy' with which union leaders had in the past regarded 'bodies upon which they were not represented and whose activities they could not control'. Thus the General Council said it aimed at 'the creation and stimulation of a general Trade Union consciousness', and clearly this was to be a 'consciousness' of a kind of which the trade union leaders could approve.[22] Although some union leaders were still heard to bemoan trades councils making 'complaints about the work of trade union head offices and officials', in general their subordinate position was increasingly accepted. During the 1920s and '30s the councils became to the TUC what the branches were to the unions themselves. The councils were seen as instruments of the wider movement, as transmission belts of orders from its leaders to the rank and file. During the 1930s they became a means of carrying out policies decided centrally by the trade union movement on such matters as unemployment, education, leisure and recruitment to the unions. Most local bodies were prepared to accept the TUC as 'the supervisory and co-ordinating body of the Trade Union Movement'. Thus in 1933 one trades council described its main work as 'receiving and considering the various circulars of the General Council'. Later in the '30s, Citrine was described by one local body as 'our General Secretary', and at Bolton it was agreed that the Trades Council was 'a clearing house for dissemination of all instructions and information from the TUC to the rank and file'.[23] The campaign against the 1927 Trade Disputes Act was a landmark in the use of the trades councils as instruments of TUC policy. An elaborate machinery of local organisers working through the trades councils and local Labour Parties was set up. The trades councils were said to have 'rendered yeoman service' and to have shown their 'usefulness and absolute necessity', although some of them complained that 'the General Council had not been sufficiently insistent'.[24] The trades councils were also used in the carefully stage-managed 1934 celebrations of the centenary of the Tolpuddle martyrs to reiterate the constitutionalist views of the union leaders.

The strictly subordinate position of the trades councils was emphasised in the running of the JCC and in its relations with the General Council. The affiliation of the trades councils to the TUC was no longer a serious possibility. The policy was put forward by the Communist Party, and remained popular in the trades councils, but was usually rejected at Congress meetings without any real discussion.[25] At the same time the JCC, as Citrine explained, 'was not an Executive body', and it came to be understood that 'all the discussions and decisions are of no avail unless the General Council agree with them'.[26] The same one-sided system operated in the JCC itself, where decisions were sometimes made without even telling the trades council delegates. This happened with the 1927 decision to ban trades council affiliation to the Minority Movement. One of the trades council members of the JCC said that though he was 'prepared to support such a line' he felt aggrieved

that although there was in being a Joint Consultative Committee with six representatives of the Trades Council[s] on it, they were never consulted at any time on this question, and as it affected the Trades Councils directly, the least the General Council could have done was to have consulted the Trades Council representatives before sending the circular out.

On this occasion a protest was entered 'against the autocratic methods adopted by the General Council', but its attitude did not change.[27] It ignored trades council protests against the altered voting method that was unilaterally introduced at the annual conference in 1927, and in 1932 it decided to set up trades council unemployed associations against the explicit vote of the previous Trades Councils' Annual Conference. Such methods were described as 'autocracy' and 'not democratic' by the trades councils themselves.[28] Nevertheless they remained evident even in the procedure of the annual conferences. Although it was reasonable enough to have trades council motions coming through the federations rather than from individual bodies, the councils soon found that they were not allowed to discuss why some motions were accepted and others were not, and they also found that extra motions could be submitted from some federations which were known to exist on paper only. In 1938 the General Council went to considerable lengths to conceal from the trades councils the extent to which many of their number were now supporting the hunger marches, and tried to justify continued opposition. In 1939 the Trades Council Annual Conference voted for a full-time organiser to deal with unemployed organisations, but the General Council did not consider it necessary in explaining its refusal to carry this out to say more than that such an arrangement was 'not necessary'. The same conference was not even allowed to express its opposition to conscription on the day after a meeting of trade union executives had done so. In response to criticisms that the proposals of the trades councils were never carried out Citrine said 'that democracy could be carried to a point where it becomes farcical'.[29]

When the Trades Council Annual Conference decided its policies it was difficult to see the purpose in doing so. A motion at the 1933 conference to have nothing to do with the National Council for Social Service was an embarrassment to the General Council, and when there were complaints that individual trades councils had ignored it with impunity the answer was that these motions were 'advisory and not executive' and that all the General Council had to do was to 'observe as closely as possible the intention behind the resolution'. Trades council delegates objected that their motions should be carried out, but there was nothing they could do to enforce this.[30] Local bodies were told that 'resolutions should deal primarily with subjects affecting the organisation of Trades Councils, and they should avoid any appearance of approaching on the prerogative of the Trade Union Executives'. In 1932 Citrine explained to the TUC that motions before the Trades Council Annual Conference were only 'prepared' from among those submitted by the trades councils, and that the General Council would 'feel free to act on these resolutions' only when they appeared 'to be of immediate importance' and 'in line with the policy of the Congress'. Otherwise they might 'require ratification'. Thus few of the motions ever considered by the Trades Council Annual Conference were in any way critical of the policies of the union leaders, and even if they were, they could not have had any effect. One motion passed in 1934 was said to be 'similar to several Congress resolutions' and was 'filed for future reference and borne in mind'. Another motion was 'on the lines of action already taken', and a general attack on the policies of the National Government was pronounced to be 'in line with the policy of the national movement'.[31] Such statements are scattered throughout the reports to the Trades Council Annual Conferences, and indicate that there was little the councils could now do to effect the policies of the trade union movement.

The control exercised over the trades councils by the TUC also altered their internal constitution and working. It was made clear that if a local body was to do 'good work' it had 'to have an understanding that the Trades Council in the locality should be the exponent of official policy'. It was also said that once a trades council 'usurped the functions of a Union it became absolutely dangerous'. Local bodies themselves came to understand that 'they should be guided by the decisions of the national body', and in Birmingham in 1933–34 policies conflicting with those of the national leaders were not even discussed. By the end of the '30s the constitution of at least one trades council did not allow it to make its own decisions but said that 'the policy of the Council should be as confirmed by the TUC'. The building of the unions themselves in this period as centralised command structures was reflected in relations between the TUC and the trades councils, and union leaders wanted 'to keep them in their place'.[32] This was not a result achieved without tension or conflict, and some of the most important disputes which arose, and which directly affected the trades councils, will now be considered.

Heresy hunting in the trades councils

The increasing control of the central organs of the trade union movement over local bodies, and in particular of the TUC over the trades councils, was an important development of the inter-war years. In previous chapters something has been said of how left-wing sections of the movement emphasised the importance of local initiative and powerful trades councils. Such views continued to be expressed in the 1920s, and to some extent in the '30s also, by the Communist Party and its associated organisations. Before 1914 they had been widely tolerated in an expanding trade union movement. Thus at Nottingham it could be said in that period of the Trades Council that 'while the debates are often keen it is fair to say that they are never acrimonious'. The impact of the world war, of the Russian revolution and the defeat of the General Strike had some effect in changing these attitudes. The centralisation and streamlined organisation of the movement represented in the 1918 Labour Party constitution and the 1921 reorganisation of the TUC left less room for local initiative than had been the case in the past. The ideals of tolerance were often replaced by the view of the trade union movement as a command structure, where loyalty to the leaders should be unquestioned. The TUC in this period saw the trades councils as 'a disciplinary problem, not a co-ordinating agency'. Struggles within the TUC can be described in terms derived from the religious history of other ages and other cultures.[33]

Nothing, it was felt, ought to be done that would in any way undermine the official leaderships of the individual affiliated unions. In the light of the antagonism to Communism, the *status quo* acquired a new sanctity.

In enforcing the general control of the leaders of the unions over the rank and file of the movement the increasing power of the TUC over the trades councils was particularly important.

The beginnings of the inter-war struggle against the heretics within the working class movement can be seen in the development of the 1918 Labour Party constitution. The position of associated political organisations, and particularly of the Communist Party, remained unclear for some years within the new arrangements. In 1920–21 the affiliation of the CPGB was refused.[34] Despite this, for a time CP members remained individual members of the Labour Party, and included a number of important public representatives such as some MPs and the leader of the Sheffield Board of Guardians.[35] However, a sharpening of attitudes developed, deriving in part from disillusionment with the first Labour government, and, it was said, also from the activities of the National Federation of Trades Councils. In October 1924 the Labour Party conference voted that those in the CP should be ineligible for membership, and a year later, at Liverpool, this change was put in the new rules of the party.[36] Many local Labour Parties refused to accept the decisions, and a number were disaffiliated. Late in 1925 these organisations set up a London Left Wing Movement, which later became the National Left Wing Movement.[37] This organisation won considerable support until the sharp change in CP policy in 1927–28 resulted in Labour leaders being characterised as 'social fascists'. As a result there was little hope of having the Liverpool decision reversed. In the interim, however, the trades councils were affected by these developments, particularly where they were still operating jointly with local Labour Parties. Communists in the Chelsea Trades Council and Labour Party were told to fight 'to show that the problems of local government cannot be settled satisfactorily to the workers until power is in the hands of the working class, the Trades Councils function[ing] as the authority in the locality'.[38]

The trades councils in the mid-'20s, whether operating as joint bodies or not, were frequently subject to the kind of radical propaganda which has been described in some detail in chapter five, and there can be no doubt that many of the ideas put forward by the CP and the Minority Movement about the work of the local organisations achieved widespread support. The MM, established in 1924 to bring together militant trade unionists, largely under the leadership of the CP, was the heir to ideas about the importance of local initiative and democratic organisation within the trade union movement.[39] Thus, as already mentioned, the proposal for affiliation to the TUC was a popular one in the trades councils. The MM call for the affiliation of workshop organisations to the trades councils was frequently discussed and often supported, as was the general demand for stronger local organisation. The threat posed to the union leaders by these policies is well set out in a pamphlet published by the Movement just before the General Strike.

Too long have these trades councils been the happy hunting ground of careerists and political opportunists. They can be made, and will be made, local co-ordinating and unifying centres of working class organisation having their delegates from the workshop committees, trade union branches and district councils and co-operative societies. They will be fashioned into weapons of struggle and will be of the greatest possible assistance to trade unionists in their everyday struggle against the exploiters.[40]

In 1925–26 the influence of the CP grew in the trades councils as in other parts of the working class movement. In the spring of 1926 the party could claim the allegiance of forty-seven delegates to the London Trades Council, as well as of five members of the executive, and over fifty trades councils were represented at the conferences run by the MM in March and August 1926. During the year conferences for young people were held under trades council auspices as a result of CP influence.[41]

The leaders of the trade unions soon began to respond to the growing strength of the MM. The GMWU in 1925 threatened to withdraw its branches from the Manchester Trades and Labour Council if it did not end its affiliation to the MM. In 1926 the union withdrew its forty-three branches from the Glasgow body when a majority of the delegates decided to remain affiliated. In London delegates were similarly withdrawn in 1927. In Newcastle a branch of the Operative Plasterers withdrew because there were Communist delegates on the Trades Council.[42] Against this background, the General Council decided at its meeting on 25 November 1925 to tell the trades councils that it did not 'approve of affiliation with the National Minority Movement', because it was 'not consistent with the policy of the Congress', though in fact the Congress had expressed no opinion on the matter. This admonition does not seem to have had much effect, since more trades councils than ever attended the MM conference in March 1926, and the activities of the local organisations during the General Strike in May confirmed some of the worst fears of the trade union leaders. One of them asserted at the TUC in the autumn that, if the General Council were to allow the trades councils to affiliate to the MM, 'within a short period the Minority Movement may become the majority movement'.[43] The General Council considered the matter at its first three meetings in 1927, and as a result issued a circular on 25 March to the trades councils informing them that

those Trades Councils which are affiliated to the Minority Movement, or which receive affiliations from branches of that organisation, or are associated with that body, shall not be accorded recognition by the General Council nor allowed to participate in any work carried on under the auspices of the General Council.

Trades Councils which refused to repudiate the MM would no longer receive communications from the General Council, nor attend the annual conferences. It was later said that at this point a number of trades councils expressed opposition to the line of the General Council. The MM leaders seized the initiative, however. They sent a circular to all trades councils on 31 March attacking the General Council for 'imposing its dictatorship on the trades councils, when at the same time it denies them the right to any decisive part in framing the policy they are asked to carry out'. At the same time, the trades councils were advised to accede to the General Council instructions so they could fight the decision at the annual conference. Meanwhile a protest signed by a number of left-wing union leaders was issued.[44] These efforts did not have the desired effect, however, because the General Council persuaded the Trades Council Annual Conference in May to accept its ruling. At the TUC meeting in September 1927 the General Council spoke out more boldly against 'dictation by any outside or irresponsible organisation', and there was an outburst from Herbert Smith of the miners about trades councils being 'manufactured by you people to destroy this union which took so much effort to build up'. The growing sharpness of feeling was made obvious by the fact that despite a moderate speech from Pollitt, leader of the MM, there were other bitter attacks on the Movement for discussing trades council business before the meetings, and the views of the General Council were endorsed.[45]

In the following period these conflicts were reflected in many local bodies, perhaps most sharply of all in the London Trades Council.[46] The strength of the CP there in 1925 has already been mentioned, and by 1927 it was such that they had a majority on the executive committee. In the previous period the delegates had supported many of the policies put forward by CP and MM. Thus there were protests about the lack of recognition for the National Federation of Trades Councils, and calls for the affiliation of the trades councils to the TUC and of shop stewards' committees to the councils. In June 1925 affiliation to the MM was agreed, but after a protracted campaign against it the decision was rejected in November.[47] However, the London Trades Council remained affiliated to the Labour Party and refused to accept its decision to ban CP delegates. Thus it sent J. Vaughan to Labour Party conferences in 1926, an action considered by the CP to be 'a vital issue for our Party'. Vaughan was a well known and popular figure, and the support he gained for his stand was an important fillip for the Left Wing Movement.[48] However, in 1927 Duncan Carmichael, the independent left-wing secretary of the Trades Council, died, and he was replaced by Alfred Wall, an ex-CP member strongly hostile to the party. In April the card vote was introduced, for probably the first and last time in the history of the trades councils, and this allowed the union officials to dominate proceedings sufficiently so that by July it was agreed that all delegates had to sign a declaration that they were not in 'the Conservative, Liberal or Communist Party'. This led to a situation where the executive committee of the Trades Council could not meet because a quorum of its members were in the CP, and a new executive committee had to be elected by selected delegates. These pressures on the London Trades Council were largely exercised at this stage because of its affiliation with the Labour Party.[49] In the future it was the TUC General Council that legislated the beliefs of trades council delegates. In 1928 the unions themselves began to take measures against the CP, starting with the Boilermakers and the Shop Assistants. Growing antagonism between right and left was shown by the fighting which was reported between CP and Labour Party supporters at the Edinburgh May Day demonstration. The General Council began to set up new trades councils where it could not secure support for its policies. This happened at Westminster in 1926, and in 1928 at Battersea, Camberwell, Hackney, Bethnal Green and Barrow. At the same time new rules were introduced in some trades councils to exclude members of the CP.[50] The Scottish TUC then decided to disaffiliate all trades councils affiliated to the Minority Movement, even though by this time none actually was, and the Edinburgh Trades and Labour Council expelled all CP delegates and supporters. In 1928 the British TUC excluded 'persons associated with the National Minority Movement' from attending the Trades Councils' Annual Conference.[51]

The growing bitterness of the CP at these measures helped its members accept the sharp turn to the left in the policies of the Communist International that took place in 1928. The party now decided to operate independently of the trade unions and to set up break-away organisations in the mining and clothing industries, thus causing the disintegration of the support it had so painfully built up in the unions.[52] There was a similar change of policy in CP activity in the trades councils. The MM call in 1927 to withdraw affiliation was now characterised by the Movement as 'a serious mistake'. It had certainly achieved very little. In March 1929 Pollitt proposed policies of

reorganisation of the Trades Councils to free them from the dominance of political reformism to transform them into local Unifying and Co-ordinating centres of the trade unions, co-operatives and unemployed movement, directly working among the masses on the Minority Movement programme.[53]

In other words, organisations completely independent of the unions were to be established. Though some of the trades councils replaced by the TUC seem to have survived at least until 1929, there was only one attempt to set up an entirely independent body under the control of the CP – the London Industrial Council. The direct intervention of the leaders of the Labour Party and the unions in the internal affairs of the London Trades Council in 1927 led to the view in the MM that the Trades Council had become 'part of the capitalist apparatus for the suppression of working-class militancy or activity' and that work within it had shown its 'complete futility'.[54] The inaugural meeting of the new body was held on 6 June 1929; represented were at least six of the unrecognised trades councils, some district committees of the Engineers, the Furniture Workers, and the break-away clothing workers. The aim of the new body was to act as 'a co-ordinating and leading centre of the industrial movement in its struggle against capitalism and Mondism'. However, its meetings varied little from those of more normal trades councils with more limited aims, in supporting wage claims, protesting about the imprisonment of foreign trade unionists, and electing representatives to working class conferences, though in this case those of the MM.[55] The Industrial Council completely failed to win away the majority of trade union organisations affiliated to the London Trades Council, and no similar effort seems to have been made elsewhere to set up break-away bodies. However, CP supporters were expelled from trades councils at Coventry and Southampton, so that by the end of 1928 it can be said that 'the MM had been rooted out of the Trades Councils' and little or nothing was heard from the CP at the Trades Council Annual Conferences or at the TUC, except on the issue of organising the unemployed. Speaking of the trades councils in 1932, Pollitt admitted that the CP was 'practically isolated from them, though it is an important field for our work'. Nevertheless he foresaw that 'we can win the masses under the influence of the trade union bureaucracy by carrying through the new approach to the problem'. As late as 1934 Citrine could still claim that 'Communism has ceased to be in almost every land a serious menace to the Labour movement', but he was soon to find that this situation would not continue for long.[56]

In 1933 the policies of the Communist International again changed. Fears that the success of fascism in Germany might be repeated elsewhere led many CPs to seek co-operation with all those elements said to be opposed to fascism. For Britain this meant a return to work in reformist trade unions and efforts at co-operation with social democracy. In March 1933 an end to attacks on the Labour leaders was ordered, and after this CP members again began to work in the trades councils, not so much to put forward policies for the role of the local organisations in the movement that had been so popular a decade before as to seek to convert other delegates to supporting the policy of the united front against fascism. Leaders of the TUC, who said they were opposed not to fascism but to an undifferentiated phenomenon known as 'dictatorship', insisted that the official organisations of the movement constituted a '*real united front*', and at the 1933 Trades Council Annual Conference a motion was passed saying that the Labour Party, TUC and co-operatives acting together 'on the fundamental principles of Freedom and Democracy' were 'capable of presenting a United Front against all forms of dictatorship', and defeating 'reaction and disruption'.[57] Soon, however, trades councils began to express support for the sort of alliance of working class political and industrial organisations being proposed by the CP. One secretary openly boasted to the 1933 TUC of the existence of such an arrangement in his town. In 1934 the TUC re-formed the Deptford Trades Council because it had pursued such policies. A circular sent out by the General Council on 5 June 1934 advocated the new principle of excluding from the trades councils altogether people associated with the Minority Movement. At the Congress meeting in September the president of the newly established Deptford body appealed to the affiliated unions to see to it that their branches reflected the opinions of union leaders, though he thought that branches should be able to choose what delegates they wished. One of the few surviving spokesmen of the left at the Congress thought such talk was dangerous and asked, 'If we agreed to this principle, where will it end?'[58] Soon after the Congress, sure enough, the General Council took the next logical step with the issue on 26 October 1934 of circulars 16 and 17, usually known by their opponents as the 'black circulars'.[59] Circular 16 told the trades councils that any of their number 'which admits delegates who are associated with the Communist or Fascist organisations, or their ancillary bodies, shall be removed from the list of Trades Councils recognised by Congress'. Circular 17 similarly asked the unions to enforce such bans within their own ranks. On 15 February 1935 the STUC sent out its own 'wee black circular', which banned co-operation with the CP, though not delegates who were members. Later the STUC forbade the trades councils to even discuss the proposal of a united front, though enforcement was left to the individual unions.[60]

The 'black circulars' and the policies they represented were important for the development of the trades councils and for their relations with the trade union movement as a whole. It was the TUC and not the unions themselves, in England and Wales at least, that adopted the role of enforcing the views of the union leadership on the branches of the unions. The individual views of trades council delegates were directly subject to the approval of the central body of the movement. Charles Dukes explained to the 1935 Trades Council Annual Conference that a trades council could now perform no useful function unless it was 'the exponent of official policy'. At the conference the circulars were accepted by a vote of eighty-nine to twenty-seven from delegates who had already been selected on the basis of their enforcement. At the 1935 TUC in Margate the importance of the issue was indicated by the length of the debate, by the passions aroused, and by the fact that the narrow vote to accept the circulars was carried, it was said, only as a result of some leaders flying in the face of the policies of their own unions.[61] A number of union leaders objected to a 'heresy hunt' and to 'interference in the democratic method of electing their officials', but Ernest Bevin stated the case for preserving the bureaucratic soul of the movement with arguments that did not stop short on the borders of mendacity.

Literally hundreds of trades councils, important bodies like Manchester, like Leeds, like London reported to the General Council that delegates were being sent from unions to those bodies, who continually obstructed, and the men who gave up their time to do the business of the Movement of those bodies found they could not get beyond the Minutes ... The problem was forced upon them, and if it were attempted, say, in a miners' branch, to do what had been done in some trades councils in the country, the Mineworkers' Federation would have been forced to discipline its members.

Thus the unions were persuaded to support these new and far-reaching powers of its central organisation.

The level of opposition to the 'black circulars' is difficult to measure, particularly in view of the vastly conflicting claims of their supporters and opponents. Among both trades councils and trade unions only a minority were actively concerned one way or the other, and it is clear that many bodies either supported or opposed the circulars by apathy or default. Thus although forty-one unions agreed with the General Council policy there were 211 affiliated to the Congress. Also the General Council claimed the agreement of 89 per cent of the trades councils, but this cannot have been based on a total of much over 200. The CP named over twenty trades councils who were against the TUC policies, but many of these bodies later rescinded their opposition, or agreed to change their rules in any case.[62] There can be no doubt, however, that many local bodies strongly opposed circular 16 and made active but unsuccessful efforts to defeat it. Less than a week after its publication the Bury Trades Council refused to accept it, and a fortnight later the St. Albans secretary replied in a tone of injured dignity by saying that theirs was 'an old organisation which was actively working on behalf of the working class for decades before the TUC took a friendly interest in it or similar Councils'. No political tests were imposed on delegates, but those of varying persuasions agreed on the 'need for a United Working Class, actively fighting against the reactionary forces of capitalism, especially against Fascism'. In the following months a small but lengthening list of local bodies expressed similar sentiments, and on 27 March 1935 the General Council decided to erase from their approved list eleven trades councils who would not operate the circular.[63] Before the new policy was confirmed at any national conference of the movement the General Council proceeded with care. However, when the Bradford Trades Council decided after two special meetings not to implement the circular its representative was excluded from the Trades Council Annual

Conference in May, as also was the delegate from Oxford. Within the Kent Trades and Labour Federation the local bodies at Dover, Chatham and Tunbridge Wells were threatened with withdrawal of recognition, and the General Council was warned of the 'danger of the dissolution of the Kent Federation if the policy of Black-Listing Trades Councils was persisted in'. Similarly, the Aylesbury Trades Council, although itself having no delegates from the CP, said it opposed the circulars on principle, and thought that their application would ruin the work of the Buckinghamshire federation. Strong opposition to the circulars also came from the Home Counties federation, particularly from Oxford, St Albans and Watford, where the dispute about the circulars reinforced a conflict that already existed between the electoral and industrial wings of the local movement.[64] When the circulars were confirmed by the trades councils and by the Congress meetings of June and September 1935 the General Council began to act more decisively against their opponents. On 18 October the Bradford Trades and Labour Council decided to capitulate 'under protest', and other bodies which held out were struck off the recognised list. On 24 October the Oxford Trades and Labour Council, 'acting in conjunction with other "disaffiliated" Trades Councils throughout the country', circularised all local bodies, urging them to attend a conference in London which would 'explain the prolonged opposition of many Trades Councils to the undemocratic action of the TUC' and where the disciplined trades councils could show 'that they are in no wise disruptionists, but are actuated by a desire to preserve and strengthen those things so necessary to effective working-class actions'. This conference took place on 9 November. Its chairman was Rodney Harrison, president of the St Albans Trades Council, who was deputed to meet TUC leaders, and who duly interviewed Citrine and Harries. At this point the rebel councils had to admit that there was no way they could enforce their views when they differed from the TUC leaders. Although the General Council agreed that they had 'no power to dictate to Trades Councils what their policy shall be', nevertheless they could 'lay down conditions under which they will recognise Trades Councils'. This power was clearly vital to the continued vigour of local bodies, as Harrison realised after his interview with Citrine, when he said that the view of the General Council

was endorsed at Margate even though we may not agree with it, and although we consider the figures to be unrepresentative, the fact remains that it *was* endorsed and cannot be altered for or by Federations or Trades Councils. You have protested on grounds which you consider to be right, and your protest has been heard and noted. Now fall into line and get on with the job that really matters.

It was with these words, perhaps, that the trades councils, in whom so many hopes had in the past been invested, who had stood on the brink of decisive power within the trade union movement and even in society as a whole, at last acknowledged their subordinate position and their inability to do anything by themselves. Soon all the local bodies accepted the new regulations, in many cases 'under protest', and agreed to carry out the wishes of the General Council.[65]

This is not to say that everybody was reconciled to the General Council's policies. In Leeds two union branches withdrew rather than accept the circular, at Plymouth the attitude of the General Council continued to be described as 'dictatorial', and at Carlisle the new regulations were effected only after 'a good deal of controversy'. Opposition also came from the unions themselves, including the AEU and the NUR. During 1936 the TUC had to put pressure in one form or another on local bodies at Clydach, Croydon, Dorchester, Wood Green and Watford to enforce the circulars. This was pressure which continued. In 1939 the Watford Trades Council was visited by Victor Feather of the TUC organisation department after being re-formed twice in four years and persuaded to pass a motion saying that it could have no policies of its own. In 1940 nine London bodies were broken up into separate industrial sections to exclude 'disruptive activities', and at Sheffield considerable pressure was necessary before the model rules were adopted. From 1940 to 1942 eleven further trades councils were reorganised.[66] Many local bodies, like those at Northampton, Wolverhampton and in the Kent federation, enforced the bans but made it clear that they were opposed to them.[67] Other local bodies showed their opposition more passively. Complaints were made about the Chatham Trades Council by leaders of the GMWU that despite agreeing to the circular Communists were still being allowed to attend. At Manchester through the period the rule was 'laxly enforced', allowing CP members to be delegates, though not on the executive committee. At the same time, there was little the General Council could do to prevent trades councils like the one at Newcastle expressing support for 'the campaign for greater working class unity' or the open defiance at Gravesend, where the rules on proscribed organisations were 'not adhered to too strictly', which 'contributed greatly to the better relations existing between the progressive bodies' of the town. In the London Trades Council a well known CP member stood as secretary in 1938 without protest, and the circular 'was not applied, nor was pressure brought to bear from the Congress' before 1941.[68] Also, to judge from material in the TUC library, it seems that there may be some truth in the claim that many trades councils honoured the circular 'in the breach rather than in the observance'. Thus many local bodies who may have agreed to the terms of the circular went on to ignore it in their rule books. This seems to have been the situation for some or all of the period of the circulars at Middlesbrough, Clitheroe, Harrogate, Bournemouth, Swindon, Durham, Accrington and Didcot.[69]

The 'black circulars' were eventually withdrawn in 1943, and though the rule about the exclusion of Communists was restored to the 1953 model rules it was no longer mandatory. By now, however, the leaders of the movement through the TUC had established their right to control all the main activities of the trades councils, and even to decide on their membership. In the early '50s there were further bitter conflicts in London, Glasgow and elsewhere, but by then a well understood machinery of central control had been established. The trades councils were accepted by then as direct instruments of the policies of the national leaders of the movement, and it is with the most important example of this role between the wars that the last part of this chapter deals.

Organising the unemployed, 1920–40

Before 1914 the trades councils gradually became more sympathetic to the plight of unemployed workers, but they did little to organise them to deal with their grievances. Unemployment inevitably became much more important for the councils in the inter-war period, when the problem dominated the lives of working people more continuously than at any other time. A number of important parallels with the pre-1914 period remained, however. Trade union leaders were still suspicious of efforts on behalf of the unemployed not organised by the unions themselves. Thus much of the work with the unemployed was begun by the left-wing political organisations of the working class movement. It was the SDF that initiated the big demonstrations of the 1880s and the 'Right to work' activities of 1905–08. In the same way it was the CP that was behind the largest and most successful political efforts of the unemployed in the '20s and '30s. When the union leaders looked for some alternative way of catering for unemployed workers they turned in this period to the trades councils, over which they were exercising increasingly rigid control. However, the imaginative publicity and the lack of narrow restrictiveness of the CP meant that in general it was more successful than the TUC-sponsored unemployed associations. The hunger marches in particular, always disliked by most union leaders, gave a focus for support to CP-influenced activity which in the end was not withheld by most sections of the working class movement, including the trades councils. This limited the councils' success in the role that union leaders sought for them.

Efforts to organise the unemployed began after the severe winter of 1919–20.[70] At a national conference in April 1921 the National Unemployed Workers' Committee Movement (NUWCM) was established. This body, which dropped the word Committee from its title in 1929, was effectively led by the CP throughout its two decades of existence and was by far the most successful and best known organisation of its kind. Throughout most of the inter-war years the NUWCM inspired large numbers of the unemployed to social and political activity, took up the cases of many individuals, and had a political impact that was greater than the more staid and hesitant efforts of the 'official' trade union and working class movement.

In the early '20s trades councils engaged in their traditional quasi-political activities on behalf of the unemployed. In Chatham the Trades Council demanded public works and a register of the unemployed from all local authorities. In Birmingham and Liverpool in 1920–21 local bodies ran demonstrations and petitions in support of activities which were initiated by left-wing organisations. In 1922 the Birmingham body called for 'adequate maintenance and recognition by the government that the burden and responsibility for the problem was a national matter and not local'.[71] In the following period the activities of local organisations were directed by an uneasy alliance between the NUWCM and TUC, who in January 1923 set up a Joint Advisory Committee. On 7 January 1923 and 1 June 1924 there were 'Unemployed Sundays', when numerous trades councils as well as national organisations took part in demonstrations. In 1924 the Communist Walter Hannington spoke to the TUC, and in the following year to the first Trades Council Annual Conference under TUC auspices.[72] However, many trade union leaders remained hostile to organisations of the unemployed, especially directed in this way. In 1925 the General Council decided that unemployed organisations as well as trades councils could not affiliate to Congress. The Joint Advisory Committee met for the last time in the same year, and in 1927 the General Council decided it was no longer 'satisfied as to the bona-fides' of the NUWCM.[73] In this period a number of local branches of the NUWCM were affiliated to trades councils or, as in Liverpool, worked in a joint committee with them. In 1923 G. D. H. Cole proposed that all trades councils should set up special organisations for the unemployed, even though he admitted that 'not a few Trade Unionists are reluctant to foster separate movements of the unemployed'.[74] In the mid-'20s, however, the problem of unemployment diminished somewhat, so few local organisations felt it necessary to take it up seriously.

In 1927 the NUWCM organised the second of its hunger marches, consisting largely of South Wales miners. The march was not backed by any official trade union organisation – though it did later secure the support of miners' leader, Arthur Cook – and was actively opposed by the General Council. Citrine thought it arose not from 'a genuine desire to ventilate the grievance of unemployment, but rather to break the back of the official movement and to show the movement was indifferent to the claims of the unemployed'. On 27 October, less than a fortnight before it was due to start, the General Council wrote to local bodies on the route of the march saying that it was 'unable to recommend trades councils to support the project'. As on many occaisons in the future, Hannington complained that this could only mean 'that the marchers were to be starved and left with no place to sleep by the trade union and Labour organisations on the route'. The London Trades Council, though it had supported the 1922 hunger march and voted on 13 October to support this one, was now firmly under the rule of its anti-Communist leadership, and issued a statement of opposition. Nevertheless support was forthcoming from local bodies at Newport, Bristol, Bath and Swindon.[75] A similar march in Scotland in September 1928 secured the grudging support of the Edinburgh Trades and Labour Council despite the initial opposition of its officials.[76] Early in 1929 the NUWCM announced that it would hold another national hunger march against the 'Not genuinely seeking work' clause, which was then being introduced by the Conservative government into unemployment payment. Again the General Council wrote to trades councils, saying they 'could not recommend the march to be supported' on the grounds that

mid-winter was inappropriate for a march of this description on account of the untold hardship imposed upon men whose physical condition was sure to be impaired by long unemployment; that no impression would be made upon the Government; and also that if Councils were to assist the marchers their already insufficient funds would be depleted.

This solicitude for the welfare of the marchers did not continue once they were on the road, since, as Hannington put it, the General Council 'professed to be opposed to the March because of its hardships, and then proceeded to create hardships by advising Trades Councils and Labour Parties not to render assistance to the Marchers'. At Leeds, Burnley, Peterborough and Southampton the trades councils followed the lead of the TUC and gave the marchers no help. In most places, however, the General Council line was ignored. At Doncaster a special delegate meeting reversed the decision of the executive, 'and splendid hospitality arrangements were made'. At Preston the Trades and Labour Council put up the marchers in their hall and said that 'they could not stand aside and see these brave men passing through Preston without rendering what help they could'. Trades councils at Sheffield, Nottingham, Reading, Oxford and Northampton were among others who actively supported the march.[77]

While the TUC leaders were opposing the efforts of others to fight on behalf of the unemployed, they tried to present some alternative. A year after severing relations with the NUWCM in 1927 the General Council studied the unemployed organisation set up by the Bristol Trades Council, and formulated a similar scheme of its own.[78] At the 1928 Congress there were criticisms of the scheme from both left and right. One delegate thought it was 'not our business' to establish organisations 'in order to counteract the influence of the Unemployed Committee Movement'. On the other hand, a representative of the Miners said that the General Council's idea would 'mean that you will have men and women paying to the Trades Council, and there will be no authority over them'. Dukes of the GMWU thought that the unemployed should be covered by the unions themselves, and that the proposed scheme might be used by 'meddlesome people', 'to the detriment of the Trade Union Movement grenerally'. The proposals were referred back to the General Council, and during the following year local bodies like the Bradford Trades Council that tried to carry them out found that 'hostility of the unions' was an important reason for their failure. Although in Bristol itself it was said with some justice that there was 'no use anyone claiming that the Trade Unions had a real scheme for the unemployed', the unions did not have enough confidence in the trades councils to help them carry out the TUC scheme. In Brighton the Trades Council thought a local organisation that was operating independently was perfectly adequate. Thus, although by 1929 the General Council considered it possible to control trades council unemployed associations, and although there was support for the scheme by the NUR, Transport Workers and others, it was nevertheless felt necessary to abandon it in the face of opposition and apathy. The General Council nevertheless encouraged others to follow Bristol and five other trades councils which had set up organisations along the lines they recommended.[79]

While the TUC was making these hesitant efforts to organise the unemployed the activities of others were increasing. The 1930 hunger march, during the period of Labour government, 'had to face a much more crystallised and brutal sabotage from the Trades Council and Labour Bureaucracy than in any previous March'. It secured support, however, though usually 'unofficially', from the local bodies of Coventry, Bristol, Leicester, Macclesfield and Guildford, and played some part in the abolition of the 'Not genuinely seeking work' clause in that year.[80] The collapse of the Labour government in 1931, not least because of its failure to deal with unemployment, must have helped to lessen faith in the constitutional methods proposed by the trade union leaders. The means test brought thousands of working people the humiliation of a Poor Law they had been able to avoid in the past. At the 1931 and 1932 Congresses marchers organised by the NUWM were kept from TUC delegates by rows of policemen, events which at least one delegate thought 'a disgrace to the whole Trade Union movement'. In this situation the TUC leaders felt constrained to do something further, despite continued opposition to their previous efforts from union leaders, and from the trades councils themselves. At its meeting in January 1932 the General Council decided it was time to re-establish the unemployed associations. They sent two representatives to a conference in Bristol in February 1932 of the few unemployed organisations which existed under the arrangements previously put forward by the TUC. The General Council representatives wanted to establish a federation of unemployed associations under TUC control. The Bristol association, the model for the original TUC scheme, was unhappy about these proposals, so no agreement was made.[81] Despite this setback a federation was set up, and the General Council in the meantime issued another Model Constitution for Unemployed Associations under the auspices of the trades councils.[82] This was presented to the 1932 Trades Council Annual Conference, where the decision of the previous year was reversed, after Citrine and Tewson pointed out that 'the Trades Councils were the only organisations available' for such work. The same proposals were considered by Congress in September, and after a debate in which the need to oppose the NUWM was emphasised the revived arrangements were again accepted.[83]

From 1932 to 1936 the General Council tried to establish unemployed organisations under its control against a background of increasingly successful efforts in this direction by its opponents. The hunger marches, despite official opposition, grew in size and popularity. The 1932 march against government economy cuts still faced official opposition to the extent that the Burton Trades Council and Labour Party sent the advance notice to the police. Despite this, some local bodies supported it. While earlier marches consisted of 'scores rather than hundreds', this time there were 2,500, who brought with them a national petition bearing over a million signatures. The harsh treatment of the marchers by the police, and the subsequent imprisonment of Hannington, the aged Tom Mann and others, gained more sympathy for the NUWM. The General Council was forced to respond to this by calling a number of demonstrations, including an enormous one in London in February 1933, which was the largest such effort it made in the period.[84]

Meanwhile the constant calls for unity from the CP after 1933 won sympathy in the trades councils and hostility from the General Council. The January–February 1934 march was again banned by the TUC, but received 'exceptionally wide' support in local working class organisations. At Bradford, where the march was defiantly supported, the Trades Council thought it was 'time the organised Movement realised that the day of demonstrating in the streets was not ended'.[85] Early in 1935 the government created new grievances by cutting the rate of benefit, setting up the Unemployment Assistance Board, and establishing training camps which were considered a threat to trade union conditions. There were nation-wide demonstrations, mostly under the leadership of the NUWM. The TUC remained hostile to these efforts, although trades councils at Abertillery and Rochdale co-operated with them. The *Times* spoke of a 'spirit of 1926', and the government was forced to announce a 'standstill order' on its cuts.[86] In 1936 the pressure on the official movement to support 'unofficial' activities became overwhleming. The National Hunger March received help from trades councils like those at Swindon and London who had taken a different attitude in the past, and also from the TUC-approved unemployment associations at Leeds and Bristol. The march was backed by the South Wales Miners' Federation and by many Labour MPs, including the party leader, Clement Attlee, who appeared on the platform at the final demonstration. Even the respectable and anti-Communist 'Jarrow crusade' going on at the same time was the object of some official hostility. According to Ellen Wilkinson, 'the TUC circularised the Trades Councils advising them against giving help' so that at Chesterfield they were ignored by the Trades and Labour Council and fed by local Conservatives. By this time, however, the General Council could not hold out much longer. Its attitude was condemned by every trades council representative who spoke at the 1937 Trades Council Annual Conference, and was finally voted down. In 1938 the TUC was forced to admit that the majority of the trades councils on the routes of the latest marches approved of them, and in 1939 it was clearly the general opinion in the councils that it was 'the militancy of the unemployed in mass demonstrations in South Wales, Glasgow, South Shields and other parts of the country that had resulted in the withdrawal of UAB orders' rather than the negotiations with Ministers undertaken by the General Council.[87]

Meanwhile, besides sponsoring their demonstrations and interviewing Ministers, the TUC had made efforts to get the trades councils to organise unemployed associations under its control. The main aim of a TUC unemployed association was to 'obtain for the unemployed persons as high a standard of living as possible', to deal with government legislation, and to provide 'educational, recreational and other facilities for its members'. The associations put forward no general policy on unemployment, though in 1934 it was said that their 'primary function' lay 'in the direction of organisation and agitation of practical work schemes being started by the local authorities', and the removal of the unemployed from the Poor Law. The associations worked directly under the trades councils, to whom they had to submit all their business, and who had control of their accounts. They were represented on the trades councils, but could speak only on unemployment. The work of the associations was restricted in other ways: a member could rejoin after a period of employment only if he had been in a union, and he could be expelled for the vague offence of jeopardising 'the proper conduct of the Association'. From 1935 he could not even join if he was a member of the CP or any organisation proscribed by the General Council, and his organisation could be disbanded if it co-operated with any such organisations.[88] The General Council made strenuous efforts to keep the local associations under its control. It never properly recognised the National Federation of Unemployed Associations, set up in 1933, and even 'regarded with some trepidation' the establishment of a federation of associations in 1935 working closely with the Yorkshire Federated Trades Councils. Since the associations in this area were by far the most successful, the arrangement was pronounced 'a success' in 1937.[89] Traces of the old attitude of superiority to the unemployed can be gathered from some of the comments about the associations at trade union conferences, when it was said that they were merely 'feeding grounds for the trade unions', and provided 'a useful auxiliary for the trade union movement'.[90] There is something in Hannington's stricture that the associations were little more than 'small unemployed social clubs'. Each year the number of footballs supplied to them was carefully tabulated, but complaints were ignored that the unemployed 'looked to the Associations to do more for their future welfare, and not to supply them with sports equipment, which was the work of a social service organisation'. However, the TUC continued to arrange the provision of sports facilities and equipment through the National Playing Fields Association, the supply of allotments and cheap seeds by the Society of Friends, and the running of classes and debates by the WEA and NCLC. Weekend schools on the UAB regulations were started in 1937.[91]

As a result of the restrictive attitude of the TUC the associations have rarely been considered a success. Michael Foot says that the NUWM 'captured the field as the leading champion of the unemployed and showed no signs of being dislodged by the feeble and tardy efforts of the orthodox Labour organisations', and Hannington asserted that the 'official' organisations were 'a dismal failure', and that the TUC 'never treated the building of its own associations seriously'. Even writers more favourably disposed to the General Council think that

the Associations did not prove a success. Their activities were narrowly defined, and the anxiety to keep them under control was evident from the beginning . . . Too much emphasis was placed on the Associations as a source of future union recruitment . . . It is difficult to escape the conclusion that the reasons for their formation were essentially negative, reflecting the narrow self-interest of individual unions, and the ideological antagonism of the TUC leadership to Communist militancy.[92]

In general it is difficult to quarrel with the latter verdict, though it is important to remember that many individual unions actually remained opposed to the associations, so that the TUC in setting them up was acting in an important way in the general interest of the union leaders rather than on behalf of any one of them. As for the trades councils, less than a quarter of them ever expressed any interest in setting up unemployed associations, and the General Council complained in 1936 that most of them preferred 'to leave the organisation of unemployed workers to non-union bodies'. In Scotland, the STUC General Council first tried to establish unemployed associations in the winter of 1932, but over a year later only two had come into existence. Three other trades councils by then were sponsoring associations not under the model rules, and twenty-three trades councils, including those of Glasgow and Edinburgh, refused to set them up at all. Even in 1936 the NUWM claimed 50,000 members in Scotland, as against only 10,000 in the 'official' organisations. In England and Wales at the end of 1932 there were said to be 'about eighty' associations, and in 1933 it was claimed that 140 existed, though only fifty-seven, with 26,267 members, could be persuaded to reply to a circular. In 1934 there were said to be 'about 120' associations, and in the following year fifty-seven of them were again persuaded to reply to a circular, with 22,420 members. In 1937 it was said that the number was now 'around the 100 mark', and in the following year 'between 120 and 140', with twenty-six in Yorkshire, and forty-five in Lancashire. In 1939, with unemployment falling, the number of associations showed a suspicious tendency to increase further, to a total of 'between 120 and 140' with an estimated membership of 25,000.[93]

These totals included many weak and insubstantial local bodies. At Luton the Trades Council Unemployed Association had 'a somewhat sad career', from 1932 to 1934; and at Earlstown during 1936 only 7s 6d out of a total Trades Council income of £71 was spent on the Unemployed Association. Some trades council delegates shared the attitudes of hostility to the unemployed also shown by their leaders. At Oldham some thought the unemployed should be in their own unions anyway. At Manchester there was 'strong opposition' to the establishment of an association because it was thought 'inadvisable to set up separate organisations for unemployed members'. There was a similar decision at Southampton 'after a careful review of all the problems involved'. At Bradford, where the TUC had tried to introduce its original scheme, considerable persuasion was necessary for the Trades Council to set up an association as late as September 1936. In 1938 it was the Trades Council itself that led delegations on behalf of the unemployed and collected money for them. Similarly, at Huddersfield, although there was an Unemployed Association in 1930, it was the Trades and Industrial Council that took up cases at the local labour exchange.[94] The TUC restrictions also caused difficulty. The Deptford Trades Council president thought them 'unworkable', and the Croydon body found its recognition withdrawn on account of 'a mistake by its unemployed organisaton'. In London in 1936 there were said to be thirty-seven unemployed associations working separately from their parent bodies 'because of the restrictions of the Model Rules laid down by the TUC which confined them only to speaking and voting on unemployment reports'. Efforts to impose the model rules could lead to 'new troubles', as was found by the Bath Trades and Labour Council, which was forced to expel the secretary of the successful Unemployed Association on the grounds of 'Communistic activities'. At Newport it was said that the rivalry of official and unofficial organisations led 'away from any agitation that was going to fight the battles for the unemployed'. From Aberdeen in 1937 the merging of the two organisations was proposed, and at Oxford for a period they did work together, though only at a time when the Trades and Labour Council was unrecognised because of the 'black circulars'. The continued success of the NUWM was probably the greatest single reason for the weakness of the associations. Thus trades councils still expressed 'pleasure' at the somewhat insubstantial stunts practiced by the NUWM in the late '30s, and at Reading efforts to set up a local association were hampered by the success of the opposing organisation. At Camberwell a number of such efforts failed for similar reasons, and at Shoreditch the Trades Council was also frustrated by the defection of all its recruits to the NUWM. At Hull in 1936 local union officials were a little shocked to find that all their recruitment leaflets were being given out by members of the NUWM, while at Heywood the local association received far less publicity in the press than the NUWM branch.[95] It seems, in general, therefore, that the trades council unemployed associations did not show the same verve or success as the activities run under the leadership of the CP, and that the restrictions placed by the leaders of the movement on the activities of the local associations were an important reason for their failure.

It must be said, however, that local associations were not uniformly unsuccessful. Thus at Battersea, Plymouth and Ashton TUC-sponsored bodies kept the flag of the official movement flying and fought off challenges from the NUWM. In Margate and Halifax successful organisations also existed for a time. The Ramsgate association in 1936 was 'well officered' and 'very active'. At Darlington 'good work' was performed in 1936, and at Preston, although the Association did not begin until May 1935, there were soon 120 members who met during the week, agitated against task work, and ran social activities. At Newcastle there was also a successful Association, even though it was only seen as 'an avenue to the Trade Union Movement'. The unemployed were even said to 'appreciate' their limited rights to attend trades council meetings. At Bristol the TUC model body continued to operate 'with the prestige and power of the Council' in 1936 and 1937, mostly by taking up individual cases and running social activities. The Birmingham association attributed its success to a permanent headquarters where it catered for sports and hobbies.[96] The most successful of all the local associations was probably the one at Leeds. During the '20s the Trades Council co-operated with the NUWCM but in 1931 began to discuss setting up a separate organisation for the unemployed based on the arrangements within the AEU. In the following year ten local members of the NUWM were arrested, and the Trades Council took the opportunity to set up an association under the TUC scheme. In the following years the Association used the Trades Hall to agitate for better conditions for the unemployed, to prepare their cases for the welfare authorities, and to organise social activities. The views of the Association were often listened to and acted upon by the Trades Council. However, although the General Council often pointed to the Leeds association as worthy of emulation, it did not always conform to the strict TUC criteria in every way. Thus when the president addressed the 1933 Congress he was careful to emphasise that they were non-sectarian, and their speakers included Communists and socialists. Further, members were allowed 'of their own free will' to speak at CP-sponsored meetings, reporters from the *Daily Worker* were invited, and the 1936 NUWM hunger march was supported. A somewhat different attitude from the one adumbrated in the TUC model rules permeates the statement of the Association's president that they were 'out for educational and agitational methods, not soothing the unemployed to sleep'.[97] Similarly, at Jarrow, CP and Labour Party members worked together in the Unemployed Associaton, and at Bath

and Abertillery there was co-operation between Unemployed
Associations and NUWM branches, a position the NUWM aimed for
from the autumn of 1935.[98] Thus even when there was some success
along the lines dictated by the General Council it was not always quite
in the way it wanted.

The issues discussed in this chapter have shown that the trades
councils continued to play an important part in the working class
movement, as forums for some of its most important internal debates and
as instruments of some of the policies of the union leaders. However, the
smothering embrace of central control now prevented the local bodies
from taking the same initiative and achieving the same expansion as they
had in the past. The final chapter will describe how this was reflected in
their internal life and work in this period.

Chapter eight

Old ideals and new realities
1926–40

After the General Strike

Despite the expanding activities of the trades councils in the decades after their exclusion from the TUC in 1895, and the central role they played in trade union development in the period up to 1926, the work of the local organisations grew more limited and their expansion more spasmodic in the period from the General Strike to the second world war. At Newcastle immediately after the General Strike the Trades Council 'slumped into lethargy and exhaustion', and in the following years there were frequent complaints of diminished enthusiasm because trades councils dealt with only 'routine matters in a dull and uninteresting way'. At Liverpool in 1948 there had been no 'spectacular gains in membership or influence' for two decades, while at Swindon in 1971 local veterans considered that the Trades Council 'never enjoyed the same influence or stature after the General Strike'.[1] The increasing power over the trades councils of union leaders who were largely opposed to decentralisation in any form has been described in the last chapter. Thus while the trades councils in the period 1926 to 1939 continued to do many of the same things they had done in the past, and though their new relationship with the TUC often helped them to function more effectively, they were now part of a more quiescent and less expansive working class movement.

Despite their less prominent role after 1926 the councils continued to express some of the ideals of their earlier period of expansion. They still called for industrial unionism and for the amalgamation of trade unions, though there was now less they could do to achieve these aims.[2] Tom Quelch was still telling the councils that local communities could be 'under the political control of the organised working class movement' if they did more to mobilise their membership, and the secretary of the Leeds Trades Council thought the local bodies were 'destined to play a big part in the emancipation of the workers from capitalism to a new order of society'. The Newcastle Trades Council president still thought that 'trades councils must become the rallying ground of labour forces in all its facets'.[3] Two pamphlets published in this period show that the tradition of radical ideas about the trades councils put forward by the syndicalists and Tom Quelch was not dead. The first was published in Glasgow in 1930, written by J. McDonald and entitled *Trades Councils*. Though showing little knowledge of the history of the councils after the 1860s, McDonald propounded many ideas that had been heard in them since that time. He thought that the TUC and the trades councils should 'take the place of the present Parliament and Municipal County Councils', and that by avoiding political parties of any kind they could develop 'workers' representation, workers' control and workers' administration of the local economic life in the interests of the workers'. In an introduction the president of the Glasgow Trades Council added that even in the short term 'they have plenty of useful and educational work to do'. Another pamphlet, written by Reg Groves and published by the Socialist League about 1933, was called *Trades Councils in the Fight for Socialism*. This still called for all-inclusive local organisations, though by that time they were becoming less common, and considered they could take up many issues facing the working class, such as the threat of war. Although Groves thought that much useful work could be performed by trades councils, it was not necessarily they themselves who would be harbingers of the future socialist society.

It is within the Councils in the battles of the working-class, on all fronts – on the front of ideas no less than others – that the political leadership will be matured which, getting increasing influence and power, will ultimately carve out the way to emancipation.

Thus other radical sections of the working class movement besides the Communist Party were coming to regard the trades councils as forums for the expression of their ideas rather than instruments for the realisation of a new society.

It would be generally true to say that in this period the trades councils and those who led them continued to express more radical sentiments than the national leaders of the labour movement. Few local bodies were happy about the Mond–Turner discussions between TUC leaders and some sections of employers in 1927. The talks were condemned at Northampton and Brighton, and the president of the latter body complained to the 1933 TUC about a 'negotiation complex' and about people 'who would sooner negotiate with the dying body of capitalism than put an end to it, and bury it decently without flowers'.[4] There were also protests from the trades councils about the acceptance of knighthoods and other honours by Citrine and national union leaders from a National Government that was uniformly and cordially detested throughout the movement.[5] At the same time, the trades councils were adapting themselves to more mundane activities within the movement. This change was reflected in the work of A. A. Purcell, once a syndicalist militant, later a TUC leader, and later still the secretary of the Manchester and Salford Trades Council. Some of his speeches and writings on the trades councils during the 1930s were published, and despite their rhetorical style they reveal a much more limited view than had been common in the past of the capacities of the local organisations. Purcell thought the trades councils should be 'the concentration point of all local power in our movement' and 'class organs in a very real sense'. They were able to make workers 'become conscious of their services to society, their rights as wealth producers, as citizens – as human beings'. Yet the practical tasks he proposed were no greater than those the local organisations already performed. Thus he opposed the setting up of special bodies uniting other working class organisations with trade union branches in ways that had been common from 1917 to 1926.[6] Generally speaking, there was a paucity of radical ideas in the councils in the 1930s by comparison with earlier periods. Perhaps the clearest indication of this is the reception just after the downfall of the Labour government in 1931 of the somewhat sterile notion put forward by the former guild socialist S. G. Hobson that there should be a 'House of Industry' to replace the House of Lords, at which would be represented unions, employers and professions. Hobson contacted Tracey of the TUC staff, who persuaded Purcell, together with Wall of the London Trades Council, to write a preface to the book outlining Hobson's views, in which they spoke of the need to restore faith in parliamentary instututions. The London Trades Council later advocated rather vaguely a 'National Economic Authority, on which should be represented workers of every grade . . . to control and co-ordinate industry'.[7]

There were other changes in the period after 1926 which limited the role and effectiveness of the councils. An important influence on their work was the Trade Disputes Act of 1927. Initially it was thought that this would involve only 'changes in our Constitution and methods of keeping accounts'.[8] But the effects were more profound than this. For one thing, the affiliation of civil service unions now ended. The Union of Post Office Workers, in particular, had often been active in the trades councils, and had to 'reluctantly withdraw' at Bolton and elsewhere. At Aylesbury, however, 'fraternal delegates' attended from 1930 to 1938, and arrangements of this kind were common during the war, when the union made various efforts to defy the Act.[9] The Trade Disputes Act forced the clear separation of finance in the industrial and electoral work of local organisations. This resulted in many union branches feeling that it was unnecessary to maintain both types of affiliation, and even worrying about the legality of maintaining affiliation to any organisation with political aims. Thus at Newcastle the Shop Assistants withdrew from the Trades Council, and two branches of Engineers at Bolton did the same. At Leeds, despite guarantees that no funds were being used for political purposes, some union branches remained outside the Trades Council as late as 1935.[10] Besides reducing the membership of the councils the Trade Disputes Act also restricted their functions, by forcing them to steer clear of some of the political matters that interested them. This brought about some important organisational changes. Ever since trade union branches had been involved in electoral work there had been a great variety and confusion in local arrangements. In the early period the demand for all-inclusive local organisations for electoral and other work had been put forward by radical sections of the movement, and the 1918 Labour Party constitution largely accepted this. In the mid-'20s Labour leaders continued to be enthusiastic supporters of joint organisation, but more radical sections of the movement began to have their doubts. Soon, however, complaints were heard within the Labour Party of the inefficiency of local bodies not exclusively devoted to electoral matters. More common was the feeling that formerly powerful bodies like the Glasgow Trades Council showed a 'complete orientation to becoming a wing of the Labour Party', their industrial activities were thus 'very weak'. Tom Mann also complained that many councils had 'become practically political agencies doing little or nothing else in the industrial field'. By 1925 leaders of the TUC favoured separate industrial and electoral organisation, and this was put forward in the early period of the JCC, including the model constitution issued in 1926.[11] The government measure of 1927 enforced this trend. At Sunderland as a result of the Act it was found necessary to establish an organisation 'catering for Trade Union interests only', and such reorganisation was necessary in many places because of the confusion between electoral and industrial work that had existed in the past. At Middlesbrough, Bury and Oxford affiliation to the Labour Party was withdrawn, and at Mansfield the Trades and Labour Council removed the words 'and Labour' from its title to show that it was now a purely industrial body. Thus there developed a clearer divison of industrial and electoral work in local organisations. There were still many exceptions, however. At Oldham it was said that the industrial organisation was 'separate only in name', and the JCC said that many local organisations in 1935 still did not have the degree of separation that was required by law, continuing to see themselves as 'mainly political bodies' in 'a state of semi-respectable inertia'. The establishment of specialist industrial bodies continued, however, so that by 1939 over three-quarters of the trades councils recognised by the General Council were distinct industrial organisations. The process continued in later years, though often for other reasons. In 1940 nine separate industrial sections in the London area were established to put an end to 'disruptive activities'. More recently those few local organisations that have retained joint industrial and electoral work have hung on tenaciously to their links with the past against centrally inspired efforts to rationalise their structure. The Liverpool body has been the most conspicuous example.[12]

In the period between the General Strike and the second world war the trades councils never again had the membership and range of functions they had developed in the two decades before. They were controlled in what they did not only by the TUC General Council but also by the government. Thus most of their activities in the period involved little that was new for them, even if they continued to be of value to a somewhat smaller and more quiescent working class movement.

Industrial, social and political activities in the 1920s and '30s

In this period the councils were more closely confined than before to their 'industrial' activities of aiding union recruitment and taking part in some of the more peripheral industrial relations activities of the movement. The TUC leaders were particularly anxious that they should play no part in bargaining about wages and conditions, and this was a point particularly emphasised in the various editions of their model rules. Many local organisations accepted a restricted role in such matters because 'the local struggle to maintain and improve living standards' was 'replaced by national agreements negotiated in the conference room', and when the Gravesend secretary was asked in 1937 to take part in negotiations during a strike of local bus workers he 'deemed it a great honour'. However, some of the larger councils continued to be actively involved in negotiations between employers and unions. The London Trades Council was perhaps most conspicuous in this respect, claiming that its 'business' included 'intervention in trade disputes' which was 'generally decisive'. This was particularly occasioned by the presence in the capital of many 'part-time officials and voluntary workers for the smaller unions without permanent offices'. The Manchester and Salford Trades Council in 1924 said it 'conducted negotiations for many affiliated branches when action by the Unions' was 'fruitless' and during the '30s continued to be asked by the management of the Belle Vue gardens to settle labour disputes. At Bolton negotiations for bus workers met with 'a certain amount of success', and at Nottingham in 1937 a complex settlement was arranged between glassworkers and their employers.[13] Trades councils also continued 'to be specially watchful of the interests of workers engaged in local public services'. In Bradford in 1931 the Trades Council organised meetings and other activities to help city employees improve their conditions, and at Earlstown in 1936 a closed shop was negotiated. 'Eternal vigilance' on the fair wages clause was felt to be necessary at Bolton, and cases of infringements were taken up at Swansea, Halifax and elsewhere. There were also discussions with local co-operative societies at Southampton, Huddersfield and Leeds about working conditions and union recognition.[14] Probably more important were the negotiations undertaken by trades councils within the trade union movement. Thus at Southampton the Trades and Labour Council in 1929 set up a joint committee of aircraft workers. The trades councils at London and Leeds acted as intermediaries in 1928 and 1936 between unofficial strikers and the official leaderships in the Tailor and Garment Workers' Union.[15]

During this period the councils also discussed problems of industrial organisation, acted as local pressure groups for the unions, and helped those workers who were on the periphery of the movement. At Newcastle in the late '20s union branches were asked to report on the state of trade in their respective industries, and the discussions that ensued created a great deal of work for the Trades Council's executive committee. Such discussions elsewhere led to an increased interest in industrial accidents and diseases, and to growing demands for shorter working hours and for holidays with pay. Although Walter Citrine claimed without much apparent justification that the trades councils played a role in improving the Factory Acts in this period, it is nevertheless true that questions of industrial safety and disease, which had been conspicuously absent from their proceedings in the past, were now commonly discussed by the trades councils, and there were often speakers from the Industrial Health Education Society, an organisation to which some local bodies were affiliated. Trades councils also discussed various schemes for work rationalisation, from Taylorism to the Bedaux schemes, and rarely had a good word for them.[16] Trades councils continued to exercise 'such powers as we possess to influence public opinion' in getting recognition for unions by multiple chain groceries at Leeds, and in many years of effort to get a union shop at the newspaper office in South Shields. Boycotts and other methods were used on behalf of shop assistants at Leicester and Weymouth, par-

A meeting of the Birmingham Trades Council, January 1939.
Courtesy Radio Times Hulton Picture Library

ticularly to improve hours of work and holidays. Similar and by now traditional methods were used on behalf of entertainment workers. For the Musicians' Union trades councils negotiated settlements at Bolton, organised non-unionists at Cardiff, issued lists of union bands at Middlesbrough, and arranged boycotts and picketing at Bradford and Manchester. General negotiations on behalf of the employees of local theatres and cinemas were also undertaken at Oldham, and there was frequent co-operation with the Theatrical Employees at Gravesend, Bradford and elsewhere.[17] The trades councils were active in the organisation of actors. In Leeds the Trades Council worked with the Actors' Association and the Entertainments Federated Council in 1924. Later in the '20s the theatrical employers tried to establish a house union, the Stage Guild. In 1929–30 a new organisation for actors on more strictly trade union lines was set up in opposition, known as Actors' Equity. The first secretary of the new organisation was Alfred Wall, the secretary of the London Trades Council, and the Trades Council worked closely with it, in 1936 claiming to have made it 'perhaps the strongest professional organisation in the country'.[18] Local bodies frequently supported the unions organising insurance collectors, and at Halifax and Bolton negotiated on their behalf.[19] Trades councils continued to act on behalf of blind workers, demanding public control of their workshops with increasing success, negotiating with the governing body of such a workshop at Middlesbrough, and being represented on a governing body at

Sunderland. The feeling among blind workers in support of proper trade union organisations was now such that when the National League for the Blind adopted charitable status in 1934 a break-away Union of British Blind was set up in the West Riding of Yorkshire. Despite strong opposition from the TUC, many trades councils were sympathetic to the new organisation, accepting branches as affiliates at Bradford and Halifax. In the end it was the Leeds Trades Council that arranged a meeting between the warring groups that settled the dispute.[20] There were other groups on the fringe of the movement that the trades councils attempted to organise in this period, usually without much success. They tried to bring hotel workers into the unions at Torquay, commercial travellers at Hull, and domestic workers at Hampstead. They also participated in somewhat abortive efforts inspired by the TUC to establish a National Union of Boxers.[21] A more important new field for the trades councils in this period was in organising health workers. Although there had been a Halifax Nursing Association as early as 1914 affiliated to the Trades and Labour Council, it was only after 1937 that the profession as a whole 'knew one of its brief moments of militancy', and nurses were recruited into the main trade unions. The TUC encouraged trades councils to be active in this work, and those at Epsom, Colchester and elsewhere reported some successes. Other groups of hospital employees were helped too. In Reading in 1931 recognition by the hospital authorities was secured for firemen and engineers, and at York and Middlesbrough in 1934 trades councils won shorter hours for the employees of the North Riding hospitals.[22]

In this period the local organisations continued to make great efforts at general union recruitment. Citrine claimed wrongly that this was the earliest function performed by the trades councils. It was true, though, that by the 1920s many local bodies in setting out their aims gave union recruitment considerable prominence. The JCC thought it 'one of the first duties' of a trades council.[23] Local organisations now often received help from the TUC in this work in ways that have been described in the last chapter. Meetings, leafleting and visits to individual homes were among the methods used. Although in smaller places like Bath new union branches were set up, in larger centres, such as Nottingham, it was felt that the duty of the Trades Council did not extend beyond introducing people to unions that already existed. This reflected a greater acceptance of the established union structure in this period and of the more subordinate position occupied by the trades councils. Since the unions themselves often refused to co-operate with local recruitment activity, at times the best the TUC could claim for it was as 'a method of creating a Trade Union atmosphere'. At Southampton, similarly, a local campaign was said only to have 'stimulated interest in the Trade Union movement of the town'.[24] Some councils found more success when they concentrated on particular groups, such as textile workers at Huddersfield in 1935, car workers at Oxford up to 1933, and shop workers at Rushden in 1939.[25] Of greater importance were the centrally directed efforts to recruit women and young persons through the trades councils. When the Women Workers' Group was established by the General Council in March 1925, work through the local bodies was discussed, and this was put forward later at the trades council annual conferences and at the conferences for women workers. In 1930, after a joint meeting between the JCC and the General Council Women Workers' Group, a National Women's Advisory Group was established, and soon trades councils were being encouraged to set up special committees to deal with women workers. In 1932 there were said to be thirty-five of these committees in existence and in 1934 thirty-nine. Successful recruitment campaigns were run through women workers' committees at Huddersfield in 1932, at Newcastle in 1933 and at Birmingham in 1939. By this time the committees were helping with other matters of interest to women workers besides recruitment to the unions. In general, however, they were not considered a success, because, as usual, 'certain Trade Unions prefer to work through their ... branches'.[26] Efforts in this period, also encouraged by the General Council, to set up Youth Advisory Councils seem to have met with greater success, at least in some places. In this period of comparative trade union weakness and limited membership there was constant talk at union conferences of how the youth were being tempted away by films and other entertainments, and were 'not coming into the Movement and taking as active an interest as was desired'. For this reason the TUC expressed itself 'very interested' in a 'Youth Trades Council' established in Bristol in 1934 and in a similar body in Bradford. It had already encouraged the establishment of a youth committee at Newcastle, and during the '30s a number of them were set up by the larger trades councils. In North Staffordshire the Youth Advisory Committee did not prove 'as successful as anticipated', and there was a lack of enthusiasm from many of the affiliated societies at Nottingham. The Birmingham Youth Advisory Committee had a similar relationship to the Trades Council as the Unemployed Association, including the same bans and proscriptions, but still did not win the support of local union officials. Greater success was reported from the London Trades Council Youth Advisory Council, which ran a conference of 200 young trade unionists in 1937 that showed 'remarkable enthusiasm', and also published a survey of working conditions and trade union membership in different parts of the metropolis.

A Walthamstow Youth Advisory Council also made use of the TUC's Youth Charter of 1938 to win new recruits to the unions and to run successful social and educational activities. Trade union leaders remained hostile even to these successful efforts to help them, and in 1939 a special conference of full-time officials in the London area persuaded the General Council that in future Youth Advisory Councils should be run only by the smaller trades councils.[27]

The councils also took part in other industrial activities of the trade union movement, though, again, their role was limited by the leaders of the movement. Support was mobilised and considerable amounts of money were raised during some of the big industrial disputes of the period. During the 1930 textile dispute over £300 was collected at both Huddersfield and Bradford. The cotton dispute of 1932 found the Huddersfield body utilising its whole 'organising ability' to raise money for those involved, at Manchester £4,734 was sent for the benefit of the strikers, and at Bolton a special committee was set up to examine police violence against pickets. Similar support was given to strikes against local bus companies – for example, in 1936 from the Halifax Trades and Labour Council to the Thames Valley bus workers, and from Bradford and Manchester to the Harmsworth miners in 1937.[28] With the increasing power of the TUC over the trades councils in this period, there was strong pressure on local organisations not to support workers in disputes deemed to be 'unofficial'. Thus trades councils were told to refer to union executives in each case despite the fact that it was 'the policy of the Trades Council Movement since its inception to support working-class activity in any direction and not to inquire into the merits or demerits of a dispute'. At Manchester in 1930 the Trades Council was persuaded to side with union officials against an unofficial dock strike. In general, however, the trades councils always lent a sympathetic ear to workers on strike whatever the attitude of union leaders to them. The London Trades Council raised £4,000 for the unofficial Rego clothing strikers in 1928 and the Birmingham body received a delegation of unofficial strikers in 1938. At Oxford in 1936 a group of unofficial strikers were supported because 'a Trade Union principle was involved'.[29] A responsibility trades councils were happier to hand over to the TUC was the settlement of inter-union disputes. A number of such efforts at Newcastle in this period were thwarted by the failure of one side to turn up at joint meetings, and in 1935 a local dispute between the GMWU and the ETU was referred to the General Council, as was a similar dispute at Bradford in the same year.[30] Another industrial role which the councils performed with more success was in allowing the legitimisation within the trade union movement of bodies which excited the rivalry of the already established unions. Such was the case with the Chemical Workers' Union, which, despite hostility from the general unions, built up support in the trades councils, by 1938 being affiliated to thirty-eight. It was because of sympathy for the Chemical Workers and the work they had done with the trades councils that in 1939 the Trades Council Annual Conference referred back a section of the JCC report which spoke of forbidding the affiliation of unions who were not in the Congress. It was through such support that the union was gradually accepted as a legitimate part of the movement.[31]

The trades councils thus retained most of their old industrial functions but failed to perform any significant new ones in this period, either because they no longer had the strength to do so, or more often because they were limited by the action of the union leaders who increasingly controlled them. Despite these constraints, the councils still felt in the 1930s that they had 'an important function in the life of the community', and continued to act as pressure groups on social issues and as representatives of local working class interests, often on local administrative and quasi-administrative bodies.[32] The role of the trade union movement in local affairs was much more readily accepted by those in power than had often been the case in the past, and for their part the trades councils showed none of the same inclination to question the way in which local communities were run, or the limited say which they were granted in community affairs. Trades councils often continued in this period to put 'representation on public bodies' among their primary aims, and supporters of the labour movement thought that 'every activity of the local council should be surrounded by its advisory committee'.[33] But despite the greater acceptance of the trade union movement by the local authorities, and the increased opportunity for representative work provided by the abolition of the Boards of Guardians in 1930 and their replacement by appointed Public Assistance Committees, there was a more limited view of what could be achieved through being represented on advisory and quasi-administrative committees and less of a struggle to obtain such representation. Nevertheless agitation and representation of local working class interests by the trades councils on general social questions went on.

At this time the chief social problems that concerned the trades councils were unemployment and poverty. Their participation in various efforts on behalf of the unemployed organised by the NUWM and the TUC has been outlined in the last chapter. At the same time they took a close interest in the welfare agencies that catered for the unemployed. They showed little of their former antipathy to employment exchanges, advocating the establishment of new ones, complaining about conditions in old ones, and at Birmingham in 1928 being consulted about their siting. In London there was a vigorous campaign against private employment agencies. They continued to be represented on local Employment Committees, as at Newcastle, or in various other bits of the machinery, as at Bolton after 1929, where an assessor was appointed by the Trades Council. During the 1920s the Employment Committees had so much to do in considering the cases of individual applicants that they appointed small rota committees from among their own members to perform the task. At Hull and Leeds in the mid-'20s trades councils wanted to withdraw from this work but were dissuaded from doing so by the TUC. Similar threats were made in London and meetings of labour representatives were arranged to discuss them.[34] Trades councils also studied closely the proceedings of courts of referees, which considered appeals from these lower bodies, even though, as at Plymouth, representation was usually through the union branches themselves. At Southampton, Middlesbrough and Manchester efforts were made to co-ordinate the work of trade union representatives on these bodies, and at Bingley the Trades Council tried to get them paid. The work of the councils around the courts of referees became so important that by 1942 the TUC was asserting that the representation of insured persons was 'a matter for local arrangement between the Trade Union branches and the Trades Council'.[35] The councils also took an interest in all the new machinery that was established in this period to deal with unemployment and poverty. The new Public Assistance Committees were watched carefully. At Middlesbrough and Nottingham it was thought unwise for trades councils to seek representation. Delegates were sent, however, to the PACs at Newcastle and Birkenhead, and threats to withdraw were used in Manchester in 1931 as a protest against cuts in benefit.[36] When the Unemployment Assistance Board was set up in 1935 to deal with the cases of those who had lost entitlement to benefit there was a network of local advisory committees. The TUC urged the trades councils to take an interest in these bodies, but there seems to have been little serious effort to be represented on them.[37] The councils were also nearly always involved in protests over the various changes in government regulations on unemployment.[38] There was particularly strong opposition to government training centres, which were considered at Bolton to be an 'insidious method of reducing wage levels', and at Reading to be 'supplying cheap labour, particularly in the building industry'. The Reading Trades Council took its protests through the Home Counties federation and the JCC to the government, and this 'apparently resulted in the suspension of the scheme'. These statements belie the claim that 'it was only the agitation of the irreconcilable communist element that kept suspicion alive' against this aspect of government policy.[39] The working class movement was also very suspicious of attempts to move young people and others from depressed areas to more prosperous ones. At Nottingham it was thought that this would 'only lead to confusion and discontent, create false hopes and serve as a menace to the organised workers'. Like the General Council, however, trades councils in the more prosperous parts of the country were reluctant to oppose the policy outright. At Watford 'a close watch' was maintained, and at Aylesbury, while the claims of those from less prosperous areas were conceded, it was nevertheless maintained that they should be aided 'without detriment to the wages, conditions, and employment of local workers'. The Aylesbury Trades Council managed to get the news as far as Middlesbrough that the conditions of local hat makers were not as good as was being pretended, and at Southampton the Trades Council got local employers in 1931 to deny national newspaper reports that there was a lot of work available in the town.[40]

The councils did more than oppose government policy on unemployment. They often put forward suggestions of their own, and though they rarely indicated much independent thinking, in many cases their ideas were more sensible and practical than those of government, academic economists, or of many of the leaders of their own movement. At Royton the secretary was clear, as many of those in positions of greater power were not, that 'reducing wages' could not 'improve trade', since 'With less money to spend the demand for goods and commodities must necessarily be less, and [this] tends to make the problem more acute'. At Macclesfield economies were described as 'probably the most sinister weapon in destroying both home and foreign markets', and at Manchester in May 1931 the Trades Council ran a 'People's Convention' against the 'economy mongers', boldly advocating high wages as a solution to unemployment.[41] It is not surprising that the Manchester and Salford Trades Council was able to gain the support of J. M. Keynes for its policies on unemployment, and letters from Keynes were read at Trades Council demonstrations in the city. Keynes would no doubt also have approved of the joint circular issued by the London and Manchester trades councils to all other local bodies in 1933 'urging them to press the Government and Municipal Authorities to plan for National and Local requirements in the matter of Roads, Housing, Bridges' so they could provide jobs for unemployed workers. Suggestions on these lines were put forward at Oldham and elsewhere, as they had been throughout the labour movement for some time.[42] Trades councils were also involved with local academics and employers in surveying conditions and proposing solutions in the depressed areas. Trade with the Soviet Union was frequently advocated by local bodies as a major part of any solution to the depression, and the president of the Glasgow Trades Council actually took active steps in negotiating it.[43]

Trades councils in the 1920s and '30s continued to take an interest in many matters beyond the direct purview of trade unionism. For many years even after this period their 'quasi-political role' has been noted, and the fact that they have remained 'almost as much concerned with political as with industrial matters'. Studies of community politics in Newcastle under Lyme and Glossop have drawn attention to the continuing role of trades councils as political pressure groups. 'Nothing does so much to keep the local authorities up to scratch as the knowledge that slackness will be noted and effectively expressed by a well organised section of the community,' it was considered at St Albans. Increasingly the trades councils took on the role not of questioning the existence or the nature of local services but of seeing they were 'up to the standard that working people have a right to expect'.[44] Thus the local organisations discussed not just industrial diseases but the health service in general. At Edinburgh in 1931 virtually all other work was stopped to take up the case of ill treatment of some patients at the local infirmary, and a pamphlet on local health service conditions was published at Middlesbrough in 1930. Though in smaller centres like Bath money was collected by the Trades Council for hospital facilities, most councils would have agreed with the secretary at Bradford that 'voluntaryism has failed; and that the time is not far removed when State ownership of the health services will be introduced'. Trades councils also continued to provide representatives for the administrative bodies of hospitals as at Huddersfield and of hospital funds as at Torquay. They were often exhorted to support the Manor House Hospital, which had close connections with the unions.[45] On housing, the councils still advocated public provision and low rents. The London Trades Council decided in 1933 to 'develop housing discontent to the utmost extent', and ran many activities, including a large conference against slum conditions and high rents. Direct labour schemes were supported at Torquay, and government efforts through private contractors were described as 'pernicious' and 'stupid' at Bradford. Local tenants' associations were supported at Halifax and Oldham, and were set up by the Industrial Council at Newport. There was an advice service for tenants at Birmingham, as also at Macclesfield. Professional legal aid was used largely for the benefit of tenants at Preston and Leeds. At Manchester many years of such work, including active support for a rent strike in 1932, were said to have 'deprived the Labour Party of leadership on rents questions'.[46] The councils seem mostly to have left questions connected with the education of children to the Labour Party, though at Bolton membership of the Education Committee was retained. Classes of various sorts for trade unionists were, however, arranged in co-operation with the labour college movement by the trades councils at Chorley, Eccles, Preston and other places. There seems to have been much less contact than in the past between the councils and the WEA.[47] Greater interest was now taken in transport facilities. Trades councils negotiated workmen's fares and the conditions on workmen's journeys at Middlesbrough and London, and agitated against fare increases at Portsmouth. One of the main activities described in the 1936 and 1937 annual reports of the Selby Trades and Labour Council concerned the placing of bus stops in the town. Local discussions of road safety and the 'difficulties and dangers surrounding our transport system' also became common.[48] The councils catered for the leisure activities of their members. Although a decline in the attendance at May Day demonstrations during the 1930s was noted at Leicester and Plymouth, young people were attracted to the trade union movement by the successful sporting activities of the Rugby, Reading and Oldham trades councils. Support was also maintained for the movement by the annual dinners and conferences which were run at Kendal and Middlesbrough and by the old folks' treat that became a 'hardy annual' at Bath.[49]

During the 1920s and '30s the trades councils continued to take the same interest in general political issues that they had done in the past. Though rarely showing much independence now, they were still active on all questions that stirred working class opinion. They could be found supporting any of the causes that might generally be deemed 'progressive', such as the abolition of the death penalty, the wider dissemination of information about birth control, and the nationalisation of the coal mines.[50] They remained concerned with the kinds of question that caused the re-establishment of the National Council of Civil Liberties in 1932. A particular interest was taken in the trials and executions of the Italian American anarchists Sacco and Vanzetti, who were widely regarded as working class heroes. At Westminster it was said that their deaths 'left a deep impression on the workers of all lands'.[51] There were similar protests against the imprisonment of Tom Mann and others in 1933, and against the treatment of Indian trade unionists.[52] On international affairs the trades councils took an attitude of rather vague pacifism. From 1922 they participated in 'No more war' demonstrations. Later the policy of a 'collective peace system' was put forward in London and elsewhere. There was a nationally organised 'Peace and freedom campaign' in 1933, and a 'Peace week' in 1936 at Bolton. Many trades councils actively supported the 'peace ballot' of 1934–35, and nearly all were sympathetic to the League of Nations, often affiliating to the League of Nations Union. Rearmament policies were nearly always opposed, at Leeds during the 1935 general election, at Bradford almost until war began. Opposition to military conscription was also maintained.[53] In 1941 George Orwell asserted that 'the most thoughtful members of the British working class are midly and vaguely pro-Russian', and it is certainly true that this attitude affected the work of the trades councils on many issues in this period. At least two councils, those at Leeds and Wolverhampton, sent their presidents to the Soviet Union to report favourably on conditions there, the latter body at a time when it said it could not even afford to send delegates to the Trades Council Annual Conference.[54] Local bodies also protested about the actions of Japanese and German militarism, often participating in boycotts of goods from those countries, though at times the efficacy of such boycotts was doubted.[55] Trades council support for the Spanish republic was later remembered as an important aspect of their work in this period, and the strongly conformist London Trades Council was even prepared to defy the TUC at the time when the latter supported a policy of non-intervention. Support for the Spanish workers was organised by methods which included collecting money for medical supplies, helping refugee children and supporting striking Spanish seamen on the north-east coast. At Gravesend and York strike action in Britain against the non-interventionist policies of the National Government was proposed, though there was little hope of such a policy being pursued by the unions in the 1930s.[56]

When war came again in 1939 the councils had a record of anti-war activity even greater than in 1914. At Ammanford the secretary wrote of 'this mad war between rival gangs of profit makers', and at Eastleigh there was talk of the 'one-sided' sacrifices being demanded. Similar sentiments were expressed at Bradford, and at Watford the Trades Council ran a conference in February 1940 that accepted overwhelmingly 'the imperialist nature of the war'. But as in 1914 the local organisations were soon brought into line by their national leaders. Distrust at Blackpool in 1940 of war savings – a common enough sentiment during the last conflict – was later seen as 'perhaps the last symptom of perpetual opposition'. In this new war the trades councils soon settled down, as they had done after 1914, to participate in activities aimed at supporting the war effort. They were accepted with little difficulty on many local bodies set up to deal with the social problems caused by hostilities.[57] However, partly because of their easy acceptance, and partly because they were now firmly under the control of the leaders of their movement, the trades councils showed much less propensity than in the past to question their role, or to express ideas of their own about how they could best serve the interests of union members. Their position thus never had the same significance as in the past, and the changes in their attitudes and activities during the war and after it never again had the same importance for the working class movement or for society as a whole.

Appendix one

A note on internal and area organisation

The form and structure of trades councils in the early part of the century were not yet so rigid and standardised as they became under the auspices of the TUC from the 1930s to the present day. Until comparatively recently they have been able to operate with a 'wise elasticity in the rules', and since they have always been 'essentially voluntary in their character and organisation' they frequently went 'considerably beyond the scope of their own rules'. With 'consultative powers only', and with no formal ability 'to direct action to the unions represented', they have nevertheless been able to exercise a certain informal moral authority. The general limits on this were well set out by one local commentator in 1912.

No compulsion whatever is used, the Council is a voluntary organisation, branches may or may not affiliate as they think best, they may instruct the delegates to act as they determine. Important measures are always referred to the Unions before the Council takes action. It is democratically constituted and elected.[1]

In this context it was impossible for even a comprehensive official definition of 1937 to get the matter quite right. A trades council was described as 'a body formed by the voluntary association of Trade Union branches in a given locality in order to promote the interests of those affiliated organisations and strengthen the position of Trade Unionism in its area'. Yet there were cases where 'kindred bodies' such as shop stewards' committees or unemployed organisations could affiliate.[2] Until comparatively recently trades councils have also been associated with local Labour Parties, at times even operating as joint bodies. Their titles too have varied a great deal. After 1914 the addition of the words 'and Labour' to the title of a trades council would indicate some electoral functions, though before then it was generally used to show that unskilled workers were admitted. The restrictions of the 1927 Trade Disputes Act made joint electoral and industrial bodies less common, though they persisted in isolated cases until the 1970s. But in the main period covered by this volume there was no close correspondence between title and function in local working class organisations.

For all the elasticity of their rules, and the differences in their forms and titles, trades councils showed a remarkable similarity not only in their activities and policies but also in their internal organisation. This was partly because they consulted equivalent bodies when they wrote their rule books, and also because they were part of a common movement with shared ideals and changes of mood.

What variations there were have largely been a function of size.[3] They all worked around meetings of delegates almost universally held monthly and endowed with ultimate authority. The number of trade unionists represented by one delegate could be as low as twenty-five or as high as 150 or more. There were always executive committees, which could be anything from meetings of delegates between regular monthly gatherings to complicated structures with network of sub-committees.[4] Thus it is not difficult to describe an 'average' trades council, and to trace a pattern on which they were organised without significant variation.

With anything from twenty to 300 delegates, trades councils had an average attendance of perhaps 50 per cent. The Halifax Trades and Labour Council of 1937 can be regarded as typical. It had 5,132 affiliates from thirty-six union branches, with ninety delegates and an average attendance of forty-four. At Chatham in 1914 the average attendance was forty-one, this 'being 48 per cent of those possible'. In the 1930s Scottish trades councils were said to get 60 per cent of delegates to their meetings.[5] Failure to attend was occasionally caused by policy disagreements, but more often by apathy.[6] The meetings were held in a variety of settings, from the headquarters of a local union to a town hall or labour exchange. Even a comparatively well established local body like the Bolton Trades Council was compelled to remain 'paripatetic' right up to the first world war.[7] The branches themselves nearly always decided how to elect their own delegates, at least until the TUC began to enforce restrictions on their political opinions during the 1930s. It was but rare for a secretary to be able to boast, as one did in Bradford in 1901, that 'the position of delegate to the Council has in many societies been bitterly contested'. Branches often, though by no means always, elected their own officers. They seem usually to have preferred people working in their trade rather than full-time union officials.[8] The Webbs considered that the lack of interest of full-time officials weakened the trades councils, and the Newcastle secretary in 1935 felt impelled to 'appeal to the full-time officials in the district to take part in the work of the Trades Council'. In Glasgow in the same period, however, officials were discouraged from participation by the Trades Council itself, and it was certainly the case that the survival and growth of trades councils in the early part of the century took place despite and not because of the attitudes of trade union officials.[9] Another important aspect of affiliation was, and indeed still remains, 'the old grievance of societies affiliating on only a proportion of their members'. At Hebden Bridge in 1916, although there were 4,450 members in branches affiliated to the Trades Council, the membership on which fees were paid was only 2,800. Similarly in 1918 the Wrexham Trades and Labour Council had a 'gross membership' of 12,593 and a 'net' one of 3,800.[10]

The executive committees, which usually met once between meetings of the delegates themselves, consisted of three or four officers, with about six to twenty delegates normally elected by ballot at the annual meeting. The original London pattern of calling this body the Trades Council and investing it with ultimate power was never repeated elsewhere and did not survive into the twentieth century.[11] Executives were usually supposed simply to prepare full meetings of delegates and to carry out whatever they 'authorised'. In practice, however, they could go beyond this, for example by giving support to strikers. Nevertheless cases of serious conflict between delegates and executive, such as occurred in Birmingham and London in the 1920s, were rare.[12] The secretaries also often exercised powers much greater than those that appeared in rule books, where they were simply allowed to keep minutes and call meetings.[13] They often spoke for the delegates to outsiders, and such secretaries as Owen Connelan of Leeds (1892–1923), and Frank Knights of Bolton (1915–41) became well known and influential both as trade unionists and as prominent members of their local communities. Most rule books allow for a small honorarium to the secretary, and in some cases it was possible to appoint someone full-time, though usually only where industrial and electoral functions were combined.[14] Other officers included a chairman or president, normally changed annually, whose main function was to preside over meetings, a treasurer, trustees, and, depending on size, vice-presidents and assistant secretaries.

Trades council finance has never been complicated. Statements of accounts are always published with annual reports and usually reveal that the sole source of income is affiliation fees. These were never high. usually 3*d* or 4*d* per head per annum, though a proposal in 1930 to fix a general minimum at 2*d* was rejected as impracticable. Efforts to increase affiliation fees are always resented, and increases have sometimes resulted in branches simply reducing the membership figure on which they affiliated.[15] Despite a TUC claim that 'shortage of money to carry on the work with maximum efficiency'[16] was a constraint for the trades councils, and frequent appeals from the secretaries to recalcitrant branches to pay up, there is no evidence that activities have ever been restricted by a lack of funds. As voluntary bodies, most of what they do is simply unaffected by such considerations, and a trades council with virtually no income could be as active as one with enough to employ a secretary.[17] An appeal on behalf of a group of embattled workers could often raise as much in a week as trades council affiliation fees did in a year. Many even built up substantial reserve funds.[18] In 1932, when there were about 358 trades councils in England and Wales, their total income was estimated at over £12,000, an average of perhaps £35.[19] A typical balance sheet at Chatham in 1914 recorded 6,303 affiliates, and a total income of just over £60, £35 of this affiliation fees. Assets included shares in the *Daily Herald* and *Daily Citizen*, and among items of expenditure were £10 on printing, £17 6*s* 9*d* on 'appeals', mostly for strikers, and £2 11*s* on affiliations to the National Housing Council, the Kent Federation of Trades Councils and the Labour Party.[20] Councils have also sometimes maintained separate funds for the support of strikers or public representatives, or to help those losing jobs or positions in pursuit of trade union aims.[21]

The chief activities of the councils and their attitudes on the issues of the day are recorded in annual reports compiled by the secretary and usually approved at an annual meeting held early in the year. Besides a report these would include information about finance, the addresses of local trade union branches and union shops, 'accompanied by such remarks and explanations as to their operations . . . as the position of the trades and the circumstances of the year may seem to require'. They could take the form of anything from an ephemeral scrap of paper to a substantial printed and bound volume, an 'institution'.[22] They provide much the richest source in explaining the life and work of the councils.

The association of the trades councils with outside bodies has always been of importance to them. Their attitudes have been affected by contact with the Land Nationalisation Society, the Minority Movement and many others. The election or nomination of council members onto such diverse administrative and quasi-administrative bodies as school boards, military tribunals and public assistance committees has been given considerable attention in this book. So also have their various efforts at co-ordination on a national level. Little or nothing has been said about the regional or county federations of trades councils which existed throughout the period covered because they have never been of more than limited importance for the trade union movement. This appendix concludes with a brief account of the work of these federations up to 1940.[23]

The first federations of trades councils were set up in the 1890s, and were seen as a means to 'supply the missing link in trade unionism', part of a general move to greater working class unity.[24] The first such organisation began in 1894 and retained until 1941 the title Yorkshire Federated Trades Councils in earnest of efforts to achieve more of a co-ordinating function than ever proved possible. It took up some matters that touched on trades councils in Yorkshire as a whole, getting greater representation in the welfare services and arranging meetings for the exiled South African trade union leaders in 1914. The Lancashire and Cheshire federation was set up between 1897 and 1902. In 1913 it organised the blacking of a furniture firm in dispute with workers in both Bradford and Nottingham, and in 1917 was able to co-ordinate the activities of working class representatives on labour exchange advisory committees well enough to arrange a simultaneous boycott in different parts of the region.[25] Such combined action, however, remained rare, and there is little evidence that before 1918 the councils looked to the federations to perform functions of any importance. There were seven federations with 361,586 affiliates in 1901, declining to five and 304,968 in 1911. There was some expansion after the first world war, when some federations which combined electoral and industrial bodies were established, along with others to strengthen trade unionism in areas where it was weak, such as Wessex, North Wales, Hampshire and the Isle of Wight.[26]

After the formation of the Joint Consultative Committee in 1925 the first serious efforts were made to stimulate the work of the federations. The full-time officials at the TUC saw these bodies as a means of building regional organisation along the lines first proposed by the Webbs in the 1890s. However, the trades councils were never reconciled to the power that such arrangements would give to full-time officials, nor with the fact that they would have to work with the regional machinery of the unions themselves. Union leaders remained suspicious of anything that seemed to give the councils greater authority. Torn between these competing suspicions, the federations were doomed, up to the 1940s at least, to inhabit a sort of bureaucratic limbo with limited value to the movement.

The JCC encouraged the establishment of new federations and the affiliation of the trades councils to them. By 1930 there were said to be nineteen in existence, and though this figure was often repeated during the '30s only ten of them could even be persuaded to reply to a circular of 1938 about expanding their work. The General Council made a number of efforts to bring them into the work of the movement, mobilising them in the abortive campaign against the 1927 trade disputes Bill, and using them to organise educational activities. A 1937 meeting of federation secretaries did not get very far, because local leaders would not agree to the affiliation of union district committees, and the TUC refused to provide any finance.[27] During the '20s and '30s the Yorkshire and Lancashire and Cheshire bodies continued to co-ordinate some local activities, but more useful work was probably done by those federations which strengthened a number of weak trades councils in a small area, as happened in

Kent, Monmouth and Essex. Efforts by the TUC to set up a larger regional organisation to cover all of South Wales were strongly resisted in the area. In London the separate trades councils began to hold their own meetings in 1928 under the auspices of the London Trades Council, to which they had always affiliated, and in 1936 voted down a TUC proposal for area organisation under full-time officials in the capital.[28] It is not surprising to find that at Leeds in 1935 'mention was made of the Federation's inability to do much in the way of co-ordinating existing Yorkshire councils', and at Aylesbury four years later so little work was being performed by the Home Counties and Buckinghamshire federation that it was thought that 'the question of continued affiliation will have to be seriously considered'.[29] In more recent times efforts to relate the work of the trade union movement to such bodies as regional health authorities, and the increasing power of the TUC, have made possible the establishment of more stable regional machinery. However, federations inevitably remain somewhat remote from rank-and-file trade unionists and dominated by permanent officials.

Appendix two

Numbers of trades councils and affiliates 1894–1938

The figures given here are for the numbers of trades councils active in each of the years from 1894 to 1938, together with their total affiliated membership. Up to 1925 these are based on figures published by the Labour Department of the Board of Trade and the Ministry of Labour in the *Abstract of Labour Statistics* and the *Labour Gazette*. From 1926 to 1938 the Ministry of Labour did not publish these totals, but continued to collect individual membership figures. The statistics section of the Department of Employment now has in its possession three manuscript folders which contain details of trades councils membership from 1911 to 1938, and the author was kindly granted access to them. They have been used to calculate numbers of trades councils and affiliated membership from 1926 to 1938, as well as the figures from 1913 for Northern Ireland. Since the latest published figures have been used in all cases before 1926, they will be found to vary somewhat from figures compiled in the past, for example by G. D. H. Cole for his *British Trade Unionism Today* (1939), p. 190. Ministry of Labour statistics have been preferred to those published by the TUC after 1926, which included only those local bodies 'recognised' by the General Council.

It is important to note that no total figures of the type given here can claim any great precision or accuracy. In the first place, many trades councils publish only approximate figures for their membership, or else give the total membership of the affiliated union branches rather than the numbers on which fees were paid. Secondly, and especially about 1918, there are considerable problems in identifying industrial as opposed to electoral bodies. An attempt has been made to include only trades councils performing industrial functions in these totals, and to exclude all bodies whose work was purely electoral, even when they had some such title as 'Trades and Labour Council'. However, the distinction between industrial and electoral activities was seldom precise, though it had to be clearer after the 1927 Trade Disputes Act. The third difficulty lies in the fact that there are many gaps in the statistics in the possession of the Department of Employment. When local organisations did not send in a figure for a particular year, those for the previous year or the one after have been used, or the nearest available one. No doubt some similar procedure was adopted in the published figures. Finally, a number of bodies with only the most fleeting existence are included, but others of the same sort could easily have been missed. The great majority of them are listed in the second part of the appendix.

The main sources used for the various years are as follows:

1894–5: Tenth Abstract of Labour Statistics, 1902–4 (PP 1905 LXXVI Cd. 2491)

1896 : Eleventh Abstract of Labour Statistics, 1905–6 (PP 1907 LXXX Cd. 3690)

1897–8: Sixteenth Abstract of Labour Statistics, 1911–13 (PP 1913 LXXX Cd. 7131)

1899–1909: Seventeenth Abstract of Labour Statistics (PP 1913 LXXX Cd. 7733)

1910–13: *Ibid.* and Eighteenth Abstract (PP 1926 XXIX Cmd. 2740)

1914–23: Eighteenth Abstract . . .

1924–5: *Labour Gazette*, 1926, p. 308.

1926–38: Calculated from manuscript folders in the possession of the statistics section of the Department of Employment.

The figures for total trade union membership are taken from H. Pelling, *A History of British Trade Unionism* (1963 edn.), pp. 268–70.

	(a) Northern counties		(b) Yorkshire		(c) Lancashire, Cheshire, IoM	
1894	12	45,005	22	77,339	39	230,618
1895	11	37,741	22	86,104	40	215,383
1896	12	46,547	22	83,888	41	221,398
1897	13	37,310	23	91,061	41	210,395
1898	13	29,276	22	85,181	41	203,041
1899	13	32,117	22	85,741	43	197,967
1900	12	30,848	24	92,888	44	198,360
1901	12	31,072	26	91,389	45	220,411
1902	13	28,202	25	95,506	47	232,014
1903	14	34,882	25	95,348	47	238,477
1904	15	38,442	26	97,676	49	235,631
1905	15	39,052	26	99,046	51	249,806
1906	14	39,067	27	103,206	53	264,873
1907	14	43,808	28	105,532	53	282,592
1908	15	44,168	28	111,869	54	296,544
1909	15	40,179	27	104,107	55	298,293
1910	12	42,000	30	107,000	55	297,000
1911	12	53,000	30	116,000	54	357,000
1912	12	43,000	32	140,000	54	374,000
1913	14	60,000	35	152,000	58	403,000
1914	16	60,000	38	179,000	62	403,000
1915	16	63,000	40	190,000	62	403,000
1916	16	59,000	40	179,000	65	424,000
1917	19	66,000	44	208,000	67	463,000
1918	25	109,000	43	251,000	69	468,000
1919	25	124,000	46	289,000	69	580,000

1920	25	144,000	47	275,000	72	635,000
1921	25	114,000	43	268,000	73	584,000
1922	24	105,000	42	265,000	71	525,000
1923	23	100,000	38	235,000	70	490,000
1924	22	101,000	38	212,000	69	459,000
1925	21	102,000	38	214,000	70	486,000
1926	23	118,588	40	193,473	72	516,422
1927	21	87,091	38	198,181	68	423,593
1928	19	61,414	36	186,057	65	368,716
1929	18	70,242	36	181,087	65	352,211
1930	19	70,767	35	174,119	63	349,433
1931	18	53,547	34	166,977	63	355,212
1932	19	61,104	34	158,285	66	349,912
1933	19	64,706	35	164,416	65	342,696
1934	22	83,842	34	176,343	63	329,258
1935	22	77,650	34	198,187	62	327,158
1936	25	87,455	36	198,417	60	314,845
1937	23	99,443	37	193,329	62	338,956
1938	23	94,627	38	210,307	62	331,658

	(d) North and West Midlands		(e) South Midlands and E. England	
1894	28	104,499	8	25,172
1895	30	120,642	7	22,938
1896	30	117,298	7	20,139
1897	30	117,649	7	18,788
1898	34	130,375	10	21,017
1899	32	120,508	10	22,158
1900	31	124,826	10	19,259
1901	32	135,928	10	17,932
1902	32	136,249	12	18,484
1903	37	145,815	15	22,012
1904	39	136,146	21	25,812
1905	37	143,857	23	22,730
1906	37	144,778	22	25,863
1907	38	152,444	26	27,029
1908	43	169,572	25	25,632
1909	45	173,660	24	27,624
1910	47	184,000	26	28,000
1911	48	193,000	28	42,000
1912	50	214,000	31	58,000
1913	53	266,000	39	74,000
1914	60	307,000	49	89,000
1915	62	333,000	48	91,000
1916	63	340,000	50	111,000
1917	68	408,000	62	149,000
1918	79	548,000	79	216,000
1919	81	611,000	87	268,000
1920	82	640,000	89	277,000
1921	79	549,000	95	244,000
1922	75	477,000	100	172,000
1923	70	436,000	97	173,000
1924	69	441,000	73	166,000

1925	69	430,000	70	161,000
1926	62	348,695	68	158,150
1927	58	319.065	57	135,163
1928	58	272,540	60	135,279
1929	54	233,000	57	132,437
1930	54	267,776	57	138,749
1931	54	253,681	57	137,807
.1032	56	255,971	59	134,324
1933	54	257,052	59	140,662
1934	54	247,490	59	143,658
1935	52	264,948	59	153,948
1936	53	281,198	61	154,909
1937	54	322,663	61	177,979
1938	55	390,548	59	171,173

	(f) London		(g) South-east		(h) South and west	
1894	4	71,432	13	11,348	3	4,904
1895	4	65,166	13	11,394	3	4,891
1896	4	58,311	13	12,813	3	4,826
1897	5	60,568	12	12,999	6	6,481
1898	4	59,833	12	11,950	6	7,270
1899	8	67,418	13	11,259	6	7,649
1900	9	78,055	13	11,904	6	9,672
1901	9	79,639	14	14,984	6	10,749
1902	10	80,989	15	15,058	6	10,693
1903	12	92,124	16	18,038	7	10,582
1904	15	107,926	16	18,021	8	10,352
1905	17	107,710	17	19,110	9	12,051
1906	19	115,408	18	18,980	9	12,021
1907	19	105,443	18	18,642	9	10,591
1908	19	102,390	18	17,232	9	10,381
1909	19	96,405	16	17,026	9	12,175
1910	16	89,000	26	30,000		
1911	16	108,000	25	38,000		
1912	16	103,000	32	44,000		
1913	17	103,000	41	67,000		
1914	19	115,000	49	79,000		
1915	18	118,000	48	86,000		
1916	20	133,000	52	94,000		
1917	20	155,000	65	143,000		
1918	22	212,000	89	216,000		
1919	25	265,000	95	260,000		
1920	24	306,000	100	274,000		
1921	24	285,000	97	230,000		
1922	24	249,000	91	186,000		
1923	24	260,000	87	156,000		
1924	26	247,000	52	91,000	28	70,000
1925	26	225,000	53	86,000	26	74,000
1926	30	239,199	52	60,726	29	59,212
1927	26	239,231	47	67,652	23	36,920
1928	25	239,967	43	59,875	20	41,192
1929	25	247,317	42	61,020	17	37,739
1930	24	223,736	43	59,349	15	32,407

1931	25	221,752	43	66,468	15	33,834
1932	25	220,886	43	67,282	15	32,960
1933	25	214,999	42	69,493	16	35,559
1934	25	211,029	43	72,195	15	33,705
1935	23	239,052	45	73,443	15	35,972
1936	22	274,987	45	70,099	19	43,788
1937	23	417,073	45	94,412	20	38,097
1938	22	424,696	48	104,899	21	46,487

	(i) Wales and Mon.		(j) Scotland		(k) Ireland (North only from 1913)	
1894	6	16,172	16	84,831	7	37,150
1895	7	15,422	16	87,128	9	36,263
1896	7	16,944	16	96,192	9	33,307
1897	6	16,705	17	102,297	9	34,074
1889	7	22,034	16	107,872	8	36,136
1899	7	23,366	18	99,759	5	37,055
1900	11	41,250	18	113,488	4	31,653
1901	11	43,782	16	120,116	6	27,071
1902	12	44,655	16	119,713	6	29,287
1903	14	47,817	17	112,862	7	27,645
1904	17	48,967	18	120,129	8	32,753
1905	18	52,383	18	121,552	7	33,822
1906	20	58,240	19	124,101	7	35,081
1907	20	67,727	20	133,269	6	37,979
1908	19	68,325	21	134,054	6	39,446
1909	20	62,961	21	135,446	7	29,243
1910	27	86,000	26	142,000	7	31,604
1911	27	84,000	30	155,000	8	39,266
1912	32	105,000	33	187,000	7	40,914
1913	36	126,000	35	230,000	1	14,000
1914	40	133,000	38	223,000	1	9,000
1915	42	139,000	41	233,000	1	10,000
1916	49	175,000	40	248,000	2	18,000
1917	64	205,000	46	300,000	2	32,000
1918	68	229,000	48	320,000	3	33,000
1919	68	237,000	51	344,000	3	26,000
1920	71	261,000	50	384,000	3	25,000
1921	67	227,000	46	360,000	3	28,000
1922	59	183,000	46	290,000	3	23,000
1923	54	177,000	45	285,000	3	27,000
1924	56	181,000	52	256,000	3	22,000
1925	52	158,000	53	284,000	2	24,000
1926	48	146,000	50	257,453	2	23,000
1927	41	132,000	42	223,310	2	13,500
1928	40	120,741	41	191,829	2	10,500
1929	41	108,755	41	186,117	2	10,180
1930	40	102,644	43	185,579	2	10,120
1931	38	92,672	43	163,951	2	8,220
1932	41	88,888	43	146,378	2	11,500
1933	37	90,061	44	163,373	2	11,250
1934	34	81,210	44	163,547	2	11,020
1935	32	75,291	45	185,600	2	10,720
1936	34	76,542	44	182,090	2	11,254

| 1937 | 33 | 76,675 | 44 | 176,448 | 2 | 11,232 |
| 1938 | 33 | 71,139 | 41 | 192,905 | 2 | 11,232 |

Totals

	(a) England and Wales		(b) United Kingdom		(c) All trade unionists
1894	135	586,603	158	708,784	1,530,000
1895	137	579,681	165	703,172	1,504,000
1896	139	582,164	164	711,663	1,608,000
1897	143	571,956	169	708,327	1,731,000
1898	149	570,077	173	714,185	1,752,000
1899	154	568,183	177	704,997	1,911,000
1900	160	607,062	182	752,203	2,022,000
1901	165	645,886	187	793,073	2,025,000
1902	172	661,860	194	810,860	2,013,000
1903	187	705,095	211	845,602	1,994,000
1904	206	718,971	232	871,853	1,967,000
1905	213	745,751	238	901,125	1,997,000
1906	219	782,438	243	941,620	2,210,000
1907	225	813,608	251	984,756	2,513,000
1908	230	846,013	257	1,019,613	2,485,000
1909	230	832,330	258	997,119	2,477,000
1910	238	863,000	271	1,036,604	2,565,000
1911	240	991,000	278	1,185,266	3,139,000
1912	259	1,081,000	299	1,308,914	3,416,000
1913	293	1,251,000	329	1,495,000	4,135,000
1914	333	1,365,000	372	1,597,000	4,145,000
1915	346	1,423,000	388	1,666,000	4,359,000
1916	355	1,515,000	397	1,781,000	4,644,000
1917	409	1,770,000	457	2,102,000	5,499,000
1918	474	2,249,000	525	2,602,000	6,533,000
1919	496	2,634,000	550	3,004,000	7,926,000
1920	510	2,812,000	563	3,221,000	8,348,000
1921	503	2,501,000	552	2,889,000	6,633,000
1922	486	2,162,000	525	2,475,000	5,625,000
1923	463	2,027,000	511	2,339,000	5,429,000
1924	423	1,980,000	478	2,258,000	5,544,000
1925	425	1,936,000	470	2,244,000	5,506,000
1926	424	2,041,326	476	2,321,779	5,219,000
1927	379	1,639,594	423	1,876,404	4,919,000
1928	366	1,485,781	409	1,688,110	4,806,000
1929	355	1,423,808	398	1,620,045	4,858,000
1930	350	1,418,980	395	1,614,679	4,842,000
1931	347	1,381,950	392	1,554,121	4,624,000
1932	358	1,369,612	403	1,527,490	4,444,000
1933	352	1,279,644	398	1,454,267	4,392,000
1934	349	1,378,732	395	1,553,299	4,590,000
1935	344	1,445,649	391	1,641-969	4,867,000
1936	355	1,502,240	401	1,695,589	5,295,000
1937	358	1,758,627	404	1,946,307	5,842,000
1938	361	1,845,534	404	2,049,671	6,053,000

II. Chief bodies included in the above totals

(a) Northern counties

Alnwick, 1917–24, 1926–28. Berwick, 1917–24. Bishop Auckland, 1905. Blaydon, 1898–1905, 1918–21, 1934. Blyth, 1904–9, 1926–28, 1934. Carlisle, 1889–92, 1897–1928, 1934. Chester le Street, 1915–27, 1934. Chopwell, 1896–?, 1920–29. Consett, 1910–37; joined Durham in 1939. Crook, 1913–21. Darlington, 1894. Durham, 1896–1910, 1932. Felling, 1918. Gateshead, 1918. Hartlepools, 1890–1910, 1916. Hartlepool West, 1917–26. Jarrow, 1921. Kendal, 1896. Maryport, 1914–34. Middlesbrough, 1880. Millom, 1918–26. Newcastle, 1873. Penrith, 1913–23, 1930. Redcar, 1917–26, 1929. Shildon, 1894–1910, 1913–16. South Shields, 1872. Stockton, 1890. Sunderland, 1884. Tynemouth, 1918–22, 1932. Workington, 1898. Windermere, 1921–31.

(b) Yorkshire

Ardsley East, 1912. Barnsley, 1891–1902, 1904. Batley, 1919 (with Dewsbury before that). Bingley, 1918. Bradford, 1872. Bridlington, 1907–12, 1921–25, 1939. Brighthouse, 1901 Birstall, 1920–30. Castleford, 1889. Chapeltown, 1918–?, 1929. Dewsbury, 1891. Doncaster, 1891–98,1901. Elland, 1916–28, 1933–35. Eston, 1915. Goole, 1908–21, 1924–30, 1939. Halifax, 1889. Harrogate, 1902. Hebden Bridge, 1900. Holmfirth, 1919. Huddersfield, 1885. Hull, 1880. Keighley, 1890. Leeds, 1860–62, 1864. Mexborough, 1891–1921, 1926. Mirfield, 1917–24. Morley, 1910. Normanton, 1893–1908, 1913–18, 1926. Ossett, 1904–09, 1912. Otley, 1912–27. Pontefract, 1910–18. Rawmarsh, 1906–31. Rotherham, 1891. Ripon, 1920–33. Saddleworth, 1914. Scarborough, 1885–86?, 1891–1928, 1936. Selby, 1913. Sheffield, 1867 (two competing bodies from 1908 to 1919 merged). Shipley, 1891. Skipton, 1907–22. Sowerby Bridge, 1892–1902, 1910. Spen Valley, 1892. Stanningley, 1897–1907. Todmorden, 1892. Wakefield, 1891. York, 1890.

(c) Lancashire, Cheshire and the Isle of Man

Accrington, 1887. Altrincham, 1895. Ashton under Lyne, 1886. Atherton, 1925. Bacup, 1904. Barrow, 1874. Birkenhead, 1892. Blackburn, 1889. Blackpool, 1893–1901, 1903. Bolton, 1859 or 1866. Bootle, 1915. Burnley, 1883. Bury, 1889. Chester, 1894. Chorley, 1890. Clayton le Moors, 1908–18. Clitheroe, 1901. Colne, 1893–1905, 1926–28. Congleton, 1906. Crewe, 1894. Darwen, 1890. Dalton, 1917. Douglas, 1894–1915, 1918–27. Droylsden, 1918–42. Earlstown, 1899. Eccles, 1897–1904, 1915. Ellesmere Port, 1913. Failsworth, 1921. Farnworth, 1894. Fleetwood, 1899–1900, 1904–22, 1925–27, 1932–35, 1937. Gorton, 1899. Great Harwood, 1905. Haslingden, 1892. Heywood, 1889. Horwich, 1891–1927. Hyde, 1881. Irlam, 1913. Lancaster, 1900. Leigh, 1895. Leyland, 1919. Littleborough, 1913–34. Liverpool, 1848. Macclesfield, 1890–1903, 1905. Manchester, 1866. Manchester Women's Trade Union Council, 1885–1918. Manchester Women's Trades and Labour Council, 1904–1918. Middleton, 1892. Milnrow, 1920–34. Morecambe, 1914–24. Northwich, 1893–1910, 1932. Oldham, 1867. Ormskirk, 1914–30. Padiham, 1893–1915, 1920. Prescott, 1916–30. Preston, 1867. Radcliffe, 1891. Ramsbottom, 1891. Rawtenstall, 1902. Rishton, 1909–19, 1922. Rochdale, 1875. Royton, 1919. Runcorn, 1894. St Helens, 1890. Sandbach, 1902–12. Southport, 1880. Stalybridge, 1887–1911? Stockport, 1889. Stretford, 1926. Swinton, 1914. Tyldesley, 1924. Ulverston, 1916–20, 1922–30, 1932. Walkden, 1914. Wallasey, 1906. Walton le Dale, 1917–36. Warrington, 1875. Westhoughton, 1906. Widnes, 1913. Wigan, 1890. Wilmslow, 1912–24. Winsford, 1905–17.

(d) North and West Midlands

Beeston, 1898–1907, 1915–21. Belper, 1898–1902, 1914–23. Bilston, 1911–26, 1932. Birmingham, 1866. Boston, 1914–23, 1924–29? Brierley Hill, 1916. Bristol, 1873. Bromsgrove, 1918–30. Burton, 1891. Buxton, 1903–22. Cannock Chase, 1913–21. Cheltenham, 1894. Chesterfield, 1893–1926, 1937. Cirencester, 1908–10, 1913. Coalville, 1894–1926, 1938. Coventry, 1889. Coleshill, 1920–30. Derby, 1891. Dudley, 1916. Evesham, 1918–26. Gainsborough, 1911–15, 1921–36. Glossop, 1892. Gloucester, 1890. Grantham, 1900. Grimsby, 1899–1908, 1909. Halesowen, 1918–27, 1934. Heanor, 1908–16, 1936. Hereford, 1903–10, 1912. Hinckley, 1894–1918, 1921. Ilkeston, 1895. Kidderminster, 1904–15, 1917. Leamington, 1903. Leek, 1902. Leicester, 1870. Lichfield, 1918–29. Lincoln, 1890. Long Eaton, 1886. Loughborough, 1892. Lydney, 1901–29. Malvern, 1919. Mansfield, 1894–1900, 1905. Newark, 1897. Newcastle, 1919. New Mills, 1909. North Staffordshire, 1892. Nottingham, 1890. Nuneaton, 1907. Oakengates, 1900–05, 1916–23. Oldbury, 1915. Oswestry, 1895. Redditch, 1908–22. Retford, 1911. Ripley, 1914. Rowley Regis, 1915. Rugby, 1903. Rugeley, 1918. Scunthorpe, 1895. Shrewsbury, 1903. Smethwick, 1904. Stafford, 1896. Stamford, 1915–26. Stapleford, 1914. Staveley, 1918. Stourbridge, 1901. Stratford, 1918. Stroud, 1908–24, 1932. Sutton Coldfield, 1903–23. Swadlincote, 1908–18. Tamworth, 1913–27. Tipton, 1913–16, 1927. Walsall, 1890. West Bromwich, 1891. Whitchurch, 1918. Willenhall, 1911–23. Wolverhampton, 1873. Worcester, 1891. Worksop, 1898–1905, 1914.

(e) South Midlands and eastern counties

Acton, 1916. Aylesbury, 1911. Banbury, 1904–09, 1914–24, 1941. Barking, 1912. Bedford, 1903. Bletchley, 1932. Brentford, 1917–27. Brentwood, 1919. Cambridge, 1916. Cambridgeshire, 1919–29. Chelmsford, 1899–1902, 1914–15, 1917–23, 1932. Cheshunt, 1917–36. Cromer, 1919. Dagenham, 1928. Dereham, 1918. Ealing, 1914. East Ham, 1903–08, 1913. Edmonton, 1915. Enfield, 1907. Felixstowe, 1902. Finchley, 1914–26?, 1936. Grays, 1904. Great Yarmouth, 1907. Halstead, 1914. Harrow, 1913–17, 1917–19, 1925. Harwich, 1918–27. Hayes, 1919–29, 1934. Hemel Hempstead, 1918–26, 1937. Hendon, 1918–21, 1926. High Wycombe, 1905. Hitchin, 1905–26, 1929 (North Hertfordshire to 1910). Ilford, 1909. Ipswich, 1885. Kettering, 1888. Kings Lynn, 1914. Letchworth, 1908. Leyton, 1914. Lowestoft, 1913. Luton, 1904. March, 1918. Northampton, 1890. Norwich, 1886. Oxford, 1887. Peterborough, 1898. Romford, 1910–24, 1927?. Rushden, 1912–27, 1939. St Albans, 1898. Slough, 1914. Southall, 1904–09, 1911. Southend, 1904–10, 1913. Stevenage, 1918. Stowmarket, 1917. Thetford, 1918–35. Tilbury, 1913–37. Tottenham, 1903. Twickenham, 1913. Uxbridge, 1918. Walthamstow, 1904. Watford, 1902 Wellingborough, 1902–06, 1911. West Ham, 1891. Willesden, 1903. Wolverton, 1911. Woodford, 1913. Wood Green, 1915.

(f) London

Battersea, 1894. Bermondsey, 1903. Bethnel Green, 1914. Brixton, 1899–1910. Camberwell, 1904–10, 1913. Chelsea, 1905–10, 1919. Deptford, 1893. Finsbury, 1919. Fulham, 1899 (known as South-western District until 1911). Greenwich, 1914–22, 1939. Hackney, 1900. Hammersmith, 1918. Hampstead, 1905–20, 1931. Holborn, 1922–26, 1937. Islington, 1903. Kensington, 1902–18. Lambeth, 1916. Lewisham, 1918. London, 1860. Marylebone, 1906. North Kensington, 1916–26?, 1938. Paddington, 1920. Poplar, 1900. St Pancras, 1900. Shoreditch, 1906. Southwark, 1904. Stepney, 1918. Wandsworth, 1904. Westminster, 1926. Woolwich, 1894.

(g) South-eastern counties

Aldershot, 1914–31? Andover, 1918. Ashford, 1912–25, 1930. Basingstoke, 1913. Bexhill, 1918. Bexley, 1908. Bournemouth, 1890. Brighton, 1890. Bromley, 1908. Canterbury, 1913–16, 1918. Chatham, 1894. Cowes, 1912–24, 1935. Croydon, 1891. Crayford, 1921. Dartford, 1911. Didcot, 1915–27. Dover, 1893–1908, 1914. Eastbourne, 1912. Eastleigh, 1913–34, 1936. Epsom, 1913. Erith, 1893. Faversham, 1915–32? (merged with Sittingbourne in 1938 as North East Kent). Folkestone, 1904–11, 1913. Gosport, 1921–28, 1933. Gravesend, 1903. Guildford, 1899. Hastings, 1894. Horsham, 1918. Kingston, 1923–24, 1926. Maidstone, 1862. Margate, 1913–27, 1935. Newbury, 1918. Newhaven, 1917. Newport, Isle of Wight, 1918–23, 1934. Penge, 1918–28. Portsmouth, 1887. Ramsgate, 1914–22, 1925. Reading, 1891. Reigate and REdhill, 1901–09, 1911. Richmond (Surrey), 1907–10, 1913–28, 1931. Sheerness, 1914–15, 1918–29. Sittingbourne, 1918 (merged with Faversham to become North East Kent in 1938). Southampton, 1890. Stone and Swanscombe, 1918–26, 1930–35. Sutton, 1918. Tonbridge, 1912. Tunbridge Wells, 1891–1916, 1918. Wimbledon, 1906. Winchester, 1918. Woking, 1913–26?, 1938. Worthing, 1918.

(h) South-western counties

Barnstaple, 1913–25, 1926–27, 1931–35. Bath, 1891. Bridgwater, 1913. Camborne, 1917–24. Castle Cary, 1918–28. Chippenham, 1912–18, 1920–23?, 1927–28. Devizes, 1916–21. Dorchester, 1918. Exeter, 1890. Frome, 1917–24, 1926. Glastonbury, 1920. Hayle, 1918–29.Melksham, 1917–29. Newton Abbot, 1914. Paignton, 1917–27. Poole, 1899–?, 1916. Plymouth, 1892–94, 1897. Radstock, 1913–27. Salisbury, 1914. Swindon, 1890. St Austell, 1916–24, 1935. Taunton, 1905–15, 1916–27, 1936. Torquay, 1912, Trowbridge, 1912. Tiverton, 1919–30. Weymouth, 1904. Westbury, 1917–25? Weston super Mare, 1867–1929, 1935. Yeovil, 1903.

(i) Wales and Monmouthshire

Abercarn, 1916. Aberdare, 1900. Aberavon, 1900–08. Abergavenny, 1918. Abergwynfi, 1916–27. Abertillery, 1903. Ammanford, 1917. Bangor, 1912–27. Barry, 1891–1903, 1914–17, 1920. Bedwas, 1915. Blackwood, 1906. Blaenavon, 1908. Blaina, 1912–35. Briton Ferry, 1900. Brynammon, 1920–25, 1928–29, 1936. Caerphilly, 1904. Cardiff, 1884. Carmarthen, 1905. Carnarvonshire, 1913–16. Colwyn Bay, 1914–27. Cwmamman, 1919. Deeside, 1911. Ebbw Vale, 1898. Gowerton, 1917–29? Holyhead, 1917–25. Llandaff, 1917–25. Llandudno, 1917–26. Llanelly, 1900. Llansamlet, 1914–30. Llantrisant, 1916. Maesteg, 1915–21. Merthyr, 1900. Mid-Rhondda, 1906–22. Milford Haven, 1916–24. Mold (Buckley), 1918. Morriston, 1904–30. Mountain Ash, 1920. Newport, 1889. Neath, 1892. Neyland, 1919–33, 1936–38. North Cardigan, 1913–26, 1930 (later became Aberystwyth). Pembroke Dock, 1912–25. Panteg, 1918–31, when it joined Pontypool. Penarth, 1911–18, 1920. Pengam, 1912. Pentre, 1907–22. Pontardulaid, 1903–33. Pontlottyn, 1916–27. Pontypool, 1904. Pontypridd, 1893. Porth, 1892–1922. Port Talbot, 1905–29. Risca, 1914–19, 1924. Rhyl, 1913–22. Rhymney, 1916. Rogerstone, 1917. Swansea, 1872, Tredegar, 1907. Tondu, 1913–23. Treherbert, 1905–23. Treorchy, 1916–22. Wrexham, 1902. Ystalyfera, 1917.

(j) Scotland

Aberdeen, 1868. Airdrie, 1924. Alloa, 1912–27. Arbroath, 1889–1909, 1912. Ayr, 1904. Ayrshire, 1897–1924, when it split into the next three and Kilmarnock. Ayr Burghs, 1924. Ayrshire South, 1924. Ayrshire North, 1924. Barrhead, 1917–25, 1937. Bathgate, 1917–19, 1923–25, 1933. Bo'ness, 1914. Bothwell, 1917–26, 1930. Burntisland, 1914. Brechin, 1923–28, 1931–36. Cambuslang, 1918–36. Carstairs, 1919–36. Clydebank, 1903. Coatbridge, 1910. Cowdenbeath, 1909.

Dumbarton, 1911–27, 1936. Dumfries, 1911. Dundee, 1885. Dunfermline, 1890. Edinburgh, 1866. Elgin, 1929. Falkirk, 1890. Galashields, 1913. Glasgow, 1858. Govan, 1890–1918. Greenock, 1889. Gretna, 1915–22. Grangemouth, 1925. Hamilton, 1910. Hawick, 1908. Inverness, 1892. Johnstone, 1910–29, 1936. Kilsyth, 1911–23, 1925–26. Kinross, 1918–31. Kirkintilloch, 1930. Kirkaldy, 1911. Kilmarnock, 1888–1901. Leith, 1904–21, when it joined Edinburgh. Methil, 1912–27. Montrose, 1891–1901, 1914–37. Motherwell, 1902. Paisley, 1891. Perth, 1897. Peterhead, 1913–26. Renfrew, 1906–20, 1925. Rutherglen, 1909. Sterling, 1907. Stornoway, 1924. Vale of Leven, 1899. Waterside, 1919. Wishaw, 1899–1922, when it merged with Motherwell.

(k) Northern Ireland

Belfast, 1881. Derry, 1916.

Notes

Chapter one. Introduction, pp. 1–7

1 There is an account of how trades councils functioned during the period covered here in appendix one.

2 B. C. Roberts, *Trade Union Government and Administration in Great Britain* (1956), p. 451; N. Barou, *British Trade Unions* (1947), p. 82; M. Turner-Samuels, *British Trade Unions* (1949), p. 80.

3 S. and B. Webb, *The History of Trade Unionism* (1894), p. 476.

4 There is more detail on what follows in A. Clinton, *Trades Councils from the beginning of the Twentieth Century to the Second World War* (London University PhD thesis, 1973), p. 8 f., and a much fuller account in W. H. Fraser, *Trades Councils in England and Scotland, 1858–1897* (Sussex University PhD thesis, 1967), partly reproduced in his *Trades Unions and Society. The Struggle for Acceptance, 1850–1880* (1974), pp. 42–9, etc. See also C. Richards, *A History of Trades Councils, 1860–75* (1920).

5 A. Aspinall, *The Early English Trade Unions* (1949), pp. 272–4; G. D. H. Cole and A. W. Filson, *British Working Class Movements, 1789–1875: Select Documents* (1951), pp. 152–8.

6 The Master and Servant campaign 'stimulated the development of trades councils as well as closer relations between them': see B. C. Roberts, *The Trades Union Congress, 1868–1921* (1958), p. 22, and D. Simon, 'Master and servant', in *Democracy and the Labour Movement* (1954), ed. J. Saville, especially pp. 176–7. The TUC was originally intended only as a meeting of representatives of trades councils 'and other similar Federations of Trades': A. E. Musson, *The Congress of 1868* (1955), p. 38.

7 Webb, p. 245. A more acceptable account of the so-called 'Junta' is given in Fraser's thesis, p. 105 f., and in his book, pp. 47–8.

8 Fraser's thesis, pp. 78–9.

9 H. A. Clegg, A. Fox and A. F. Thompson, *A History of British Trade Unions since 1889*, volume I, *1889–1910* (Oxford, 1964), p. 488.

Chapter two. Servants of the trade unions, pp. 8–28

1 What follows is intended to complement and extend the account of these matters that appears in Fraser's thesis, pp. 200–12. There is also a little on the topic in E. H. P. Brown, *The Growth of British Industrial Relations* (1959), pp. 185–6.

2 This is suggested in H. A. Turner, *Trade Union Growth Structure and Policy* (1962) pp. 271–2.

3 E. Dolléans and G. Dehove, *Histoire du Travail en France* (Paris, 1953), vol. I, pp. 161–2. S. Pollard and C. Holmes, *Documents of European Economic History*, vol. I, p. 537, give the 1806 law that set up the Lyons Conseil. A. L. Dunham, *The Industrial Revolution in France, 1815–48* (New York, 1955), p. 202, shows that British advocates may have overstated their success.

4 L. Amulree, *Industrial Arbitration in Great Britain* (1929), pp. 60, 65, 68.

5 On Dronfield see Mendelson *et al.* (1958), p. 24, and on Gilliver, who spoke to the 1866 Social Science Congress on the matter, see Corbett (1966), p. 37.

6 The quotations are in *Beehive Newspaper*, 25 August 1866, and given in C. Richards, *A History of the Trades Councils, 1860–75* (1920), p. 19. See also Fraser's thesis, p. 206, and his book, pp. 109–10.

7 Richards, p. 20. Fraser in *BSSLH* autumn 1969, p. 38, wrongly states that the Manchester body was the only one that existed before the '90s.

8 V. L. Allen, 'Origins of industrial conciliation and arbitration' in *International Review of Social History*, 1964; J. H. Porter, *Industrial Conciliation and Arbitration, 1860–1914* (Leeds University PhD thesis, 1968), summarised in 'Wage bargaining under conciliation agreements, 1860–1914', *Economic History Review*, second series, XIII, 1970. The quotation is on p. 475 of the article.

9 Porter's thesis, p. 87; Mendelson *et al.*, pp. 36–7; S. Pollard, *A History of Labour in Sheffield* (Liverpool, 1959), p. 134.

10 H. Crompton, *Industrial Conciliation* (1876), pp. 132–3, who wanted legal intervention, and L. L. F. Price, *Industrial Peace* (1887), p. 29, who favoured voluntarism.

11 This is most noticeable in the RSLO for 1890 (PP 1890–91 LXXVIII), especially p. 48.

12 RCL minutes of evidence (PP 1893–94 XXXIX), pp. 328–39; S. B. Boulton on 'Labour disputes and chambers of commerce' in *Nineteenth Century* June 1890. On the attitude of the London TC see Fraser's thesis, p. 210.

13 London CC ARs for 1901, p. 47 and 1904, p. 18; RSLO for 1905 (PP 1906 CXII); London CC ARs for 1915, p. 48 and 1912, p. 61.

14 C. E. Musgrove, *The London Chamber of Commerce from 1881 to 1914* (1914), p. 77; *The Chamber of Commerce Journal* July 1915, pp. 247–8.

15 Amulree, *op. cit.*, p. 98; London CC 1922 AR, p. 44.

16 Buckley (1955), pp. 44–5; L. Bather, *A History of the Manchester and Salford Trades Council* (Manchester University PhD thesis, 1956), pp. 28–9 and 296–8; RSLO for 1891 (PP, 1893–94 LXXXIII), pp. 325, 331, 352; Leeds TC Minutes for 7 June 1895 and 20 May 1897; Liverpool TC March 1891 AR, p. 14; Corbett (1966), pp. 56–7, and Birmingham TC June 1899 AR, p. 4.

17 RSLO for 1894 (PP 1895 XCII), p. 275, and for 1895 (PP 1896 LXXX) p. 237; S. Boulton 'The genesis of the Conciliation Act' in *Chamber of Commerce Journal* September 1896.

18 *Report on Rules of Voluntary Conciliation and Arbitration Boards and Joint Committees* (PP 1908 XCVIII), pp. xiii, 268–70.

19 Bolton TC 1916 JS, pp. xxxix–xl, and November 1914 AR, p. 6; *Eleventh Report of the Board of Trade Proceedings under the Conciliation Act 1896* (PP 1914 LXXIX), p. 106; RSLO for 1913 (PP 1914–16 XXXVI), p. xlix.

20 This information is on a typed sheet with the 1916 AR of the Nottingham TC in the LRD.

21 E. H. P. Brown (1959), p. 185, and Turner (1962), pp. 270–2 and 316.

22 Brown, pp. 117–18, 123.

23 T. Mann, 'The development of the labour movement' in *Nineteenth Century* May 1890, giving a verdict on the London plan; RSLO for 1891 (PP 1893–94 LXXXIII), p. 331, on Leeds. See also H. Crompton, *op. cit.*, p. 113, and Brown, p. 186.

24 On Cardiff and Leeds see RCL, *Minutes of Evidence before Group C* (PP 1892 XXXVI, c. 6795), pp. 38, 48, 173. On Hull see R. Brown, *The Labour Movement in Hull, 1870–1900, with special reference to New Unionism* (Hull University MSc (Econ.) thesis, 1966), p. 203.

25 R. Brown, p. 184, and RSLO for 1892 (PP 1894 LXXXIII), p. 186.

26 W. M. Burke, *History and Functions of Central Labor Unions* (New York, 1899), p. 118.

27 Sheffield T&LC April 1922 AR, pp. 5–6.

28 The quotation is from Connah's Quay T&LC 1917 Rules, p. 4, but similar statements can be found in Halifax T&LC 1890 Rules, and Wakefield T&LC 1920 and 1936 Rules. G. Howell (1896), p. 423.

29 W TU Coll E, Vol. IV, p. 316, for examples of bringing disputants together at Wrexham and Birmingham, and Preston T&LC 1917 AR, p. 7, for an example of acting as chairman. The Coventry quotation is in *Coventry Times* 23 July 1913.

30 RCL *Minutes of Evidence before Group C* (PP 1892 XXXVI), p. 557; Kettering TC Rules, nd but after 1893; Hartlepool Trade Union Council delegates card 1916–17; Oxford TC 1922 Constitution, p. 2.

31 Quoted in G. Tate, *London Trades Council, 1860–1950, A History* (1950), p. 90.

32 Aylesbury T&LC Rules, nd but before 1934, p. 8; D. Hardman, *1912–1937. The First Twenty-Five Years in the History of the Cambridge Borough Trades Council and Labour Party* (Cambridge, 1937), p. 12.

33 Liverpool TC 13 August 1919 Minutes.

34 See Fraser's thesis, pp. 105–6.

35 *LWC* 9 January 1914; Bather's thesis, p. 45.

36 Birmingham TC June 1898 AR, p. 3; Tate, *op. cit.*, p. 81, and London TC *Report of National Trade Union Conference held on Saturday January 1st 1898*, which mentions the attendance of forty trades councils. See also J. B. Jefferys, *The Story of the Engineers, 1800–1945* (1945), p. 147.

37 The dispute is described in H. Clegg, A. Fox and A. Thompson, *A History of British Trade Unions since 1889*, vol. 1 (1964), pp. 212–13. The Bradford TC collected over £200 in 1902 and £300 in 1903 (1903 YB, p. 8, 1904 YB, p. 25). It also circularised other local bodies – see Birmingham TC 4 April 1903 Minutes. Substantial amounts were raised at Liverpool (Hamling (1948), p. 34), at Leeds (1903 AR, p. 23), and elsewhere.

38 H. R. Hinkins, 'The Liverpool general transport strike, 1911' in *Transactions of the Historic Society of Lancashire and Cheshire*, 113, 1961, p. 181.

39 On the Black Country strike see J. Leask and P. Bellars, *'Nor shall the sword sleep ...' An Account of Industrial Struggle* (Birmingham ? nd, *c.* 1954), p. 14, R. Hyman, *The Workers' Union, 1898–1929* (Oxford University DPhil, 1968), p. 73, and *The Workers' Union* (Oxford, 1971), p. 53, and Birmingham TC 1912 AR, p. 9, 1913 AR, p. 4. On Leeds see J. E. Williams, 'The Leeds Corporation strike in 1913' in *Essays in Labour History, 1886–1923* (1971), ed. A. Briggs and J. Saville, and Leeds TC, 13 December 1913 and 2 April 1914 Minutes.

40 Wood Green TC 1923 Constitution.

41 L. Ulman, *The Rise of the National Trade Union* (Cambridge, Mass., 1955), p. 342.

42 T. Mann on 'The labour problem' in *Labour Elector*, 25 January 1890. A. Bennett, *Oldham Trades and Labour Council Centenary, 1867–1967* (Oldham, 1967). *LWC* 28 February 1913 for a Yorkshire Trades Councils Federation conference on hours of work and Leeds TC 27 April and 30 August 1912 Minutes on 'systematic overtime'.

43 Leicester TC 1913 YB, p. 11, and Connah's Quay T&LC 1917 AR wanted a forty-eight-hour week, and Liverpool TC 14 November 1917 Minutes and March 1918 AR, pp. 26–30, discussed the six-hour day. For a later call for shorter hours as a solution to unemployment see H. McShane, *Glasgow District Trades Council Centenary Brochure, 1858–1958* (Glasgow, 1958), p. 37.

44 Bennett, *op. cit.*, mentions such a list in Oldham in 1895, and Nottingham TC 1930 TUC Souvenir, p. 31, and July 1919 AR, pp. 23–30, the difficulty of getting trades to agree to one. Leeds TC 31 January and 27 February 1911 Minutes on disagreements about what firms were 'fair', and TUC 1891 Report, p. 63, for opposition to trades councils issuing fair lists.

45 Liverpool TC March 1918 AR, p. 7; Burton TC 1915 AR, p. 5.

46 For more on insurance collectors and shopworkers see below, pp. 24–5. On Blackpool see Blackpool TC *75th Anniversary History Report and Directory* (Blackpool, 1966), p. 10, and Liverpool TC 10 July 1912 Minutes.

47 E. Howe and H. Waite, *The London Society of Compositors. A Centenary History* (London, 1948), p. 197; Clegg *et al.*, p. 288; Brown's thesis, pp. 144, 180; W. A. Daley and A. Eades, *History of the Birmingham Trades Council, 1866–1916* (Birmingham, 1916), p. 30.

48 Bennett, *op. cit.*; Derby TC 1910 YB; Leeds TC Fair Contracts Committee Minute

Book 1894–1912 is with the TC Minutes in the City Archives and is summarised in R. Turner, *The Development of the Leeds Trades Council, 1889–1914* (Leeds University BA thesis, 1972).

49 Birmingham TC 6 December 1902 and 13 June 1908 Minutes for examples and Oxford TC 16 November 1904 Minutes for a letter from Leicester TC about whether contracts from their town were being carried out by 'fair' firms.

50 Manchester T&LC 1912 AR, p. 10; Birmingham TC 1912 AR, p. 8; *LWC* 2 March 1917.

51 Bennett, *op. cit.*; W. H. Chaloner, *The Social and Economic Development of Crewe, 1780–1923* (Manchester, 1950), p. 219; S. Maddock, *The Liverpool Trades Council and Politics, 1878–1918* (Liverpool University MA thesis, 1959), pp. 100–3, 177, Liverpool T&LC March 1896 AR, p. 6; *LWC* 2 and 23 August and 27 September 1912, and Leeds TC, 25 September 1912 Minutes.

52 E. P. Thompson, 'Homage to Tom Maguire', pp. 296–8 in *Essays in Labour History* (1960), ed. A. Briggs and J. Saville, makes some thinly substantiated suggestions along these lines. They are corrected for Leeds in Turner's thesis and in general in Fraser's, pp. 135 f. New unionists were 'warmly welcomed' to membership, according to Minutes for 2 October 1889, at Leeds. For even earlier examples see Fraser (1974), p. 211.

53 Nottingham TC 1930 TUC Souvenir, p. 31.

54 Brown thesis, p. 348; *Coventry Herald*, 7 October 1899, R. Hyman's book, p. 21; Oxford TC 1913 AR and 18 December 1912 Minutes; G. E. Cheshire, *Twenty Five Years of Progress. The History of the Aylesbury and District Trades Council* (Aylesbury, 1936), p. 16; Northampton TC June 1917 AR, p. 17.

55 Crewe T&LC 1906 AR; Hardman (1937), p. 13; Motherwell TC October 1913 AR, p. 3.

56 Newport T&LC 1909 Rules, p. 4. There is an identical form of words in Chapeltown T&LC 1919 Rules, p. 3, and similar formulations in Chorley T&LC 17 May 1918 LRD Reply, Burnley T&LC 1903 Rules, p. 3, Macclesfield TC 1928 Rules, p. 3, and Bristol T&LC 1922 Rules, p. 3, where the first object is 'to promote the organisation of workers within the appropriate Trade Unions'.

57 Huddersfield T&LC 1911 AR, p. 2; Aberdeen TC 1912 AR, p. 9; Manchester T&LC 1912 AR, p. 11; *LWC* 25 May and 23 August 1912. There are similar complaints mentioned in Leicester TC 1915 YB, p. 4.

58 Leeds TC, 29 June and 14 July 1904 Minutes. Similarly the Birmingham TC rebuffed charges that extra pay for overtime was leading to the loss of orders to local firms (1905 AR, p. 5).

59 Bristol TC Minutes, quoted in 1931 TUC Souvenir; Bradford T&LC 1899 YB, p. 54; Bennett (1967); E. Button in *Industrial Review* October 1931.

60 TUC 1905 Report, pp. 53–4, describes some of the local meetings; Birmingham TC 3 May 1902 Minutes.

61 Sunderland T&LC February 1910 AR, p. 13; York T&LC 1911 YB, p. 5.

62 Peterborough TC, *Diamond Jubilee, 1899–1959* (Peterborough, 1959), p. 15; Birmingham TC 1910 AR, p. 5.

63 Aberdeen TC 1913 AR, p. 6; *LWC* 2 December 1911; Liverpool TC 13 December 1911 and 8 January 1913 Minutes.

64 Examples in Motherwell TC October 1913 AR, p. 10, and Bournemouth TC 1939 Constitution.

65 S. and B. Webb (1920), pp. 444–5; K. D. Buckley (1955), p. 28; Liverpool T&LC March 1909 AR, p. 6; Edinburgh TC 1918 AR, p. 7; Birmingham TC 2 May 1923 Minutes.

66 Cheshire (1936), p. 24; Northampton TC 1924 AR, p. 6, and 1925 AR, p. 4.

67 Lancashire and Cheshire Federation of TCs January 1914 HYR, p. 4.

68 On the MEA see Clegg *et al.*, pp. 449–50. For support at Liverpool TC see Maddock's thesis, pp. 171–2, as well as many references in the Minutes for 1917

and 1918 and March 1919 AR, pp. 7–8; and at Rawtenstall TC *50th Anniversary, 1902–52* (Rawtenstall, 1952), p. 10. On the AUCE see F. Hall and H. P. Watkins, *Co-operation* (1937), pp. 17–19, together with H. B. Williams, *History of the Plymouth and District Trades Council from 1892 to 1952* (Plymouth, 1952), pp. 17–19, on a particularly bitter local dispute where the Trades Council supported the co-operative society against a union branch which had seceded after a decade of membership. For sharp arguments in Leeds about the AUCE see *LWC* 5 November 1915 and 14 January 1916.

69 *CFT* 31 January, 25 April and 1 August 1890 on negotiation and agitation on this question by the Bolton and Heywood trades councils. In later years trades councils negotiated rearrangements (Bradford T&LC 1909 YB, p. 3, and 1931 YB, p. 9; Batley T&LC 1928–29 AR, p. 7), and organised ballots to find out what periods were favoured by the workers (Radcliffe TC 1906 AR; Huddersfield T&LC August 1914 AR, p. 6, and *CFT* 30 January 1914 on Hebden Bridge TC).

70 Birmingham TC 4 November 1899 Minutes and *Town Crier* 9 February 1923; Liverpool TC 19 and 26 February 1908 and 12 October 1910 Minutes; Oxford TC 30 April 1902 Minutes; Oldham T&LC 1917 YB, p. 29.

71 For May Day demonstrations see Coventry T&LC 1919 AR, p. 16, when many workers struck, and Bolton TC 1925 AR, when £20 was spent. On the bands see Peterborough TC (1959), pp. 15–17, and A. Tuckett, *Up with all that's down! A History of Swindon Trades Council, 1891–1971* (Swindon, 1971), p. 10.

72 Bradford T&LC 1906 YB, p. 7; Manchester T&LC 1919 AR, p. 3.

73 Bennett (1967); Bather's thesis, p. 88; Warrington T&LC September 1904 AR, p. 5; Stockton T&LC 1911 AR, pp. 59–61.

74 Croydon T&LRC 1914 AR, pp. 16–18; Blackpool TC (1966), p. 21.

75 Leeds TC 26 May 1899 and 13 March 1901 Minutes, T&LC 1923 AR, p. 11, and 1931 AR, p. 2; Hebden Bridge TC 1916 AR; Hull TC 1926 TUC Souvenir, pp. 74–6; *The Worker* (Bournemouth) March 1914 describes conditions at a number of halls, including Barrow.

76 B. T. Hall, *Over Sixty Years. The Story of the Working Men's Club and Institute Union* (1922), mentions co-operation with the WEA and Ruskin College but nothing on other parts of the movement. In Blackpool the secretary resigned in 1925 rather than work with the Union – TC (1966), p. 29.

77 Rochdale TC *Victory Bazaar Handbook* 1929, p. 3, mentions such problems.

78 Spen Valley T&LC 1924 AR; E. Burns, *The General Strike, May 1926. Trades Councils in Action* (1926), p. 100; Watford TC *Souvenir Programme of the Official Visit of the Prime Minister* (Watford, 1931).

79 Bradford T&LC 1913 YB, p. 11; Leeds TC 25 June and 6 September 1911 Minutes; Birmingham TC 1927 AR, p. 18, and R. P. Hastings, *The Labour Movement in Birmingham, 1927–45* (Birmingham University MA thesis, 1959), pp. 40–1; Wolverhampton T&LC 1915 YB, p. 23.

80 Support for the *Citizen* is in Bradford T&LC 1913 YB, p. 11, and Birmingham TC 1912 AR, p. 9, and 1913 AR, p. 29. Examples of action in support of the *Herald* can be found in *Herald* 24 April 1915 from Tamworth TC, and Cardiff T&LC 1923 YB, p. 25.

81 Motherwell TC October 1913 AR, p. 5; Manchester TC 1938 AR, p. 1, 1937 AR, p. 2.

82 *Dictionary of Labour Biography*, vol. 1 (1972), ed. J. Bellamy and J. Saville, p. 287, on Bevin; McShane (1958), p. 3, for Shinwell. On Manchester, Bather's thesis, pp. 229–30.

83 Middlesborough T&LC 1916 AR, p. 3; Bradford T&LC 1915 YB, p. 5.

84 The history of the union can be read in two duplicated documents issued by the Musicians' Union; E. S. Teale, *The Story of the Amalgamated Musicians' Union* (originally published in 1929), and H. Radcliffe, *Notes on the Musicians' Union* (1969). See also Clegg *et al.*, pp. 228–9.

85 Brown thesis, p. 375; Birmingham TC 1913 AR, p. 5; Leicester TC 1915 YB, p. 18; Plymouth TC December 1915 HYR, 1923 AR, p. 9; Hyde T&LC March 1915 AR.
86 Liverpool TC March 1897 AR, p. 10; Bolton TC 1923 AR, p. 8.
87 For an example of the former see Birmingham TC 1907 AR, p. 29, and of the latter Birkenhead T&LC 1909 AR, p. 5, Burton T&LC 1915 AR, p. 20, and Cardiff T&LC 1925 YB, p. 36.
88 Birmingham TC 19 October 1907 Minutes; *Herald* 1 May 1915; Liverpool TC 8 March 1918 Minutes.
89 Birmingham TC 1924 AR, p. 6, *Town Crier* 12 September 1924; Wolverhampton T&LC 1915 YB; Manchester T&LC 1924 AR, p. 3.
90 *Southern Worker* June 1919 on the establishment of a branch of insurance agents by the Bournemouth TC. Wartime claims are mentioned in *LWC* 3 May 1918 and Oldham T&LC 1917 YB, pp. 25–6. For negotiations for the Prudential agents see Birmingham TC 1905 AR, pp. 5–6, and for the Britannic agents, Stockton T&LC 1924 AR.
91 Examples include Birmingham TC 3 December 1898 Minutes, *LWC* 26 September 1913 and Bolton TC 1922 AR, p. 7.
92 The Bolton TC started a campaign for half-day closing in 1897 with ultimate success (1916 JS p. xxix, and *Centenary Brochure* [1966] p. 11). Carlisle T&LC February 1914 AR for an appeal to shop early. For discussion of a boycott of the Home & Colonial Stores see Oxford TC 12 January 1915 Minutes. On Swansea and Cardiff see Clegg *et al.*, p. 227, and on Liverpool, Maddock's thesis, p. 90.
93 Support for the shop hours Bill is described in Birmingham TC 5 March 1899 Minutes and action against the living-in system in Liverpool TC 31 July 1907 Minutes. Successful negotiation with local firms is mentioned in Stockport T&LC 1906 AR and Leeds TC 30 January 1907 Minutes, and a successful boycott in East Ham TC&LP 1925 AR, securing union recognition and higher wages.
94 Oxford TC 21 August and 28 September 1904, 31 May and 28 June 1905, 24 June, 22 July, 28 October 1908, 29 March 1911, 30 December 1914, 24 February and 30 June 1915 Minutes; Aberdeen T&LC 1917 AR, p. 6, for a local joint committee and Brighton TC 1907 AR, p. 6, for the settlement of a 'misunderstanding'. For the AUCE see above, p. 21.
95 The Women's Trades Council existed from 1895 to 1918. There was also a Women's Trade Union Council from 1904, which was more militant on the question of women's suffrage. (Bather's thesis, pp. 93–113.)
96 Bradford T&LC 1903 YB, p. 13; Oxford TC 1913 AR. In 1907 the Rochdale Trades and Labour Council stopped those who had members of their family not union members from being officers. (*Industrial Review* July 1931, pp. 10–11.)
97 *Herald* 27 March 1915 on such efforts at Walthamstow and 6 March 1915 on efforts at Deptford, Greenwich and Lewisham; Liverpool T&LC March 1908 AR, p. 3; Halifax TC 1914 AR; Great Harwood T&LC 1916 AR, pp. 4–5.
98 *LWC* 31 July 1918; A. Tropp, *The Schoolteachers* (1957), p. 150. For unsuccessful efforts at affiliation see Huddersfield T&LC 1918 AR, p. 8, and Blackpool TC 1917 TUC Souvenir, p. 63. For affiliations see Nottingham TC 1908 TUC Souvenir, p. 81, where association with the CTA is claimed to be the first, *LWC* 5 April 1918, Bolton TC November 1917 AR, p. 7, Liverpool TC 20 October 1917 Minutes. In Northampton in 1917 a CTA delegate was president and the Head Teachers' Association joined. The CTA remained active. (TC June 1917 AR, pp. 2, 13 and 1921 AR, p. 1.)
99 Northampton TC 25 June 1915 AR, p. 19, records that the organiser of the Agricultural Labourers' Union 'cordially thanked delegates for what they had done for his Union', a role which continued in later years – 1921 AR, p. 7, 1923 AR, p. 5, 1924 AR, p. 8. Hardman (1937), p. 15, mentions the work of the Cambridge body with the Agricultural Wages Board in 1917–21 and 1924.
100 Birmingham TC *Enquiry into the Condition of Labour in Bakehouses* (Birmingham,

nd, 1910?). Support for legislation in London TC in *Daily Herald* 9 March 1911, and Liverpool TC 26 April 1911 Minutes. Cardiff T&LC 1923 YB, p. 23, supports a law to prohibit night baking altogether.

101 Birmingham TC 20 August and 1 October 1898 Minutes.

102 Birmingham TC 5 September 1908 Minutes and 1913 AR, p. 5; Bradford T&LC 1909 YB, p. 5; Stockton T&LC 1924 AR.

103 *LWC* 2 June 1916; Bolton TC 1924 AR, p. 5, 1925, AR, p. 5, 1933 AR, p. 7.

104 Liverpool TC 12 May 1909 Minutes on a conference. Nottingham TC 1910 AR, p. 5, on a march. Manchester T&LC 1923 AR, p. 4, for negotiations.

105 Coventry T&LC 1910 AR, p. 10, for the setting up of a branch and Motherwell TC October 1913 AR, pp. 15–16, and October 1916 AR, pp. 10–11, for negotiations on their behalf.

106 Maddock's thesis, pp. 90–1, and Liverpool TC March 1916 AR, pp. 5–8; Oxford TC 26 March 1913 Minutes; J. E. Williams (1971); *Plebs* March 1924, p. 100.

107 Hamling (1948), p. 23, and *YFT* 1 September 1899 on efforts to reduce the number of deliveries on Saturday by the Huddersfield TC. There were numerous protests during the war against the proposed abolition of Sunday deliveries (e.g. Liverpool TC 8 March 1916 Minutes, Oldham T&LC 1917 YB, pp. 24–5 and Bolton TC November 1916 AR, p. 6, where it was claimed that this agitation had been successful).

108 Birmingham TC 21 July 1906 Minutes for a protest about conditions and Portsmouth T&LC 1912 AR, pp. 22–3 for the Grievance Committee.

109 The main sources on this are V. L. Allen 'The National Union of Police and Prison Officers' in *Economic History Review*, 1953 (2nd series, XI), and G. W. Reynolds and A. Judge, *The Night the Police went on Strike* (1968). The latter account, though more detailed, is inaccurate and undocumented.

110 At Birmingham the TC once supported a 'Police and Citizens' Friendly Association' which aimed 'to secure one day's rest in seven for the Police forces of this country' (5 February 1910 and 6 May 1911 Minutes, and 1911 AR, p. 8) and at Carlisle the T&LC protested about the failure of the local Watch Committee to receive a delegation on police grievances (February 1914 AR, p. 11).

111 Liverpool TC 10 January 1917 Minutes and Maddock's thesis, p. 170 (Reynolds and Judge, p. 156, wrongly state that the Liverpool branch was not set up until after the London strike of August 1918); on Manchester see Reynolds and Judge, p. 36; Rawtenstall TC (1952), p. 12; Watford TC&LP 1918 Handbook, p. 9.

112 Birmingham TC 1918 AR, p. 6; Reynolds and Judge, p. 65; *Times* 31 August 1918. *LRDMC* October 1918. says that the success of the strike 'was very largely due to the support of the London Trades Council and its officials'.

113 The Birmingham meeting is reported in *Town Crier* 10 October 1919. (Their efforts were 'highly appreciated' by the branch secretary, who got the highest vote in the election for the TC executive early in 1919 [26 October and 2 November 1918 and 4 January 1919 Minutes]). *CFT* 23 August 1918 on the Lancashire federation and 7 March and 29 August 1919 on the Ashton branch, including its ultimate winding up. B. Roberts (1958), p. 326, on the TUC.

114 On the last point see Allen, p. 137, and Reynolds and Judge, pp. 129, 131–3. W. J. Davis later claimed to have been active in breaking the 1919 strike (TUC 1919 Report, p. 143).

115 Reynolds and Judge, pp. 114, 121, 142; Allen, p. 143.

116 T. L. Drinkwater, *A History of the Trade Unions and Labour Party in Liverpool, 1911 to the Great Strike* (Liverpool University BA thesis), pp. 45–6, *Times* 5–7 August 1919, Hamling, *op. cit.,* pp. 39–40, and Liverpool TC 3 August and 13 August Minutes.

117 Preston T&LC 1919 AR, p. 7, Finchley TC 1919 AR, p. 8, and Doncaster T&LC 1920 AR give examples of appeals of this type. In Birmingham Municipal Library with the TC Minutes in the collection entitled *Circulars Leaflets, etc. 1866–1966*

there are a number of leaflets issued by the TC on behalf of the dismissed strikers together with a letter of 27 August 1919 signed by 120 of them which repudiates their union in a pathetic but vain attempt at reinstatement.

Chapter three. From individualism to social reform, pp. 29–53

1 J. B. Jeffreys, *Labour's Formative Years, 1849–1875* (1948), pp. 135–6, reprinting *Reynolds Weekly Newspaper* 10 November 1861; G. Howell, *The Conflicts of Capital and Labour Historically and Economically Considered* (1876), p. 426; *Industrial Review* October 1931 on Nottingham. On trades councils and politics in the 1860s and '70s, see Fraser (1974), pp. 122 f.

2 *Manchester City News*, 11 January 1879, quoted in Bather's thesis, p. 17; B. Webb, *Our Partnership* (1948), p. 21, on George Shipton; on Liverpool, Maddock thesis, p. 72; on Leeds, Thompson (1960), p. 295 f. See also above, pp. 15 and 202 n. 52.

3 Cardiff TC 1889 AR, p. 3; Swansea Labour Association 1928 TUC Souvenir, p. 47; Maddock thesis, p. 270.

4 Quotations given in Maddock, p. 65; Liverpool TC March 1895 AR, p. 8.

5 Liverpool TC March 1915 AR, p. 7; Nottingham TC 1908 TUC Souvenir, p. 37; Bennett (1967; Birmingham TC June 1900 AR, p. 10; Harrogate TC 1909 Rules.

6 Corbett (1966), p. 79; Tuckett (1971), p. 24; S. and B. Webb (1920), p. 420; E. Halévy, *History of the English People in the Nineteenth Century*, vol. 5 (1951), p. 220.

7 Newcastle T&LC 1907–8 AR, p. 13.

8 C. L. Mowat, *The Charity Organisation Society 1869–1913. Its Ideas and Work* (1961), chapter 6 and p. 168. Few trades councils would have disagreed with the view of *The Syndicalist* of July 1914 of 'the doctrine-ridden inhuman pedants who belong to the Charity Organisation Society; people whose feelings and instincts are not strong enough to enlighten their brains as to the absurd narrowness of their economic theories'.

9 The Workmen's National Housing Council is dealt with below, p. 38. The Oxford TC (Minutes, 24 June 1908) affiliated to the National Anti-Sweating League, and the Birmingham TC attended conferences run by it and co-operated with the local branch in running an exhibition (1906 AR, p. 7; 1907 AR, p. 4, and 9 December 1909 Minutes). For the National Committee for the Break-up of the Poor Law and the National Committee for the Prevention of Destitution, Webbian front organisations set up to publicise their views on the welfare services, see Birmingham TC 3 September 1910 Minutes; Northampton TC 20 June 1915 AR, p. 14, B. Webb (1948), p. 422 f; and A. M. McBriar, *Fabian Socialism and English Politics* (Cambridge 1962), p. 277.

10 They also supported such proposals as amalgamating all local charities under the control of the municipality in York in 1912 (*Victoria History of the County of Yorkshire. The City of York* (1961), ed. P. M. Tollett, p. 44) and at Bolton six years later (TC 1918 AR, p. 3).

11 McShane (1958), pp. 16–17; *YFT* 7 July 1897; Birmingham TC June 1893 AR, pp. 3–5, and 4, 13 October 1902 Minutes; Oxford TC 24 May 1905 Minutes.

12 Bradford T&LC 1902 YB, pp. 5, 51 f, 1903 YB, p. 62 f. Leeds TC 5 July 1900 Minutes for support for a Manchester TC view about the need for more direct labour, a sentiment which may have arisen from efforts to enforce FWCs.

13 On this movement see E. E. Barry, *Nationalisation in British Politics. The Historical Background* (1965), especially chapters 2 and 10. Local bodies seem to have had less to do with the Georgeite 'English Land Restoration League' which in 1902 became the 'English League for the Taxation of Land Values' – but for exceptions see Stockton T&LC 1911 YB, pp. 28–33, and Portsmouth T&LC 1912 AR, p. 29.

14 *Land and Labo[u]r* June 1891, July 1893, May 1895, May and July 1896.

15 *Ibid.,* May 1896, June and November 1897, June 1900, June 1902, Leicester TC

1919 YB, p. 11. 'The Nationalisation of Land should be the first plank on any political platform of Labour,' said the president in TC 1922 YB, p. 15.

16 *Land and Labour* March and June 1899, Leeds TC 21 May 1901 Minutes, 1903 AR, p. 12. For 'Housing and Land Reform' conferences see *Land and Labour* April, May and November 1901, May 1902, Birmingham TC 19 August 1899 Minutes, Liverpool TC 7 November 1906 Minutes.

17 Bennett (1967);Warrington T&LC September 1904 AR, p. 21; Dorchester TC 1918 Rules, p. 3.

18 LNS May 1917 AR, pp. 12–15; *Land Nationaliser* January 1920; Bennett; Leeds T&LC 1923 AR, p. 3; *Town Crier*, 2 March 1923 for an address to the Birmingham TC on 'Land – the Master Key'; Northampton TC 1919 AR, p. 2, 1922 AR, p. 6, 1925 AR, p. 4.

19 Barry, p. 100 f on this. For examples of affiliation see Birmingham TC 5 September 1913 Minutes and Peterborough TC (1959), p. 15. For support for the policy see Birmingham TC 1907 AR, p. 5, Wolverhampton TC 1913 YB, p. 9, Carlisle TC February 1917 AR, p. 6, and Hastings T&LC 1918 AR.

20 McShane (1958), pp. 16–17; Accrington T&LC January 1905 AR, p. 7; Newcastle T&LC 1907–08 AR, p. 9; Birmingham TC 1907 AR, p. 3. Connah's Quay 1917 AR gives a list of industries that should be taken over.

21 Leicester TC 1916 YB, p. 6; Bolton TC 1919 AR, p. 3; Nottingham TC July 1918 AR, p. 5. For an example of support for 'Mines for the nation' see Bradford T&LC 1921 YB, p. 5.

22 Tate (1950), pp. 79–80; Liverpool TC March 1915 AR, pp. 8–9.

23 For protests in the Mann case see Sheffield T&LC 23 April 1912 Minutes, *Daily Herald* 13 May 1912 on the Dartford T&LC, and Coventry T&LC 1912 AR. For protests on the Tom Mooney case see London TC 1918 AR, p. 4, Liverpool TC March 1919 AR, pp. 8–9 and Birmingham TC 10 August 1918 Minutes.

24 *LWC* 30 May 1914 for Leeds TC protesting against the imprisonment of Mrs Pankhurst because the 'women's movement had the same great ideals as ours'. Similar support is in Liverpool TC 25 July 1906 and 23 July 1910 Minutes.

25 For support for Irish nationalism at Manchester see T&LC 1917 AR, p. 3, and S. Bünger, *Die sozialistiche Antikriegebewegung in Grossbritannien, 1914–17* (Berlin 1967), p. 153, and at Leeds, *LWC* 30 April 1920. Visits of Annie Besant to many local organisations just after the war led to support for the Indian cause – Northampton TC 1919 AR, pp. 7–9, Bradford T&LC 1918 YB, p. 3, and Bolton TC 1919 AR, p. 4, which was convinced by Mrs Besant to support 'the self-determination of all nations.'

26 On the 'coolie labour' issue see Leeds T&LC 1903 AR, p. 11 and Warrington T&LC September 1904 AR, p. 9. For protests against the employment of foreigners on British ships during the war see Leicester TC 1917 YB, p. 19, on 'moral social and industrial considerations', and Southampton TC on 'using the workers of other countries to lower the wages in this country' (*LWC* 30 June 1916).

27 On the Congo, Birmingham TC 1907 AR, p. 29; on China, Portsmouth T&LC 1912 AR, p. 5; on anti-semitism and the Czar see Bather's thesis, pp. 121–2; on the anti-alien resolutions see J. A. Gerrard, *The English and Immigration, 1880–1910* (1971), pp. 173, and on the Boer war, R. Price, *An Imperial War and the British Working Class. Working Class Attitudes and Reactions to the Boer War, 1899–1902* (1972), pp. 74, 82–9.

28 For examples see Belfast Trade Union Council *1851–1951. A Short History* (Belfast, 1951), p. 14, and Blackpool TC, *75th Anniversary History Report and Directory* (Blackpool, 1966), p. 21. For other examples, including correct prognostications about the lack of effect of such motions, see Sheffield T&LC 24 September 1912 Minutes and A. Clinton 'Trades councils during the first world war' in *IRSH*, xv, 1970, p. 204.

29 *Daily Herald* 2 March 1914 and *Federationist* April 1914 on London; Birmingham

TC 16 August 1913, 7 March 1914 Minutes; Huddersfield T&LC August 1914 AR, p. 5, on a local meeting, and *Industrial Review* February 1932, on another, remembered many years after as an 'outstanding event', at Doncaster.

30 R. Brown's thesis, p. 78; Bellamy and Saville (1972), p. 283; Fraser's thesis, p. 158; J. Walton and R. Clements, *Hats off to the People!* (Leicester, 1951), p. 13; W. H. Chaloner (1950), pp. 270–2.

31 Brown, p. 395; Leicester TC 1894 AR, pp. 14–15, 1895 AR, pp. 14, 19, 24–5; Leeds TC 6 April 1895 Minutes.

32 Birmingham TC 12 November 1904 Minutes, and Corbett (1966), p. 90; Bradford T&LC 1905 YB, p. 13. For other examples of support for public works programmes see Liverpool T&LC 1904 AR, pp. 14–17 and Bolton TC 1916 JS pp. xxxv–xxxvi. On support for this policy in the labour movement in this period see D. Mackay, D. Forsyth and D. Kelly, 'The discussion of public works programmes, 1917–35: some remarks on the labour movement's contribution' in *IRSH,* XI , 1966, p. 9.

33 K. D. Brown, *Labour and Unemployment, 1900–14* (Newton Abbot, 1971), pp. 23, 40, 44, 64; Carlisle TC February 1909 AR, p. 7; Oxford TC 20 December 1905, 31 January and 28 February 1906 and 23 September 1908 Minutes.

34 On the Act see R. C. Davison, *The Unemployed* (1929), p. 37. On local attitudes see Birmingham TC 1907 AR pp. 5–6, and Liverpool TC 27 June 1907 Minutes. The latter quotation is in I. Mitchell 'Organised labour and the unemployed problem' in *Nineteenth Century* July 1905. K. D. Brown, 'Conflict in early British welfare policy: the case of the Unemployed Workmen's Bill of 1905' in *Journal of Modern History* 42, 1971, p. 625, says that 1,000 local protest meetings took place the winter before the Act was passed and many of them were sponsored by the trades councils.

35 Sunderland T&LC February 1909 AR, p. 8.

36 Hamling (1948), pp. 27, 35, T&LC March 1894 AR, p. 5 March 1903 AR, pp. 14–17, March 1909 AR, pp. 3–4, 26 September 1906 and 16 September 1908 Minutes, Maddock's thesis, p. 179, Drinkwater's thesis, pp. 64–7.

37 D. G. Hanes, *The First British Workmen's Compensation Act, 1897* (New Haven, Conn., 1968), p. 114; Bennett (1967); Birmingham TC June 1900 AR, p. 6, June 1901 AR, p. 3; Bradford T&LC 1907 YB, p. 7, 1908 YB, p. 2, 1909 YB, p. 71; *LWC* 6 August 1915.

38 Bradford T&LC 1899 YB, pp. 34, 54–6, 1901 YB, pp. 37, 40–3, 1902 YB, pp. 37–40, 1906 YB, p. 7, 1912 YB, p. 53 f; Birmingham TC 6 August 1898, 2 December 1899 Minutes; Huddersfield TC August 1918 AR; Halifax T&LC 1914 AR, 1928 AR, 1928 Rules, 1935 AR, p. 7.

39 The North Staffordshire TC used some of the surplus from the money collected for running the 1905 TUC to give donations to local hospitals (1942 JS, p. 10), the Bolton TC celebrated its fiftieth anniversary in 1916 by a levy of $\frac{1}{2}d$ per member for the infimary (1916 JS, p. xxxix), and the Peterborough body ran a fete in 1918 which bought the first x-ray equipment for the local hospital (TC (1959), p. 15).

40 B. Abel-Smith, *The Hospitals, 1800–1948* (1964), pp. 135–6; Belfast Trades Union Council (1951), p. 5; Liverpool TC 8 July 1908 Minutes and March 1914 AR, p. 12; Birmingham TC June 1903–December 1904 AR, pp. 8–9, and 1909 AR, p. 26; Oxford TC 30 May 1900, 28 May 1902, 26 March 1903 Minutes; Leicester TC 1910 YB, pp. 26–8.

41 Blackpool TC 1938 TUC Souvenir, p. 77, and (1966), p. 31; Mackinven, (1959), p. 55; Sheffield T&LC 1925 AR, p. 39.

42 Birmingham TC 26 March and 4 June 1898 Minutes and Paisley T&LC May 1913 AR, p. 3, for sub-committees. Southampton T&LC 1906 AR, p. 3, and Liverpool T&LC March 1914 AR, p. 11, and TC March 1915 AR, pp. 10–14, for systematic investigation into specific cases.

43 In Birmingham demands for such representation were made as early as the 1880s (Corbett (1966), p. 46), and they are also recorded in Sunderland T&LC February

1909 AR, p. 6. The Leicester Trades Council got a representative in 1909 apparently because of their work on the Saturday Fund (1910 YB, p. 10, and *LWC* 28 March 1913). A Huddersfield delegate was on a governing body in 1913 (T&LC August 1913 AR, p. 3) and at Oldham there was a representative at least from 1915 (T&LC 1916 YB, p. 28).

44 For example, Northampton TC 1924 AR, p. 9.
45 On this see F. Brockway, *Socialism over sixty years. The Life of Jowett of Bradford (1864–1944)* (1946), p. 84, and *Federationist* June 1914.
46 Middlesbrough T&LC 1915 AR, and Oldham T&LC 1917 YB, pp. 16–20 and secretary's letter to delegates of 30 July 1917 on maternity centres. J. H. H. Williams, *A Century of Public Health in Britain, 1839–1929* (1932), on the Royal Commission, and Liverpool TC 10 April Minutes and Northampton TC 1920 AR, p. 9, and 1921 AR, p. 6, on various meetings and discussions. The Leeds TC had a representative of the Leeds Committee for Combating Venereal Disease, but he soon resigned on the grounds that it was dominated by 'Chapel and Church-going people prepared to condemn and trying to force a remedy in connection with this ailment which was not a remedy in his opinion' (*LWC* 29 June 1917).
47 Leeds TC 25 August 1909 Minutes; *Victoria County History of the County of Yorkshire. East Riding*, vol. 1 (1969), ed. K. J. Allison, p. 266; Hackney TC 1900 Rules, p. 2; E. Cheshire (1936), p. 17; Clydebank T&LC 1913 AR, p. 9; Ripley T&LC 1915 AR; W. H. Chaloner (1950), p. 277.
48 Workmen's National Housing Council 1912 AR for details of policy, including efforts to implement the 1909 Housing Act. It was set up in 1898 and the secretary was Fred Knee, later for a short while London Trades Council secretary. Birmingham TC 5 October 1901 Minutes mentions a special delegate meeting, and Southampton T&LC & LRC 1919 AR the organisation of a conference in association with it. Other affiliates included Liverpool (T&LC 18 September 1916 Minutes), Sunderland (T&LC February 1909 AR, p. 6) and Northampton (TC June 1917 AR, p. 17). McShane (1958), p. 19, says that a Scottish association was set up as the result of meetings run by the Glasgow Trades Council in 1899 and 1900. In 1918 the organisation changed its name to the National Labour Housing Council and came almost entirely under the wing of the Labour Party. For other influences see p. 32 above.
49 Birmingham TC *Housing of the Working Classes* (leaflet of 28 October 1896); Oxford TC 27 June 1900 Minutes; Bradford T&LC 1914 YB p. 53 f; Ripley T&LC 1915 AR; Carlisle T&LC February 1914 AR, p. 5; *Federationist* December 1914; Rawtenstall TC (1952), p. 13.
50 The origin of the story is perhaps W. Gallacher, *Revolt on the Clyde* (1936), pp. 52–8.
51 *LWC* 23 January 1914 for the first quotation and 30 January and 13 March on the local rent strike that followed. W R&P, p. 205, on Camberwell. On the claimed responsibility see *Woolwich Pioneer* 24 June 1921 and Coventry TC 1915 AR, p. 7. There are numerous references in the *Federationist* during 1915 to local agitation on the question and the Manchester T&LC issued a pamphlet entitled *Report on the Increase of House Rents in Manchester and Salford since the commencement of the War.*
52 Bennett (1967) and material on tenants' meetings with the Oldham T&LC Reports in the LRD Collection.
53 Hartlepools Labour League 1917 AR; Hull TC 1924 TUC Souvenir, p. 6.
54 Preston TC 1919 AR, p. 6; Doncaster T&LC 1920 AR; Manchester T&LC 1919 AR, p. 5, 1923 AR, pp. 6–7, 1924 AR, pp. 5–6, and Bather's thesis, p. 199; Birmingham TC 1918 AR, p. 4, and Northampton TC June 1917 AR, p. 16.
55 Coventry T&LC, 1894 AR, p. 3. For the Act see H. C. Barnard, *A History of English Education from 1760* (1969 edn), p. 179, and for representation see Maddock's thesis, p. 105, on Liverpool, Southport TC 1940 TUC Souvenir, and

Blackpool TC 1917 TUC Souvenir, p. 59; G. A. N. Lowndes, *The Silent Social Revolution* (1969), p. 164, mentions the importance of the involvement of trade unionists in the success of the committees. Local technical courses were advertised in 1917 at Edinburgh (Mackinven, p. 53) and advocated at Connah's Quay (T&LC 1917 AR).

56 Wolverhampton T&LC 1913 YB, p. 17.

57 R. Brown's thesis, pp. 354 and 396, on anti-clerical feeling at Hull, and York T&LC 1911 YB, p. 10, where a protest about lack of representation on the Town's Education Committee was in these terms: 'Religious denominationalism is evidently preferred to special knowledge, wide experience and broad sympathies.' The Manchester T&LC was on the Manchester Association for Unsectarian Education from 1895 to 1897, until it refused to support an FWC.

58 VCH Yorkshire, East Riding (1969), p. 259; Leeds TC May 1886 AR, p. 4; S. Bryther, *The Labour and Socialist Movement in Bristol* (Bristol, 1929), p. 35; Nottingham TC 1930 TUC Souvenir, p. 27; Birmingham TC 3 June 1899 Minutes.

59 See W. P. McCann *Trade Unionist, Cooperative and Socialist Organisations in relation to Popular Education, 1870–1902* (Manchester University PhD thesis, 1960), p. 395, on defence of the Higher Grade schools from the trades councils of London, Manchester, Birmingham and the Yorkshire Federation, and pp. 439–441 on enormous meetings in Leeds and Manchester at which trades council speakers were prominent in opposition to the 1902 Bill. See also Birmingham TC 5 July and 6 September 1902 Minutes; Bradford T&LC 1902 YB, p. 9; Tuckett (1971), p. 25.

60 Bather thesis, p. 120, and Manchester T&LC 1912 AR, p. 12; Birmingham TC, 21 March 1903 Minutes for the election of the first delegate, and 1906 AR, pp. 20–3, for his report; Liverpool TC March 1911 AR, p. 13 f, and March 1915 AR, pp. 17–28; Warrington T&LC September 1904 AR, p. 8; Cheltenham T&LC 13 October 1918 reply to LRD circular.

61 For efforts along these lines see Leeds TC 18 May 1909 Minutes and Liverpool T&LC March 1913 AR, p. 12 f.

62 *Report of the National Conference for the State Maintenance of Children, 20 January 1905*; twenty-eight trades councils were represented at this conference which, according to Ramsay MacDonald, was arranged by 'the SDF working through the London Trades Council' (quoted in P. Thompson, *Socialists, Liberals and Labour. The Struggle for London, 1885–1914* (1967), p. 266). For similar conferences run at Bradford and Liverpool in 1905 see *Federationist* June 1916 and Liverpool T&LC March 1905 AR, pp. 15–17. On the SDF campaign in general see M. E. Buckley, *The Feeding of Schoolchildren* (1914), pp. 25–6, and on the support for the campaign from trades councils see L. Andrews, *The Education (Provision of Meals) Act, 1906* (London University MEd thesis 1966), pp. 119, 161, 238. On attempts to improve details of its working see Liverpool TC March 1913 AR, p. 11, and for efforts to get it applied, Grimsby T&LC 1915 YB, p. 5.

63 Liverpool TC March 1902 AR, p. 11, records a series of lectures to the TC itself by an Extension lecturer and Connah's Quay T&LC 1916 and 1917 ARs, and 21 May 1918 LRD Reply refer to classes arranged by the T&LC. Nottingham TC 1930 TUC Souvenir, p. 35, on support for local authority classes.

64 A Mansbridge, *The Kingdom of the Mind. Essays and Addresses, 1903–37* (1944), p. 15; Bolton TC 1916 JS, p. xxxix; Birmingham TC June 1907 AR, p. 7; W. J. Souch, *The History of the Reading Branch of the Workers' Educational Association, 1904–54* (Reading, 1954), pp. 6–7 and A. Mansbridge, *An Adventure in Working-class Education, being the Story of the Workers' Educational Association, 1903–1915* (1920), p. 17; Belfast Trades Union Council (1951), p. 11; A. J. Allaway, *The First Fifty of the WEA in Leicester* (Leicester, 1959), p. 5; Northampton TC 1920 AR, p. 8; Blackpool TC (1951), p. 19; A. J. Allaway, *Challenge and Response. WEA Midland District, 1919–69* (Leicester 1969), p. 61; M. Stocks, *The Workers' Educational Association. The First Fifty Years* (1953), p. 99.

65 J. F. C. Harrison, *Workers' Education in Leeds. A History of the Leeds branch of the Workers' Educational Association, 1907–57* (Leeds, 1957), pp. 7–9.

66 G. D. H. Cole and R. Postgate, *The Common People, 1746–1946* (1971 edn), p. 560; Blackpool TC (1966), p. 21.

67 Bolton TC 1924 AR, pp. 3–4; Northampton TC 1925 AR, pp. 5–6; Leeds T&LC 1923 AR, p. 3, 1929 AR, p. 2; Nottingham TC 1930 TUC Souvenir, p. 35, 1929 YB, p. 16. A visitor to the Glasgow TC in 1920 found the two groups coexisting there: W. Williams, *Full up and Fed up. The Workers' Mind in Crowded Britain* (1921), p. 157.

68 On South Wales see B. Simon, *Education and the Labour Movement, 1870–1920* (1965), p. 335, and Cwmannan T&LC 1925 Draft Rules, which aim to provide 'Independent Education'. The Glasgow TC Rules, nd, *c.* 1943 wanted education 'building up the Trade Union Movement to make it capable of taking control of production and distribution'.

69 Examples include Halifax T&LC 1914 AR and Doncaster T&LC 1920 AR, where there was also a small library.

70 On Liverpool see March 1902 AR, pp. 14–16 and Maddock thesis, pp. 41–3, and on Birmingham there is a great deal of material in the Municipal Library collection, including leaflets on the exhibition of 1901, the Minutes of the Finance Committee for 1901–02 and of the TC Bursaries' Standing Committee, 1902–36. See also Corbett (1966), pp. 62–4, 184.

71 Luton TC *Thirty Years of Progress. Short History of the Trade Union Movement in Luton and District* (Luton, 1941), p. 14, shows the TC chairman in such a position of authority as to address the local Adult School Movement on their work. For similar expertise see E. Button, *Trade Union Education* (Nottingham, 1924) – the reprint of a speech first heard at the Trades Council by a future secretary and regional WEA leader.

72 Nottingham TC 1930 TUC Souvenir, p. 35, July 1919 AR, pp. 3–4; Huddersfield T&LC August 1916 AR, p. 7; Tuckett (1971), p. 55; Middlesbrough T&LC 1917 AR.

73 *Federationist* June 1916, Bradford T&LC 1917 YB, pp. 49–58 and Labour Party 1917 Report, pp. 135–6. For a discussion of these proposals at Leeds see *LWC* 27 October 1916.

74 Above p. 35; J. E. Williams, *The Derbyshire Miners* (1962), p. 455; Reading T&LC March 1909 AR; Leicester TC 1910 YB, p. 10; Portsmouth T&LC 1912 AR, pp. 22, 50; Oxford TC 21 January, 21 December 1907, 3 November 1909 and 26 October 1910 Minutes; Birmingham TC 1905 AR, p. 4, 1906 AR, p. 7; Davidson (1929), p. 38; W. A. Orton, *Labour in Transition* (1921), p. 13.

75 Fraser's thesis, p. 420; Bolton TC 1916 JS, p. xxx; Nottingham TC 1930 TUC Souvenir, p. 33; Birmingham TC 1906 AR, p. 6.

76 R. V. Sires 'The beginnings of British legislation for old-age pensions' in *Journal of Economic History*, XIV, 1954, p. 234; A. Wilson and G. S. MacKay, *Old Age Pensions. An Historical and Critical Study* (1941), pp. 15, 21 f; T. S. and M. B. Simey, *Charles Booth, Social Scientist* (1960), pp. 160–9.

77 TUC 1896 Report, p. 50.

78 On the beginnings of the campaign see F. H. Stead 'A free State pension for every aged person: the demand of organised labour. A campaign of conferences' in *Review of Reviews* April 1899. In the Birmingham Municipal Library are the manuscript minutes of the local conference, which was run by the Trades Council. The main source on what follows is F. H. Stead, *How Old Age Pensions Began to Be* (1909) and a bound volume of NCLOAP publications in the British Museum entitled *Ten Years' Work for Old Age Pensions, 1899–1909*.

79 Corbett (1966), pp. 80–1; Birmingham TC 1 April and 6 May 1899, 6 April and 2 September 1905 Minutes, 1905 AR, p. 6, 1907 AR, p. 6, NCLOAP July 1900 AR, pp. 4, 11–21.

80 NCLOAP July 1904 AR, p. 5, July 1901 AR, *YFT* 4 August 1899 and Sires, p. 244.
81 *Report of the Old Age Pension Conference held in the Memorial Hall . . . January 1902*, at which twelve trades councils were represented was an example of activity before the election. J. E. Williams (1962), p. 242, on the Derbyshire miners. For examples of activity during the 1906 general election see Rotherham T&LC 1906 AR, Doncaster TC 1906 AR and NCLOAP July 1906 AR. For local protests about the delay that followed in granting the measure see Leeds TC 27 March 1907 Minutes, Mansfield TC 1955 YB, p. 10 (in November 1907), and TUC 1907 Report, pp. 181–2, 1908 Report, p. 57.
82 Sunderland T&LC February 1909 AR, p. 12; Liverpool TC 24 April 1907 and 13 May 1908 Minutes.
83 H. J. Hoare, *Old Age Pensions* (1915), pp. 150–9; Wilson and McKay, p. 47.
84 Stead, p. 113.
85 K. D. Brown (1971), pp. 139–40; Bradford T&LC 1911 YB, p. 7; York T&LC 1911 YB, p. 7; Liverpool TC 14 September 1910 Minutes; Birmingham TC 1 October 1910 Minutes. Leeds TC also worried that the local exchange was used to break a strike at Leicester (*LWC* 26 September 1913).
86 Leicester TC 1910 YB, pp. 6, 8. Visits are reported in Carlisle TC February 1910 AR, p. 9, Clydebank T&LC 1913 AR, p. 12, Birmingham TC 10 December 1909 and 23 July 1910 Minutes, Leeds TC 5 January and 27 April 1910 Minutes. The quotation is from Stockton T&LC 1911 AR, pp. 46–8.
87 York T&LC 1911 YB, p. 7; Birmingham TC 1909 AR, p. 7.
88 Huddersfield T&LC August 1911 AR, p. 9, and Plymouth T&LC December 1913 HYR. On Oxford see 29 January 1913 and 7 and 14 July 1914 Minutes. On Liverpool see T&LC March 1910 AR, p. 9, March 1911 AT, pp. 4, 7, March 1916 AT, p. 28, and 22 February 1911 Minutes, for a similar threat to withdraw, only defeated by the casting vote of the chairman.
89 T. S. Chegwidden and G. M. Evans, *The Employment Service of Great Britain* (1934), pp. 31–2, 92–7, 259–60. See also A. Clinton (1970), pp. 214–15. For representation see Nottingham TC 1917 AR, p. 26, and Bolton TC 1917 AR, p. 5, and for a struggle to secure it, Finchley TC 1919 AR, pp. 7–8.
90 *CFT* 17 September 1920. Demands for such facilities came from Crewe TC in 1912 (Chaloner (1950), p. 212) and Hull in TC 1926 AR, p. 9.
91 'The Picket' on 'The labour exchanges: are they a failure?' in *CFT* 29 June 1917; Blackpool TC (1960), p. 28; Gainsborough T&LC 1921 AR; *Town Crier* 26 May 1922.
92 Report of the Committee of Enquiry into the Work of Employment Exchanges (PP 1920 XIX) and W. H. Beveridge, *Unemployment. A Problem of Industry* (1931), pp. 303–4.
93 Quoted in S. Pollard, *The Development of the British Economy, 1914–67* (1969), p. 35. For similar sentiments at a trades council see Aberdeen TC 1913 AR, p. 9.
94 Liverpool TC 8 March and 24 May 1911 Minutes; Birmingham TC 1 July 1911 Minutes and Corbett (1966), p. 84.
95 North Staffordshire TC JS (1938), p. 10; Birmingham TC 1912 AR, p. 7; Aberdeen TC 1913 AR, p. 9; Leicester TC 1913 YB, p. 4; Birmingham TC 6 and 26 April 1912 Minutes; Manchester T&LC 1912 AR, p. 11; Bradford TC 1912 YB, p. 5, with original emphasis.
96 Liverpool T&LC March 1912, p. 12; Leicester TC 1912 YB, p. 4; Sheffield TC 1913 AR, p. 4.
97 It had 500 members in 1912 (Bradford T&LC 1912 YB, p. 5). Birmingham TC 6 April 1912 Minutes also discussed a scheme on these lines.
98 P. Cohen, *The British System of Social Insurance* (1932), pp. 3, 27; W. J. Braithwaite, *Lloyd George's Ambulance Wagon* (1957), pp. 128, 134, 320; Halévy, *op. cit.*, Vol. 6, pp. 300–1.

99 Plymouth T&LC December 1913 HYR and 1936 TUC Souvenir, p. 46; Carlisle T&LC February 1916 AR, p. 9.
100 Cohen, p. 145; F. Tillyard and F. N. Ball, *Unemployment Insurance in Great Britain, 1911–48* (Leigh on Sea, 1949), pp. 6–7.
101 Birmingham TC 1912 AR, p. 7, and 6 July 1912, 4 January 1913 Minutes; *CFT*, 27 June 1917.
102 Liverpool T&LC March 1913 AR, p. 10.
103 For a full account see Fraser's thesis, pp. 321–525.
104 A. W. Humphrey, *A History of Labour Representation* (1912), pp. 96–103; G. D. H. Cole, *British Working Class Politics, 1832–1914* (1941), p. 113. On London see P. Thompson (1967), pp. 102–6, and G. Tate (1950), p. 79.
105 E. P. Thompson (1960), p. 309; P. Thompson, p. 155. B. Barker, 'Anatomy of reformism: the social and political ideas of the Labour leadership in Yorkshire', *IRSH*, XVIII, 1973, p. 7, also emphasises the role of Yorkshire trades councils as 'the focal point for trade union participation in politics'.
106 LRC 1900 Report, pp. 2–7, 17–18, 1901 Report, pp. 7, 16. The Leeds TC 1 July 1900 Minutes for a decision to affiliate which was apparently not thought to depend on support for independent representation, although the Derby TC left the LRC over this issue in 1903 – C. F. Brand, *The Labour Party. A Short History* (1965), p. 17.
107 Cole (1941), pp. 174, 228–32; F. Bealey and H. Pelling, *Labour and Politics 1900–06* (1958), pp. 236–9; R. T. MacKenzie, *British Political Parties* (1963), pp. 463, 468; Carlisle TC February 1905 AR, p. 9; Accrington TC January 1905 AR, p. 6; R. Gregory, *The Miners and British Politics, 1906–14* (1968), p. 156, on Chesterfield; D. Cox, 'The Labour Party in Leicester: a study in branch development', *IRSH*, VI, 1961, p. 210.
108 LRC 1902 Report, p. 8, 1903 Report, p. 26, 1905 Report, p. 43.
109 Grimsby T&LC 1906 AR; Liverpool TC 30 May 1906 Minutes and Maddock's thesis, p. 197.
110 Oldham T&LC 1906 AR, p. 3; Radcliffe TC 1908 AR, p. 15.
111 R. I. McKibbin, *The Evolution of a National Party. Labour's Political Organisation, 1910–24* (Oxford University DPhil, 1970), pp. 75–83, 52–3; Labour Party 1914 Report, p. 3; Bather's thesis, p. 172, and *Manchester Guardian* 10 March 1910; Leicester TC 1911 YB, p. 7.
112 G. D. H. Cole, in C. Richards (1920), pp. 6–9; McKibbin thesis, pp. 196–7; Liverpool T&LC March 1913 AR, p. 9, and Maddock's thesis, pp. 227–38; Rochdale T&LC 1914 AR, p. 6; Oldham T&LC 1914 AR, pp. 5–7; Burton T&LC 1915 AR, pp. 4–5; Woolwich T&LC&LP *Memorandum on Unification of Industrial and Political Forces* (Woolwich, 1917). R. McKibbin, *The Evolution of the Labour Party, 1910–24* (1974), pp. 28–31, 33–9, describes in more detail the efforts to modify local electoral machinery and make it strong enough to affiliate to the national Party. The situation varied a great deal according to the relative strength of trades councils, ILP branches and other working class bodies.
113 Bury St Edmunds T&LC 9 May 1918 LRD Reply; Ipswich T&LC 1918 AR, p. 3.
114 Clydach T&LC, Hendon TC and Hereford TC LRD Replies of 22 May and 1 and 6 June 1918. D. Carmichael's opposition to such fusion is given in *CFT* 29 March 1918 and there is a debate on these and related issues in *CFT* 12 April, 19 April, 3 May, 31 May 1918. The best report of the conference is in *The Guildsman* April 1918.
115 *Carlisle Journal* 4 June 1915 and *CFT* 5 April 1918 for suggestions along these lines at the time and McKenzie (1963), p. 480, and Maddock's thesis, p. 233, for later repetitions of it.
116 *Labour Organiser* October 1922, p. 14, August 1923, p. 3; *Plebs* February 1924, pp. 61–3.
117 For an example see M. Cole in *New Standards* January 1924, p. 87. See also pp. 00–00 below.

118 H. Morrison on 'Trades councils: should they be separate from borough Labour Parties?' in *Labour Organiser* October 1924, pp. 14–15.

Chapter four. Recognition and radicalisation, pp. 54–80

1 A. Marwick, *The Deluge. British Society and the First World War* (1967), pp. 217–18.
2 See also p. 34 above. Birmingham TC 5 August 1914 Minutes; Bennett (1967); Nottingham TC July 1914 AR, p. 6.
3 Memorandum on Steps taken for the Prevention and Relief of Distress Due to the War (PP 1914 LXXXI Cd. 7603), p. 4.
4 For an account of some aspects of the work of this body see R. Harrison on 'The war emergency workers' National Committee, 1914–20' in *Essays in Labour History 1886–1923* (1971), ed. A. Briggs and J. Saville.
5 WEWNC *Report August 1914 to March 1916* (1916), p. 4; Liverpool LRC 1914 AR, p. 7; Peterborough TC (1959), p. 15; STUC 1916 Report, p. 37.
6 W R&P vol. I, pp. 197–204. In Bethnal Green eight trade union representatives out of sixty were 'not considered enough' (pp. 183–95).
7 H. MacKinven (1959), p. 53; Huddersfield T&LC August 1915 AR, p. 4; Grimsby T&LC 1915 YB, pp. 10, 29.
8 Wolverhampton T&LC 1915 YB, p. 12; *Federationist* January 1915; G. D. H. Cole, *Labour in Wartime* (1915), p. 86; W R&P, pp. 183–95. See also p. 31 above.
9 WEWNC 11 September 1914 Minutes; *Federationist*, February and March 1915; Fulham Labour Council, January 1917 AR.
10 WEWNC *The War Emergency: Suggestions for Labour Members in Local Committees* (1914), written by Webb; W R&P, p. 191; C. M. Lloyd on 'Doles and degradation' in *The Nation* 31 October 1914; Cole (1915), pp. 91–2.
11 Motherwell TC October 1914 AR, p. 11; WEWNC 14 January 1915 Minutes.
12 For later work on the committees see Leicester TC 1916 YB, p. 48, Great Harwood T&LC February 1916 AR, p. 6, Cowes T&LC March 1916 AR, and Hammersmith Labour Council March 1916 AR. On these developments in general see Marwick (1967), p. 213.
13 *Herald* 20 March 1915; Oldham T&LC 1914 AR, p. 9; Great Harwood T&LC February 1916 AR, p. 5; Coventry TC 1914 AR, p. 6; *Federationist* February and May 1915 and June 1916; *Herald* 9 October 1915 and 19 February 1916.
14 LGB Report on Special Work Arising out of the War (PP 1914–16 XXV), p. 14; First Report of the Departmental Committee … to consider … the Reception and Employment of Belgian Refugees (PP 1914–16 VII); Minutes of Evidence Taken before the Departmental Committee (*ibid.*), pp. 33, 86, 118; Newport TC 1915 AR, p. 2; Oxford TC 12 January 1915 Minutes; Wrexham T&LC 1914 AR, p. 2.
15 Birmingham TC 5 September 1914 Minutes for support for the Poplar motion, *Herald* 31 October 1914 and *Daily Citizen* 2 October 1914 for subsequent developments, and for local conferences see Cole (1915), pp. 107, 129, WEWNC 9 November 1914 Minutes and Bradford T&LC 1915 YB, p. 13.
16 E. T. Devine and L. Brandt, *Disabled Soldiers and Sailors Pensions and Training* (New York, 1919), pp. 102, 121, 128–37. Oldham T&LC 1916 YB, pp. 41–4 gives a summary of the Act and of the attitude of the labour movement towards it.
17 'Circular to Counties, County Boroughs etc., by the Statutory Committee on War Pensions, 19th February 1916', reproduced in W. Milne Bailey, *Trade Union Documents* (1929), p. 473.
18 Edinburgh TC March 1917 AR; Devine and Brandt, p. 136; Leicester TC 1917 YB, pp. 3, 50–1. Harrison (1971), p. 242 says that Labour councillors rather than genuine labour representatives were chosen, though this does not seem to have been a common complaint in the trades councils.
19 TUC 1916 Report, pp. 118–26.
20 Devine and Brandt, p. 156.

21 *Federationist* October 1917; Northampton TC June 1916 AR, p. 4, July 1917 to December 1918 AR, p. 2 and LRC 1916 AR, pp. 4–5; Ayr Labour Council 1916 AR, p. 4.
22 Liverpool TC March 1918 AR, p. 36; Dewsbury TC 1916 AR; Hampstead T&LC March 1917 AR; Finchley TC 1919 AR, p. 7.
23 'The work of the Soldiers' and Sailors' Family Associations' in *Edinburgh Review* January 1917, p. 156.
24 Finchley TC 1919 AR, pp. 7–8. For the committees, see above pp. 00–00.
25 On this and much of what follows see M. I. Thomis, *The Labour Movement in Britain and Compulsory Military Service, 1914–16* (London University MA thesis, 1959).
26 Liverpool TC March 1914 AR, p. 4. Plymouth TC HYR July 1913 describes a series of meetings against conscription held locally, and the Oxford TC 26 January 1910 and 5 June 1913 Minutes refer to meetings to which delegates were sent.
27 *Herald* 10 July and 18 December 1915; *Federationist* July and September 1915.
28 Thomis, p. 88; Northampton TC 26 June 1915 AR, p. 8, June 1916 AR, pp. 10, 12; Birmingham TC 1915 AR, p. 5; Carlisle T&LC February 1916 AR, pp. 7–8; *Herald* 13 November 1915; Huddersfield T&LC August 1916 AR, p. 3; *Labour Leader* 4 November 1915; Sheffield T&LC 19 October 1915 Minutes.
29 TUC 1915 Report, pp. 79–92; Thomis, pp. 154, 166, 183, 190, 199.
30 Labour Party 1916 Report, p. 124; Thomis, p. 220.
31 McShane (1958), pp. 26–7; Birmingham TC 10 January 1916 Minutes; *Federationist* March 1916; Maddock thesis, pp. 182–7, Liverpool TC March 1916 AR, pp. 4–5, and LRC 28 January 1916 letter in LRD; Huddersfield T&LC August 1916 AR, p. 4.
32 The Colchester leaflet is in the LRD and the Reading motion in *Federationist* June 1916. For some later protests see *Herald* 20 May 1916, Sheffield T&LC 15 January 1918 Minutes, J. Hinton (1973), p. 257, Birmingham TC 22 March 1918 Minutes, and *LWC* 20 June 1919.
33 The quotation is in J. M. Rae, *The Development of Official Treatment of Conscientious Objectors to Military Service, 1916–45* (London University PhD thesis 1965), p. 158. On p. 160 Rae gives his assessment of the work of the tribunals. He does not deny that cruel treatment was meted out, but considers that it was untypical. He repeats this view in his book *Conscience and Politics. The British Government and the Conscientious Objector to Military Service* (1970).
34 Rae's thesis, pp. 168, 160–5.
35 Rae's book, p. 56; J. W. Graham, *Conscription and Conscience* (1922), p. 65; Oxford T&LC 24 November 1915 and 23 February 1916 Minutes; *Federationist* April 1916; W. H. Chaloner (1950), p. 277.
36 For complaints on this score see *Federationist* June and July 1916 and Liverpool TC 7 May 1916 Minutes. At Aylesbury there were protests against the conscription of a union official who was 'blind in one eye, and partially blind in the other and had a wife and eleven children to support' (E. Cheshire (1936), pp. 21–2).
37 *Leeds Mercury* 21, 24, 28 March 1916; *Glasgow Herald* 16 March 1916; *LWC* 31 March 1916.
38 For accounts of this complex topic see A. L. Bowley, *Prices and Wages in the United Kingdom, 1914–1920* (Oxford, 1921) and S. Litman, *Prices and Price Control in Great Britain and the United States during the World War* (New York, 1920).
39 Bradford T&LC 1915 YB, pp. 9, 11; *Federationist* November 1914 and February 1915; Burnley T&LC 2 February 1915 Delegate Meeting Agenda (LRD).
40 Trades councils constantly referred to the WEWNC-issued *Memorandum on the Increased Cost of Living during the War* which went through various editions from 1915 to 1917. For the local meetings see Cole (1915), pp. 115–33, Harrison (1971), pp. 231–2, WEWNC Minutes and annual reports of the trades councils of Bradford,

Northampton, Oldham, Sheffield and elsewhere. *Herald* 20 February 1915 in
reporting the London meetings says they expressed more interest in opposition to the
war.

41 Cole, pp. 115–6.

42 *Herald* 11 December 1915 on Bethnal Green and H. Carter, *The Control of the
Drink Trade in Britain* (1919) for the quoted report. The Burton Trades and Labour
Council was a strong opponent of control for obvious reasons (1915 AR, p. 4),
although the Northampton body participated in the Liquor Control Board of that
town (TC June 1916 AR, p. 3) and the Carlisle one in more permanent local efforts
(Carter, p. 287, and T&LC February 1917 AR, p. 5).

43 Committee appointed by the Board of Trade to investigate . . . the increase in the
Price of Commodities . . . Interim Report (PP 1916 XIV); A. Marwick (1967), p.
187.

44 S. Litman (1920), p. 98. For examples see Battersea T&LC 1916 AR, p. 8, Leicester
TC 1917 YB, p. 5, and *Herald*, 23 September 1916.

45 *Federationist* July and December 1916; Bradford T&LC 1917 YB, p. 7; Chatham
T&LC June 1917 AR; PP 1917–8 XII for the Commission of Enquiry into
Industrial Unrest Reports and Cd. 8665, p. 2, for the quotation.

46 R. Smillie, *My Life for Labour* (1925), pp. 174–80; W. H. Beveridge, *British Food
Control* (1928), pp. 51–8, where figures on representation are given; S. Litman, pp.
129–38; F. Coller, *A State Trading Adventure* (Oxford, 1925), p. 77; N. B. Dearle,
Dictionary of Official Wartime Organisations (1928), p. 95.

47 *CFT* 5 October 1917. Similar grievances about the war pensions committees were
discussed at the Federation meeting reported in the paper on 6 July 1917.

48 *CFT* 7 September 1917; Leicester LP 1917 AR, p. 9; H. B. Williams (1952), p. 16;
Luton TC (1941), p. 14..

49 Edinburgh TC 1918 AR, p. 7; Ayr Labour Council 1917 AR, p. 5; G. Cheshire,
(1936), p. 20; Bather's thesis, p. 178; A. Tuckett (1971), p. 51.

50 W. H. Beveridge, pp. 196, 224; S. Pollard (1969), p. 52; Birmingham TC 1
December 1917 Minutes and *Hats off to the People!* (Birmingham, 1951), p. 7.

51 H. W. Clemensha, *Food Control in the North West Division* (Manchester, 1922),
pp. 7, 22. For a visit of the Yorkshire Commissioner to the Yorkshire Federated
Trades Councils see *LWC* 18 October 1918.

52 Nottingham TC June 1918 AR, p. 4. The Hereford TC Delegate Meeting Agenda
for 5 May 1918 (in LRD) refers to the discussion of 'Supplementary, Invalid and
Overtime Rates; Butter and Margarine Distribution; Registered Transfers; and other
matters affecting the work of the Food Control Committee'. The Trades Council
itself thus took a close interest in this work.

53 A. Marwick (1967), pp. 207–8, describes the entire rather bizarre 'food economy'
episode and Gallacher (1936), pp. 72–5, the abandonment of efforts to set up a
committee in Paisley because of the bitter comments of trades council
representatives.

54 National War Savings Committee First Annual Report (PP 1917–8 XVIII), pp. 6,
15; Leeds LP 1916 YB, p. 51; Liverpool T&LC March 1917, AR, p. 10; Fulham
Labour Council January 1917 AR; *Federationist* December 1916.

55 On this see Beveridge, p. 235. For trades council support see Nottingham TC June
1918 AR, p. 4, and Liverpool T&LC March 1918 AR, p. 24.

56 On the committees see Beveridge, p. 289, and Dearle (1928), p. 271, with the
quotation from Coller (1925), pp. 229–32. On Leeds see *LWC* 27 February 1920
and, on Smethwick, *Town Crier* 6 February and 16 July 1920.

57 Middlesbrough T&LC 1916 AR, p. 3; Northampton TC 26 June 1915 AR, pp. 1–2;
Newport TC 1916 AR, p. 10; Hereford TC 6 June 1918 LRD Reply; Liverpool TC
March 1918 AR, pp. 23, 25.

58 Bournemouth T&LC 1915 AR, quoted in *Southern Worker* April 1916; Labour
Party 1918 Report, p. 137; Northampton TC 1920 AR, pp. 4–5.

59 *Federationist*, September 1915, May 1916.
60 G. Wootton, *The Politics of Influence* (1963), pp. 78, 95, 121; *LRDMC* November 1917, p. 7.
61 Great Harwood T&LC February 1917 AR, p. 4; Oldham T&LC letter of 12 October 1917 in LRD; *LRDMC* August 1917, p. 7; Hebden Bridge TC, 21 May 1918 LRD Reply; Middlesbrough T&LC 1917 AR; Chesterfield T&LC 1917 Balance Sheet.
62 These developments are described in Wootton, pp. 107–13.
63 Birkenhead TC March 1916 AR, p. 3; Plymouth TC 1915 AR, p. 5; Coventry TC letter of 20 November 1916 in LRD.
64 Rotherham T&LC 1914 AR, p. 4; Northampton TC June 1917 AR, pp. 19, 22.
65 M. Carritt, *Brighton Trades Council. The History of Sixty Years* (Brighton, 1950), p. 12; Liverpool TC and LRC circular of November 1918 in LRD. On the Trade Union Rights Committee see *LWC* 30 July 1915 and *Herald* 25 September 1915 for discussion and 25 March 1916 for affiliation of the Deptford TC. Chatham T&LC June 1917 AR. For a protest against the expulsion and imprisonment of Russian political refugees who would not join the army see Sheffield T&LC 6 June 1916 and 5 June 1917 Minutes, and for a call for strike action on these and other matters, Chatham TC 18 June 1918 Minutes.
66 H. Wolfe, *Labour Supply and Regulation* (Oxford 1923), p. 130.
67 J. Mendelson *et al.* (1958), p. 67, describe the development of the Sheffield shop stewards' movement without reference to the trades and labour council, though Hinton (1973) pp. 162, 237, 248, 263 quotes a number of examples of co-operation, and on p. 223 an example from Coventry. On Glasgow see W. Kendall *The Revolutionary Movement in Britain, 1900–1920* (1969), p. 140, and Hinton, p. 138.
68 W. Gallacher and J. Paton, *Towards Industrial Democracy. A Memorandum on Workshop Control* (Paisley, 1918); *Federationist* April 1915; Sunderland T&LC 1916 AR; Drinkwater's thesis, p. 33.
69 Chorley T&LC 17 May 1918 LRD Reply; Birmingham TC 6 July and 13 September 1918 Minutes and 1918 AR, p. 5. For a conference addressed by Murphy and others and partly sponsored by the Coventry TC see Ruskin College, Oxford, *The Trade Unions Organisation and Action* (1919).
70 Liverpool T&LC March 1918 AR, pp. 31–4, and 13 February 1918 Minutes.
71 Liverpool T&LC 11 April 1917 Minutes on the 'struggles and heroism' of the revolution, and Manchester T&LC 1917 AR, p. 3, and Bünger (1967), p. 153, on a meeting in its support at which James Connolly was also enthusiastically remembered. On the Leeds Convention and its aftermath, see below pp. 115–16.
72 H. H. Hanak, 'The Union of Democratic Control during the first world war' in *Bulletin of the Institute of Historical Research*, 1963, vol. 36, pp. 177–8; H. N. Swanwick, *Builders of Peace, being Ten Years History of the Union of Democratic Control* (1924), p. 51; W. A. Orton (1921), p. 110; M. Swartz, *The Union of Democratic Control in British Politics during the First World War* (Oxford, 1971), pp. 228–9.
73 Swartz, pp. 148–9, 152–3, 174. On Poplar see R. Barker, *Education and Politics, 1900–1951. A Study of the Labour Party* (Oxford, 1972), p. 142, and on Bradford see *Bradford Pioneer* 24 November and 1 December 1916, T&LC 1918 YB, p. 5, and Swartz, pp. 205–6. See also H. Winkler, *The League of Nations Movement in Great Britain, 1914–19* (New Brunswick, 1952), p. 198. Liverpool T&LC March 1919 AR, p. 4, thought President Wilson someone 'to whom mankind owes so much for his farsighted policy and his earnest desire to establish a real and lasting peace'.
74 Nottingham TC July 1918 AR, p. 3.
75 On the role of the Glasgow and other trades councils in the Scottish struggle for the forty-hour week see H. McShane (1958), pp. 31–2, and A. Tuckett, *The Scottish Carter* (1967), pp. 147–9. On the Belfast body and the strike there for forty-four hours see Belfast Trades Union Council (1951), p. 14.

76 On growing support for national self-determination in the trades councils, see above, pp. 33–4.
77 The 'Memorandum on the Causes and Remedies of Labour Unrest' by Arthur Henderson and G. D. H. Cole is given in A. Gleason, *What the Workers Want. A Study of British Labour* (1920) with the quotation on p. 389. *The Times* 25 September 1917. Quotations from the Cabinet reports are given in D. Mitchell, *1918: Red Mirage* (1970), pp. 371–8 and B. E. Gilbert, *British Social Policy, 1914–39* (1970), pp. 17–45.
78 Wolverhampton T&LC 1915 YB, p. 18; Huddersfield T&LC August 1916 AR, p. 6; Chatham T&LC June 1917 AR. The *Herald* of 21 August 1915 reports some similar attacks on the leaders of the movement at a meeting of the Hull Trades Council.
79 Wrexham T&LC 1915 AR, p. 2; Bradford T&LC 1917 YB, p. 13; Hyde T&LC March 1915 AR; Liverpool T&LC March 1919 AR, p. 5; Northampton TC 1920 AR, p. 7; Huddersfield T&LC August 1918 AR, p. 5; Aldershot T&LC 1921 Rules.
80 Commission of Enquiry into Industrial Unrest (PP. 1917–18 XII Cd. 8668), p. 17 (with original emphasis); Manchester T&LC 1920 AR, pp. 5–6; *LWC* 19 September 1919.
81 Luton TC (1941), p. 4; Bolton TC 1919 AR, p. 1; Manchester T&LC 1920 AR, p. 3; Bradford TC 1921 YB, p. 3.

Chapter five. Ideology and organisation, pp. 81–113

1 Aberdeen TC 20 June 1883 Minutes, quoted in K. D. Buckley (1955), p. 32; C. Richards (1920), p. 36.
2 Bather's thesis, p. 150; Leeds TC 14 April 1897 and 11 May 1898 Minutes; J. E. Williams (1962), p. 254.
3 *Trade Unionist*, 4 April and 4 July 1891.
4 *Clarion*, 28 May and 4 June 1892. For support for the trade union reorganisation scheme of this paper see Leicester TC 1897 AR p. 4.
5 T. Mann on 'The labour problem' in *Labour Elector* 4, 11, 18, 25 January 1890; T. Mann and B. Tillett, *The 'New' Trade Unionism* (1890), p. 12; T. Mann on 'Trade unionism and co-operation' in *Forecasts for the Coming Century* (Manchester, 1897), ed. E. Carpenter.
6 T. Mann, *From Single Tax to Syndicalism* (1913), p. 42, and *Memoirs* (1967 edition), p. 42.
7 On this see F. F. Ridley, *Revolutionary Syndicalism in France* (Cambridge, 1970), pp. 65–71, 74–5, G. Lefranc, *Le Syndicalisme en France* (Paris, 1953), and F. Pelloutier, *Histoire des bourses de travail* (Paris, 1902). The quotation is from M. Kritsky, *L'Evolution de syndicalisme en France* (Paris, 1908), p. 197.
8 Ridley, p. 73, and A. B. Spitzer on 'Anarchy and culture: Ferdinand Pelloutier and the dilemma of revolutionary syndicalism' in *International Review of Social History*, 1963, VIII, pp. 380, 386.
9 This direct translation, which is of questionable accuracy, is also to be found in G. D. H. Cole, *The World of Labour* (1913), pp. 353, 409.
10 On this and much of what follows see E. Burdick, *Syndicalism and Industrial Unionism in England until 1918* (Oxford University DPhil thesis, 1950). There is some mention of the attitude of the syndicalists to the trades councils in B. Pribicevic, *The Shop Stewards' Movement and Workers' Control, 1910–22* (Oxford, 1959), p. 20.
11 E. J. B. Allen, *Revolutionary Unionism* (1909), p. 15.
12 *The Industrial Syndicalist* September 1910, p. 18.
13 *Times* 16 April 1912.
14 *Industrial Syndicalist* December 1910, especially pp. 7–9, 24–5, 32–3.

15 *Ibid.*, March 1911, pp. 3, 10; Stockton T&LC 1911 AR, p. 7; Leicester TC 1912 YB, pp. 21, 23.
16 Trades council protests at the prosecution of Mann are mentioned above, p. 33. P. Thompson (1967), p. 62, on Walthamstow, and *The Syndicalist* November 1912 for an example of activity after then.
17 Burdick's thesis, p. 22.
18 *The Syndicalist* February 1912.
19 *Ibid.*, July 1912; *The Worker* (Bournemouth) October 1912; *LWC* 13 July 1912.
20 *The Syndicalist* November 1912.
21 *Ibid.*, December 1912. The use of the trades councils to oppose careerism in the movement is also advocated in *Herald* 12 June 1915.
22 Burdick, p. 101.
23 *The Syndicalist* March–April and December 1913; Huddersfield T&LC, August 1913 AR, p. 4; *Solidarity* May 1914.
24 H. Pelling, *Popular Politics and Society in Late Victorian Britain* (1968), p. 157.
25 Ridley (1970), p. 1.
26 Bradford T&LC 1914 YB, p. 17, 1912 YB, p. 7 (with original emphasis); *The Worker* (Huddersfield) 31 July 1915; Nottingham TC, July 1914 AR, p. 4, July 1916 AR, p. 3; Halifax T&IC 1921 Rules, p. 4.
27 Bournemouth TC 1913 AR, quoted in *The Worker* (Bournemouth) March 1914. For discussions see Oxford TC, 24 June 1914 Minutes and *LWC* 30 May 1913, and for a list of motions on the matter see Bennet (1967) and Oldham T&LC 1917 YB, p. 39. At Plymouth in 1914 'unification of forces was the battle cry on all sides' (H. B. Williams (1952), p. 14). For the advocacy of industrial unionism see Brighton T&LC 1914 Rules, p. 2, and Blackpool TC (1951), p. 17. On unity see the Bournemouth TC Secretary quoted in *Southern Worker* March 1920, and Dorchester T&LC 1918 Rules, p. 3.
28 'Demos' on 'Trades councils' in *The Worker* (Bournemouth) October 1912; Liverpool T&LC, March 1912 AR, p. 7, March 1913 AR, pp. 8 and 9; Maddock's thesis, p. 169.
29 Clydach T&LC 22 July 1918 LRD Reply; Portsmouth T&LC 1912 AR, p. 13, 1914 AR, p. 5; Oxford TC, 24 June 1914 Minutes; Reading T&LC March 1915 AR; *LWC* 13 July 1912; *Herald*, 18 November 1916; 1932 TCAC, p. 23.
30 N. Carpenter, *Guild Socialism. An Historical and Critical Analysis* (New York, 1922), pp. 175–6, 199, outlines the theory which itself is in 'Guild socialism: the Storrington document' in A. Briggs and J. Saville (1971), p. 339; W. Gallacher and J. Paton (1918).
31 *LWC* 6 August 1915 (Cole coll. gives authorship); G. D. H. Cole, *Self Government in Industry* (1920), pp. 73–4.
32 *Herald* 23 September 1916; *Guildsman* January 1917 and November 1919; the programme of a lecture school on trade unionism arranged by the Croydon TC and given by guild socialists in September 1917 is in LRD and Cole coll.; London TC *Conference on National Guilds and Industrial Control* (nd, 1921); Leicester TC 1917 YB, p. 6; M. B. Reckett and C. E. Bechhofer, *The Meaning of National Guilds* (1920), pp. 93–5.
33 Hinton (1973) shows how these influences manifested themselves in the wartime workers' committee movement.
34 C. W. Guilleband, *The Workers' Councils. A German Experiment in Industrial Democracy* (Cambridge, 1928), especially pp. 5–8; A. Gramsci on 'Soviets in Italy' in *New Left Review*, 51, September–October 1968, p. 37; R. Thal, 'Sur les conseils ouvriers' in *Bulletin Communiste* 20 May 1920, p. 15 (with original emphasis).
35 *The Socialist*, April 1917; J. T. Murphy, *The Workers' Committee* (Sheffield, 1918), p. 12; A. Gleason (1920) p. 208.
36 *Federationist* October 1914, October 1915 and March 1916. Quelch put forward similar views in the left wing papers of the movement. See 'The possibility of the

trades council' in *Justice* 20 April 1916 and also *The Call* 14 October 1919.
37 R. P. Arnot, *Trade Unionism. A New Model* (1919), p. 13.
38 Communist Unity Convention *Official Report*, pp. 6–9, gives the debate and H. Pelling, *The British Communist Party. A Historical Profile* (1958), p. 9, mentions it. On the search for a soviet see E. E. Barry (1965), pp. 220, 274. On 1920 see W. Paul, *Communism and Society* (1922), pp. 174–5, and on later hopes see R. P. Arnot on 'A parliament of labour' in *Labour Monthly* October 1921, p. 338.
39 On Cole see McKibbin's thesis, p. 356, and on the LRD and guild movement in general see W. Kendall (1969), chapter 16, and M. Cole on 'Guild socialism and the Labour Research Department' in A. Briggs and J. Saville (1971).
40 B. Pearce, *Early History of the Communist Party of Great Britain* (1966), pp. 28–31, describes the policies of the CP in this period, including their attitude to the trades councils. See also R. Hyman on 'Communist industrial policy in the 1920s' in *International Socialism*, 53, October–December 1972.
41 A. Hutt, *The Post-war History of the British Working Class* (1937) p. 44; *The Worker* 18 November 1922; statement of September 1921 quoted in *The Communist International, 1919–43. Documents* (vol. 1), ed. J. Degras (1956), p. 296.
42 CPGB, *Communist Industrial Policy* (nd, 1922) p. 8; T. Quelch on 'The trades councils: the need for the extension of their scope and work' in *Labour Monthly* March 1922. For a similar policy statement see *The Worker* (Glasgow) 24 March 1923.
43 *All Power* January 1922 and T. Quelch on 'Resurrect the trades councils' in *ibid.*, March 1922.
44 J. T. Murphy, *Stop the Retreat!* (nd, 1922). The RILU document is given in H. Pollitt, *Serving my Time* (1940), pp. 157–63.
45 R. Harrison, *Before the Socialists* (1965), p. 292.
46 Amalgamated Society of Carpenters and Joiners, *Monthly Report*, January 1875, quoted in W. H. Fraser's thesis, p. 222; B. C. Roberts (1958), p. 82; *Beehive* 31 January 1874; Fraser, p. 531; G. Howell, *Trade Unionism Old and New* (1891), p. 227.
47 Mendelson *et al.* (1958), p. 39; Fraser's thesis, p. 96; Birmingham TC, *A Trades Council Federation for Birmingham* (Birmingham, nd, 1893), p. 3.
48 *Labour Magazine* May 1924, p. 39.
49 For a detailed proof of these propositions see Fraser, pp. 526–50.
50 See above, p. 83. In Germany at least the equivalent local organisations do seem to have remained more powerful, at least up to 1914 – see W. S. Saunders, *Trade Unionism in Germany* (1916), pp. 20–1, and C. M. Lloyd, *Trade Unionism* (1921), pp. 62, 121.
51 TUC 1924 Report, p. 181; TUC Parliamentary Committee Minutes, quoted in McCann's thesis, pp. 415–16; Leeds TC, 23 May 1910 Minutes; TUC 1910 Report, p. 11, and 1916 Report, p. 121. See also above, pp. 20–1 and 60.
52 S. and B. Webb, *The History of Trade Unionism* (1894 edn), pp. 224, 440, 466.
53 S. and B. Webb, *Industrial Democracy* (1897), pp. 269, 274–5, 296.
54 J. H. Greenwood, *The Theory and Practice of Trade Unionism* (1911), pp. 62–3; W. Citrine, *Men and Work. An Autobiography* (1964), p. 37; Tynemouth TC 1937–8 AR.
55 S. and B. Webb, *The History of Trade Unionism* (1902 impression) p. xiii, (1911 impression), p. xi.
56 W TU Coll E vol. IV, pp. 309–23.
57 S. and B. Webb, *The History of Trade Unionism* (1920 edn), pp. 557–9.
58 G. D. H. Cole, *Organised Labour. An Introducton to Trade Unionism* (1924), p. 12. This is in a passage when he compares the situation to what it was when he wrote *An Introduction to Trade Unionism* (1918), which is really the first edition of the same work.

59 See elsewhere pp. 64, 118 f and 33. For examples of such activity see *LWC* 23 January 1920 and Bradford T&LC 1919 YB, p. 9; 1920 YB, p. 5.
60 Lovell and Roberts (1968), p. 79, consider that closer contact with the trades councils was 'the main concrete result of the campaign'.
61 Manchester TC 1923 AR, p. 4; Cardiff T&LC 1924 YB, p. 39; Birmingham TC 1923 AR, p. 8; *LWC* 23 February, 2 November 1923.
62 Fraser (1974), p. 70; Tate (1950), p. 78; Roberts (1958), p. 79; *Industrial Review* March 1932. *Beehive* 17 January 1874 reports the meeting.
63 Corbett (1966), p. 43; Maddock's thesis, pp. 33–4; Bather's thesis, pp. 68–9, 237–8.
64 TUC 1889 Report, pp. 58–9; *Trade Unionist* 4 April 1891; *Labour Gazette* 1893, p. 116.
65 For an example of the aspirations involved in the establishment of a federation see Birmingham TC, *A Trades Council Federation for Birmingham* (Birmingham, nd, 1893). On the subsequent development of the federations see appendix one, pp. 187–8.
66 Quoted in Maddock's thesis, p. 136.
67 Fraser's thesis, p. 547; Leicester TC 1895 AR, p. 15; Turner thesis, pp. 47–8, Leeds TC 4 September 1895 Minutes; W TU Coll vol. IV, p. 303.
68 *Labour Gazette* 1894, p. 142. Many Irish unions were pleased at the establishment of a body where they did not have to be represented through the trades councils – J. D. Clarkson, *Labour and Nationalism in Ireland* (New York, 1925), pp. 186–7.
69 This account is taken from the reports of the STUC for 1919 to 1939, and the quotations are from 1925 Report, p. 97, 1934, p. 131, 1925, p. 107, 1936, pp. 36, 32, 1927, pp. 81, 209–10, 1938, p. 40.
70 *Herald* 26 August 1916.
71 These events are described in the issues of *Federationist* and *LRDMC* for October 1917.
72 See the same periodicals for November 1917.
73 *Herald* 10 November 1917 favoured a National Federation but did not want 'to see it dominated by the GFTU'. *Labour Leader* 8 November 1917 was also 'not at all sure that such a reactionary body as the GFTU is the best godfather for the new infant', and on 15 November published a letter from a federation secretary who repudiated the support his organisation was supposed to have given to it.
74 *Federationist* February 1917.
75 *CFT* 3 October 1919.
76 *Town Crier* 8 October 1920; Birmingham TC 1920 AR, p. 12.
77 Birmingham TC, 19 May 1922 Minutes; *Town Crier* 26 May 1922.
78 There are accounts of this conference in Birmingham TC 1922 AR, p. 5, and *Town Crier* 14 July 1922.
79 The account of this conference is based on *Town Crier* 30 October 1922, *LRDMC* 1 November 1922 and *Daily Herald* 16 October 1922.
80 Bather's thesis, p. 191; *Town Crier* 12 May 1922; *Sheffield Forward* March and April 1922; D. J. Ward, 'A move forward' in *The Post* 25 November 1922. For other organisational discussions in the trades councils in this period, see below pp. 121–2.
81 Sheffield T&LC 23 April 1923 AR, pp. 3, 9; Wolverhampton T&LC 1923 YB pp. 6–7; Stepney TC 1922 AR, p. 2. At Northampton a special meeting was held which unanimously approved of a report from the October conference (1922 AR, pp. 2, 8).
82 *Town Crier* 18 August 1922; *Workers' Weekly* 26 October 1923.
83 *Town Crier* 14 September 1923.
84 Margaret Cole in *New Standards* January 1924 said that the effect of the TUC snub on the Federation was 'to push the Trades Councils into Communist arms'.
85 The information about Dutt was obtained in an interview of R. Page Arnot by the author.
86 What follows is based on a printed *Report of the Second Annual Conference of the National Federation of Trades Councils* and *Town Crier* 17 November 1923.

Accounts of the conference vary in many particulars, notably on the numbers of those present. The figure given here has been computed by adding to the list given in the report the delegate from Halifax, who seconded one of the motions. A particularly inaccurate account can be found in J. Klugmann, *A History of the Communist Party of Great Britain*, vol. I (1968), pp. 113–14, where motions are inaccurately transcribed and the wrong number of delegates is given.

87 This is not in the report, but was reprinted separately, and there is a copy of the reprint in the Marx Memorial Library. It is also given in H. Pollitt (1940), pp. 169–71, and *Workers Weekly* 23 November 1923.

88 This aspect is especially emphasised in the report in *Daily Herald* 19 November 1923, which speaks 'of how anxious trade unionists, "right" or "left", are to hasten the establishment of closer unity of the whole trade union movement'.

89 Manchester T&LC 1923 AR, p. 3; Bolton TC 1923 AR, p. 3, 1924 AR, p. 8; Wolverhampton T&LC 1926 YB; *Sheffield Forward*, February 1924; Drinkwater thesis, p. 73; Cwmamman T&LC 1925 Draft Rules, p. 1; Hull TC&LP 1924 AR, p. 3; anon, *An Historical Sketch of the Birmingham Trades Council, 1866–1926* (Birmingham, nd, 1927), p. 31.

90 *Town Crier* 1 February 1924; *Streatham Leader* July 1924.

91 *International Press Correspondence* 28 August 1924; RILU *International Labour Movement, 1923–24*, typewritten report of which there is a copy in the TUC library.

92 MM Conference Report, 23–4 August 1924 (duplicated document in Tanner Coll. at Nuffield College, Oxford).

93 *All Power* February, March, April, June, July, September, October, December 1923 and January 1924. An article in the July 1923 issue on 'The conquest of power' explained how local 'Workers' Councils' could take 'charge of the municipalities'.

94 *Ibid.*, October and December 1923. The importance of the affiliation of workshop committees was also emphasised at the first conference of the MM, and in the new organisation Quelch continued to put forward these ideas: *The Worker* (Glasgow) 20 September and 4 October 1924.

95 M. Starr, *Trade Unionism, Past and Future* (1923), p. 31, with original emphasis.

96 *Plebs* February and March 1924. See also pp. 52–3 above.

97 *Daily Herald* 24 November 1923.

98 This view had been put forward by G. D. H. Cole as early as in the *Daily Herald* 7 July 1922. See also p. 53.

99 *Plebs* May 1924. See also W. Citrine, *The Trade Union Movement of Great Britain* (Amsterdam, 1926), pp. 55–6, 60, which makes clear the distrust of all major union leaders for independent activities by trades councils, especially when they acted together.

100 J. T. Murphy in *The Worker* (Glasgow) 13 September 1924.

101 *Plebs* January 1925.

102 *Labour Magazine* May 1924; H. Tracey in Wandsworth TC 1928 AR, p. 12.

103 Quotation in Lovell and Roberts (1968), p. 80. On Bramley's suggestion see *LRDMC* April 1925.

104 For this see Lovell and Roberts, pp. 79–80, and TUC 1924 Report, pp. 180–2.

105 Birmingham TC, 28 March 1925 Minutes.

106 Drinkwater's thesis, p. 74, and Birmingham TC, 21 March 1924 Minutes.

107 F. Bramley on 'Trades councils and the Trades Union Congress ' in Cardiff T&LC 1924 YB, pp. 32–3.

108 The debate is given in TUC 1924 Report, pp. 324–7.

109 For this and what follows see *Report of the National Trades Councils Conference*, 27 February 1925. This became the first in the series of TUC trades council conferences referred to here as TCAC.

110 *The Worker* (Glasgow) 7 March 1925.

111 *Ibid.* See also J. R. Campbell on 'The employers' offensive and how to meet it' in *Communist Review* March 1925.

112 Eccles T&LC 1925 AR, p. 3; Leeds T&LC 1925 AR, p. 3; Newport Industrial Council 1924 AR.

Chapter six. The 'hour of glory', pp. 114–37

1 Quoted in G. Tate (1950), p. 90, and above, p. 14.
2 H. R. Hikins (1961), pp. 181, 191–4; T. Mann (1913), p. 80; D. Torr, *Tom Mann* (1936), pp. 38–41. B. Holton 'Syndicalism and Labour on Merseyside, 1906–14' in *Building The Union* (Liverpool, 1973), ed. H. R. Hikins, p. 139 also argues for the limited importance of the permit system.
3 *LWC* 29 June 1917; Council of Workers' and Soldiers' Delegates, *What happened at Leeds* (1917).
4 Drinkwater's thesis, p. 36; Chatham T&LC June 1917 AR.
5 See the leaflet from the Council of Workers' and Soldiers' Delegates in the British Library of Economic and Political Science and *LWC* 6 July 1917.
6 For accounts of these meetings and of the events that surrounded them see *Labour Leader* 9, 16 August 1917, *The Times* 30 July and 14 August 1917 and *Western Mail* 30 July 1917. See also J. Hinton (1973), p. 241.
7 *LWC* 13 July and 2 November 1917. For an account of other reasons why the councils failed see W. Kendall (1969), pp. 174–6, 378–9. There is much more detail on all this in S. White 'Soviets in Britain: the Leeds Convention of 1917', *IRSH*, XIX, 1974, including the efforts to set up the councils. White emphasises the pacifist character of the convention, but underestimates its implications by concentrating on the intentions of those involved. He also ignores the difficulties the councils had in fitting into the system of existing organisations.
8 R. K. Middlemas, *The Clydesiders* (1965), p. 91; Kendall, p. 140; Belfast Trade Union Council (1951), p. 14.
9 Middlesbrough T&LC 1919 AR, p. 6; Finchley TC 1919 AR, p. 8; Huddersfield T&LC, August 1920 AR, p. 3.
10 Many of the publications of these organisations are in a box at the LRD entitled *Soviet Intervention, etc.* See also Kendall, pp. 242, 251, 412; A. Hutt (1937), p. 36.
11 Oldham T&LC *Report of the Speeches at Special Organisational Conference* (1918); Chatham TC, 18 June 1919 Minutes, supported a strike call on this and other issues; London TC and LP sponsored demonstration in Trafalgar Square on 20 July 1919 called 'to demand the immediate cessation of the intervention against the socialist Republics' (leaflet in LRD box). For other examples of opposition to the intervention, Sheffield TC 16 July 1918 Minutes; Bolton TC 1919 AR, p. 4; Northampton TC 1919 AR, pp. 9–10, 1920 AR, pp. 7, 10; *Town Crier*, 19 March 1920, and J. Corbett, 'The Birmingham Council of Action' in *Birmingham Trades Council Journal*, August and September 1952; Bather's thesis, p. 187.
12 Finchley TC 1919 AR, p. 9; Huddersfield T&LC, August 1918 AR, p. 8; Coventry T&LC 1919 AR, p. 3; Bradford TC 1922 YB, p. 3.
13 Northampton TC 1919 AR, p. 34; Drinkwater's thesis, pp. 71–2; Birmingham TC, 2 February 1924 Minutes; Blackpool TC (1951), p. 31.
14 The two best accounts of this are S. White 'Labour's Council of Action, 1920', *Journal of Contemporary History*, 9, 4, 1974, and L. J. Macfarlane, 'Hands off Russia: British labour and the Russo-Polish war, 1920' in *Past and Present*, 38, December 1967. See also S. R. Graubard, *British Labour and the Russian Revolution* (1956).
15 The text of Henderson's telegram is in W. P. and Z. Coates, *A History of Anglo-Soviet Relations* (1943), p. 42. Much of the rest is from a duplicated eight-page document by F. Bramley, J. S. Middleton and H. S. Lindsey entitled *Report of the Council of Action. August to October 1920*, 18 October 1920. There are copies at the LRD and in the TUC library.

16 Council of Action, *Report of the Special Conference on Labour and the Russo-Polish War* (1920).
17 Copy in the LRD *Soviet Intervention, etc.* box.
18 Macfarlane, p. 149, on the frequency of local demands. The quotations are from a Council of Action leaflet of 26 August entitled *Labour and Russia. Report to the Local Councils of Action, Executes of Trade Unions etc,.* (copy in LRD) and the report by Bramley *et al.*, p. 7.
19 J. Wedgwood, 'The Council of Action – a triumph for labour unanimity' in *Review of Reviews*, LXII, 1920. The Birmingham TC 1920 AR, p. 10, said that 'the national leaders modified their attitude' so that the local organisations 'more or less soon became moribund'.
20 G. D. H. Cole, *History of the Labour Party from 1914* (1948), p. 105; W. Williams, *Full up and Fed up. The Workers' Mind in Crowded Britain* (1921), p. 156; Liverpool TC 8 August 1920 Minutes; Bennett (1967). For other examples see White, p. 107.
21 Bradford T&LC 1921 YB, pp. 5–7; *LWC*, 20, 27 August 1920; Bather's thesis, p. 187; Manchester T&LC 1920 AR, p. 4; *Manchester Guardian* 20 October 1920; *Town Crier* 17 December 1920.
22 The story of the Birmingham Council of Action is in the 1952 article by Corbett, cited in n. 11 above, and the minutes of this body as well as of some of its sub-committees are in the Trades Council minute books. The quotations are from these minutes, and from leaflets given there, as well as in *Town Crier* 1 October 1920 and 11 March 1921.
23 The Sheffield T&LC Minute Book (EC Minutes, vol. 10a) contains the Council of Action minutes for 15 August, 14 September, 19 October 1920 and 14 January and 1 February 1921.
24 Macfarlane, pp. 143–4, after examining the Cabinet papers, considers that the labour movement did not have the direct effect on the situation that it thought, but was not without influence. The local view quoted is in Doncaster T&LC 1920 AR, and similar sentiments are in Manchester T&LC 1920 AR, p. 4, Huddersfield T&LC August 1920 AR, p. 6, and Birmingham TC 1920 AR, p. 10.
25 *The Pioneer* (Merthyr Tydfil) 4, 18 September 1920; W. Paul, *Communism and Society* (1922), pp. 174–5. See also W. and E. Paul, *Creative Revolution* (1920), which outlines a plan for a system of worker's councils as an alternative to parliamentary government, and S. White, *loc. cit.*, pp. 107–8, which gives details from Cabinet Paper sources.
26 V. Lenin, 'Speech delivered at a congress of leather industry workers, 2 October 1920' in *Collected Works*, vol. 31 (1966), p. 308; Macfarlane, p. 149; J. Wallace, 'The Council of Action – an attempt to impose soviet rule' in *Review of Reviews*, LXII, 1920; J. H. Thomas, at the Council of Action conference (n. 16); W. Williams (1921), p. 147; Frank Hodges on 'What we mean by the Council of Action' in *Sunday Express* 15 August 1920.
27 Manchester T&LC 1920 AR, pp. 5–6. White (*loc. cit.*) again argues that pacifism was the predominent sentiment but ignores the implications of what was planned independently of the national Council of Action.
28 For a full account see R. P. Arnot, *The Miners: Years of Struggle* (1953), pp. 300–21.
29 The Manchester call was in the coal dispute in October 1920 (see Bather, p. 39, and *Manchester Guardian* 20 October 1920). On Barrow see *The Communist* 8 July 1922, and on Liverpool, TC 21 April 1921 Minutes and Drinkwater's thesis, p. 63.
30 Doncaster T&LC 1921 AR; Bradford T&LC 1922 YB p. 5.
31 Birmingham TC 1921 AR, p. 4, and 14 April 1921 *et seq.* Minutes.
32 Northampton TC 1922 AR, pp. 7–8; *LWC* 31 March 1922; *Town Crier* 7 April and 12 May 1922.
33 Sheffield T&LC 23 March 1923 AR, pp. 3, 8–9; *Sheffield Forward* April, May and

July 1922 (with original emphasis).

34 *The Communist* 10 June 1922; M. Carritt (1950), p. 13; *LRDMC* October 1925; E. Burns (1926), p. 107.

35 *Workers' Weekly* 7 April 1923.

36 Kendal T&LC 1924 AR; T. Mann, *Power through the General Strike – a Call to Action* (1923), p. 11. Above, p. 103 ff.

37 *The Communist* 7 October 1922; *Town Crier* 9 March 1923, and *Workers' Weekly* 31 March 1923, on efforts in Birmingham during the Ruhr crisis; *Workers' Weekly*, 12, 19, 26 May 1923, and Klugmann (1968), vol. I , pp. 148–57, on Poland; Liverpool TC, 15 July 1925 Minutes, on China.

38 L. D. Thomson, *Relations between Government and Trade Unions in the General Strike of May 1926* (London University PhD thesis, 1952), p. 629, quoting *The Economist* 29 November 1924: Lovell and Roberts (1968), pp. 83–6.

39 Bennett (1967); Liverpool TC Minute Book, vol. 14, especially 31 July 1925, for these details; *Town Crier* 17 July 1925. L. J. Macfarlane, *The British Communist Party. Its Origins and Development until 1929* (1966), p. 155, gives details of local bodies set up at that time under CP influence.

40 This phrase is in G. D. H. Cole, *British Trade Unionism Today* (1939), p. 187.

41 The chief accounts of the general strike are in R. P. Arnot, *The General Strike. Its origins and history* (1926); R. Postgate, E. Wilkinson and J. F. Horrabin, *A Workers' History of the Great Strike* (1927); W. H. Crook, *The General Strike* (Chapel Hill, N.C., 1931); Thomson's thesis; J. Symons, *The General Strike. A Historical Portrait* (1957); A. Mason, 'The government and the General Strike' in *International Review of Social History*, XIV , 1969, and C. Farman, *The General Strike, May 1926* (1972). [No attempt is made here to repeat the story of events during the strike itself, which can be found in these volumes, nor to take account of those works, especially by M. Morris, P. Renshaw and G. Phillips, which have appeared since the time of writing, though these do not alter the general lines of the argument.]

42 History Group of the Communist Party, *The General Strike in the North-east* (1961), is largely based on this document (hereafter *Account*), together with some comments by R. P. Arnot, whose many works on the period nearly always reproduce it. His *The Miners. Years of Struggle*, pp. 436–44, contains extracts together with other interesting local material. Detailed recent accounts are to be found in A. Mason, *The Miners' Union of Northumberland and Durham, 1918–31, with special reference to the General Strike of 1926* (Hull University PhD thesis, 1967), and *The General Strike in the North-east* (Hull, 1970).

43 D. E. Baines and R. Bean, 'The General Strike on Merseyside, 1926' in *Liverpool and Merseyside. Essays in the economic and social history of the port and its hinterland* (1969) ed. J. R. Harris; T. Woodhouse, *Leeds in the General Strike* (Leeds University BA dissertation, 1971); R. P. Hastings, *The General Strike in Birmingham, 1926* (Birmingham University BA dissertation, 1954); P. Wyncoll, 'The General Strike in Nottingham' in *Marxism today* June 1972; R. Hyman, *Oxford Workers in the Great Strike* (Oxford, 1966). [For numerous more recent examples see *BSSLH*, 34, 1977, pp. 86–7.]

44 For such assessments see Klugmann (1968), vol. II , pp. 147–53, Symons, pp. 124–33, 143–9, and Farman, pp. 152–66.

45 Besides the boxes of reports and messages in the TUC Library (which subsequent quotations are from unless otherwise stated) there is also a small collection in the British Library of Economic and Political Science, and some useful documents in the appendix of Mason's thesis, in the Willesden Public Library, and in a folder of printed reproductions entitled *The General Strike, 1926*, ed. J. F. Clarke and J. W. Leonard (Newcastle upon Tyne, 1971).

46 Lovell and Roberts (1968), p. 88; Thomson's thesis, pp. 1617–18.

47 *Town Crier* 11 September 1925; Bradford T&LC 1926 YB, p. 3; 1925 TCAC pp. 15–16.
48 Quotation in Thomson, p. 728; R. Martin, *Communism and the British Trade Unions, 1924–33. A Study of the National Minority Movement* (Oxford, 1969), p. 69; *Report of Special Conference of Action.* Calls for the setting up of councils of action can be found in *Workers' Weekly* 23, 30 April 1926, though they are less prominent before that date.
49 B. Davies, *Pages from a Worker's Life* (1961), p. 15; Burns, p. 112; Leeds TC, 20 July 1925, 5, 11 March 1926 Minutes, Crook, p. 371, and Woodhouse thesis, p. 7.
50 Bolton TC 1925 AR, p. 8; STUC 1926 Report, p. 102; Birmingham TC 6, 17 March 1926 Minutes.
51 Postgate *et al.*, p. 46; Huddersfield T&LC, *75th Anniversary, 1885–1960, and Programme of Events* (Huddersfield, 1960), p. 11; notice of March meetings with Liverpool T&LC Minutes and General Strike Collection; Wyncoll, p. 74; Bather's thesis, pp. 40, 44, Manchester T&LC 1925 AR, p. 5; Burns, pp. 11, 145.
52 *St Pancras Bulletin* 12 May.
53 Hastings, p. 99; Burns, pp. 185–6, 179, 121, 56; Birmingham TC 1927 AR, p. 7.
54 Crewe CoA 4 May letter to Citrine; Burns, p. 146; St Albans Emergency Committee MS Minute Book and notes on its work; Woodhouse, pp. 9–14; N. Connole, *Leaven of Life. The Story of George Henry Fletcher* (1961), p. 148.
55 TUC 7 May Intelligence Committee Report; Merseyside CoA *Strike Bulletin* 7, 13 May; Farman, p. 171.
56 G. Glasgow, *General Strikes and Road Transport* (1926), p. 103, quoting a Ministry of Health circular of 20 November 1925; W. Citrine (1964), p. 178.
57 P. S. Bagwell, *The Railwaymen* (1965), pp. 472–3; Crook, pp. 377, 398.
58 *British Worker* 6 May says 'No Trades Council may issue permits' and 10 May that the transport committees were 'the sole authority to deal with Permits'. Similar statements are in the General Council circular to affiliated organisations of 2 May and the General Council bulletins of 7 and 8 May.
59 Symons, p. 64; Chatham TC, 6 May Report; Swansea Strike Committee, 8 May message.
60 Masons's thesis, p. 305, and Darlington T&LC, 9 May letter to TUC; Burns, p. 123; reports from separate Cheltenham Council of Action and Strike Committee (of rail unions) with similar reports from the T&LC and Joint Strike Committee of Gloucester.
61 *Westminster Worker* 6 May; Burns, p. 104; W. D. Buxton, *The Part played by the Coventry Trades Council in the 1926 General Strike* (typescript in the possession of the TC); Hastings, p. 56; *Huddersfield Workers' Bulletin* 7 May; Exeter Central Strike Committee, 7 May letter to TUC; Peterborough T&LC, 7 May letter to Citrine; Burton on Trent Joint Strike Committee, 8 May letter to TUC; Kendal Strike Committee *Daily Report* 3 May; TUC Intelligence Committee Report, 7 May; Farman, p. 162.
62 TUC 8 May, Intelligence Committee Report; Clegg (1954), p. 23; *LRDMC* May 1926; Burns, p. 117; TUC *Progress of the Strike Report* 10 May; Baines and Bean, p. 253.
63 Farman, pp. 136–7.
64 Burns, pp. 123, 169; Birmingham TC, 18 May 1926 Minutes.
65 TUC, *The Mining Crisis. Proposals for Co-ordinated Action of Trade Unions,* 30 April 1926; *Account*, p. 12; Burns, pp. 120, 107; Hastings, p. 114.
66 TUC 1926 Report, pp. 166, 345; TUC National Strike Special Conference Report (January 1927), p. 58; Crook, p. 399. Charles Ammon of the Union of Post Office Workers reported to the TUC in letters of 5 and 10 May on the influence of the CP in Bedford and Camden Town, though he claimed this led to fewer people being on strike than would otherwise have been the case.
67 Hamling (1948), p. 45; Bather's thesis, p. 44; L. Paul, *Angry Young Man* (1951),

p. 87; Burns, pp. 187, 154, 122, and similar reports in Postgate *et al.*, p. 24.
68 Hamling, p. 45; Burns, p. 138.
69 *General Council Bulletin,* 4 May; Farman, pp. 159–60; TUC Publicity Committee, 10 May message to Wood Green TC; Burns, p. 160, on Preston, and an (undated) letter from H. Tracey about their printed *Strike News.*
70 Burns, p. 103; L. Paul, p. 87.
71 Postgate *et al.*, p. 23; Hastings, p. 64; Merseyside CoA notice of 10 May; Bristol TC, 10 May Report; *Birmingham Central Strike Bulletin* 7 May; Leeds TC, 5 May message, and TUC Progress of Strike Report, 10 May; Chiswick TCCoA, 7, 10 May messages to the TUC.
72 On Coventry see E. Wilkinson on 'Ten days that shook the Cabinet' in *Lansbury's Labour Weekly* 22 May 1926, and Coventry TC, 9 May Report; 'Warrington Central Strike Committee urge withdrawal of all workers' in a telegram of 6 May; North Staffordshire T&LC Strike Advisory Committee wrote on 7 May asking for all building workers to be called out; Southampton TC, 7 May report of feeling against people still at work; Abertillery T&LC, 10 May letter to the TUC calls for 'Postal Workers ETU and non-essential parts of Municipal Employees to be called out at once'.
73 Burns, p. 190; Crook, p. 450; Arnot (1926), p. 233; *The Times* 15 May; Woodhouse, p. 29; Burns, pp. 124, 127; Baines and Bean, p. 262; Symons, p. 216.
74 Burns, pp. 101, 184, 166, 157, 189; H. McShane (1958), p. 36; Keighley TC&LP February 1927 AR, p. 8; Blackpool TC (1951), p. 54; Sheffield Disputes Committee, 13 May letter to TUC; Rawtenstall TC (1952), p. 17; *Workers' Chronicle* (Newcastle) 14 May (now reproduced opposite the title page of Mason's book); Crook, p. 448; Postgate *et al.*, p. 88; St Albans T&LC Emergency Committee, 14 May Minutes; W. D. Buxton typescript on Coventry and G. Hodgkinson, *Sent to Coventry* (1970), p. 99.
75 J. T. Murphy, *A Revolutionary Workers' Government* (1929), p. 13; *Communist Review* July 1926, p. 126; Hastings, p. 41; Klugmann (1969), vol. 2, p. 159 (original emphasis); Arnot, *The Miners,* p. 443; R. Miliband, *Parliamentary Socialism* (1961), p. 141; *Daily Telegraph* 19 May (referring to the Poplar Strike Committee).
76 Hodgkinson, p. 97; *Westminster Worker* 10 May; Cwmamman T&LC, 11 May message to TUC.
77 *Croydon Worker* 12 May; *Westminster Worker* 11 May; *St Pancras Bulletin* 12 May; Burns, p. 119
78 A. Moffat, *My Life with the Miners* (1965), p. 45; *Workers' Chronicle* (Newcastle) 8, 9 May, and letter from J. C. Ludbrook to A. Mason, 8 June 1963, in the appendix to his thesis, pp. 53–4; Crook, pp. 416–17.
79 Burns, pp. 143, 176; Moffat, p. 47; Cheltenham CoA Report (nd); St Pancras CoA, 5 May letter to TUC; Symons, pp. 150–1; Klugmann, vol. 2, pp. 200–2; Birmingham TC, 30 October, 27 November 1925, 2 January 1926 Minutes; Farman, p. 156.
80 Burns, p. 137; TUC *Official Bulletin* 7 May; *Progress of Strike Report* 10 May. On police sympathy see Symons, pp. 109–10, Citrine (1964), p. 178. On Swindon see Burns, p. 181, and A. Tuckett (1971), p. 68.
81 Crook, pp. 422, 454, and Farman, pp. 185–7, 192–3, who well describes the escalating pattern of violence at that time; TUC *Progress of Strike Report* 8 May on STUC deputation. On the Birmingham arrest see Corbett (1966), pp. 128–9, and on earlier attacks of this sort there see *Town Crier* 27 May, 1 July 1921, 13 January 1922.
82 Arnot's 'Plan of campaign' in his *The Miners,* p. 439.
83 Crook, p. 361; D. J. Robertson, 'A narrative of the General Strike of 1926' in *Economic Journal,* vol. 38, 1926, p. 385; Farman, pp. 164–5; Burns, pp. 56, 121; 'C.B.', *The Reds and the General Strike* (1926), p. 17. On electricity supply see *British Worker* 7 May, and Farman, pp. 118–19.

84 Wyncoll, p. 174; TUC *Progress of Strike Report* 10 May; Hastings, p. 41; Edinburgh Strike Committee, *Official Bulletin* 8 May; Symons, pp. 146–7; Crook, p. 412; Swansea TC, 7 May message; Darlington Strike Committee Rota Committee Minutes for 7 May, reproduced in J. F. Clarke and Leonard (1971).

85 Merseyside CoA *Strike Bulletin* 7 May; Farman, p. 164; Baines and Bean, p. 250.

86 On the events in Newcastle see *Account*, pp. 7–10, and, for assessments, Crook, pp. 410–11, Symons, pp. 124–33, and Mason's thesis, pp. 293–300.

87 Crook, p. 402 (original emphasis); Woodhouse, p. 26; Merseyside CoA *Strike Bulletin* 6 May; Eccles T&LC 1926 AR, p. 7; L. Paul, p. 86; Bradford T&LC 1927 YB, p. 5.

88 C.B. (1926), pp. 15–16; Baines and Bean, p. 260.

89 Klugmann, vol. 2, p. 171. For some other criticisms see A. Mason on 'The General Strike' in *BSSLH*, 20, 1970.

90 *Workers' Daily* 3 May; *Workers' Bulletin* 4 May; Farman, p. 169; R. Martin (1969), p. 72; Arnot's 'Plan of campaign' in *The Miners*, p. 436.

91 Arnot (1926), p. 102; Macfarlaine (1966), p. 166.

92 *Workers' Bulletin* 13, 14 May; Klugmann, vol. 2, pp. 138, 224; C.B., p. 36.

93 Eccles T&LC 1926 AR, p. 6; H. B. Williams (1952), p. 24; Burns, p. 185.

Chapter seven. The establishment of authority, pp. 138–67

1 Cardiff T&LC 1926 YB, p. 17; J. Yarwood, *A Retrospect and an explanation* (Newcastle, 1932), p. 7. See pp. 110–13 above for the establishment of the JCC.

2 1929 TCAC, pp. 4–5. For other complaints see TUC 1928 Report, pp. 349–51.

3 Sunderland T&LC, June 1930 AR.

4 The first two issues of this periodical, dated June and July 1925, have recently been located by the TUC librarian.

5 1933 TCAC, p. 10.

6 TUC 1931 Report, p. 124; 1932 TCAC, pp. 14–15; 1936 TCAC, pp. 14–15, 26; 1934 TCAC, pp. 14, 36; TUC 1939 Report, p. 184.

7 1937 TAC, p. 13; TUC 1938 Report, p. 152.

8 1936 TCAC, pp. 15, 27; 1937 TCAC, p. 23; TUC 1932 Report, pp. 156–7.

9 1925 TAC, pp. 14–15; TUC Reports for 1927, p. 150, 1928, p. 141, 1930, p. 106, 1931, p. 123 and 1932, pp. 100–1; 1933 TCAC, p. 17 and 1936 TCAC, p. 30. On the success of the sports activity of the trades council at Reading see 1933 TCAC, p. 17, and similarly at Rugby, 1932 TCAC, p. 19.

10 1932 TCAC, p. 12; TUC 1932 Report, pp. 100, 260–1 and 1933 Report, pp. 290–1.

11 Lovell and Roberts (1968), pp. 130–1; TUC 1933 Report, p. 232, 1936 Report, pp. 100–1; *Labour Magazine* January 1931; 1935 TCAC, pp. 33–9.

12 TUC 1929 Report, p. 14.

13 Clegg (1954), pp. 292–3, 297.

14 1926 TCAC, p. 19; 1932 TCAC, p. 9; 1934 TCAC, p. 20. See below, p. ooo f., on some of what was done locally.

15 1930 TCAC, p. 12; 1934 TCAC, p. 20; Newcastle TC 1933–34 AR.

16 TUC 1932 Report, p. 99, and 1931 Report, pp. 512–33, 122–3; 1930 TCAC, p. 12; 1935 TCAC, p. 7; TUC 1938 Report, pp. 289–91.

17 1930 TCAC, p. 10; TUC 1939 Report, p. 120; 1931 TCAC, pp. 6–7; 1935 TCAC, pp. 13–14, 28; 1936 TCAC, pp. 7–8.

18 See appendix one, on trades council federations.

19 The 1926 edition of the model rules is given in W. Milne Bailey (1929), pp. 172–80. 1926 TCAC, pp. 15–18; TUC 1926 Report, p. 165; 1927 TCAC, pp. 11–13; Redcar TC 1926 Rules; Southampton TC 1928 Rules.

20 There are copies of the TUC Model Rules in the TUC Library for 1934, 1935, 1937,

1943, 1947, 1953, 1960 and 1963. Bath TC 1937 Rules allow for the settling of industrial disputes, as do the Middlesbrough T&LC 1936 Rules, apparently unrevised until 1949. On affiliation other than trade·union branches see below, p. 184.

21 Manchester T&LC 1924 AR, p. 3. Similar hopes are expressed in the *Labour Bulletin of Industrial and Political Information* September 1925, p. 59.

22 H. Tracey in *Labour Magazine* May 1924, p. 40; TUC 1925 Report, p. 215.

23 STUC 1934 Report, p. 129; TUC circular of 27 March 1927 to the trades councils; Sunderland TC June 1933 AR, p. 10; Tynemouth TC 1936–37 AR; Bolton TC 1927 AR, p. 6.

24 *Industrial Review* July 1927; Bradford TC 1928 YB, p. 7; 1930 TCAC, p. 6.

25 For support for affiliation see Hull TC&LP 1924 AR, p. 12, Taunton TC 1925 Rules and 1930 TCAC, pp. 12–13. For examples of the demand being put forward by the CP see MM 1924 Conference Report, p. 5, and TUC 1926 Report, p. 340. A *Bulletin* sent out by the CP London District Committee on 24 June 1926 and later reproduced by Arthur Henderson in a circular of 2 July (in the TUC Library) says that such affiliation would be of 'untold value in extending our influence with greater force upon the General Council and the Central leadership as a whole'. For rejection of the proposal at meetings of the Congress see TUC 1924 Report, pp. 324–7, 1926 Report, pp. 465–6, 1927 Report, pp. 331–2, 1928 Report, pp. 351–2. A proposal that trades council members of the JCC should attend the Congress was similarly rejected in 1934 without much discussion (Report, pp. 235–6).

26 TUC 1932 Report, p. 260; Watford TC 1939 AR, p. 12.

27 1927 TCAC, pp. 7–8, 10.

28 Protests on the voting system are referred to on p. 138 above. On the unemployed associations see 1931 TCAC, p. 15; 1932 TCAC, pp. 9–12. Complaints about dictating to unaffiliated bodies are in 1927 TCAC, pp. 7, 14, and undemocratic methods in Huddersfield T&LC 1929 AR and 1934 TCAC, p. 32.

29 1929 TCAC, pp. 14–15; 1938 TCAC, pp. 10, 22; 1939 TCAC, p. 43; Bradford TC 1940 YB, p. 13; 1940 TCAC, pp. 3, 13.

30 1934 TCAC, p. 18.

31 *Industrial Review* December 1927; TUC 1932 Report, p. 260; 1934 TCAC, p. 5.

32 1935 TCAC, p. 23; 1934 TCAC, p. 21; *Town Crier* 1 April 1933, 12 October 1934; Hendon TC 1939 Constitution; Clegg (1954), p. 287.

33 Nottingham TC 1908 TUC Souvenir, p. 38; R. Martin, *The National Minority Movement. A Study in the Organisation of Trade Union Militancy in the Inter War Period* (Oxford University DPhil, 1964), p. 326; Lovell and Roberts (1968), p. 94.

34 LP 1920 Report, pp. 74–83. On this and what followed see Macfarlane (1966), pp. 94–109 and Klugmann (1968), vol.I, pp. 230–4.

35 N. Connole (1961), pp. 136–7.

36 LRD, *The Workers' Register of Capital and Labour* (1923), pp. 49–50; LP 1924 Report, pp. 123–31, 1925 Report, pp. 38, 181–9.

37 The best account of this is in J. Redman, *The Communist Party and the Labour Left, 1925–29* (Hull, 1957).

38 This is from a duplicated document in the LRD of the Left Wing Group in the Chelsea TC&LP headed *Municipal and Local Government Elections*. It is undated, but probably 1925.

39 R. Martin (1969). Martin's thesis contains information about the activities of the MM in the trades councils, at least at London and Birmingham.

40 For discussions of workshop affiliation see Liverpool TC 27 November 1925 Minutes and Leeds TC 29 July, 30 September 1925 Minutes. T. Quelch in *Workshop Organisation* (1926), p. 11, argues that they should 'ultimately become the backbone of the Trades and Labour Councils'. For the other quotation see NMM *Is Trade Unionism Played Out?* (1926), p. 8.

41 *International Press Correspondence*, 18 April 1928; Macfarlane (1966), p. 323;

MM August 1926 Conference Report, pp. 26, 32, 56; M. McCarthy, *Generation in Revolt* (1953), p. 76.

42 Bather's thesis, p. 190; CPGB, *Orders from Moscow?* (1926), pp. 26–7; Newcastle TC 1927–28 AR, p. 4.

43 TUC 1926 Report, pp. 163, 342.

44 The TUC circular is in the TUC library. The MM circular is in the Tanner Collection, together with a letter of 5 April explaining it to the MM EC. See also J. T. Murphy, *Modern Trade Unionism* (1935), p. 29, and *The Worker* (London) 15 April 1927.

45 1927 TCAC, pp. 7–8, 10; TUC 1927 Report, pp. 151, 321, 325–6, 336.

46 There is an account of this in Martin's thesis, pp. 303–11. However, this is based almost entirely on the two main published histories of the London Trades Council. The reason for this lack of documentation is given in a misleading footnote which asserts that 'the records of the Council were removed by the Secretary, Mr. Julius Jacobs, when the Council was reconstituted in 1950' (p. 303). The event referred to occurred in 1952, and Mr Jacobs has since frequently made these records available to researchers. Besides this, there was quite a full selection of the printed minutes of the Trades Council for the 1920s available in the TUC library, and the annual reports are widely available. [London TC records are now on microfilm, with originals at the TUC.] One other important defect in Martin's account for these matters is that on pp. 306–7 he gives a list of motions passed by the London Trades Council and supposed to show its domination by the CP. It can only be said that few of these motions would have been rejected by any local body in this period.

47 London TC 26 June 1924 Minutes, 1925 AR, pp. 4–5, 11 June 1925 Agenda, 30 July 1925 Minutes; Martin's thesis, p. 305.

48 London TC 26 August 1926 Minutes; letter from R. W. Robson of the CP London District of 30 August 1926 in TUC library.

49 Secretary's Report on the Resolutions Adopted at the Delegate Meeting on 14 July 1927 (with minutes), London TC, 15 September 1927 Agenda; Tate (1950), p. 133; letter from Egerton Wake to A. M. Wall of 21 July 1927.

50 *Labour Magazine* July 1928; Mackinven (1959), p. 59; Westminster TC March 1927 AR; TUC 1928 Report, pp. 140–1, 348–9; Martin's thesis, p. 301 (on Barrow); Wandsworth TC 1927 AR; Shoreditch TC 1929 AR, p. 7.

51 STUC 1929 Report, p. 63; *Labour Magazine* November 1928; TUC 1928 Report, p. 143.

52 The story is described in the latter part of Martin (1969), and S. W. Lerner, *Breakaway Unions and the Small Trade Union* (1961), pp. 85–143 and *A History of the United Clothing Workers Union* (London University PhD thesis, 1956).

53 Above, p. 148 on the 1927 decision. NMM 1929 Conference Report, p. 17, and 29 March 1929 circular in Tanner coll.

54 NMM 1929 Conference Agenda, pp. 13–14, and *Preliminary Notes on the Need for a London Industrial Council* (duplicated document of 14 March 1929 in Tanner coll). See Martin's thesis, pp. 309–10, for quotations from related documents in the Tanner collection.

55 These quotations are from reports of a London Industrial Council meeting of 4 July 1929 and a conference of 20 April in the Tanner collection. See also Martin's thesis, p. 310.

56 Coventry TC 1930 AR; Southampton TC 1934 Report, p. 2; Martin's thesis, p. 324; *RILU Magazine*, 1 February 1932; TUC 1934 Report, p. 249.

57 *Daily Worker* 8 March 1933 and 1933 TCAC, p. 6 (with original emphasis).

58 TUC 1933 Report, pp. 64–5, 1934 Report, pp. 101–2, 282–4. *Daily Worker* 11 February 1935 on events at Deptford.

59 They are given in full in TUC 1935 Report, pp. 110–12.

60 STUC 1935 Report, pp. 50, 140, 1936 Report, p. 57.

61 1935 TCAC, p. 23; TUC 1935 Report, pp. 260–80; V. L. Allen on 'The centenary

of the British Trades Union Congress, 1868–1968' in his *The Sociology of Industrial Relations* (1971), p. 201, and *Daily Worker* 14 September 1935 for similar claims.
62 T. Bell, *The British Communist Party. A Short History* (1937), p. 168; *Daily Herald* 2 March 1935; *Daily Worker* 10 May 1935. The file of correspondence between the St Albans TC and the TUC on circular 16 shows the reluctance of the General Council to reveal the precise number of trades councils who were supporting them.
63 *Daily Worker* 2 November 1934; St Albans TC to the General Council, 19 November 1934; *Times* and *Daily Herald* for 28 March 1935.
64 Bradford TC 1935 YB, pp. 7, 9–11, and 1935 TCAC, p. 5; *Daily Worker* 27 May 1935; Kent T&L Federation, 15 July 1935 Minutes; Aylesbury TC 1935 AR and G. E. Cheshire (1936), pp. 32–3; Watford TC&LP Industrial Section letter of August 1935 with the Chatham TC Minutes.
65 Bradford TC 1936 YB, pp. 3–4; Oxford T&LC circulars of 24 October and 6 December 1935 and letter of 23 August 1935 from Harries to the Stockton TC (copies with the Chatham TC Minutes in Marx House); Oxford T&LC 1935 AR, p. 3; St Albans TC 1935 AR.
66 Leeds TC 28 November 1934 Minutes; *Daily Herald* 23 April 1935; Carlisle TC January 1937 AR; *Daily Herald* 6 June, 4 July 1935; TUC 1936 Report, p. 113; 1936 TCAC, p. 13; Watford TC 1939 AR, p. 17; 1939 TCAC, pp. 20–1; TUC 1940 Report, p. 108, 1942 Report, p. 30.
67 Northampton TC 1935 AR, pp. 6–7; Wolverhampton TC 1939 YB; Kent T&L Federation June 1936 AR.
68 Chatham TC, 11 May 1935 Minutes; L. Bather on 'The Manchester and Salford Trades Council from 1880' in *BSSLH*, 6, 1963, and his thesis, pp. 198–9; Newcastle TC 1936–37 AR, p. 6; Gravesend TC&LP 1937 AR, p. 16; London TC 1941 AR, pp. 18–19.
69 J. A. Mahon, *Trade Unionism* (1938), p. 74; Middlesbrough T&LC 1936 Rules; Clitheroe TC 1936 Rules; Harrogate TC 1938 Rules; Bournemouth TC 1939 Constitution and Rules; Swindon TC 1939 Rules; Durham TC 1939 Rules; Accrington TC&LP Industrial Section 1941 Constitution; Didcot TC 1943 Rules.
70 Much of the history of the unemployed movement is in R. Hayburn, *The Responses to Unemployment in the 1930s, with particular reference to South East Lancashire* (Hull University PhD thesis, 1970), and in the various works of Hannington.
71 Chatham TC 20 November, 12 December 1920, 9 January 1921 Minutes; W. Hamling (1948), pp. 41–2; *Town Crier* 9 December 1921, Birmingham TC 1922 YB, p. 4.
72 TUC 1924 Report, pp. 342–6, and 1925 TCAC, p. 13.
73 TUC 1925 Report, p. 408, 1928 Report, p. 113.
74 L. J. Macfarlane (1966), p. 124; Liverpool TC 19, 25 August 1925 Minutes; G. D. H. Cole, *Out of Work* (1923), pp. 77–9.
75 TUC 1928 Report, pp. 149–51, 364–5; W. Hannington, *Unemployed Struggles, 1919–36* (1936), pp. 159–61 (hereafter *US*) and *The March of the Miners. How we smashed the opposition* (1927), pp. 14, 25.
76 *US*, p. 178; W. Hannington, *Our March against the Starvation Government* (1928), p. 13; J. Sorel, 'Miners under Castle Rock: the Scottish hunger march of September 1928' in *Marx Memorial Library Quarterly Bulletin*, 59, July 1971.
77 TUC 1929 Report, p. 119; W. Hannington, *The Story of the National Hunger March* (1929), from which all quotations are taken. See also *US*, cap.IX .
78 TUC 1928 Report, pp. 111–13, 311–13; W. Milne Bailey (1929), pp. 184–6, gives the model constitution. The Bristol Association was established in 1921 and in 1927 came directly under the wing of the Trades and Labour Council. It worked with some success to direct the local unemployed into 'constitutional channels' and took up large numbers of individual cases. By the early '30s it had lost some ground to the NUWM. For details, Large and Whitfield (1973), pp. 22–7, and Bristol T&LC 1928 AR.

79 1929 TCAC, pp. 12–13; 1930 TCAC, p. 7; Brighton TC&LP 1928 AR, pp. 6, 13; TUC 1929 Report, pp. 96–9.
80 *Daily Worker* 31 March 1930; W. Hannington, *Achievements of the Hunger March against the Labour Government* (1930), pp. 14, 6, and on 'The unemployed' in *British Trade Unionism Today* (1939), ed. G. D. H. Cole, p. 158. Ministry of Health file 37/99 (1930) in the Public Record Office gives details of trades council support. (I am indebted to Miss Josephine Smith for this information.)
81 *US*, p. 219; TUC 1932 Report, p. 298; A. Hutt (1937), pp. 216, 222–3; *Labour Magazine* February 1932; W. Hannington, *Crimes against the Unemployed. An Exposure of the TUC Scab Scheme and the Crimes committed against the Unemployed by the TUC General Council* (1932), p. 4; 1932 TCAC, p. 12.
82 No copies of the 1932 Model Rules have been found by the author, though there is a summary in 1932 TCAC, p. 10. In the TUC library there is a copy of the 1934 edition, which probably shows little significant change from 1932, and of the 1935 edition, which does.
83 1932 TCAC, pp. 20–4 and TUC 1932 Report, pp. 121–2, 277–80. The initial view of the NUWM can be gathered from the title of Hannington's pamphlet of 1932, cited above, although this attitude later changed.
84 *US*, pp. 244–5; W. Hannington, *Never on our Knees* (1967), pp. 258–9; R. Graves and A. Hodge, *The Long Weekend. A Social History of Great Britain* (1941), p. 258. On the TUC's 1933 demonstrations see Hayburn's thesis, pp. 267–72. For support for the hunger march see Wolverhampton TC 1933 YB and for opposition Birmingham TC 1931 AR, pp. 7–8, after bitter debate.
85 A. Hutt (1937), p. 252; N. Branson and M. Heinemann, *Britain in the Nineteen-thirties* (1971), p. 31; 1934 TCAC, pp. 13, 30.
86 *US*, pp. 310–11; Hayburn's thesis, p. 536; Hutt, pp. 264–7.
87 A. Tuckett (1971), pp. 73–4; Leeds TC 1936 AR, p. 6, and Unemployment Association Propaganda and Educational Committee Minute Book for 1936–37 in Leeds City Archives; Bristol TC 1936 AR; R. Hayburn, 'The police and the hunger marchers' in *International Review of Social History*, XVII , 1972, pp. 630–1, 641–2; E. Wilkinson, *The Town that was Murdered* (1939), pp. 205–6; 1937 TCAC, pp. 9, 19–21; 1938 TCAC, p. 22; 1939 TCAC, p. 41.
88 These quotations are taken from the model rules, details of which are given in n. 82. The policies are in 1934 TCAC, p. 11.
89 1935 TCAC, p. 22; 1937 TCAC, p. 8.
90 1939 TCAC, p. 42; TUC 1935 Report, p. 123.
91 Hannington in G. D. H. Cole (1939), p. 161; 1936 TCAC, p. 21. On education in Leeds see J. F. C. Harrison, *Learning and Living, 1760–1960* (1961), p. 286: classes in philosophy and the welfare system were run, but had to be abandoned because of 'members failing to turn up' (Leeds TC 1937 AR, p. 11, and Unemployment Association Propaganda and Education Committee, 3 March 1937 Minutes). On the weekend schools see 1937 TCAC, p. 8; 1938 TCAC, p. 10; 1939 TCAC, p. 12.
92 M. Foot, *Aneurin Bevan*, vol. I (1966 edn), p. 137; W. Hannington, *A Short History of the Unemployed* (1938), pp. 93–4; Lovell and Roberts (1968), p. 129.
93 1936 TCAC, p. 12; STUC 1933 Report, pp. 35–8, 1934 Report, pp. 40–1, 91–2, 1936 Report, p. 127; *Labour Magazine* December 1932; TUC 1933 Report, pp. 122, 282; 1934 TCAC, p. 29; TUC 1935 Report, p. 122; 1937 TCAC, p. 9; 1938 TCAC, pp. 9–10; 1939 TCAC, pp. 11, 42:
94 Luton TC (1941), p. 17; Earlstown TC&LP 1936 AR; Hayburn's thesis, p. 292; Manchester TC 1932 AR, p. 8, 1933 AR, p. 7, 1934 AR, pp. 8–9, 1935 AR, p. 7; Southampton TC 1932 AR; Bradford TC 1930 YB, p. 7, 1933 YB, p. 5, 1937 YB, p. 5, 1939 YB, p. 7, 1940 YB, p. 3; Huddersfield T&IC August 1930 AR, pp. 2, 7; Hayburn's thesis, pp. 294–308.

95 TUC 1932 Report, p. 278; 1939 TCAC, p. 40; 1936 TCAC, p. 21; Bath T&LC 1939 AR; 1939 TCAC, p. 40; STUC 1937 Report, p. 40; Oxford T&LC 1935 AR, p. 3; 1939 TCAC, pp. 40, 42; Camberwell T&LC 1934 AR, 1937 AR; 1933 TCAC, p. 28; Hull TC 1936 AR, p. 8; Hayburn's thesis, p. 292.

96 1933 TCAC, p. 27; H. B. Williams (1952), p. 25; *Town Crier* 1 January 1932; Margate TC 1935 TUC Souvenir, p. 17; Halifax T&LC 1937 AR, p. 3; Kent T&L Federation, 11 January 1936 Minutes; Darlington TC 1936 AR; Preston T&LC 1935 AR, p. 8; Newcastle TC 1934–35 AR, p. 7; Bristol T&LC 1936 AR, 1937 AR; Birmingham TC 1932 AR, pp. 5–6.

97 This information is taken from the Leeds T&LC Minute Books (1928–37), ARs from 1928 to 1939, from the speech by Durant in TUC 1933 Report, pp. 279–81, and the Minutes of the Unemployment Association Propaganda and Educational Committee for 1936 and 1937. Quotations are from the two latter sources.

98 E. Wilkinson (1939), pp. 192–3; T. Bell (1937), p. 146; Hayburn's thesis, p. 357.

Chapter eight. Old ideals and new realities, pp. 167–83

1 J. Yarwood (1932), p. 3; 1935 TCAC, p. 26; W. Hamling (1948), p. 46; A. Tuckett (1971), p. 69.

2 *Industrial Review* March 1927 and 1927 TCAC, pp. 15–16; Swindon TC 1928 Rules, p. 5; Bradford TC 1931 YB, p. 9; Manchester TC 1929 AR, p. 2.

3 T. Quelch on 'Trades councils' in Wandsworth TC 1927 AR, p. 10, and also in London TC 1929 AR, p. 21; *Daily Herald* 31 July 1935, and for similar sentiments Halifax T&IC 1935 AR, p. 3, Newcastle TC 1932 TUC Souvenir, p. 111.

4 Northampton TC 1927 AR, p. 2, 1928 AR, p. 6; Brighton TC&LP 1927 AR, p. 7 and TUC 1933 Report, p. 64. For similar sentiments see Macclesfield TC 1927 AR, p. 3.

5 Southall and Deptford Trades Councils protested about the knighthoods (*Daily Worker* 8 July 1935), as also did the Kent federation (15 July 1935 Minutes). Manchester T&LC 1932 AR, p. 4, speaks of 'the staggering colossal ineptitude of our ruling class', and 1935 AR, p. 3, of 'unswerving hostility' to the National Government.

6 A. A. Purcell, *The Trades Councils and the Local Working Class Movement* (Manchester, 1931), p. 12; Manchester TC, *The Workers' Battle for Livelihood and Life* (Manchester, 1935), p. 28.

7 *Daily Herald* 22 July 1930; S. G. Hobson, *Pilgrim to the Left* (1938), pp. 246–9 and *The House of Industry* (1931), pp. vii–xxi; London TC, *The Trade Unionist's Modern Catechism* (1932), p. 5, and *Conference on Industrial Policy in relation to the present crisis* . . . 17 October 1931.

8 South Shields TC&LP 1928 AR; Keighley TC&LP 1928 AR.

9 Bolton TC 1927 AR, p. 4; G. Cheshire (1936), pp. 29–30, Aylesbury TC 1937 AR.

10 Newcastle TC 1927‑8 AR, pp. 4, 6; Bolton TC 1928 AR, p. 7; Leeds T&LC 1927 AR, p. 3, T C 1935 AR, p. 2.

11 McKibbin's thesis, pp. 253–7; STUC 1924 Report, pp. 97, 107; T. Mann on 'The future of the trades councils' in *Trade Union Unity* February 1926; W. Citrine, *The Trade Union Movement of Great Britain* (Amsterdam, 1925), p. 61; 1926 TCAC, pp. 15, 18, 1927 TCAC, pp. 11–12, 15; W. Milne Bailey (1929), pp. 172–80. For the history of earlier attitudes on these matters, see above pp. 49–53 and 109–10.

12 Sunderland TC June 1931 AR; Middlesbrough T&LC 1928 AR; Bury TC 1928 AR, p. 4; Oxford T&LC February 1929 AR, p. 3; Mansfield Trades Union Council 1965 YB, p. 15; Bennett (1967); 1936 TCAC, p. 13; 1937 TCAC, p. 28; TUC 1939 Report, p. 137, 1940 Report, p. 108; E. Heffer on 'Tearing up 100 years of history' in *Tribune* 24 January 1969.

13 H. B. Williams (1952), p. 26; Gravesend TC&LP 1937 AR, p. 8; London TC 1928

AR, p. 119, 29 March 1928 Minutes, 1929 AR, p. 86, 1932 AR, p. 16; Manchester TC 1924 AR, p. 4, 1931 AR, p. 5; Bolton TC 1927 AR, p. 5; 1929 AR, p. 5; Nottingham TC 1938 YB, p. 6.

14 Manchester TC, *Memorandum on Municipal Rationalisation* (Manchester, 1930); Bradford TC 1932 YB, p. 5; Earlstown TC&LP February 1937 AR; Bolton TC 1924 AR, p. 4; Swansea Labour Association 1933 AR, p. 8; Halifax T&LC 1937 AR; Southampton TC 1935 AR; Huddersfield T&LC August 1929 AR; Leeds TC 29 December 1926 Minutes.

15 Southampton T&LC&LRC 1929 AR; S. Lerner, *Breakaway Unions and the Small Trade Union* (1961), pp. 111, 112–3, 130; Leeds TC, 11 March 1936 Minutes and 1936 AR, pp. 3–4.

16 Newcastle TC 1927–8 AR, p. 6, and J. Yarwood (1932), p. 9; Birmingham TC 1935 AR, p. 7, on the establishment of an Industrial Hygiene Research Committee; Citrine in Tynemouth TC 1937–38 AR; Macclesfield TC 1927 AR, p. 6, and Earlstown TC&LP March 1930 AR on the IHES; 1932 TCAC, pp. 30–1, Macclesfield TC 1932 AR, p. 5, London TC 25 July 1935 Minutes and Leeds TC 27 March 1935 Minutes on shorter hours; Manchester TC 1935 AR, p. 7, and North Staffordshire T&LC AR 1937 on holidays with pay; for opposition to rationalisation schemes see *Town Crier* 8 February 1924 (Birmingham TC), Leeds T&LC 1929 AR, p. 3, Leicester TC 1932 YB, p. 1, and London TC 13 April 1933 Minutes supporting a strike against the 'Bedaux' system.

17 Leeds T&LC 30 March 1927 Minutes; South Shields TC 1937 AR; Leicester TC 1931 YB, p. 11; Weymouth TC 1934 TUC Souvenir, p. 83; Bolton TC 1923 AR, p. 8; Cardiff T&LC 1926 YB, p. 20; Middlesbrough T&LC 1923 AR; Bradford TC 1938 YB, p. 5; Manchester TC, *Our Centenary, 1854–1955* (Manchester, 1955); Oldham T&LC Industrial Section 1935 AR; Gravesend TC&LP 1937 AR, p. 16; Bradford TC 1931 YB, p. 6.

18 Leeds T&LC 30 April, 24 September 1924 Minutes; *Labour Magazine* September 1932; 'A Delegate', *Short History of the London Trades Council* (1935), pp. 108–11; London TC 1935 AR, p. 15.

19 London TC, 29 May 1924 and 8 September 1938 Minutes; West Ham TC 1929 AR, p. 4; Bolton TC 1928 AR, p. 6; Halifax T&LC 1937 AR, p. 2, 1938 AR, p. 4.

20 Dewsbury TC 1927 AR, p. 5; Middlesbrough T&LC 1931 AR; Sunderland TC June 1933 AR; Bradford TC 1935 YB, p. 7; Halifax T&LC 1934 AR, p. 5; Leeds T&LC 1934 AR, p. 4, 1935 AR, p. 5; 1934 TCAC, pp. 14, 24–5; TUC 1934 Report, p. 101.

21 Torquay T&LC January 1938 AR; Hull TC&LP Industrial Section 1926 AR, p. 8; Hampstead TC 1936 AR and 1933 TCAC, p. 15; Nottingham TC 1937 YB, p. 5, 1938 YB, p. 7, and Tynemouth TC 1936–7 AR.

22 Halifax T&LC 1914 AR; B. Abel Smith, *A History of the Nursing Profession* (1960), pp. 208, 142–5; TUC *Report of the Seventh Annual Conference of Unions Catering for Women Workers* (1937), p. 9; Epsom TC 1938 AR; Colchester TC 1937 AR, p. 2; Reading TC&LP 1931 AR; Middlesbrough T&LC 1934 AR.

23 Manchester TC 1935 AR, p. 1; Macclesfield TC 1928 Rules, p. 3; Bristol TC 1922 Rules, 1930 Rules; 1937 TCAC, p. 2.

24 Bolton TC 1928 AR, p. 3, on visits to homes; Bath T&LC 1936 AR; Nottingham TC 1930 TUC Souvenir, p. 31; 1934 TCAC, p. 20, and 1935 TCAC, p. 10, on complaints about lack of union assistance; TUC 1936 Report, p. 97; Southampton TC 1933 AR, p. 8.

25 Huddersfield T&LC August 1935 AR, p. 2; TUC 1934 Report, p. 227; Rushden TC 1939 AR.

26 TUC 1925 Report, pp. 223, 410; 1926 TCAC, pp. 9–10; TUC *Report of the Second Annual Women's Trade Union Conference* (1927), p. 18; TUC *Women in the Trade Union Movement* (1955), p. 80; TUC 1932 Report, p. 104; 1934 TCAC, p. 15; Huddersfield T&IC August 1932 AR, p. 5; Newcastle TC 1933–34 AR, p. 5;

Birmingham TC 1939 AR, pp. 39–43; *Industrial Newsletter for Women* January 1939; TUC *Report of the Seventh Annual Conference of Unions catering for Women Workers* (1937), p. 12.

27 1937 TCAC pp. 27–31; Bristol T&LC 1934 AR; TUC 1934 Report, p. 97; Newcastle TC 1927–28 AR, p. 8; North Staffordshire T&LC 1938 AR, 1939 AR; Nottingham TC 1938 YB, p. 3; Birmingham TC 1938 AR, pp. 10–11, 1940 AR, p. 13; London TC, 9 September 1937 Minutes and Trades Union Youth Advisory Committee *Memorandum concerning an Industrial and Commercial Survey of Greater London* (1937); *Labour* November 1937 and February 1939; TUC 1939 121–2.

28 Huddersfield T&IC August 1930 AR, p. 6; Bradford TC 1931 YB, p. 7; Huddersfield T&LC August 1932 AR, p. 5; Manchester TC 1932 AR, pp. 10–11, and 1933 TCAC, p. 16; Bolton TC 1932 AR, p. 6; Halifax T&IC 1936 AR, p. 3; Bradford TC 1938 YB, p. 5; Manchester TC 1937 AR, p. 9.

29 1937 TCAC, pp. 13, 24–6; Bather's thesis, p. 43; S. Lerner (1961), p. 109; Birmingham TC 1938 AR, p. 8; Oxford TC 1936 AR.

30 Newcastle TC 1927–28 AR, p. 4, 1928–9 AR, p. 4, 1933–34 AR, p. 6, 1934–35 AR, p. 6; Bradford TC 1936 YB, p. 4.

31 Lerner, pp. 27–32; Hull TC&LP Industrial Section 1926 AR, p. 5, and Gravesend TC 1938 AR for refusals; Leeds T&LC 1932 AR, p. 5, for increasing interest; 1939 TCAC, pp. 60–1.

32 Darwen TC&LP 1935 AR.

33 Barnstaple T&LC Rules, nd, post–1939; H. Laski, *A Grammar of Politics* (1925), p. 422.

34 Hull TC&LP Industrial Section 1926 AR, p. 9, calls for a new exchange, Heywood TC 1928 AR and Sunderland TC June 1936 AR on conditions; Birmingham TC 1928 AR, p. 4; London TC 1929 AR, pp. 96–8, 11 June 1931 and 27 January 1938 Minutes; Newcastle TC 1929–30 AR, p. 7; Bolton TC 1929 AR, p. 2; E. M. Burns, *British Unemployment Programs, 1920–38* (Washington, D. C., 1941) pp. 96–7; Leeds T&LC 1924 AR, p. 5; London TC, 25 June, 30 July 1925 Minutes.

35 Plymouth T&LC 1923 AR, p. 11, and H. B. Williams (1952), p. 24; Southampton LP&TC 1931 AR; Middlesbrough T&LC 1934 AR; Manchester TC 1936 AR, p. 6; Bingley TC&LP 1929 AR; TUC *Trades Councils and Wartime Conditions* (1942).

36 Middlesbrough T&LC 1930 AR; Nottingham TC 1932 YB, p. 4; Newcastle TC 1929–30 AR, p. 7; Birkenhead TC&LP March 1930 AR, p. 11; Manchester TC 1931 AR, p. 14.

37 A. W. Fleet, 'The use of advisory bodies by the Unemployment Assistance Board' in *Advisory Bodies. A Study of their Uses in relation to Central Government, 1919–1939* (1940) ed. R. V. Vernon and N. Manseigh; E. M. Burns, *op. cit.*, pp. 229–31; 1936 TCAC, p. 10.

38 Wolverhampton TC 1936 YB, and Blackpool TC (1951), p. 36, on the means test; Manchester TC 1929 AR, p. 6, on the 'not genuinely seeking work' clause; Southampton TC 1933 AR and Middlesbrough T&LC 1932 AR on transitional benefits; Bradford TC 1936 YB, p. 3, and Great Harwood T&LC 1936 AR for protests against the 1934 Act and the UAB. London TC, *The Unemployed Regulations Must Go* (1936) for more general policies.

39 Bolton TC 1933 AR, p. 9; Reading TC&LP 1931 AR. On the opposition of the working class movement to occupational schemes in general see Hayburn's thesis, pp. 247–9, 1931 TCAC, p. 14, 1933 TCAC, pp. 13–14, 31, where they were described as 'a menace to the Trades Councils'. Also R. C. Davison, *British Unemployment Policy. The Modern Phase since 1930* (1938), p. 118, on the 'communist element'.

40 TUC 1936 Report, p. 136, 1937 Report, pp. 116–9; Nottingham TC 1935 YB, p. 2; Watford TC 1936 AR, p. 16; Aylesbury TC 1936 AR; Middlesbrough T&LC 1935

AR; Southampton LP&TC 1931 AR.

41 Royton T&LC 1929 AR; Macclesfield TC 1930 AR, p. 4; Manchester TC 1931
    AR, pp. 6, 10–11; Manchester TC, *Economy!!!* (Manchester, 1931), and
    Unemployment and the Coming Winter (1930), attacking proposals from the
    Associated Chambers of Commerce.

42 *Labour Magazine* August 1932 and Bather's thesis, p. 203; Manchester TC 1934
    AR, p. 7, and for support, Coventry TC 1933 AR and Leeds T&LC 1934
    AR, p. 3; Bennett (1967); D. McKay *et al.* on 'The discussion of public works
    programmes, 1917–35; some remarks on the labour movement's contribution' in
    International Review of Social History, XI, 1966.

43 Newcastle TC 1929–30 AR, p. 7, and Middlesbrough T&LC 1931 AR, 1932 AR,
    the latter body being on the Teesside Development Board. On support for Soviet
    trade see Leeds T&LC 1929 AR, p. 4, and Manchester TC 1931 AR, pp. 51–2, and
    1932 AR, p. 6, and for its negotiation at Glasgow, TUC 1933 Report, p. 243.

44 N. Barou, *British Trade Unions* (1947), p. 82; F. Bealey, J. Blondel and W. P.
    McCann, *Constituency Politics. A study of Newcastle under Lyme* (1965), p. 380;
    A. H. Birch, *Small Town Politics. A Study of Political Life in Glossop* (1959), p.
    174; St Albans TC 1936 AR; G. Woodcock in J. Corbett (1966), p. 5.

45 McKineven (1959), p. 59; Middlesbrough T&LC 1930 AR; Bath TC 1937 AR;
    Bradford TC 1938 YB, p. 9; Huddersfield T&IC August 1937 AR, p. 2; Torquay
    T&LC June 1936 AR; on Manor House see *LWC* 29 September 1922, St Albans
    T&LC 1928 AR and Southampton TC 1936 AR.

46 London TC 1933 AR, pp. 3–5; Torquay T&LC June 1938 AR; Bradford T&LC
    1924 YB, p. 4; Halifax T&IC 1928 AR; Oldham T&LC 1923 AR, p. 2;
    Birmingham TC 1922 AR, p. 33; Macclesfield TC 1934 AR, p. 5; Preston T&LC
    1927 AR, p. 7; Leeds T&LC 1933 AR, p. 5; Manchester TC 1923 AR, p. 7, 1929
    AR, pp. 48–53, *Labour Magazine* February 1932, 1938 AR, p. 13, and Bather's
    thesis, p. 202.

47 Bolton TC 1924 AR, p. 4; Chorley TC 1935 AR; Eccles T&LC 1935 AR, p. 6;
    Preston T&LC 1935 AR, p. 9.

48 Middlesbrough T&LC 1935 AR, London TC 1931 AR, p. 14, and Portsmouth TC
    January 1938 AR; Bolton TC 1924 AR, p. 5, 1925 AR, p. 4; Manchester TC, *The
    Massacre on the Roads* (Manchester, 1935).

49 Leicester TC 1935 YB, p. 9; H. B. Williams (1952), p. 26; 1932 TCAC, p. 19; 1933
    TCAC, p. 17; Bennett (1967); Kendal TC February 1936 AR; Middlesbrough
    T&LC 1930 AR; Bath TC 1937 AR.

50 Macclesfield TC 1927 AR, p. 4, and Bradford TC 1929 YB, p. 9, on the death
    penalty; Leeds T&LC 30 March 1927 Minutes on birth control; Dewsbury TC
    1927 AR, p. 5, on nationalisation of the mines.

51 London TC 25 August 1927 Minutes; Keighley TC&LP February 1929 AR, p. 7;
    Bradford T&LC 1928 YB, p. 9; Westminster TC March 1928 AR.

52 Manchester TC 1933 AR, p. 7; Northampton TC 1933 AR, p. 6.

53 On 'No more war' activities see *LWC* 4 August 1922, Cardiff T&LC 1923 AR, p.
    21, and 1925 YB, p. 7; Brighton TC&LP 1935 AR; London TC, *The War Menace*
    (1935), p. 3; 1934 TCAC, p. 17, on the Peace and Freedom campaign;
    Wolverhampton TC 1935 YB and Reading TC&LP 1934 AR on the 'peace ballot';
    North Staffordshire T&LC 1927 AR, p. 7, on the League as a means 'to bring about
    everlasting peace', and Batley T&LC 1928–9 AR, p. 2, and Preston T&LC 1927
    AR, p. 7, for membership of the League of Nations Union; Leeds TC 29 May 1935
    Minutes and 1935 AR, p. 4; Bradford T&LC 1937 YB, p. 7; on conscription, South
    Shields TC 1936 AR and A. Tuckett (1971), p. 80. At Bristol, the 1938 Munich
    Settlement was strongly opposed — Large and Whitfield (1973) p. 29.

54 G. Orwell, *Collected Essays, Journalism and Letters*, vol. II (1970 ed), p. 174; Leeds
    TC 1938 AR, p. 3, and Wolverhampton TC 1937 YB. For sentiments which
    expressed more than 'mild' approval of the Soviet Union see Ammanford TC&LP

March 1940 AR and Northampton TC 1941 AR, p. 3.
55 Keighley TC&LP February 1929 AR, p. 7, and Nottingham TC 1933 YB, p. 3, on opposition to foreign troops in China; Manchester TC 1937 AR, pp. 12–13, and Gravesend TC Industrial Section 1938 AR, p. 4, for boycotts against Japan, and Great Harwood T&LC 1935 AR and Leeds TC 30 May 1934 Minutes for a similar boycott against Germany.
56 H. Collins, *Trade Unions Today* (1950), p. 112; London TC 1936 AR, p. 13, 10 September 1936 Minutes; Huddersfield T&IC August 1937 AR, Southampton TC 1936 AR and Earlstown TC&LP January 1939 AR on support activities; Middlesbrough TC 1936 AR and Hull TC 1936 AR, pp. 4, 5, on the strike of seamen; Gravesend TC&LP 1937 AR, p. 12, and *Daily Herald* 28 January 1936 for the strike calls.
57 Ammanford TC&LP March 1940 AR; Eastleigh TC 1939 AR; Bradford TC 1940 YB, p. 9; Watford TC 1939 AR, pp. 17, 21–42; Blackpool TC (1951), p. 37; Rushden TC 1939 AR and 1941 TCAC, p. 11, for representation on food control committees, and H. B. Williams (1952), p. 25, and Leeds TC 1939 AR, p. 6, on the general acceptance of the trades councils in wartime administration.

Appendix one. A note on organisation, pp. 184–8

1 G. Howell, *The Conflicts of Capital and Labour Historically and Economically Considered* (1876), pp. 422, 420; Report of the Labour Correspondent of the Board of Trade in PP 1900 LXXXIII, p. xxxix; G. Drage, *Trade Unions* (1905), p. 107; 'Demos' on 'Trades councils' in *The Worker* (Bournemouth) October 1912.
2 1937 TCAC, p. 27; Macclesfield TC 1928 Rules, p. 3; Halifax T&IC 1935 Rules; Barrow TC Constitution, nd, c. 1922.
3 Retford T&LC 1912 AR for consulting other bodies on a new rule book, and Kettering TC 1906 AR, p. 2, or Luton TC *Thirty Years of Progress* (1941), p. 15, for co-operation with Northampton and London respectively. The TUC Library has hundreds of (mainly twentieth century) rule books, and the W TU Coll. a good number of nineteenth century examples.
4 Dorchester TC 1918 Rules, p. 7, has one delegate for twenty-five, and Glasgow TC Rules (nd, c. 1943), p. 2, provision for up to six per thousand. Kettering TC Rules (nd, c. 1918) have an executive of all delegates, and Yeovil T&LC March 1916 AR and Plymouth T&LC 1916 Rules, p. 4, arrangements for one delegate from each affiliated society. Manchester T&LC 17 June 1925 Agenda and Mountain Ash TC 1934 Rules, p. 30, for trade groups. For systems of sub-committees see Edinburgh TC 1918 AR p. 4 (when it was abandoned in favour of working more through the executive), Bristol T&LC 1928 AR (membership, disputes and policy) and Northampton TC 1935 AR (housing, unemployment and transport).
5 Halifax T&LC 1937 AR, p. 7; Chatham T&LC June 1914 AR, p. 3; STUC 1935 Report, p. 42.
6 During the first world war pro-war delegates refused to attend the anti-war Bradford T&LC (1917 YB, p. 3, 1918 YB, p. 3). In Manchester in 1934 and Brighton in 1935 branches withdrew when delegates were barred for their political views. (See 1937 TUC Report, p. 322, and Brighton TC&LP 1935 AR, p. 4.) Halifax T&LC 1936 AR, p. 2, contains a characteristic complaint from a secretary about affiliated branches who never send a delegate at all.
7 Nottingham TC met in the town hall from 1890 (1930 TUC Souvenir, p. 37), and the North Staffordshire body from 1893 (TC *Jubilee Souvenir 1892–1942* (Hanley, 1942) p. 8). *Southern Worker* September 1919 speaks of a 'pernicious' atmosphere when the Bournemouth TC met in the labour exchange, and Bolton TC *Jubilee Souvenir, 1866–1916* (Bolton 1916) gives details of numerous efforts to find a permanent home.

8 Bradford T&LC 1901 YB, p. 12, and 1904 YB pp. 33–6, which shows that twenty-four out of forty-six local branch secretaries were delegates. Chatham T&LC 1918 Rules say that delegates should be working in their trade and be elected by branch members and not executives, but such rules were rare.
9 S. and B. Webb, *The History of Trade Unionism* (1920), p. 454; Newcastle TC 1934–5 AR, p. 4; STUC 1934 Report, p. 131, on the failure of delegates to attend 'because of the influence of full time officials and executives', and p. 134 for the consequent efforts to exclude them.
10 Bradford T&LC 1913 YB, p. 12; Hebden Bridge Reply to Labour Year Book Circular of 15 February 1918 (in LRD); W TU Coll E, vol. IV , p. 314. Bradford T&LC 1923 YB pp. 3, 5, appeals to branches to affiliate 75 per cent. of their membership.
11 W. H. Fraser, *Trade Unions and Society. The Struggle for Acceptance, 1850–80* (1974), p. 45, for this, and his thesis, pp. 34–5, for more detail.
12 Macclesfield TC 1929 Rules, p. 6; Birmingham TC Rules in 1921 AR, pp. 10–11. Leeds TC 20 August 1909 Minutes for strikers, and chapter seven, p. 238, for the London dispute.
13 Connah's Quay T&LC 1917 Rules, pp. 7–8; Northampton TC 1936 Rules, p. 7.
14 The first full-time secretary seems to have been the one appointed in Bradford in 1907, and the second in Birmingham in 1913 (*Federationist* June 1914; Birmingham TC 1912 AR, p. 4).
15 1930 TCAC, p. 13, 1926 TCAC, p. 9.
16 TUC 1926 Report, p. 165.
17 Ayr TC 1917 AR shows an income of £16 10s but a range of activities as great as any with an income ten times the size.
18 The tiny Connah's Quay T&LC recorded reserves of £64 in its 1917 AR, and Carlisle TC January 1938 AR shows more than half its income coming from a surplus accumulated in previous years.
19 The financial estimate, in 1932 TCAC, p. 15, is probably a little low. The total figure for affiliates is from appendix two.
20 Chatham T&LC June 1914 AR, pp. 4, 5, 7.
21 Examples of each of these can be found in the Bacup T&LC Rules, p. 3, Huddersfield T&IC August 1911 AR, pp. 6–7, Bury TC 1924 AR, p. 9.
22 Burnley T&LC 1903 Rules, p. 13; Bradford T&LC 1909 YB, p. 53.
23 There is a more detailed account of what follows in my thesis, pp. 357–66.
24 *CFT* 1 September 1893. See also pp. 100–1 above.
25 *Daily Citizen* 5 November 1912; *LWC* 6 February 1914; Lancashire and Cheshire Federation of TCs, January 1913 HYR, p. 3; *CFT* 6 July, 5 October 1917, 27 May 1919.
26 Statistical and other information can be found in the *Seventeenth Abstract of Labour Statistics* (PP 1914–16 LXI) as well as the *Eighth Annual Abstract* (PP 1902 XCII) and material in the Department of Employment folders, summarised in my thesis, pp. 359–60.
27 These details, meetings and activities can be traced in 1930 TCAC, p. 17, 1936 TCAC, pp. 26–7, 1938 TCAC, pp. 12–13, 16–17, 26–7, 31–2, 1939 TCAC, pp. 7, 15, 23, and TUC 1928 Report, pp. 139–40.
28 Full details of these developments in the TUC and TCAC reports, and they are outlined in my thesis, pp. 362–4.
29 Leeds TC 25 July 1935 Minutes; Aylesbury TC 1939 AR, p. 2. My thesis, pp. 365–6, gives a number of similar references.

Bibliography

I. Collections of primary sources

Trades Union Congress Library

1. Boxes containing trades council annual reports, histories and related material (JN 1129).
2. Boxes containing trades council rule books and related material (JN 1129).
3. Boxes containing Trades Councils Annual Conference reports and some associated publications, including Congress Souvenirs (HD 6661).
4. Collections of reports and papers on the General Strike (HD 5366).

Much other relevant material is scattered throughout the library under such headings as 'Women's Trade Unionism', 'Communism', and 'TUC Publications'.

Labour Research Department

1. Boxes containing what survives of the documents and completed forms collected during the 1917 survey of trades councils, together with some later reports and connected material.
2. Box entitled 'Soviet Intervention etc' containing leaflets, pamphlets, and mimeographed material on the topic dating from 1919–21.

British Museum

1. (Printed) Minutes of the War Emergency Workers National Committee 1914–18.
2. National Committee of Organised Labour for Old Age Pensions – collections of pamphlets and leaflets.

There are also good runs of annual reports of the trades councils of London and Northampton, and other relevant material, such as many of the publications of the NUWM.

Marx Memorial Library

1. Chatham Trades Council Minutes, 1918–23, 1936–40, and Kent Trades and Labour Federation and Medway Joint Labour Council Minutes, 1936–40.
2. Various other relevant items are contained in the library's pamphlet collection, such as the reprint of Pollitt's speech to the 1923 National Federation of Trades Councils conference, and the publications of the London Trades Council Youth Advisory Committee of the late 30s.

British Library of Political and Economic Science

1. Webb Trade Union Collection. Section B vol. XIV contains some trades council publications. Section C vol. 113 contains trades council rule books from the 1890s and before. Section D 288–334 contains trades council annual reports and year books, mostly before 1900.
2. S. and B. Webb Reports and Papers on the Felief of Distress, 1914–15.
3. General Strike Collection.

The Municipal Library, Birmingham

1. Birmingham Trades Council Minute Books from 1869, together with numerous annual reports and other related material.

2. Birmingham Trades Council and Allied Labour Organisations, Circulars, Leaflets, etc, 1866–1956.
3. Birmingham Trades Council, General Fund Expenditure, 1897–1919 and 1942.
4. Birmingham Trades Council, 1899 Old Age Pensions Conference Minutes.
5. Birmingham Trades Council Industrial Polytechnic Bursaries, material on 1901 exhibition, finance committee minutes 1901–02, and standing committee minutes and reports, 1902–36.

The Picton Library, Liverpool

1. Liverpool Trades Council Minutes, 1878–1901, 1906–13, 1916–24, 1925–29, and annual reports 1890–1909.
2. Miscellaneous records on the General Strike in Merseyside.
Some other material, such as Labour Representation Committee Minutes, TC correspondence, 1913 and 1925–50, papers 1900–39, and correspondence relating to the 1925 Liverpool Congress.

Leeds City Archives Department, Sheepscar, Leeds

1. Leeds Trades Council Minutes, 1882–1937.
2. Leeds Trades Council Contribution Book 1938–44, EC Minute Book 1911–13, Out of Work List 1917–30, Fair Contracts Committee Minute Book 1894–1912, Reception Committee Minute Book 1904, Daily Citizen Week Minute Book 1913, Unemployment Association Propaganda and Educational Committee Minute Book 1936–37, Income-Expenditure Book 1903–21, Trades Club Cash Book 1915–55 and Minute Book 1912–17.

Bradford Central Library

Bradford Trades and Labour Council Year Books since 1899.

Sheffield Trades and Labour Council Offices, Fargate, Sheffield

1. Minutes of the Trades and Labour Council from 1903, with separate volumes for executive and delegate meetings for most of the period. Moved in 1975 to Sheffield Central Library.
2. Various related files including minutes and accounts of the Central Dispute Committee of the 1926 General Strike and papers of the 1925 Trade Union organising committee.

Sheffield Central Library

Trades and Labour Council Annual Reports, 1903–11, 1913, 1916, Amalgamated Trades and Labour Council Annual Reports, 1921, 1923, 1926–28, 1930–35, 1940, 1943, 1947, 1950–date; *Sheffield Guardian*, 1906–15; *Sheffield Forward*, 1921–27 (incomplete); some trades council publications and newspaper cuttings relevant to its history.

Coventry Local History Library

Files of 'personal notes on the industrial history of Coventry', collections of newspaper cuttings and other materials relevant to the history of the local working class movement.

In the possession of the Coventry Trades Council

A selection of annual reports together with some other material of which the most important is some of the papers of Billy Buxton, including a typescript account of local events in the General Strike.

The Library of Nuffield College, Oxford

1. The Tanner Collection.
2. The Cole Collection.

London Chamber of Commerce, Cannon Street, London EC4

Annual Reports and Journal of the Chamber of Commerce.

Department of Employment, Statistics Division

Manuscript folders giving the membership of individual trades councils from 1911 to 1938.

Willesden Public Library

Documents on the General Strike, including accounts of most BBC news broadcasts, and Willesden Council of Action Strike Bulletins.

In the possession of Mr H. D. Belton

Notes on the Minutes of the Oxford Trades Council from 1898 to 1918, and on annual reports and related documents.

In the possession of Mr M. Friesner

St. Albans Trades Council Emergency Committee Minutes and related reports 1926, and Trades Council–TUC correspondence of 1934–36 on circular 16.

II. Reports from organisations and conferences

Communist Unity Convention *Official Report* (1920)
Council of Action *Report, August to October 1920* (18 October 1920)
—*Report of the Special Conference on Labour and the Russo-Polish War* (1920)
Council of Workmen and Soldiers' Delegates *What Happened at Leeds* (1917)
Labour Representation Committee and Labour Party Reports to and of Conferences from 1900.
Land Nationalisation Society Annual Reports 1892–1920.
London Chamber of Commerce Annual Reports 1890–1922.
London Trades Council *Conference on National Guilds and Industrial Control* (1921).
—*Conference on Industrial Policy in relation to the present crisis* (1931).
—*Report of National Trade Union Conference held on Saturday January 1st 1898*.
National Minority Movement Conference Reports and Agendas, 1924–9.
National Committee of Organised Labour for Promoting Old Age Pensions for all Annual Reports 1900–1909.
National Federation of Trades Councils *Second Annual Conference Report*, 15th October 1923.
Northumberland and Durham Joint Strike Committee *The General Strike* (1926).
Oldham Trades and Labour Council *Report of Speeches at a Special Organisation Conference* (1918).
Red International of Labour Unions, *The International Labour Movement 1923–4*.
(Ruskin College, Oxford) *The Trade Unions: Organisation and Action* – Report of Conference held in Coventry in May 1919.

Scottish Trades Union Congress Reports and Conference Proceedings since 1916.
Trades Union Congress Reports and Conference Proceedings from 1886.
TUC Souvenir Volumes: produced by local sponsoring organisations: 1908 Nottingham
    TC; 1917 Blackpool TC; 1920 Portsmouth T&LC; 1924 Hull TC (Industrial
    Section); 1928 Swansea Labour Association; 1930 Nottingham TC; 1931 Bristol
    TC; 1932 Newcastle on Tyne TC; 1934 Weymouth TC; 1935 Margate TC; 1936
    Plymouth TC; 1938 Blackpool TC; 1940 Southport TC&LP.
(TUC) Annual Conferences of Trades Councils since 1925. (The report for 1928 is
    missing in the TUC library, and the reports to the conferences are only printed with
    the conference proceedings from 1932).
(TUC) Annual Women's Trade Union Conference, 1926 and 1927, and Annual
    Conferences of Unions catering for Women Workers, 1937 onwards.
(TUC) *Report of the Old Age Pensions Conference held at the Memorial Hall . . . 14th
    and 15th January 1902.*
War Emergency Workers' National Committee Report, *August 1914 to March 1916.*
Workmen's National Housing Council (1898–1918) Annual Reports.
*Report of the National Conference on the State Maintenance of Children 20th January
    1905.*

III. Parliamentary papers

The Labour Department of the Board of Trade, which was set up in 1886, and became
the Ministry of Labour in 1916, issued numerous reports containing information about
trades councils. These give details of the numbers and size of the trades councils, of the
names of their secretaries and of their work in local boards of conciliation. A series of
Reports on Strikes and Lock-outs was published from 1889 onwards, a series of general
reports of the Chief Labour Correspondent of the Board of Trade from 1896, and a series
of statistical reports began in 1894. These often repeat one another, but changes in format
mean that useful information in some editions is often not contained in others. The
reports of proceedings under the 1896 Conciliation Act, the first of which was published
in 1897, and the twelfth and last in 1914, contain useful information, as also do the
reports on conciliation board rules published in 1908 and 1910. Very little information
was published in Parliamentary Papers by the Ministry of Labour about the trades
councils, except in the Eighteenth Abstract of Labour Statistics of 1926. Some other
information about the trades councils is to be found in the Directories of Industrial
Associations issued by the Chief Registrar of Friendly Societies from 1900 to 1919. The
list that follows gives the chief of these sources that have been used, together with a few
other parliamentary papers where information about the trades councils or about matters
of interest to their history is to be found.

1890–1 LXXVIII C. 6476. Report on the Strikes and Lock-outs of 1890.
1892 XXXIV–XXXVI; 1893–4 XXII–XXXIV, XXXIX;1894 XXXV. Reports of the
    Royal Commission on Labour.
1893–4 LXXXIII, part I, C. 6890. Report on the Strikes and Lock-outs of 1891.
1894 LXXXI, part I, C. 7403. Report on the Strikes and Lock-outs of 1892.
1895 XCII C. 7901. Report on the Strikes and Lock-outs of 1894.
1896 LXXX, part I, C. 8231. Report on the Strikes and Lock-outs of 1895.
1897 LXXXIII C. 8533. First Report of Proceedings under the 1896 Conciliation Act.
1897 LXXXIV C. 8643. Report on the Strikes and Lock-outs of 1896.
1897 XCIX C. 8460. Ninth Report by the Chief Labour Correspondent of the Board
    of Trade.
1898 LXXXVIII C. 9012. Report on the Strikes and Lock-outs of 1897.
1898 CIII C. 9013. Report by the Chief Labour Correspondent of the Board of Trade.
1899 LXXXVIII (275). Second Report of Proceedings under the 1896 Conciliation Act.
1899 XCII C. 9437. Report on the Strikes and Lock-outs of 1898.
1899 XCII C. 9443. Report by the Chief Labour Correspondent of the Board of Trade.

1900 LXXXIII Cd. 422. Report by the Chief Labour Correspondent of the Board of Trade.

1901 LXXIV Cd. 773. Report by the Chief Labour Correspondent of the Board of Trade.

1901 LXXIV (296). Third Report of Proceedings under the 1896 Conciliation Act.

1902 XCVII Cd. 1124. Eighth Annual Abstract of Labour Statistics, 1900–01.

1902 XCVII Cd. 1348. Report by the Chief Labour Correspondent of the Board of Trade.

1904 LXXXIX Cd. 1846. Fourth Report of Proceedings under the 1896 Conciliation Act.

1905 LXXVI Cd. 2491. Tenth Abstract of Labour Statistics for 1902–4.

1906 CXII Cd. 3065. Report on the Strikes and Lock-outs of 1905.

1906 CXIII Cd. 2838. Report by the Chief Labour Correspondent of the Board of Trade.

1907 LXXX Cd. 3065. Eleventh Abstract of Labour Statistics.

1908 XCVIII Cd. 3788. Report on the Rules of Voluntary Conciliation and Arbitration Boards and Joint Committees.

1908 XCVIII Cd. 4413. Twelfth Abstract of Labour Statistics 1906–07.

1908 XCVIII Cd. 4253. Report on the Strikes and Lock-outs of 1907.

1909 XLIX Cd. 4980. Report on the Strikes and Lock-outs of 1908.

1909 LXXXIX Cd. 4651. Report by the Chief Correspondent of the Board of Trade.

1910 XX Cd. 5346. Second Report on Voluntary Conciliation and Arbitration Boards.

1910 XXI Cd. 5366. Seventh Report of Proceedings under the 1896 Conciliation Act.

1910 LVIII Cd. 5325. Report on the Strikes and Lock-outs of 1909.

1910 LXXX Cd. 5006. Directory of Industrial Associations in the United Kingdom in 1910.

1911 XLI Cd. 5850. Report on the Strikes and Lock-outs of 1910.

1911 LXXI Cd. 5619. Directory of Industrial Associations in the United Kingdom in 1911.

1912–13 XLVII Cd. 6109. Report on the Strikes and Lock-outs of 1911.

1912–13 LXVII Cd. 6546. Directory of Industrial Associations in the United Kingdom in 1913.

1913 LXXX Cd. 7131. Sixteenth Abstract of Labour Statistics.

1914 LXXX Cd. 7658. Directory of Industrial Associations in the United Kingdom in 1914.

1914 LXXI Cd. 7603. Memorandum on Steps taken for the Prevention and Relief of Distress due to the War.

1914 LXXIX (89). Eleventh Report of Proceedings under the 1896 Conciliation Act.

1914–16 VII Cd. 7750. First Report of the Departmental Committee to consider the reception and employment of Belgian refugees.

1914–16 VII Cd. 7779. Minutes of Evidence before the Departmental Committee on Belgian Refugees.

1914–16 XXV Cd. 7763. Local Government Board Report on Special Work arising out of the War.

1914–16 XXXVI Cd. 7658. Report on Strikes and Lock-outs in 1913.

1914–16 LXI Cd. 7733. Seventeenth Abstract of Labour Statistics.

1916 XIV Cd. 8358. Committee appointed by the Board of Trade to investigate the principle causes which led to the increase in the price of commodities since the beginning of the War. First Report.

1917–18 XII Cd. 8662–9 and 8696. Reports of the Commissioners of Enquiry into Industrial Unrest.

1917–18 XVIII Cd. 8561. National War Savings Committee First Annual Report.

1920 XIX Cmd. 1054. Report of the Committee of Enquiry into the Work of Employment Exchanges.

1926 XXIX Cmd. 2740. Eighteenth Abstract of Labour Statistics.

IV Unpublished theses

Andrews, L., *The Education (Provision of Meals) Act 1906. A Study of the Education (Provision of Meals) Act, 1906, against its Social, Political and Economic Background.* London M.A. (Ed.), 1966.

Atkinson, B. J., *The Bristol Labour Movement, 1868–1906.* Oxford D.Phil., 1969.

Bather, L. A., *A History of the Manchester and Salford Trades Council.* Manchester Ph.D., 1956.

Brown, R., *The Labour Movement in Hull, 1870–1900, with special reference to New Unionism.* Hull M.Sc. (Econ.) 1966.

Burdick, E., *Syndicalism and Industrial Unionism in England until 1918.* Oxford D.Phil., 1950.

Clinton, A., *Trades Councils from the beginning of the twentieth century to the Second World War.* London Ph.D., 1973.

Drinkwater, T. L., *A History of the Trade Unions and Labour Party in Liverpool, 1911 to the Great Strike.* Liverpool B.A., 1940.

Fraser, W. H., *Trades Councils in England and Scotland, 1858–97.* Sussex Ph.D., 1967.

Hastings, R. P., *The General Strike in Birmingham, 1926.* Birmingham B.A., 1954.

—*The Labour Movement in Birmingham, 1927–45.* Birmingham M.A., 1959.

Hayburn, R., *The Responses to Unemployment in the 1930s, with particular reference to South-east Lancashire.* Hull Ph.D., 1970.

Howard, M., *The History of the Labour Movement in Birmingham, 1900–06.* Birmingham B.A., 1953.

Hyman, R., *The Workers' Union, 1898–1928.* Oxford D.Phil., 1968.

Lerner, S., *A History of the United Clothing Workers' Union. A Case Study of Social Disorganisation.* London Ph.D., 1956.

McCann, W. P., *Trade Unionist, Co-operative and Socialist Organisations in relation to Popular Education; 1870–1902.* Manchester Ph.D., 1960.

McKibbin, R. I., *The Evolution of a National Party. Labour's Political Organisation, 1910–24.* Oxford D.Phil., 1970.

Maddock, S., *The Liverpool Trades Council and Politics, 1878–1918.* Liverpool M.A., 1959.

Martin, R., *The National Minority Movement. A Study in the Organisation of Trade Union Militancy in the Inter-war Period.* Oxford D.Phil., 1964.

Mason, A., *The Miners' Unions of Northumberland and Durham, 1918–31, with special reference to the General Strike of 1926.* Hull Ph.D., 1967.

Porter, J. H., *Industrial Conciliation and Arbitration, 1860–1914.* Leeds Ph.D., 1968.

Rae, J. M., *The Development of Official Treatment of Conscientious Objectors to Military Service, 1916–45.* London Ph.D., 1965.

Schofield, J., *The Labour Movement and Educational Policy, 1900–31.* Manchester M.Ed., 1964.

Thomis, M. I., *The Labour Movement in Great Britain and Compulsory Military Service, 1914–16.* London M.A., 1959.

Thomson, L. D., *Relations between Government and Trade Unions in the General Strike of 1926.* London Ph.D., 1952.

Turner, R., *The Development of the Leeds Trades Council, 1889–1914.* Leeds B.A., 1972.

Woodhouse, T., *Leeds in the General Strike.* Leeds B.A., 1971.

V Newspapers and periodical publications

This list does not include local papers temporarily issued during the 1926 General Strike.

All Power, 1922–24. *British Worker*, May 1926. *The Communist*, 1920–23. *Communist Review*, 1921–35. *Cotton Factory Times*, 1885–1937. *Daily Herald*,

1911–14; *Herald*, 1914–19; *Daily Herald*, 1919 on. *Daily Worker*, 1930 on. *The Federationist*, 1913–19. *The Guildsman*, 1916–21, *The Guild Socialist*, 1921–23, *New Standards*, 1923–24. *Industrial Newsletter for Women*, 1938 on. *Industrial Review*, 1927–33. *Industrial Syndicalist*, 1910–11. *Labour Bulletin of Industrial and Political Information*, 1925–33. *Labour Gazette*, 1893 on. *Labour Magazine*, 1922–33, *Labour* 1933 on. *Labour Monthly*, 1921 on. *Labour Organiser*, 1920 on. *Labour Research Department Monthly Circular*, 1917 on (called the *Fabian Research Department Monthly Circular* until October 1918). *Land and Labo[u]r*, 1889–1912. *Land Nationaliser*, 1913–21. *Leeds Weekly Citizen*, 1911 on. *Manchester Guardian*. *Plebs* 1909 on. *Sheffield Forward*, 1921–27. *Streatham Leader*, 1924–25. *The Syndicalist*, 1912–14. *The Times*. *Town Crier* (Birmingham) 1919 on. *The Worker* (paper of the Clyde Workers' Committee and later of the Minority Movement) 1918–31. *The Worker*, (Bournemouth) 1912–14; *Southern Worker*, 1916–18, 1919–21. *Workers' Weekly*, 1923–27.

Some isolated references will also be found to the following publications: *The Beehive*, *Bradford Pioneer*, *The Call*, *Clarion*, *Coventry Herald*, *Daily Citizen*, *Glasgow Herald*, *International Press Correspondence*, *Justice*, *Labour Elector*, *Labour Leader*, *Lansbury's Labour Weekly*, *Leeds Mercury*, *The Pioneer* (Merthyr Tydfil), *RILU Magazine*, *The Socialist*, *Solidarity*, *The Trade Unionist* (1891), *Western Mail*, *Woolwich Pioneer*, *The Worker* (Huddersfield).

VI Articles in periodical publications and books

Anon., 'Labour notes: the importance of trades councils', *Carlisle Journal*, 4 June 1915.

Anon., 'Trades council or Labour Party? Which shall it be?', *Labour Organiser*, October 1922.

Anon., 'The work of the Soldiers and Sailors Family Associations', *Edinburgh Review*, January 1917.

Allen, V. L., 'The National Union of Police and Prison Officers', *Economic History Review*, second series, XI, 1958.

—'Origins of industrial conciliation and arbitration', *International Review of Social History*, IX, 1964.

—'The centenary of the British Trades Union Congress, 1868–1968', in his *The Sociology of Industrial Relations* (1971).

Arnot, R. P., 'A parliament of labour', *Labour Monthly*, I, October 1921.

Baines, D. E., and Bean R., 'The General Strike on Merseyside, 1926', in *Liverpool and Merseyside. Essays in economic and social history of the port and its hinterland*, ed. J. R. Harris (1966).

Barker, B., 'Anatomy of reformism: The social and political ideas of the Labour leadership in Yorkshire, *International Review of Social History*, XVIII, 1973.

Bather, L., 'Manchester and Salford Trades Council from 1880', *Bulletin of the Society for the Study of Labour History*, 6, 1963.

Boulton, S., 'The genesis of the Conciliation Act', *Chamber of Commerce Journal*, September 1896.

Boulton, S., 'Labour disputes and chambers of commerce', *Nineteenth Century*, June 1890.

Brown, K. D., 'Conflict in early British welfare policy: the case of the Unemployed Workmen's Bill of 1905', *Journal of Modern History*, 42, 1971.

Clinton, A., 'Trades councils during the first world war', *International Review of Social History*, XV, 1970.

—'Trades council bibliography', *Bulletin of the Society for the Study of Labour History*, 29, 1974.

Cole, G. D. H., 'Some notes on British trade unionism in the third quarter of the nineteenth century', *International Review of Social History*, II, 1937.

Cole, M., 'Guild socialism and the Labour Research Department' in *Essays in Labour History* (1971), ed. A. Briggs and J. Saville.

Corbett, J., 'The Birmingham Council of Action', *Birmingham Trades Council Journal*, August and September 1952.

Cox, D., 'The Labour Party in Leicester: a study in branch development', *International Review of Social History*, VI, 1961.

'Demos', 'Trades councils', *The Worker* (Bournemouth), October 1912.

Dutt, R. P., 'The future of the trades councils', *Labour Monthly*, IV, February 1924.

Flanders, A., 'Great Britain', *Comparative Labour Movements* (New York, 1952), ed. W. Galenson.

Fleet, A. W., 'The use of advisory bodies by the Unemployment Assistance Board', in *Advisory Bodies. A Study of their Uses in relation to Central Government 1919–1939* (1940), ed. R. V. Vernon and N. Manseigh.

Fraser, W. H., 'Scottish trades councils in the nineteenth century' in *Bulletin of the Society for the Study of Labour History*, 14, 1967.

—Review of the Minutes of the Edinburgh Trades Council, 1859–1873, (Edinburgh, 1968), ed. I. McDougall, in *Bulletin of the Society for the Study of Labour History*, 19, 1969.

Grant, B., 'Trades councils, 1860–1914', *The Amateur Historian*, 3, 1957.

Gramsci, A., 'Soviets in Italy', *New Left Review*, 51, 1968.

Hanak, H. H., 'The Union of Democratic Control during the first world war', *Bulletin of the Institute of Historical Research*, 36, 1963.

Harrison, R., 'The War Emergency Workers National Committee, 1914–20' in *Essays in Labour History 1886–1923* (1971), ed. A. Briggs and J. Saville.

Hayburn, R., 'The police and the hunger marchers', *International Review of Social History*, XVII, 1972.

Heffer, E., 'Tearing up 100 years of history', *Tribune* 24 January 1969.

Humphrey, A. W., 'Trades councils and the Trades Union Congress', *The Post*, 28 June 1924.

Hikins, H. R., 'The Liverpool general transport strike, 1911', *Transactions of the Historic Society of Lancashire and Cheshire*, 113, 1961.

Hodges, F., 'What we mean by the Council of Action', *Sunday Express*, 15 August 1920.

Hyman, R., 'Communist industrial policy in the 1920s', *International Socialism*, 53, 1972.

Lenin, V., 'Speech delivered at a congress of leather industry workers, 2 October 1920', in his *Collected Works*, vol. 31 (1966).

Lloyd, C. M., 'Doles and degradation', *The Nation*, 31 October 1914.

MacFarlane, L. J., 'Hands off Russia. British Labour and the Russo-Polish war' in *Past and Present*, 38, 1967.

McKay, D., Forsyth, D., and Kelly, D., 'The discussion of public works programmes, 1917–35: some remarks on the labour movement's contribution', *International Review of Social History*, XI, 1966.

Mann, T., 'The development of the labour movement', *Nineteenth Century*, May 1890.

—'The future of the trades councils', *Trade Union Unity*, February 1926.

—'The Labour problem', *Labour Elector*, 4–23 January 1890.

—'Trade unionism and co-operation', *Forecasts for the Coming Century* (Manchester, 1897), ed. E. Carpenter.

Mason, A., 'The General Strike', *Bulletin of the Society for the Study of Labour History*, 20, 1970.

—'The government and the General Strike', *International Review of Social History*, XIV, 1969.

Mitchell, I., 'Organised labour and the unemployed problem', *Nineteenth Century*, July 1905.

Morgan, K., 'The Merthyr of Keir Hardie', in *Merthyr Politics. The Making of a Working Class Tradition* (Cardiff, 1966), ed. G. Williams.

Morrison, H., 'Trades councils: should they be separate from boro' parties?'; *Labour Organiser*, October 1924.

Peet, F. H., 'Our tasks in the trades councils', *Communist Review*, May 1926.
Porter, J. H., 'Wage bargaining under conciliation agreements, 1860–1914', *Economic History Review*, second series, XIII, 1970.
Quelch, T., 'The importance of the trades councils', *Labour Monthly*, VI, May 1926.
——'The possibilities of the trades council', *Justice*, 20 April 1916.
——'Resurrect the trades councils', *All Power*, March 1922.
——'The trades councils: the need for the extension of their scope and work' in *Labour Monthly*, March 1922.
——'A workers' General Staff', *The Call*, 16 October 1919.
——'What the trades councils should be', *All Power*, December 1923.
Robertson, D. J., 'A narrative of the General Strike of 1926', *Economic Journal*, 38, 1926.
Saville, J., 'Trades councils and the labour movement to 1900', *Bulletin of the Society for the Study of Labour History*, 14, 1967.
Sires, R. V., 'The beginnings of British legislation for old age pensions', *Journal of Economic History*, 1954.
Simon, D., 'Master and servant' in *Democracy and the Labour Movement* (1954), ed. J. Saville.
Sorel, J., 'Miners' lamps under Castle Rock: the Scottish hunger march of September 1928', *Marx Memorial Library Quarterly Bulletin*, 59, 1971.
Spitzer, A. B., 'Anarchy and culture: Ferdinand Pelloutier and the dilemma of revolutionary syndicalism', *International Review of Social History*, VIII, 1963.
Stead, F. H., 'A free State pension for every aged person: the demand of British organised labour. A campaign of conferences', *Review of Reviews*, April 1899.
Thel, R., 'Sur les conseils ouvriers', *Bulletin Communiste*, 20 May 1920.
Thompson, E. P., 'Homage to Tom Maguire', in *Essays in Labour History* (1960) ed. A. Briggs and J. Saville.
Tracey, H., 'The world of industry: trades councils and the Congress', *Labour Magazine*, May 1924.
Wallace, J., 'The Council of Action: an attempt to impose Soviet rule' in *Review of Reviews*, September–October 1920.
Ward, D. J., 'A move forward', *The Post*, 25 November 1922.
Wedgewood, J., 'The Council of Action: a triumph for Labour unanimity', *Review of Reviews*, September–October 1920.
White, S., 'Labour's Council of Action 1920', *Journal of Contemporary History*, 9, 4 October 1974.
——'Soviets in Britain: The Leeds Convention of 1917', *International Review of Social History*, XIX, 1974.
Whitley, G., 'Time to make full use of the trades councils?' *The Guardian*, of late 1967, reprinted by the TUC.
Williams, J. E., 'The Leeds corporation strike in 1913', in *Essays in Labour History 1886–1923* (1971) ed. A. Briggs and J. Saville.
Wyncoll, P., 'The General Strike in Nottingham', *Marxism Today*, June 1972.

VII Books and pamphlets

All are published in London unless otherwise stated.
Anon, *An Historical Sketch of the Birmingham Trades Council, 1866–1926* (Birmingham, 1927).
'A Delegate', *Short History of the London Trades Council* (1935).
Allaway, A. J., *Challenge and Response. WEA Midland District, 1919–69* (Leicester, 1969).
——*The First Fifty Years of the WEA in Leicester* (Leicester, 1959).
Allen, E. J. B., *Revolutionary Unionism* (1909).
Amulree, L., *Industrial Arbitration in Great Britain* (1929).

Arnot, R. P., *The General Strike. Its Origins and History* (1926).
—*The Miners. Years of Struggle. A History of the Miners' Federation of Great Britain (from 1910 onwards).* (1953).
—*Trade Unionism. A New Model* (1919).
Ashraf, M. *Bradford Trades Council, 1872–1972* (Bradford, 1972).
Aspinall, A., *The Early English Trade Unions* (1949).
Bagwell, P. S., *The Railwaymen. The History of the National Union of Railwaymen* (1965).
Bailey, W. Milne, *Trade Union Documents* (1929).
Barker, R., *Education and Politics, 1900–51. A Study of the Labour Party* (Oxford, 1972).
Bernard, H. C., *A History of English Education* (1969 ed.).
Barou, N., *British Trade Unions* (1947).
Barry, E. E., *Nationalisation in British Politics. The Historical Background* (1965).
Bealey, F., Blondel, J., and McCann, W. P., *Constituency Politics. A Study of Newcastle under Lyme* (1965).
—and Pelling, H., *Labour and Politics, 1900–06* (1958).
Belfast Trades Union Council, *1851–1951. A Short History* (Belfast, 1951).
Bell, T., *The British Communist Party. A Short History* (1937).
Bellamy, J. M., and Saville, J., *Dictionary of Labour Biography*, vol. I (1972).
Bennett, A., *Oldham Trades and Labour Council Centenary, 1867–1967.* (Oldham, 1967). (Without pagination.)
Beveridge, W. H., *British Food Control* (1928).
—*Unemployment. A Problem of Industry* (1931).
Birch, A. H., *Small Town Politics. A Study of Political Life in Glossop* (1959).
Birch, L., *The History of the TUC, 1868–1968. A Pictorial Survey of a Social Revolution* (1968).
Birmingham Trades Council, *A Trades Council Federation for Birmingham* (Birmingham, nd, 1893?).
—*Enquiry into Conditions of Labour in Bakehouses* (Birmingham, nd, 1910?).
—*Hats off to the People!* (Birmingham, 1951).
Blackpool Trades Council, *Diamond Jubilee History Report and Directory* (Blackpool, 1951).
—*75th Anniversary History Report and Directory* (Blackpool, 1966).
Bolton Trades Council, *Centenary Brochure* (Bolton, 1966).
—*Jubilee Souvenir, 1866–1916* (Bolton, 1916).
Bowley, A. L., *Prices and Wages in the United Kingdom, 1914–20* (Oxford, 1921).
Braithwaite, W. J., *Lloyd George's Ambulance Wagon* (1957).
Brand, C. F., *The Labour Party. A Short History* (1965).
Branson, N., and Heinemann, M., *Britain in the Nineteen-thirties* (1971).
Brockway, F., *Socialism over Sixty Years. The Life of Jowett of Bradford, 1866–1944* (1946).
Brown, E. H. Phelps, *The Growth of British Industrial Relations* (1959).
Brown, K. D., *Labour and Unemployment, 1900–14* (Newton Abbot. 1971).
Brown, R., *Waterfront Organisation in Hull, 1870–1900* (Hull, 1972).
Bryther, S., *The Labour and Socialist Movement in Bristol* (Bristol, 1929).
Buckley, K. D., *Trade Unionism in Aberdeen, 1878 to 1900* (Edinburgh, 1955).
Buckley, M. E., *The Feeding of Schoolchildren* (1914).
Bunger, S., *Die sozialistiche Antikreigsbewegungen in Grossbritannien, 1914–17* (Berlin, 1967).
Burke, W. M., *History and Functions of Central Labor Unions* (New York, 1899).
Burns, E., *The General Strike, May, 1926. Trades Councils in Action* (1926).
Burns, E. M., *British Unemployment Programs, 1920–38.* (Washington, D.C., 1941).
Button, E., *Trade Union Education* (Nottingham, 1924).
Carritt, M., *Brighton Trades Council. The History of Sixty Years* (Brighton, 1950).

Carter, H., *The Control of the Drink Trade in Britain. A Contribution to National Efficiency during the Great War, 1915–18* (1919).
'C.B.', *The Reds and the General Strike* (1926).
Chaloner, W. H., *The Social and Economic Development of Crewe, 1780–1923* (Manchester, 1950).
Chegwidden, T. S., and Evans, G. M., *The Employment Exchange Service of Great Britain* (1934).
Cheshire, G. E., *Twenty-five Years of Progress. The History of the Aylesbury and District Trades Council* (Aylesbury, 1936).
Church, R. A., *Economic and Social Change in a Midland Town. Victorian Nottingham, 1815–1900* (1966).
Citrine, W. M., *Democracy or Disruption? An Examination of Communist Influences in the Trade Unions* (1928).
—*Men and Work. An Autobiography* (1964).
—*The Trade Union Movement of Great Britain* (Amsterdam, 1925).
Clarke, J. F., and Leonard, J. W., *The General Strike, 1926* (Newcastle upon Tyne, 1971). (Folder of reproduced documents.)
—and McDermott, T. P., *The Newcastle and District Trades Council, 1873–1973. A Centenary History* (Newcastle upon Tyne, 1973).
Clarkson, J. D., *Labour and Nationalism in Ireland* (New York, 1925).
Clegg, H. A., *General Union. A Study of the National Union of General and Municipal Workers* (Oxford, 1954).
—Fox, A., and Thompson, A. F., *A History of British Trade Unions since 1889*, vol. I, 1889–1910 (1964).
Clemesha, W. H., *Food Control in the North West Division* (Manchester, 1922).
Cohen, P., *The British System of Social Insurance* (1932).
Cole, G. D. H., (ed.) *British Trade Unionism Today. A Survey* (1939).
Cole, G. D. H., *British Working Class Politics, 1832–1914* (1941).
—*History of the Labour Party from 1914* (1948).
—*An Introduction to Trade Unionism* (1918).
—*An Introduction to Trade Unionism* (1953).
—*Labour in Wartime* (1915).
—*Organised Labour. An Introduction to Trade Unionism* (1924).
—*Out of Work* (1923).
—*Self-government in Industry* (1920).
—*The World of Labour* (1913).
—and Filson, A. W. (ed.), *English Working Class Movements, 1789–1875. Select Documents* (1951).
—and Postgate, R., *The Common People, 1746–1946* (1971 edn).
Coller, F. H., *A State Trading Adventure* (Oxford, 1925).
Collins, H., *Trade Unions Today* (1950).
Connole, N., *Leaven of Life. The Story of George Henry Fletcher* (1961).
Corbett, J., *The Birmingham Trades Council, 1866–1966* (1966).
CPGB, *Communist Industrial Policy* (nd, 1922).
—*Orders from Moscow?* (1926).
Crook, W. H., *The General Strike* (Chapel Hill, N.C., 1931).
Crompton, H., *Industrial Conciliation* (1876).
Cunnison, J., *Labour Organisation* (1930).
Dailey, W. A., and Eades, A., *History of the Birmingham Trades Council, 1866–1916* (Birmingham, 1916).
Davies, B., *Pages from a Worker's Life* (1961).
Davison, R. C., *British Unemployment Policy. The Modern Phase since 1930* (1938).
—*The Unemployed. Old policies and New* (1929).
Dearle, N. B., *Dictionary of Official Wartime Organisations* (1928).
Degras, J., *The Communist International, 1919–43 Documents.* Vol. I, 1919–1922 (1956); vol. II, 1923–28 (1960).

Delion, M., *Le Trades Unionisme en Angleterre depuis 1914* (Paris, 1926).
Devine, E. T., and Brandt, L., *Disabled Soldiers and Sailors, Pensions and Training* (New York, 1919).
Diack, W., *History of the Trades Council and Trade Union Movement in Aberdeen* (Aberdeen, 1939).
Dolléans, E., and Dehove, G., *Histoire du travail en France* (Paris, 1953).
Drage, G., *Trade Unions* (1905).
Dunham, A. L., *The Industrial Revolution in France* (New York, 1955).
Eagle, E. C., *The East Midlands District of the Workers' Educational Association. An Outline of its Origin and Growth* (Leicester, 1953).
Essex Federation of Trades Councils, *Twenty-one Years of Progress, 1938–59* (1959).
Farman, C., *The General Strike, May 1926* (1972).
Flanders, A., *Trade Unions* (1965 edn.).
—*Trade Unions and Politics* (1961).
—and Clegg, H. A., *The System of Industrial Relations in Great Britain. Its History, Law and Institutions* (1956).
Foot, M., *Aneurin Bevan. A Biography*, vol. I, 1897–1945 (1966 edn.).
Fraser, W. H., *Trade Unions and Society. The Struggle for Acceptance, 1850–1880* (1974).
Gallacher, W., *Revolt on the Clyde. An Autobiography* (1936).
—and Paton, J., *Towards Industrial Democracy. A Memorandum on Workshop Control* (Paisley, 1918).
Gerrard, J. A., *The English and Immigration, 1880–1910* (1971).
Gillespie, F. E., *Labour and Politics in England, 1850–75* (1927).
Glasgow, G., *General Strikes and Road Transport* (1926).
Gleason, A., *What the Workers Want. A Study of British Labor* (1920).
Graham, J. W., *Conscription and Conscience. A History, 1916–19* (1922).
Graubard, S. R., *British Labour and the Russian Revolution* (1956).
Graves, R., and Hodge, A., *The Long Weekend. A Social History of Great Britain, 1918–39* (1941).
Greenwood, J. H., *The Theory and Practice of Trade Unionism* (1911).
Gregory, R., *The Miners and British Politics, 1906–14* (1968).
Groves, R., *Trades Councils in the Fight for Socialism* (nd, ?1933).
Guilleband, C. W., *The Workers' Council. A German Experiment in Industrial Democracy* (Cambridge, 1928).
Halévy, E., *A History of the English People in the Nineteenth Century*, vol. 5, *Imperialism and the Rise of Labour, 1895–1905* (1951 edn.), and vol. 6, *The Rule of Democracy, 1905–14* (1961 edn).
Hall, B. T., *Over Sixty Years. The Story of the Working Men's Club and Institute Union* (1922).
Hall, F., and Watkins, W. P., *Co-operation* (1937).
Hamling, W., *A Short History of the Liverpool Trades Council, 1848–1948* (Liverpool, 1948).
Hanes, D. G., *The First British Workmen's Compensation Act, 1897* (New Haven, Conn., 1968).
Hannington, W., *Achievements of the Hunger March against the Labour Government* (1930).
—*Crimes against the Unemployed. An Exposure of the TUC Scab Scheme and the Crimes Committed against the Unemployed by the TUC General Council* (1932).
—*The March of the Miners. How we Smashed the Opposition* (1927).
—*Never on our Knees* (1967).
—*Our March against the Starvation Government* (1928).
—*A Short History of the Unemployed* (1938).
—*The Story of the National Hunger March* (1929).
—*Unemployed Struggles, 1919–36* (1936).

Hardman, D., *1912–37. The First Twenty-five Years in the History of the Cambridge Borough Trades Council and Labour Party* (Cambridge, 1937).

Harrison, J. F. C., *Learning and Living, 1760–1960* (1961).

—*Workers Education in Leeds. A History of the Leeds Branch of the Workers Educational Association, 1907–57* (Leeds, 1957).

Harrison, R., *Before the Socialists* (1965).

Hikins, H. R., (ed.) *Building the Union. Studies of the Growth of the Workers' Movement, Merseyside, 1756–1967* (Liverpool, 1973).

Hinton, J., *The First Shop Stewards' Movement* (1973).

History Group of the Communist Party, *The General Strike in the North East* (1961).

Hoare, H. J., *Old Age Pensions. Their Actual Workings and Ascertained Results in the United Kingdom* (1915).

Hobsbawm, E. J., *Labouring Men. Studies in the History of Labour* (1964).

Hobson, S. G., *The House of Industry* (1931).

—*Pilgrim to the Left* (1938).

Hodgkinson, G., *Sent to Coventry* (1970).

Howe, E., and Waite, H., *The London Society of Compositors. A Centenary History* (1948).

Howell, G., *The Conflicts of Capital and Labour Historically and Economically Considered* (1876).

—*Trade Unionism Old and New* (1891).

Huddersfield Trades and Industrial Council *75th Anniversary, 1885–1960, and Programme of Events* (Huddersfield, 1960).

Humphrey, A. W., *A History of Labour Representation* (1912).

Hutt, A., *The Post-war History of the British Working Class* (1937).

Hyman, R., *Oxford Workers in the Great Strike* (Oxford, 1966).

—*The Workers' Union* (Oxford, 1971).

Jefferys, J. B., *The Story of the Engineers, 1800–1945* (1945).

—*Labour's Formative Years, 1849–75* (1948).

Jenkins, C., and Mortimer, J. E., *British Trade Unions Today* (Oxford, 1965).

Kendall, W., *The Revolutionary Movement in Britain, 1900–20* (1969).

Klugmann, J., *A History of the Communist Party of Great Britain*, vol. 1, *Formation and Early Years* (1968); vol. 2, *The General Strike* (1969).

Kritsky, M., *L'Evolution de syndicalisme en France* (Paris, 1908).

Large, D., and Whitfield R., *The Bristol Trades Council, 1873–1973* (Bristol, 1973).

Larkin, E., *James Larkin. Irish Labour Leader, 1876–1947* (1965).

Laski, H. J., *A Grammar of Politics* (1925).

Leask, J., and Bellars, P., *"Nor shall the sword sleep . . ." An account of industrial struggle* (Birmingham?, nd, c. 1954).

Lefranc, G., *Le Syndicalisme en France* (Paris, 1953).

Lerner, S., *Breakaway Unions and the Small Trade Union* (1961).

Litman, S., *Prices and Price Control in Great Britain and the United States during the World War* (New York, 1920).

Lloyd, C. M., *Trade Unionism* (1915 and 1921).

London Trades Combination Committee, *Combinations Defended* (1838).

London Trades Council, *The Trade Unionist's Modern Catechism* (1932).

—*The Unemployed Regulations Must Go* (1936).

—*The War Menace* (1935 and 1936).

London Trades Council Youth Advisory Committee, *Memorandum concerning an Industrial and Commercial Survey of Greater London* (1937).

Lovell, J., and Roberts, B. C., *A Short History of the TUC* (1968).

Lowndes, G. A. N., *The Silent Social Revolution* (1969).

LRD, *The Workers' Register of Capital and Labour* (1923).

Luton, Dunstable and District Trades Council, *Thirty Years of Progress. Short History of the Trade Union Movement in Luton and District* (Luton, 1941).

McBriar, A. M., *Fabian Socialism and English Politics* (Cambridge, 1962).
McCarthy, M., *Generation in Revolt* (1953).
MacDermott, T. P., *Centuries of Conflict. The Story of Trade Unionism on Tyneside* (Newcastle upon Tyne, 1965).
McDonald, J., *Trades Councils* (Glasgow, 1930).
Macfarlane, L. J., *The British Communist Party. Its Origin and Development until 1929* (1966).
McKibbin, R., *The Evolution of the National Labour Party, 1910–24* (1974).
McKenzie, R. T., *British Political Parties. The Distribution of Power within the Conservative and Labour Parties* (1963 edn).
Mackinven, H., *The Edinburgh and District Trades Council Centenary, 1859–1959* (Edinburgh, 1959).
McShane, H., *Glasgow District Trades Council. Centenary Brochure, 1858–1958. A Hundred Years of Progress* (Glasgow, 1958).
Mahon, J. A., *Trade Unionism* (1938).
Manchester and Salford Trades Council, *Economy!!!* (Manchester, 1931).
—*The Massacre on the Roads* (Manchester, 1935).
—*Memorandum on Municipal Rationalisation* (Manchester, 1930).
—*Our Centenary, 1854–1955* (Manchester, 1955).
—*Report on the Increase of House Rents in Manchester and Salford since the Commencement of the War* (Manchester, 1915).
—*Unemployment and the Coming Winter* (Manchester, 1930).
—*The Workers' Battle for Livelihood and Life* (Manchester, 1935).
Mann, T., *From Single Tax to Syndicalism* (1913).
—*Memoirs* (1967 edn.).
—*Power through the General Strike. A Call to Action* (1923).
—and Tillett, B., *The 'New' Trade Unionism* (1890).
Mansbridge, A., *An Adventure in Working Class Education, being the Story of the Workers Educational Association, 1903–15* (1920).
—*The Kingdom of the Mind. Essays and Addresses, 1902–37* (1944).
Martin, R., *Communism and the British Trade Unions, 1924–33. A Study of the National Minority Movement* (Oxford, 1969).
Marwick, A., *The Deluge. British Society and the First World War* (1967 edn.).
Marwick, W. H., *Economic Developments in Victorian Scotland* (1936).
Mason, A., *The General Strike in the North East* (Hull, 1970).
Mendelson, J., Owen, W., Pollard, S., and Thornes, V., *The Sheffield Trades and Labour Council, 1858–1958* (Sheffield, 1958).
Miliband, R., *Parliamentary Socialism* (1961).
Mitchell, D., *1919: Red Mirage* (1970).
Moffit, A., *My Life with the Miners* (1965).
Mowat, C. L., *The Charity Organisation Society, 1869–1913. Its Ideas and Work* (1961).
Murphy, J. T., *Modern Trade Unionism* (1935).
—*A Revolutionary Workers' Government* (1929).
—*Stop the Retreat!* (nd, 1922?).
—*The Workers' Committee. An Outline of its Principles and Structure* (Sheffield, 1918).
Musgrove, C. E., *The London Chamber of Commerce from 1881 to 1914* (1914).
Musson, A. E., *The Congress of 1868. The Origins and establishment of the Trades Union Congress* (1955).
North Staffordshire Trades Council, *Jubilee Souvenir, 1892–1942* (Hanley, 1942).
Northampton Trades Council, *1888–1938. Golden Jubilee and 49th Annual Report* (Northampton, 1938).
Orton, W. A., *Labour in Transition. A Survey of British Industrial History since 1914* (1921).
Orwell, G., *Collected Essays, Journalism and Letters* (1970, ed,), vol. 2.

Paul, L., *Angry Young Man* (1951).
Paul, W., *Communism and Society* (1922).
—and E., *Creative Revolution* (1920).
Pearce, B., *Early History of the Communist Party of Great Briatin* (1966).
Pelling, H., *The British Communist Party. A Historical Profile* (1958).
—*A History of British Trade Unionism* (1963 edn).
—*Popular Politics and Society in Late Victorian Britain* (1968).
Pelloutier, F., *Histoire des bourses de travail* (Paris, 1902).
Peterborough and District Trades Council, *Diamond Jubilee, 1899–1959* (Peterborough, 1959).
Pollard, S., *The Development of the British Economy, 1914–67* (1969).
—*A History of Labour in Sheffield* (Liverpool, 1959).
—and Holmes, C. (eds.) *Documents of European Economic History* (1968), vol. I.
Pollitt, H., *Serving my Time* (1940).
Postgate, R., Wilkinson, E., and Horrabin, J. F., *A Workers' History of the Great Strike* (1927).
Pribicevic, B., *The Shop Stewards' Movement and Workers' Control, 1910–22* (Oxford, 1959).
Price, L. L. F., *Industrial Peace* (1887).
Price, R., *An Imperial War and the British Working Class. Working Class Reactions to the Boer War, 1899–1902* (1972).
Purcell, A. A., *Onward to Socialism* (Manchester, nd, 1931?).
—*The Trades Councils and the Local Working Class Movement* (Manchester, 1931).
Quelch, T., *The Militant Trades Council. A Model Constitution for Trades Councils* (1925).
Radcliffe, H., *Notes on the Musicians' Union* (1969).
Rae, J. M., *Conscience and Politics. The British Government and the Conscientious Objector to Military Service* (1970).
Rawtenstall Trades Council, *Fiftieth Anniversary, 1902–52* (Rawtenstall, 1952).
Reckitt, M. B., and Bechhofer, C. E., *The Meaning of National Guilds* (1920).
Radman, J., *The Communist Party and the Labour Left, 1925–29* (Hull, 1957).
Reynolds, G. W., and Judge, A., *The Night the Police went on Strike* (1968).
Richards, C., *A History of the Trades Councils, 1860–75* (1920).
Ridley, F. F., *Revolutionary Syndicalism in France* (Cambridge, 1970).
Roberts, B. C., *The Trades Union Congress, 1868–1921* (1958).
—*Trade Union Government and Administration in Great Britain* (1956).
Royal Commission on Trade Unions and Employers' Organisation, *Selected Written Evidence Submitted to the Royal Commission* (1968).
Samuels, M. Turner, *British Trade Unions* (1949).
Saunders, W. S., *Trade Unionism in Germany* (1916).
Simey, T. S. and M. B., *Charles Booth. Social Scientist* (1960).
Simon, B., *Education and the Labour Movement, 1870–1920* (1965).
Smith, B. Abel, *A History of the Nursing Profession* (1960).
—*The Hospitals, 1800–1948* (1964).
Souch, W. J., *The History of the Reading branch of the Workers Educational Association* (Reading, 1954).
Starr, M., *Trade Unionism. Past and Future* (1923).
Stead, F. H., *How Old Age Pensions began to be* (1909).
Stocks, M., *The Workers' Educational Association. The First Fifty Years* (1953).
Swanwick, H. N., *Builders of Peace, being Ten Years History of the Union of Democratic Control* (1924).
Swartz, M., *The Union of Democratic Control in British Politics during the First World War* (Oxford, 1971).
Symons, J., *The General Strike. A Historical Portrait* (1957).
Tate, G., *London Trades Council, 1860–1950. A History* (1950).

Teale, E. S., *The Story of the Amalgamated Musicians Union* (nd, originally published in 1929).
Thompson, P., *Socialist, Liberals and Labour. The Struggle for London, 1885–1914* (1967).
Tillyard, F., and Ball, F. N., *Unemployment Insurance in Great Britain, 1911–48* (Leigh on Sea, 1949).
Torr, D., *Tom Mann* (1936).
Tropp, A., *The Schoolteachers* (1957).
TUC, *Trades Councils and Wartime Conditions* (1942).
—*Trade Union Structure and Closer Unity* (1947).
—*Trades Councils Guide* (1948, 1st edn).
—*Women in the Trade Union Movement* (1955).
Tuckett, A., *The Scottish Carter. The History of the Scottish Horse and Motormen's Association, 1898–1964* (1967).
—*Up with all that's down! A History of the Swindon Trades Council, 1891–1971* (Swindon, 1971).
Turner, H. A., *Trade Union Growth Structure and Policy* (1962).
Ulman, L., *The Rise of the National Trade Union* (Cambridge, Mass., 1955).
Victoria County History of the County of Yorkshire, East Riding, vol. 1 (1969), ed. K. J. Allison.
—*The City of York* (1961) ed. P. M. Tollett.
Walton, J., and Clements, R., *Hats off to the People!* (Leicester, 1951).
War Emergency Workers' National Committee, *Memorandum and Recommendations on the Increased Prices of Wheat and Coal* (1915).
—*Memorandum on the Increased Cost of Living during the War* (1915, June, July and September 1916, and 1917).
—*The War Emergency. Suggestions to Labour Members on Local Committees* (1914).
Webb, B., *Our Partnership* (1948).
Webb, S. and B., *The History of Trade Unionism* (1894, 1st ed; 1902, new impression; 1911, new impression; 1920, 2nd ed.).
—*Industrial Democracy* (1897).
Wilkinson, E., *The Town that was Murdered* (1939).
Williams, H. B., *History of the Plymouth and District Trades Council from 1892 to 1952* (Plymouth, 1952).
Williams, J. E., *The Derbyshire Miners. A Study in Industrial and Social History* (1962).
Williams, J. H. H., *A Century of Public Health in Britain, 1839–1929* (1932).
Williams, W., *Full up and Fed up. The Workers' Mind in Crowded Britain* (1921).
Wilson, A., and McKay, G. S., *Old Age Pensions. An Historical and Critical Study* (1941).
Winkler, H., *The League of Nations Movement in Great Britain, 1914–19* (New Brunswick, 1952).
Wolfe, H., *Labour Supply and Regulation* (Oxford, 1923).
Woolwich Trades and Labour Council and Labour Party, *Memorandum on Unification of Industrial and Political Forces* (Woolwich, 1917).
Wootton, G., *The Politics of Influence. British Ex-servicemen, Cabinet Decisions and Cultural Change, 1917–58* (1963).
Yarwood, J., *A Retrospect and an Explanation* (Newcastle upon tyne, 1932).
Young, A. F., *Social Services in British Industry* (1968).

Index

Trades councils are referred to by their towns, and unions generally by occupations. Items **in heavy type** contain only the most important examples. Individual chambers of commerce, co-operative societies, ex-servicemen's organisations, federations of trades councils and labour newspapers are given under those headings. References to the notes are included where they do not duplicate those in the main text. Individual items in appendix two are not included.